I0820036

COWINNER OF
THE JULES AND FRANCES LANDRY AWARD FOR 2026

LOUISIANA STATE UNIVERSITY PRESS
BATON ROUGE

Inquisition for Blood

The Making of a Black Female Serial Killer in the Jim Crow South

LAUREN NICOLE HENLEY

Published with the assistance of the V. Ray Cardozier Fund

Published by Louisiana State University Press
lsupress.org

Manufactured in the United States of America
First printing

Designer: Michelle A. Neustrom
Typefaces: Minion Pro, text; Meno Display Extra Condensed, display
Printer and binder: Sheridan Books, Inc.

Jacket illustration courtesy the author and Adobe Stock/Uuganbayar.

Cataloging-in-Publication Data are available from the Library of Congress.

ISBN 978-0-8071-8618-3 (cloth: alk. paper) — ISBN 978-0-8071-8673-2 (pdf) —
ISBN 978-0-8071-8672-5 (epub)

For those gone too soon

Contents

Inquisition for Blood

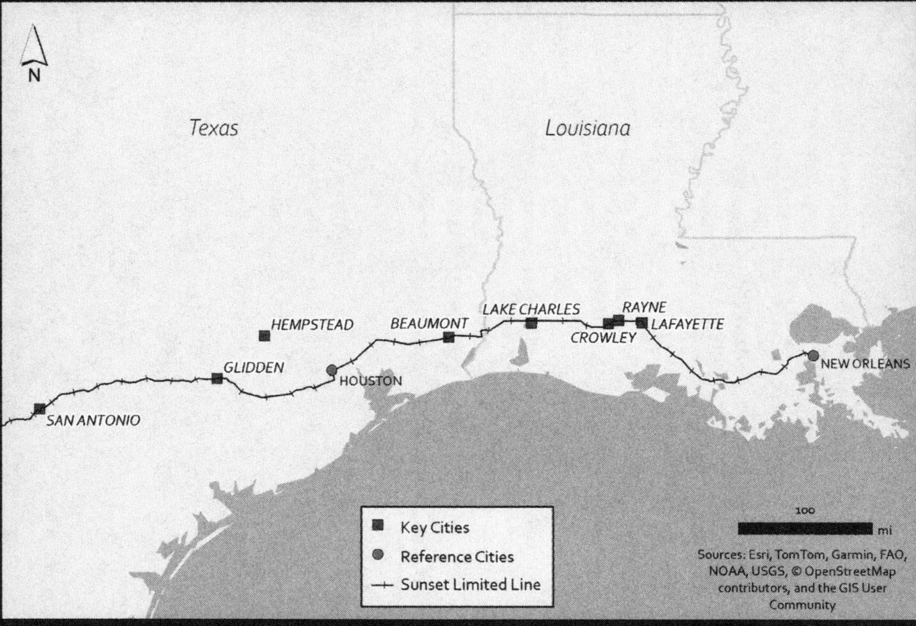

The sites of the Louisiana-Texas ax murders in relation to the Sunset Route of the Southern Pacific Railroad. The Sunset Limited is the train that travels the Sunset Route. (Map created by the Spatial Analysis Lab, University of Richmond)

Introduction

In April 1912, newspapers across the globe printed headline after headline proclaiming a sensational story: a young Black woman named Clementine Barnabet had confessed to murdering over a dozen people in the rice belt region of the United States. Supposedly, the nineteen-year-old Louisiana native had been driven by religion to slaughter entire families up and down the Southern Pacific Railroad's Sunset Route, using an ax to wreak havoc on unsuspecting victims. Although Clementine claimed she killed four families—comprising seventeen people—along a twenty-five-mile stretch of the railroad in southwestern Louisiana, newspapers quickly exaggerated her victim count and geographic reach.[1] In so doing, the press made Clementine Barnabet into an even more notorious serial killer.

Yet, manufacturing Clementine into a murderous monster was not simply a matter of journalistic flair. For years, entire Black families had been brutally axed in their own homes, the assailant slipping away in the night only to reappear in another rice belt town in southwestern Louisiana or southeastern Texas with a similar mission. Eventually dubbed the "axman," the elusive killer seemed to be both everywhere and nowhere at the same time.[2] The axman was not only unknown, but *unknowable.* Thus, when a young Black woman took credit for some—although not all—of the axman crimes, it was not surprising that the press immediately latched onto a known perpetrator as the target of its sensationalistic campaign.[3] If the killer had a name and had been caught, then presumably the madness would end. It did not matter that Clementine's narrative was full of inconsistencies. It did not matter that more murders happened after her confession. It did not matter that she was sitting in jail when over half of the axman crimes occurred. What mattered was that she was a known entity who served as a convenient—if contradictory—contrast to the intangible and terrifying axman.

This strategy of proclaiming a party as guilty despite evidentiary shortcomings was not novel in the case of Clementine Barnabet. By the early 1900s, the press had a decades-long history of printing narratives of violent crime that prioritized sensationalism, confirmed social norms, and offered worried readers believable if unsubstantiated explanations of lawbreaking.[4] As such, factual reporting was neither guaranteed nor expected: newspapers simultaneously covered *and* created the news. This duality also meant that the media defined who was and wasn't newsworthy. That the white press deemed a young Black woman important enough to grace the front page of papers from New Mexico and South Dakota to Pennsylvania and Florida offers strong evidence of the uniqueness of this case.[5] The liberties of *how* information was reported evinces historical continuity; *what* was reported appears to be unprecedented.

In constructing Clementine as a serial killer, newspaper reporters' sloppy ignorance of factual evidence did more than create a false sense of finality to the axman crimes. It also afforded an otherwise obscure young Black woman a disproportionate level of perceived power. Clementine Barnabet was effectively a random young Black woman in a random town in Jim Crow America. She was employed as a domestic servant in white households around Lafayette, Louisiana, joining the majority of Black women in the country who were relegated to backbreaking, low-paying work—either agricultural or domestic—during the early 1900s.[6] Had she not confessed to murder, it seems reasonable to conclude that Clementine would have blended in with the millions of Black women who lived, loved, and labored under the shackles of Jim Crow.

Clementine's confession thrust her into the national limelight in contradictory ways, but her decision to come forward may not have played out that way under other circumstances. Her notoriety emerged in response to two distinct contexts: the seemingly unceasing nature of the axman's rampage and her identity as a young Black woman from Louisiana. By the time of Clementine's April confession, the ax murders had rocked the rice belt for roughly two and a half years. That was a long time for entire communities to live under siege, perpetually scared of an unknowable assailant while responding to both real and constructed threats about the axman. That someone—*anyone*—had confessed to the crimes meant that the multiyear whodunit case had theoretically been solved.

Almost overnight, Clementine Barnabet became a household name. Her tripartite identity—succinctly understood as young, Black, and female—positioned her as both a scapegoat and mastermind as soon as she confessed. She defied social convention regarding who had the propensity to kill, and to do so violently, repeatedly, and without detection. Through print media and self-presentation, Clementine came to represent an amalgamation of perceived social ills, including religious deviance, racial admixture, and youthful depravity. Newspapers struggled to understand how someone *like her* could have been responsible for crimes that required both a fiendish disregard for human life and intentional cunning to escape without getting caught. In the minds of white society, a young Black woman *should not* have been capable of the kind of transgressive behavior that led to ax murder. In trying to make sense of Clementine's culpability, the press empowered her beyond the scope of what she said she did.

The press's empowerment of Clementine was a product of her confession, her identity, *and* the communities she impacted. For months on end, Black folks in the rice belt had constructed the axman to be the embodiment of unknowable fear. Eventually, they would also come to construct Clementine as the embodiment of known fear. In so doing, they established strategies of community care that prioritized communal- and self-defense, local knowledge, and cautious alliances. That they did not rely on white authorities for protection, but instead worked alongside *and* in opposition to formal investigative institutions, highlights how the axman murders functioned as both a community-making and community-breaking experience.

Inquisition for Blood: The Making of a Black Female Serial Killer in the Jim Crow South uses the saga of Clementine Barnabet to argue that gendered Black criminality was constructed by the press, local communities, the state, and even the perpetrator herself. Although it would be easy to dismiss Clementine as an exceptional case of historical notoriety, analyzing how she became a Black female serial killer and what that label tells us about constructing crime is more productive. Ultimately, criminalizing Black folks by gender was a legal, social, and cultural process in early twentieth-century America.

/ / /

To say that Clementine Barnabet was "made into a serial killer" is not to say that she committed the crimes attributed to her. Maybe she did; maybe she didn't. Instead, offering this moniker not only highlights the role of the media in constructing a particular narrative, but it invites broader considerations of stereotypes and assumptions about who does and does not commit serial murder. Clementine's story appeared in newspapers from Canada to India and from England to New Zealand, yet her legacy as a murderess has been overshadowed by her white female contemporaries, such as Jane Toppan, Belle Gunness, and Linda Hazzard. This whitewashing of serial murder has been reinforced by American popular culture and the genre of true crime. Even scholars have fallen victim to this trope.

Inquisition for Blood thus draws on Black women's criminal history to fill a void within scholarship on historical serial murder. For the past two decades, literature delineating the contours of Black female criminality in post-Reconstruction America has examined northern cities, southern carceral institutions, and the boundaries of Black womanhood itself.[7] Scholars have reckoned with the intersections of class, race, and gender, highlighting how urban sites served as contested spaces for autonomy, dignity, and survival.[8] They have parsed how Black women's incarceration in the Jim Crow South was a project of both modernization and criminalization, complete with racialized and gendered dynamics. More recently, a Black feminist lens has been used to interpret Black women's criminal history during slavery and its aftermaths to consider how and why some Black women chose violence, and what those choices say about the societies they inhabited.[9] This literature agrees that the criminalization of Black women has never been exclusively a product of the crimes attributed to them. Instead, social, cultural, and legal factors have shaped this process.

Meanwhile, scholarship on historical serial murder has yet to intersect in any meaningful way with Black women's criminality. Although it would be easy to suggest that this lack of engagement is due to a paucity of cases to explore, such an explanation is shortsighted and overly simple. Instead, there are at least two ways to conceptualize this dearth. First is the fact that literature on serial murder is saturated by both nonacademic and practice-based works. Much of the nonacademic research is rigorous and well-supported, but much of it also tends toward the true crime genre.[10] Likewise, practice-based literature, typically from psychologists, law enforcement professionals, criminologists, journalists, and more, focuses on the practical implications of identifying, catching, profiling, and understanding serial killers.[11] Where scholars of *historical* serial murder enter this conversation, it is almost always in the broader context of either violent crime or popular media.[12]

As such, researchers of serial murder have routinely addressed low-evidence examples, unnamed culprits, and tenuous threads. Academic, nonacademic, and practice-based authors have considered both Black and female serial killers with moderate interest, and some have even offered one-paragraph analyses about the Louisiana-Texas axman and/or Clementine Barnabet.[13] Yet, literature on historical serial murder has focused overwhelmingly on the most well-known serial killers in history, reinforcing the stereotype that serial murder is the purview of white men.

Indeed, the mainstream image of a serial killer conjures the Ted Bundys and Jeffrey Dahmers of the world, erroneously pigeonholing these offenders as hyper-intelligent and charismatic young white men. When the curious probe deeper, they may encounter either stories of an individual Black male or white female serial killer outlier, content that these individuals represent anomalies from the typical offender. At the time of the writing of this book, the reality is that over 20 percent of serial killers are Black and roughly 15 percent are women (either acting alone or with an accomplice), suggesting that neither is as atypical as stereotypes suggest.[14] Asked to name an individual from either of these groups, people may pause for a moment before spouting Wayne Williams or Aileen Wuornos as notable examples. When it comes to Black female serial killers, however, the American popular imagination is blank. The construction of serial murder as the domain of white men—with occasional deviations thrown in—does a disservice to Black female offenders and their victims. This is not to suggest that Black female serial killers should receive the same problematic celebrity as their white male counterparts.[15] Rather, this book highlights the dangers of racializing crime and perpetuating these biases in popular culture, thereby denying Black women's ability to be fully human.

Black men and women have been criminalized in the United States since the earliest days of an African presence on colonial soil. Labeled as animalistic, brutish, savage, and uncivilized, Black people's criminalization has historically relied on depicting them as inferior. Stereotypes about serial killers imply not only that they are more intelligent than the average citizen, but that they possess a level of alluring charm that enables them to get away with murder. This dichotomy has prevented reckoning with Black serial killers—both male and female—as a legitimate phenomenon. It is as if certain types of crimes have been gatekept by those who manufacture criminal stereotyping itself. I hope to rectify this oversimplification, not by unequivocally naming Clementine Barnabet as a Black female serial killer, but by showing that women like her have existed throughout American history. As uncomfortable as that fact might seem, it provides a more nuanced—and therefore more realistic—portrait of the history of violent crime in the United States.

The case of Clementine Barnabet disrupts more than stereotypes and assumptions about serial killers. At the height of her notoriety in the media, Clementine was at the nexus of Black girlhood and Black womanhood, which requires considerations of Black women and crime that are attentive to age. That a roughly nineteen-year-old Black female was described by the press as both a "silly child" and a "Black Amazon" is a product of her identity at the intersection of two unique life stages.[16] This positionality meant that she was not constructed as innocent or guilty, but simultaneously innocent *and* guilty. This is not a contradiction, but an outcome of the spectrum of human behaviors attributed to her by virtue of her identity as a young Black woman. It was Clementine Barnabet's youthfulness that captivated and terrified newspaper audiences, and it is this same youthfulness that permits this study of her to serve as a bridge between scholarship on Black girlhood and scholarship on criminalized Black womanhood. Differentiating this developmental stage within this literature can help us to better understand the full spectrum of Black girls' and women's lives on the criminalized margins of Jim Crow society.

Although early scholarship on the history of criminalized girlhood in the early twentieth century glossed over or briefly acknowledged Black girls, studies over the last fifteen years have explored Black female juvenile delinquency in northern and southern contexts.[17] These works reveal that Black middle-class ideals were often at odds with the lived experiences of Black girls and young women deemed incorrigible or delinquent. Even those who were not sent to formal institutions for criminalized circumstances or actions navigated their childhood and adolescence in race-, gender-, and age-specific ways. Thus, scholarship on Black girlhood in post-Reconstruction America emphasizes that this life stage was contestable, shaped by the geospatial differences between the North and the South, by the girls and young women themselves, and by the various people and institutions that sought to control their behaviors.[18] I use these frameworks about Black girlhood to explain how and why the press was able to imagine Clementine Barnabet as both innocent and guilty of the crimes ascribed to her.

In aggregate, *Inquisition for Blood* uses the role of print media—and the saga surrounding Clementine Barnabet—to push conversations about *young* Black women's criminality and Black female serial killers more generally.

These contributions do not require a definitive statement regarding her guilt or innocence, but instead highlight how knowledge about Clementine was constructed, for what purpose, and based on what evidence. Ultimately, then, this is as much a story about Clementine herself as it is about who she was imagined to be.

/ / /

Almost forty years ago, Black women's historians identified two of the biggest challenges of their work: a lack of findable manuscript collections in archives and institutional validation of the field as a worthwhile academic enterprise.[19] Since then, scholars have responded by "[doing] much with very little," "re-assessing the historical record," and "reading *along the bias grain*" (emphasis in original).[20] What has emerged has been a fascinating arc of the discipline: a self-critical field that privileges middle-class and respectable Black womanhood, while being acutely aware of the power structures that have created this imbalance in the first place. What has not emerged, however, has been an interrogation of the *way* records on Black women's history are found.

Scholars of Black women's history scour an impressive array of primary source materials looking for their subjects. Typically, this approach requires an identity-first methodology: find evidence of Black women's existence within given records, and *then* determine who they were, what they did, and why these fragments of their lives are preserved in this particular manner. Within the subfield of Black women's criminal history, this strategy has yielded many fruitful works over the last two decades. Yet, embracing this approach requires the perpetrator's identity to be known, or at least suspected, in the first place. In most cases of serial murder, however, anonymity is a necessity. This means that scholars interested in Black female serial killers cannot rely on an identity-first framework, but must consider an action-based strategy. In other words, we must think more like detectives and less like academics.

Practically, this action-based approach to *Inquisition for Blood* has resulted in a robust yet curious collection of primary sources. More than three thousand newspaper articles spanning the forty-eight contiguous United States, seven countries, nine languages, and hundreds of cities and towns comprise the bulk of the evidence presented here. A significant number of these clippings do not name Clementine Barnabet explicitly or implicitly. Instead, they focus on an unknown and unknowable perpetrator. Typically gendered male, the assailant would eventually be dubbed the axman. It was not until Clementine confessed to murder that a young Black woman became associated with the years-long reign of terror. That Clementine is not specifically named in newspaper articles about her supposed crimes is not a weakness of the sources, but a key feature of serial murder.

To fully capture the scale and scope of the Louisiana-Texas ax murders, I combed local and regional newspapers not for stories of Clementine, but for the actions that were eventually attributed to both her and the axman. I read hundreds of crime scene analyses, parsed how local communities connected the dots, and followed investigators' collaborations across jurisdictional lines. In aggregate, a stark picture of serial murder emerged *independent* of Clementine's confession, suggesting that whoever committed these crimes benefited from linkage blindness and rudimentary forensic science. It also confirmed that the scant secondary literature specifically exploring this case tends to employ an identity-first framework, ultimately leaving essential parts of the narrative obscured by sensationalism.

Still, newspapers are imperfect sources, though scholars of Black women's history have deftly demonstrated their utility in uncovering everyday experiences of marginalized and criminalized populations.[21] Moreover, print media itself played an essential role in how knowledge about the axman and Clementine Barnabet was created and circulated, suggesting that news outlets functioned as secondary investigators who sought to solve the whodunit paradigm. *Inquisition for Blood* thus prioritizes local newspapers' details about the murders while exploring how regional, national, and international media crafted increasingly sensational narratives of the crimes and the motives behind them.

The near omission of the Black press in a book about a Black female serial killer and Black community responses reflects available sources. Less than 1 percent of the articles I have about this case come from Black newspapers. Certainly, some Black press coverage has simply been lost to time and nature. Yet, evidence from white papers perhaps reveals the cause of the scarcity of Black media engagement: unimaginable fear. Black communities in the rice belt were ground zero for the pandemonium that had tangible consequences for their daily lives. For much of the saga that follows, both the authorities and lay folks believed the perpetrator was a Black man. Thus, to make public news about the axman in the Black press risked tipping off the unknown assailant, thereby jeopardizing Black communities' sense of safety. It also risked undermining racial uplift narratives that anchored many Black newspapers. Because white communities believed they were immune from being slaughtered, the voyeuristic lens of the white press is actually a productive window into what Black communities *knew* but were afraid to publish.

Although newspapers comprise the largest record type used in this book, additional primary sources piece this saga together. Court records, prison ledgers, Federal Writers' Project materials, censuses, death certificates, city directories, maps, photographs, archival collections, and more contribute to a fuller picture of the axman's crimes and legacy. At times, contradictions within and between these materials highlight the ambiguities of serial murder. I have found that *messy* is the most succinct way to describe these conundrums. Thus, I intentionally use messiness to emphasize how various types of evidence intersect to tell complicated—and sometimes competing—narratives of murder and its consequences.

At the outset, however, I want to acknowledge that some kinds of records are frustratingly absent from this story. It seems police reports from the crime scenes, for example, were not preserved. Likewise, even after more than a decade-long search, a transcript of Clementine's trial has not been located. Specifics regarding Clementine's incarceration periods—whether in the Lafayette jail or the state penitentiary—are also conspicuously missing.

Still, I commit to "doing more with less" while acknowledging the longstanding conversation in Black women's history that "certain subjects are avoided because they have been deemed either dangerous or damaging."[22] Although this critique was originally aimed at the seemingly taboo topic of sexuality, I suggest it applies decades later to sincere interrogations of Black female serial killers. While fear of reinforcing racist pathologies likely explains the reticence to explore those often lauded as the worst of the worst, omitting these individuals from narratives of the Black female experience unwittingly commits the same kinds of erasures Black women's historians criticized in the 1980s. Thus, *Inquisition for Blood* takes seriously the existence of Black female serial killers as a productive way to push the discipline's boundaries of telling inclusive histories.

/ / /

Although this saga proceeds chronologically, the press did not associate the initial murders with one another, though Clementine Barnabet would later suggest they should have been connected. That her timeline was imprecise never seemed to matter to either the authorities or reporters. Eventually, local lawmen would draw connections between crimes in their own and/or neighboring jurisdictions, but it was not until 1912 that they recognized that the pattern crossed the entire rice belt region. Additionally, the crimes that occurred in the early months of 1912 were definitively *not* committed by Clementine, though they bore an uncanny resemblance to their predecessors. The local press attempted to resolve this conundrum by naming the assailant the axman, but this descriptor faced its own challenges by the time of Clementine's springtime confession. Weirder still, the later crimes in the summer and fall of 1912 had glaring inconsistencies when compared to previous assaults, though by this point they were *known* to have been committed by the axman. All of that is to say, what follows is both a temporally linear story and one that is conceptually and evidentiarily messy.

Arguably, this linearity requires a significant disclaimer about serial murder itself: uncertainty is a required feature of the experience, especially in the beginning. Not only do multiple crimes have to occur for a series to exist, but commonalities connecting them must be acknowledged too. When these parameters are contextualized against the backdrop of turn-of-the-century policing and racial stereotyping, a curious juxtaposition emerges: the authorities were certain they knew who killed the first axman victims—multiple Black men. The lack of conceptual awareness that the assailant could be anyone else, let alone a single person, caused linkage blindness to cloud the early investigations. Thus, although this book chronicles Clementine's involvement in these crimes, it does so by first considering the way the authorities made assumptions about who was capable of committing murder in Black communities during the early 1900s. Stereotypes about Black *men's* criminality possibly allowed a Black *woman* to get away with serial murder for nearly two years.

The near-invisibility of Black women's criminality at the beginning of this saga stands in stark contrast to Clementine's headline-grabbing story by the end. This shift itself is a testament the power she was given and the power she claimed. Much uncertainty, madness, terror, and panic were created by the wholesale murder of Black families along the Southern Pacific Railroad. Clementine's power was a direct product of this fear: how communities experienced it, how the press covered it, and, ultimately, how she engaged with it.

Thus, although this is a book about the making of a Black female serial killer, Clementine Barnabet's name does not appear throughout every chapter: the first five murders were not originally attributed to her, and she was physically in jail when all of the 1912 crimes occurred. Still, she would eventually be labeled the axwoman and imbued with far more murderous power than evidence can confirm. Through the unknowable, the uncertain, and the elusive, Clementine became a serial killer.

Structurally, this book is divided into two parts: pre-confession and post-confession. A background chapter first sets the scene before the murders, contextualizing Black life in the rice belt as both unique and representative of broader themes in the New South. Then, part I outlines *how* a narrative of serial murder developed in the region, exploring the extent to which each crime contributed to this theory. These five chapters function as concentric circles that grow bigger and bigger, revealing how knowledge about the killings shifted from local and tenuous to national and sensationalized. Part II starts with Clementine Barnabet's April 1912 confession and then analyzes the end of the axman's reign, her October 1912 trial, and what is knowable about her decade-long imprisonment at the Louisiana State Penitentiary. Rather than functioning as concentric circles, these four chapters explore what kind of knowledge circulated once Clementine Barnabet became a household name. Combined, these parts reveal how a Black female serial killer was made in early-twentieth-century America.

Disclaimer on Conventions

Scholarship typically favors referring to historical actors by their last names. As entire families were killed by either the axman or Clementine Barnabet, this book uses first names for the victims for ease of comprehension. Similarly, multiple members of the Barnabet family were implicated as potential suspects, so these individuals are also referred to by their first names. For consistency's sake, therefore, members of the local communities who were impacted by the axman's madness are also discussed using their first names. Only individuals with titles affixed to their names—sheriffs, deputies, preachers, coroners, etc.—are discussed using surnames (plus, two of the main sheriffs involved share the same first name).

At the outset, it is worth mentioning that hundreds of law enforcement personnel worked these ax murders. The decision has been made to focus primarily on the county or parish sheriffs who oversaw much of the logistical handling of these cases, with references to their city and/or town counterparts as needed. For every crime, both the local sheriff's department and police department worked together. Therefore, mention of a given sheriff and "his" officers should be understood as shorthand for the many layers of officials assigned to the cases, not as a declaration of a subordinate relationship.

Similarly, the number of people who were arrested in connection with these crimes is astronomical. Some were detained as suspects, while others were held for the knowledge they were believed to hold. Still others were apprehended seemingly for being at the wrong place at the wrong time. Arguably, more unnamed people—overwhelmingly Black men—were arrested for the ax murders than were people whose names are known. Many times, newspapers did not bother to list out everyone sitting in a parish, county, or city jail who was connected to the axman. Nor, for that matter, did they report on when people were released. Yet, the fact that the slaughters continued—and that they were believed to be the product of the same killer—means that those who were incarcerated at the time of the latest murder could not have physically committed any of them. To improve readability and offer some imprecise conclusions, this book focuses primarily on suspects whose names were known. They represent the tip of the iceberg of those who got ensnared in the axman's wrath in nonfatal ways.

Speaking of names, the sheer volume of people and places identified by this research may feel overwhelming. In some ways, this is the point. The folks who lived through the chaos were continually overwhelmed by the unknowable nature of it all. However, we have the benefit of both hindsight and finality. So, a guide to the people, places, and crimes is included in appendix A. I encourage returning to this reference whenever a question arises about the setting or involved parties.

And now, let the messiness begin.

Setting the Scene

Life Before the Murders

This is a story about murder. And terror. And intraracial crime. It is an uncomfortable account of how local communities dealt with the unknowable over the course of three years in the early twentieth century. It is an exploration of a young Black woman's entanglement with Louisiana's criminal justice system, culminating not in her serving out the terms of her life sentence to the infamous Louisiana State Penitentiary, but in her release after roughly ten years. Yet, the events that transpired in this complex and sometimes contradictory saga did not occur in a vacuum. At the turn of the twentieth century, southwestern Louisiana and southeastern Texas underwent significant transformation, informed by both post-Reconstruction politics and technological advancement. Although different cities and towns experienced specific events that contributed to their unique characteristics—like the discovery of oil outside of Beaumont, Texas, and Rayne, Louisiana's shipments of regional delicacies nationwide—the rice belt as a whole changed significantly in the postbellum era.

Indeed, although other agricultural commodities were, and continue to be, produced in the alluvial marshy lowlands of the region, the significant cultivation of rice makes the area distinct. In 1909, Louisiana, Texas, and Arkansas produced 96.7 percent of the American rice crop. Within this near-monopoly, more than 95 percent of the grain came from the first two states, further highlighting the consolidation of rice production in a relatively small geographic area. Perhaps most important to this study, however, is the fact that the locations with the highest percentage of rice-cultivating farms—including Acadia and Calcasieu parishes in Louisiana and Jefferson County in Texas—were also locales visited by the axman. In the Pelican State, these two municipalities cultivated more than 60 percent of the state's rice crop in the first decade of the twentieth century. Across the Sabine River, this single county was responsible for more than a quarter of Texas's grain production during those years.[1] This is not to suggest the unknown killer *only* attacked in areas heavily dependent on rice irrigation, but that the grain's centrality to this story is a function of topography, geography, and technology. Crucially, the rice belt was simultaneously a rural region and one that was heavily industrialized by the early 1900s.

Thus, the rice belt is best understood as a distinctive setting driven by environmental conditions, technological innovation, and cultural syncretism. Aided by the expansion of the Southern Pacific Railroad (SPRR), the arrival of rice in the region altered the local economic and cultural landscape as towns and cities sprang up along the tracks. Simultaneously, Black life in the region shifted from the antebellum era through roughly the first decade of the twentieth century, reflecting the unique religio-cultural context of Louisiana's French Catholic and African American histories. Combined, these legacies confirm the distinctiveness of the rice belt and its utility to studies of turn-of-the-century Louisiana and Texas.

Yet, the intersection of Jim Crow norms and interracial violence situates the region in its broader context, suggesting that intraracial terror is an essential but understudied part of this conversation. Ultimately, understanding the rice belt as a cultural and agricultural site—as both a unique place and one that is inseparable from the New South—helps explain why and how the axman murders unfolded the way they did. I contend that it is precisely *this* context that not only allowed, but perhaps required, the contradictory sagas of Clementine Barnabet and the axman to coalesce.

/ / /

The rice belt region is a geographic area not defined by state, county, or parish borders. Instead, it is an amorphous place marked by environmental conditions.[2] In particular, moist clay soil, decent rainfall, relatively mild winters, and high humidity are necessary for the long-term successful cultivation of rice. Although these characteristics existed in the Carolina Lowcountry in colonial America and throughout the antebellum era, rice production in that region declined rapidly in the mid-nineteenth century.[3]

The destruction of South Carolina's rice farms during the Civil War shifted the grain's viability westward, initially settling in the delta along both sides of the Mississippi River.[4] Technological innovation, including the introduction of steam-powered pumps, increased the crop's profitability in Mississippi and Louisiana. Such improvements allowed water to be pumped into rice fields rather than relying on the gravity-driven flooding that had characterized East Coast rice production since at least the late seventeenth century.[5] In the decades following the Civil War, rice cultivation in the United States centered on the rich soils radiating out along the mighty Mississippi. In Louisiana, however, the only rice mill—the actual site where the grain was transformed from a plant into a sellable commodity—was in New Orleans.[6]

The westward push of the Southern Pacific Railroad helped unleash the floodgates of rice production into southwestern Louisiana and southeastern Texas.[7] In 1880, the completion of a line by the Texas & New Orleans Railroad between Houston and New Orleans connected otherwise disparate markets—and small towns along the way sprang up rapidly.[8] The next year, the Southern Pacific Railroad Company purchased the T&NO. Vermilionville, which was later renamed Lafayette, was not only one of the largest and oldest towns along the route, but located halfway between the two termini. In 1880, it maintained a modest population of roughly eight hundred people.[9] Lafayette was quickly dubbed "a convenient location for repair shops and a division terminal," solidifying the town's centrality to rail development and expansion in the region.[10]

Within two decades of the railroad's arrival, the population of Lafayette increased by more than 400 percent, transforming the once modest town into a robust city.[11] Just one decade later, the population had again doubled, making it the second-most populous Louisiana city in this study.[12] By 1912, however, Lafayette was pushed to its breaking point as ax murders swept through the region. Although the city was neither the first nor last location to be visited by the axman, it became the epicenter of the rice belt's saga. Not only was Clementine Barnabet from Lafayette, but the murders she took credit for occurred within a twenty-five-mile radius of the bustling parish seat.

The scale and scope of the railroad explains how a single site figured so prominently in a murderous rampage that spanned more than four hundred miles. By 1890, 90 percent of southerners resided in counties with railroads, and according to historian Tera Hunter, such technology was considered "one of the most modern symbols of the era."[13] By that same year, the Southern Pacific Railroad had purchased the smaller lines that pieced together a route from New Orleans to San Francisco.[14] The company had been chartered in 1865 with a singular if ambitious dream: to carve a railroad across the southern United States, linking goods and people from Louisiana, Texas, Arizona, New Mexico, and California to the more robust train system east of the Mississippi River.[15] Although the goal was realized in less than thirty years, it came with a price. Two decades later, the very railroad that was designed to connect cargo and passengers in the southwestern United States also provided easy access for an unknown killer to strike and escape without a trace.

Developing in tandem with the Southern Pacific route, the region's rice production exploded. Elites and boosters touted the must-see modernity sweeping through the marshlands, linking the area's growth to the broader South via the railroad.[16] The Louisiana Commissioner of Agriculture and Immigration, William H. Harris, started a concerted campaign in the 1880s to attract white Americans and European immigrants to the southwestern part of the state.[17] Drawing on the railroad to craft a narrative of technological and agricultural innovation, Harris propagated that "progress is the watchword in this land."[18] Yet, he operated under the capitalist colonizing mentality that the region was uninhabited and barren, therefore ripe for settlement. In reality, the indigenous Ishak peoples (commonly known as the Atakapa) had been ravaged from their native lands centuries before, Acadian refugees from Canada had claimed the area in the mid-eighteenth century, and enslaved people—some of whom could have been Clementine Barnabet's ancestors—had labored on sugar and cotton plantations and cattle ranches until the end of the Civil War.[19] Southwestern Louisiana might have been prime for rice cultivation, but by no means was it an ahistorical region waiting for a white civilizing mission.

By the end of the nineteenth century, it was Black laborers, not white businessmen, who drove rice production in southwestern Louisiana and southeastern Texas.[20] Following the end of the Civil War, roughly 4 million freedmen and freedwomen—perhaps including Clementine's parents—staked claim to their rights as newfound U.S. citizens.[21] They stayed in the South, they moved to the North and West, they reconnected with family, and they looked to the future without forgetting the past.[22] In Louisiana in particular, the state's unique history of a sizeable population of free persons of color, French empirical foundations, and Catholic ideologies helped facilitate a robust restructuring of political leadership during Radical Reconstruction.[23] At the local level, Black men were given political appointments as police officers, town marshals, postal workers, and other jobs, ushering a brief but significant moment in which people of African descent were afforded some of the liberties guaranteed to them by the Thirteenth, Fourteenth, and Fifteenth Amendments.[24]

By the time the Southern Pacific Railroad forged through the southwestern part of the state, the gains of this decade-long experiment had been decimated by white supremacy couched in a narrative of "redemption."[25] By the mid-1890s, Louisiana, once a state considered distinctive for its racial classifications and Catholic foundations, confirmed its commitment to the subjugation of Black folks by upholding the *Plessy v. Ferguson* decision. Based on a case involving Homer Plessy, a man of one-eighth Black ancestry who deliberately bought a first-class ticket and rode in a train's white carriage before being arrested for violating the state's separate car law, the decision reflected rollbacks from Reconstruction. Eventually, the Louisiana Supreme Court determined that "separate but equal" policies were constitutional. Segregation had gained a significant legal victory. The railroad, it seemed, had served as a marker of both technological progress and racial oppression.[26] As an ax murderer swept through the rice belt region in the early twentieth century, the train's dichotomous purpose would continue to make itself known.

/ / /

Despite erroneous claims that southwestern Louisiana was a barren land opened up by the Southern Pacific Railroad, the transportation technology did impact the region's accessibility.[27] Once reachable only by carriage, foot, or flat-bottomed boats known as pirogues, the marshy outposts of the area quickly developed into profitable communities by the turn of the twentieth century. A number of these towns, up-and-coming in the early 1900s, would be ensnared in a series of unfathomable ax murders within the next decade. Crowley, for example, touted itself as the "Rice Capital of America." Then it was struck by the axman. Twice. Rayne, which has the unfortunate claim of being the first town visited by the nocturnal killer, cultivated rice but was known for its unique regional export: frogs' legs. Lake Charles, located along its eponymous lake, the Calcasieu River, and the Southern Pacific Railroad, grew rapidly as timber was logged from mills upstream and sent with the current to the railyards, joining thousands of pounds of rice irrigated throughout the parish. Indeed, one of the axman's victims had labored at a timber mill just north of town.

Across the state line in Texas, Beaumont's logging industry was readily replaced with the discovery of oil, leading to an astonishing population boom of more than 600 percent from 1890 to 1910. Then, the discovery of axed bodies led to understandable panic. Glidden, established for no other reason than servicing SPRR trains, found itself in the news for something much more nefarious in the spring of 1912. San Antonio, known for cotton and sugar, and on the western edge of the rice belt, almost doubled its population in the first decade of the twentieth century.[28] It also experienced the predations of the axman more times than any other town or city along the railroad. Arguably one of the most significant technologies that reshaped the rice belt region at the turn of the twentieth century, the Southern Pacific Railroad's transportive potential shifted regional centers and led to uneven but substantial development as it connected the southwestern United States to New Orleans.

As much as the Southern Pacific Railroad restructured how agricultural commodities from the rice belt were sent to market from the late nineteenth century onward, the demographics of the laborers looked incredibly similar to that of the antebellum era. Rice might have come to southwestern Louisiana and southeastern Texas after the Civil War, but people of African descent already had an established—and distinctive—presence in the area. Although this project uses the broader American dichotomy between "Black" and "white" to distinguish community responses to the regional ax murders, the history of Louisiana affords a more nuanced understanding of racial and cultural identities in the rice belt. Colloquially known as Acadiana, southwestern Louisiana saw an influx of French refugees from Nova Scotia (Acadia) into the area starting in the mid-eighteenth century.[29] There, they encountered people of African descent who had already been in the territory for decades. Over centuries, a unique rural culture developed in what became the rice belt that was distinct from that of New Orleans.[30] From the outside looking in, a flawed and simplified dichotomy emerged: Cajuns became the descendants of the Acadian refugees while Creoles became the descendants of African and European heritages.[31] In reality, both Cajun and Creole people understood—and continue to understand—their identities to be more complicated, predicated on cultural continuities including foodways, music, geographies, ancestries, and religion.

While the term Cajun has generally maintained its association with Acadian refugees, even as many people who call themselves Cajun cannot trace their ancestry to French Canada, the term Creole has been applied to nearly every combination of people in what was once French Louisiana territory. White Creoles, Black Creoles, Creoles of color, Catholic Creoles, and other descriptors have attempted to redefine the term, complicating its meaning in the process. To make matters more muddied, even Cajuns have been identified as Creoles. And, in the broader history of Atlantic exploration, settlement, and enslavement, the term Creole has been applied to anyone—regardless of heritage—born in the New World, anyone of exclusively European ancestry born in various colonies/territories, and anyone of partial African heritage caught in this larger system of exploitative labor.[32] Not surprisingly, therefore, the term Creole has come to represent myriad and sometimes contradictory groups of people throughout Louisiana's history. Yet, in the southwestern part of the state, it is important to recognize the distinct legacy the term Creole maintains even in the modern era. Perhaps summarized as the belief that "black identity and French heritage are thought of not only as compatible but as inseparable," Creole has come to represent both pride and struggle for those who embrace the term.[33]

It is this legacy of Creole identity in the rice belt region that undergirds the unspoken racial characterizations present throughout this project. Indeed, Clementine Barnabet was often identified as Creole (though such a term was never applied to her father or brother). In the context of the ax murders, the term was more than racialized—it was politicized. While it is impossible to know if Clementine herself identified as Creole, when the label became associated with her in print media during the early 1910s, it represented not a proud heritage of African American and French identities, but the fact that such an amalgamation had presumably constructed a killer. At a national moment in which antimiscegenation ideologies proliferated, Clementine became Creole not because of her ancestry, but because anxieties about race-mixing were rooted in conversations regarding degeneracy and impurity. Given this context, Clementine is generally not described as Creole throughout this project. Nor, for that matter, are the terms Creole or Cajun used to describe others in this work. Instead, the terms Black and white are employed to contextualize people's experiences in the Jim Crow South.

This larger American racial binary permits general assessments of the towns and cities visited in this study. None of the Louisiana locations discussed at length in this work—Crowley, Lafayette, Lake Charles, and Rayne—had a majority Black population in the first decade of the twentieth century. Lafayette, the second largest Louisiana city in this study and the one that receives the most sustained attention, was roughly 44 percent Black in 1910.[34] The only Texas locale discussed here with a majority Black population was Waller County, which was 55 percent Black in 1910.[35] The county seat, Hempstead, was supposedly visited by the axman in the spring of 1912, and yet this was also the only crime that did not occur along the Sunset Route of the SPRR, but on a subsidiary line. It was also the first attack in which people survived, leading some to question whether it was actually committed by the infamous killer.

Combined, the technological and racial contexts of the rice belt paint a unique picture of a rapidly growing region that was highly dependent on the railroad, specialized in its industrialization, and culturally distinctive from New Orleans and San Antonio. Although the latter city does figure into this study due to three axman attacks, the differences between them and their eastern counterparts confirm the Bexar County seat's presence as an outlier in this saga. San Antonio's population of almost one hundred thousand residents in 1910 makes it the biggest city in this story, dwarfing the most populous Louisiana site—Lake Charles—more than eight times over.[36] That San Antonio was also only 11 percent Black in 1910 adds to the distinctiveness of the Alamo City in the broader axman narrative.[37] Still, as subsequent chapters reveal, what happened in San Antonio traveled east along the Sunset Route of the Southern Pacific Railroad, linking the south-central Texas city to the murderous madness sweeping the rice belt.

/ / /

Although an expansive history of the region's enslaved population is beyond the scope of this project, cultural continuities like religion shaped the rice belt's Black communities into the early twentieth century. After all, faith served as a key feature in the ax murder cases as both a source of comfort and a cause for concern. Protestantism, Catholicism, Pentecostalism, Voodooism, and hoodooism all swirled amid the unknowable nature of the crimes, with different faith communities celebrated or condemned, depending on their perceived proximity to the violence. That these groups appeared at all was a product of Louisiana's rich religious history, informed by both slavery and colonization.[38]

In Louisiana, the religious ideologies of people of West African descent stem from the region's history as a French colony, a brief Spanish possession, and then an American state. These worldviews are also informed by the indigenous communities that lived in the area pre-colonization. Enslaved laborers who arrived in French Louisiana—whether from the West African coast or from Caribbean islands—brought with them faith practices that differed from European Christianity.[39] Just as West African communities were not monolithic in their cultures, languages, gender roles, and participation in the transatlantic slave trade, they were also highly diverse in their religious practices.[40] Nonetheless, a few generalizations conclude that, though many West African cosmologies were monotheistic, they also believed in lesser deities to access the highest power.[41] Thus, while praying to a supreme deity might have been allowed in specific cases, the majority of faithful supplications were made to intermediary gods and goddesses. In different West African societies, these mediating deities went by different names, but their purposes were similar: they helped navigate life on earth and required a series of rituals, traditions, and knowledge bases for the faithful.[42] Known as *orishas* in Yoruba cosmologies—which, along with other West African deities, became *loas/lwas* in many diasporic communities—these middle-tier gods and goddesses wielded (and continue to wield) incredible power for believers.[43] Understood to have domain over certain realms—like love, war, health, reproduction, and more—orishas and loas/lwas also have personalities (sometimes represented through animals and/or natural forces) and temperaments that must be considered whenever offerings and prayers are made.

During the transatlantic slave trade, enslaved laborers carried the concept of intermediary deities to their respective boat stops, ushering in a diaspora of West African-derived religions ranging from Santería to Candomblé to Voodoo.[44] Try as they might, enslavers could not eradicate the vestiges of something so personal and engrained—an individual's faith. Thus, enslaved communities found different ways to integrate their own ideologies into the dominant religious milieus of their local environments. In French Catholic Louisiana, enslaved believers associated their intermediary deities with Catholic saints, allowing them to continue many of their religious rituals cloaked by the territory's acceptable faith. Attending mass, for example, provided an opportunity to communicate with a given orisha or loa/lwa under the guise of Catholic obedience, but finding the time and resources to act on the deity's instructions presented another hurdle.[45] Often reliant on components of herbalism that promoted a more holistic worldview in which earthly products—plants, animals, and their byproducts—could be used to elicit divine responses, West African religions typically demanded tactile engagement.[46] Praying to a given deity might resemble a Catholic ritual, but the necessity of, for instance, acquiring an ingredient for a specific mixture represented a connection to diasporic roots. At the same time, entirely separating Catholic rituals and diasporic practices might have represented one way some communities developed their own religious philosophies. Seemingly incongruous to outsiders, the reality of the various faith practices that comprised diverse, fluid, and yet essential religious ideologies among people of African descent in Louisiana must not be pigeonholed into Catholicism, Protestantism, or Voodoo.

Yet, it was not the overly simplified one-to-one imposition of West African orishas and Voodoo loas/lwas onto Catholic saints that defined the distinctiveness of Louisiana's—specifically southern Louisiana's—Black communities. It was also the backdrop of Protestant Christianity that further complicated the area's uniqueness.[47] Although Louisiana had (and continues to have) the largest percentage of Black Catholics in the United States, Protestant faiths have historically maintained strongholds in the rice belt region too.[48] In the *rural* South, however, the geographic distance between churches—not to mention individual families/farms—meant that religious communities were sustained not through Sunday services, but through daily practice. Building on John Hayes's concept of a "folk Christianity" that emerged in the poor rural South in the postbellum era, the nuances of southern Louisiana's history suggest a unique iteration of such faith practices developed in the region's marshy rice fields by the turn of the twentieth century.[49] The southern and western parts of Louisiana, though informed by the robust history of New Orleans, represent distinct cultures and communities that emerged *outside* of the purview of this urban center.[50] In the small towns that dotted the landscape—and the bayous and swamps in between—Black communities sustained their faiths through various mechanisms.[51] Thus, Black folks in the rice belt drew from Catholic, West African, Protestant, and practical considerations when developing religious ideologies that allowed them to make sense of their world. It was these ideologies that they turned to as ax murders swept the region—both to explain the violence and to save themselves from it.

Perhaps nowhere is this amalgamation more understood than in the proliferation of hoodoo in and beyond southwestern Louisiana. Described by historian Jeffrey Anderson as the outcome of "creolization and syncretism" in the nineteenth-century America South, hoodoo blends African, European, and Native American cultures.[52] Indeed, if Voodoo is best understood as an organized and holistic religion, hoodoo is more aptly characterized by historian Carolyn Marrow Long as "magical practices" undertaken by individual practitioners for specific clients.[53] Also known as mojo, tricking, fixing, rootwork, and conjure, hoodoo represents a way of interacting with and manipulating one's circumstances or situation through the use of artifacts, potions, spells, rituals, and more. Early twentieth-century hoodoo "doctors" recognized their ability to help believers in the realms of love, money, health, and more, and concocted specific charms—often with equally specific instructions—to bring about the desired result. Though not a formal religion, hoodoo nonetheless informed how many Black folks in the rice belt understood their world. In the axman madness, hoodoo functioned as proof of Clementine Barnabet's criminality, an exploitable form of self-defense for Black communities, and a shorthand for religious deviance offered by undiscerning white authorities.

In rural southwestern Louisiana, the monolithic misnomer "the Black church" actually reflects how Christian and non-Christian faith practices emerged in a specific geographic, racial, and religious context.[54] Given the complex setting of the region by the early twentieth century, a snapshot of local Black communities' ideologies suggests deep faithful devotion, belief in herbal remedies and folk medicine, acceptance of a supreme deity, acknowledgment of the appearance of spirits in the realm of the living, and adherence to cultural practices rooted in rationalizable superstition and inherited knowledge.[55] These themes reappeared at different points throughout the axman saga as people turned to their faith to make sense of the unknowable.

Ultimately, this legacy of fluidity allowed Clementine Barnabet to simultaneously say that she had grown up Catholic and believe that a conjure prohibited her from speaking at length about her crimes. It was not just in Clementine's mind that these religious worldviews could, and arguably must, coexist. It was an accepted way that people in the region navigated their worlds. Given these norms, then, it is not surprising that the Sacrifice Church—a religious explanation for the axman madness—came to represent both a hidden yet aberrant faith *and* a figment of people's imaginations. Clearly, the religious milieu of the area is at once the sum of these parts and entirely different from them: a spectrum of beliefs that has been erroneously mystified and criminalized by those who seek to read a single "truth" onto rich syncretic worldviews. The consequences—and promises—of this religious diversity were laid bare for three terrifying years in the rice belt in the early twentieth century.

/ / /

As much as religious diversity and racial categorizations gave the rice belt its unique character, the reality remains that southwestern Louisiana and southeastern Texas were still part of the New South. This necessarily meant that the region was defined by both the establishment and maintenance of Jim Crow ideologies. Jim Crow comprised laws, beliefs, and practices that, when combined, constituted a sociopolitical program of white supremacy in post-Reconstruction America. Although segregation—defined by historian C. Vann Woodward as the "physical separation of people for reasons of race"—represented one of the most pervasive and legally enforceable mechanisms of Jim Crow, other forms of racial discrimination pervaded daily life.[56] From fears of Black degeneracy and narratives of race-based extinction to convict leasing and sharecropping, Woodward notes that Jim Crow beliefs and practices not only "anticipated and sometimes exceeded the laws" governing discrimination and segregation, but they ensured white supremacy was perpetuated and sustained.[57] While detailing the scale of the Jim Crow regime is beyond the scope of this project, two components of its maintenance were essential to the broader context of the axman murders: fear of Black criminality and the widespread embrace of interracial violence.

The construction of Jim Crow ideologies required justification. To declare Black Americans inferior and criminal was as much an intellectual process as it was a legal one. Indeed, when Nathaniel Southgate Shaler penned "The Negro Problem" in the November 1884 issue of the *Atlantic Monthly,* he bemoaned that "there can be no doubt that for centuries to come the task of weaving these African threads of life into our society will be the greatest of all American problems."[58] To Shaler and many of his contemporaries, the topic of American race relations required both immediate and scientific study, leading to a wave of interest in racial science. Across disciplinary boundaries, social scientists took to early-modern penology, new statistical analyses, and postemancipation census data to construct an enduring and nefarious justification for Jim Crow ideologies: Black criminality.[59] Thus, when Frederick L. Hoffman published *Race Traits and Tendencies of the American Negro* in 1896—the same year the Supreme Court ruled "separate but equal" was constitutional—historian Khalil Gibran Muhammad asserts that the statistician merged "crime statistics with a well-crafted white supremacist narrative" to argue Black criminality was pathological.[60]

Although much of the turn-of-the-century racial science research was conducted in northern cities like Philadelphia, Chicago, and New York, the findings effectively criminalized Black migrants who'd left the South in search of better opportunities. Few white Progressive writers were willing to argue that the difference in Black folks' mortality rates, health outcomes, educational attainments, employment prospects, living conditions, and more were the product of environmental factors. Instead, many intellectuals and reformers latched onto the seemingly objective data of racial scientists, content that Black Americans were to blame for their own plight. If slavery had restrained the criminal impulse inherent in those of African descent, the logic went, then the sudden imposition of freedom had inadvertently unleashed a flood of criminality based on race. Now, at the dawn of a new century, three decades of postemancipation data seemed to confirm that surging Black criminality was indeed something to fear. Simultaneously, theories of biological criminality—promulgated by Italian criminologist Cesare Lombroso—offered physical markers of deviance as evidence of the "born criminal."[61] Thus, the leap from fearing Black criminality to condemning and controlling it was supported by a turn toward violence. That this fear was the product of white anxiety and essentialist interpretations of statistical data did not matter. As historian Douglas Flowe notes, the "crucible of black criminality" had been born.[62]

Given the way fear of Black criminality was created and sustained, it follows that Jim Crow ideologies did not develop in the rice belt peacefully. As coined by W. E. B. Du Bois, the "brief moment in the sun" of Radical Reconstruction gave Black Americans a taste of self-determination, political participation, and community autonomy, no matter how short-lived.[63] Woodward agrees the "cross currents and contradictions" of the decade-long experiment ensured the backlash was not necessarily swift, but it was undeniably violent.[64] Indeed, many have studied interracial violence in Louisiana, with particular foci on lynching statewide and policing in and around New Orleans. Within the New South, the Pelican State maintained a perverse distinction: having the third highest number of lynching victims from 1877 to 1950, exceeded only by Georgia and Mississippi.[65] From the 1873 Colfax Massacre of up to 150 Black men and the 1877 Thibodaux Massacre of at least thirty-five Black residents, to the 1891 New Orleans lynching of eleven Italian-Americans and the 1922 Mer Rouge lynching of two white men, Louisiana has a sordid history of resorting to extralegal brutality to maintain white supremacy.

Although the number of lynching victims in Texas was fewer than in its eastern counterpart, the Lone Star State still experienced significant levels of extralegal violence in the late nineteenth and early twentieth centuries. From 1877 to 1950, for example, more than three hundred Black folks were lynched in Texas, with the ten most active counties located in the eastern part of the state.[66] While only one of these counties—Waller—was visited by the axman, the region's culture of extralegal violence permeated municipal boundaries. Indeed, numbers alone do not fully capture the significance of lynching in and beyond the rice belt states.

Historian George Frederickson argues that lynching during the Jim Crow era was "an ultimate sociological method of racial control and repression," proof that only by resorting to extralegal violence could white supremacists maintain power.[67] Enacted as displays of punishment, warning, spectacle, and dominance, lynchings were public mechanisms to adjudicate perceived transgressions.[68] Importantly, the validity of the offense was irrelevant to the execution of extralegal violence, confirming the action itself as key to social control. While cases of multivictim homicide—like serial, mass, or spree murder—may be committed to rectify perceived wrongdoings, said justification is offered at the individual, rather than community, level. That is to say, the axman murders, although aimed at Black families, should not be understood as lynchings, but as a form of violence that coexisted alongside other types of harm Black folks experienced and recognized in Jim Crow society.

Moreover, not all interracial violence in the rice belt region occurred in extralegal contexts. Some of it was both legal and state sanctioned. From convict leasing and chain gangs to executions and local policing, the modern state has been constructed via the brutalization and subjugation of Black bodies. Many of these mechanisms evince the ways white lawmen abused and assaulted Black citizens, highlighting how the criminalization of Black men and women often rendered them guilty until proven innocent.[69] Scholars note that, in early twentieth-century America, the police typically functioned as an extension of both white supremacy and the carceral state, symbolizing a punitive regulatory entity that was emblematic of—and often above—the law itself.[70]

/ / /

Perhaps the most illustrative example of interracial violence that blurs the line between legal and extralegal in turn-of-the-century Louisiana is the New Orleans riot of 1900. Although this project intentionally decenters the state's most famous city, Robert Charles's revolt and subsequent murder offer precedent for the level of panic that swept local communities, as well as the headline-grabbing news coverage that followed the seemingly unthinkable crimes. Over the course of four tension-fueled days in late July, Robert Charles killed seven white people, including four New Orleans police officers, before being cornered in a burning building and riddled with bullets upon his attempted escape. Alongside the murder of Robert Charles, white mobs killed another seven Black victims and injured "several dozen more," according to historian K. Stephen Prince.[71] Scholars who have explored this case rightfully parse its significance for the city's "tinderbox" race relations as "a bold act of political resistance," and emblematic of "an outbreak of racial terror" in the South.[72] While no noose was ever literally tied around Robert Charles's neck, the (extra)ordinary violence he experienced as a Black man in Jim Crow America contributed to both his final rebellion and public execution.[73]

Important for the axman saga, however, is the fact that Robert Charles's actions have yet to be understood as those of a spree murderer.[74] Often confused as serial killers in popular discourse, spree killers are differentiated from their more sensationalized counterparts by the lack of return to normalcy following the first homicide. Like serial killers, however, the victim count need only exceed one for the FBI's definition of spree murderer to apply.[75] Robert Charles, upon realizing he had killed a white policeman, stayed on the run, aware that turning himself in risked being lynched or sentenced to a chain gang. In less than a week, he claimed an additional half dozen lives, reaching the preliminary victim count of perhaps the most well-known Black male spree killers: John Allen Muhammad and Lee Boyd Malvo, the D.C. beltway snipers. Roughly one hundred years before audiences fixated on the seemingly random murders gripping the nation's capital and trickling down Interstate 95, a "habitually armed" Robert Charles staked claim to and was killed by a complicated form of interracial violence.[76] While it may seem curious to end an assessment of extralegal, legal, and quasilegal violence in the rice belt during Jim Crow by suggesting that Robert Charles should be understood as a spree killer, the axman story seeks to inspire this kind of nuanced historical reckoning. Including Black men and women in the history of spree and serial killing, not to mention mass murder, paints a more comprehensive, if troubling, picture of how extreme violence functioned *and was investigated* alongside its everyday counterpart.

Indeed, the ability to recount these seemingly exceptional moments of violence stems from the broader context of interracial terror that swept the rice belt specifically—and the New South more generally—in the maintenance of Jim Crow ideologies. Though lynching was the "most violent form of racial harassment," it was far less common than nonfatal assaults on both people and property.[77] Yet, people's day-to-day experiences with myriad kinds of harms—from lethal to just plain loathsome—fundamentally shaped how they understood violence in distinctively racialized terms. Tellingly, however, this same racialization nearly prohibits Black men (and women) from being seen as serial and spree killers today and in the past, even as they were regularly lynched for being suspected of murder, one of the defining requirements for both of these designations.[78] To fully interrogate interracial violence in this era, all people must be understood as capable of committing all kinds of crimes. This is not to say that the rationales and motives beyond said crimes are independent of people's identities and experiences, but that criminalization is a social and political project rooted in beliefs about human capacity to cause harm.

Arguably, it follows that one of the unintentional consequences of focusing on interracial violence in Louisiana and Texas has been separate attention paid to its intraracial counterpart in histories of the region. This strategy implicitly ignores telling instances when intraracial violence elicited a distinct awareness of collective terror that competed with fears of interracial lynch mobs, police brutality, and everyday injury. A more complete history of Black life in the Jim Crow South must take seriously when inter- and intraracial violence *simultaneously* impacted people's sense of safety and community. While the axman murders represent perhaps one of the most publicized examples of this duality, additional works are needed to bring more nuance to this discussion.

/ / /

Returning to the larger context of the unfolding saga, the distinctiveness of the rice belt region contributes to localized historical studies of the New South. Indeed, part cliché and part earnest description, the setting of this project is perhaps best understood as Louisiana's iconic staple: a pot of gumbo. A mixture of Western African, French/European, Native American, and southern ingredients, cooking methods, spices, and more, gumbo eludes simple description but makes immediate sense to individuals who grew up on the comforting dish. Just as gumbo represents the region's interwoven and complex history, so too does the context of southwestern Louisiana defy a straightforward interpretation of the past. Many have addressed the nuanced social realities of the well-documented urban centers of Louisiana; fewer have parsed the understudied rice belt region in the post-Reconstruction era.

Southwestern Louisiana—and the rice belt region as a whole—represents a particular subsection of the New South informed by specific religious, cultural, social, political, economic, and agricultural contexts. Centering the narrative that follows within this environment provides a unique and provocative way to understand how, even against the backdrop of such amalgamations, a single person's claims forced the state—and the nation—to grapple with numerous challenges to define what kinds of communal values could and would be upheld. Indeed, in the pages that follow, dichotomies are contested, resisted, and broken. Questions of girlhood versus womanhood, religious devotion versus insanity, genetic criminality versus environmental corruption, and murder versus faithful sacrifice permeate this book. Few of these queries have comforting answers.

PART I

Pre-Confession

1

The First Crimes

Interpersonal Violence and Serial Murder

It was between 1:00 and 2:00 a.m. on a crisp mid-November night in 1909 when heart-pounding screams awakened the neighborhood. The shrill sounds raised concern, if not outright panic, on the Black side of town. Neighbors bolted from their beds to determine the source of the commotion, no doubt worried that the helpless cries of children foretold something bad.[1]

When they arrived, they were greeted by a gruesome scene: Edna Opelousas, a young mother of three, had been brutally murdered with an ax. Her skull had been split open, and some reports claimed her body had been hacked to pieces. Edna's young children—ranging in age from four to nine—had also been attacked with an ax, though they still clung precariously to their lives.[2] Blood covered the small cabin, evidence of the murderous assault.[3]

Neighbors sent for a doctor, but it was too late. Two of Edna's children perished by that afternoon. The third followed the next day. Within forty-eight hours, all four victims of this violent attack were dead.[4]

In the next fifteen months, another nine individuals in three families across southwestern Louisiana would meet their end in a nearly identical manner. The similarities and differences between these first four crimes explain how linkage blindness criminalized Black men while perhaps letting a Black female serial killer escape undetected. Ultimately, white press coverage of these crimes provides insights into Black communities' knowledge about both the murders themselves and local authorities' responses to them.

/ / /

Even in 1910 America, it didn't take long for news of the quadruple murder of the Opelousas family to spread. Rayne, Louisiana, was a small town with a big advantage: proximity to the Southern Pacific Railroad's southernmost route. Rayne's famous frogs' legs were shipped on ice, ready to grace the finest dining tables from New Orleans to Manhattan. In the aftermath of the Opelousas murder, however, both updates and gossip rode the rails along with amphibian limbs, titillating audiences from the Gulf Coast to the East Coast.

The day after the local newspaper published its account of the crimes, the *Sedalia Democrat-Sentinel* ran a sensational story from the Hearst News Service that claimed Edna Opelousas was not only a white woman, but a "daughter of a famous Louisiana family," for whom the town of Opelousas had been named.[5] As such, it was not surprising that two hundred men with dogs had been hunting for the killer and traced him to the piney woods. When they found the man, the paper concluded, he would be lynched in a matter of hours.[6] Accusations of murder were regularly used to justify mob violence in the era.[7]

That the small-town Missouri paper—and others subscribed to the Hearst service—managed to print such a story, no matter its veracity, was a testament to the way newspapers filled their pages in the early twentieth century. National newswires like the Hearst News Service (later the International News Service), the United Press, the Associated Press, and others conveyed must-read pieces to local papers that subscribed to their wires. These arrangements allowed small-town printers to carry stories from far-flung corners of the country, enticing their readers with titillating headlines and curious reports.

Yet, sometimes newswires were more concerned with breaking a story than confirming its accuracy. This race to publication occasionally led to sensational reprints across the United States that ranged from abysmally researched to entirely fabricated. Such was the case with Hearst's misidentification of the Opelousas family. The wire wasn't mistaken that folks were looking for the assailant, however. Apparently, a neighbor had seen a Black man "hurriedly passing" as the children's screams lingered in the air.[8] Another report confirmed that "the murderer fled and was seen by the neighbor next door south running with his hat in his hand."[9] Likely these accounts described the same person, imbued with journalistic flair to captivate readers. Despite the known limitations of eyewitness testimony today, in early 1900s policing, the neighbors' descriptions were good enough.[10] People followed footprints they believed to be the killer's out of town, but the man was never located.[11]

Whether the elusive man in the pine thicket or the hurried man with the hat were the same remains speculation. What is clear is that vigilante justice—the kind enacted by local communities who refused to wait for legal processes to proceed—bore no fruit. Instead, hundreds of curious visitors flocked to the scene, morbidly excited to witness the "grewsome sight."[12] At the same time, the authorities arrived and began scouring for clues. A single bloody ax had been left as a "reminder of the crime."[13] It was not until a couple days later that Rayne Marshal Lyman Clark revealed the victims had also been stabbed with a knife, which was now in his possession.[14]

In an era before fingerprinting, DNA profiling, and forensic pathology, the presence of the murder weapons was not enough for Acadia Parish Sheriff Louis Fontenot to determine who killed the Opelousas family. A mustachioed first-generation French American who had been elected sheriff the previous year, Fontenot likely hadn't visited too many murder scenes before.[15] Acadia Parish had its fair share of crimes—"seeking and soliciting orders for intoxicating liquors," "horse stealing," "wife desertion," and "cutting and stabbing with intent to kill," for example—but this was something else entirely.[16] When convened, the coroner's jury was at a loss.[17]

The case was perplexing. Edna was a twenty-some-year-old mother, the eldest living daughter of Demosthene and Georgiana Opelousas, two Louisiana natives.[18] It seemed that the Opelousas family was like other Black families in the region—one generation removed from slavery and building a life for themselves in the Jim Crow South. Edna and her children lived in a small outhouse—reportedly just ten feet by twelve feet—located behind her father's property. There were neighbors on either side and a Black church not too far away. The southern side of town, where the Opelousases lived, extended half a mile south of the Southern Pacific Railroad's tracks. Surely someone knew something about what had transpired that dark Saturday morning.[19]

It turned out that one of Edna's sisters heard the cabin door open and "saw a man entering the place."[20] She immediately summoned help, and the women's father headed toward the house, but it was not long before the screams of a little girl rang out into the nighttime air. Demosthene had been too slow—his daughter was dead and his grandchildren had been attacked.

If one of Edna's sisters had indeed seen a man go inside the cabin, it is surprising that Sheriff Fontenot had two Black women "arrested on suspicion" the day after the murder.[21] Likely, these women were America and Estelle Washington. Their arrest coincided with that of George Washington, their husband and father, respectively. It seemed that, although the Opelousases were an ordinary family living an ordinary life, there had recently been an altercation between Estelle and Edna for which the former had been arrested for assault, having threatened to kill the latter—and with an ax, no less.[22] Worse for the Washingtons was the claim that the ax used to kill the Opelousas family had been sold to either America or Estelle.[23] Still worse was the fact that "conflicting evidence" regarding their whereabouts on the night of the crime emerged, though George was believed to have an alibi. Plus, the two families had lived near one another for over a decade and it was reported that Edna and Estelle sought the affections of the same man. Since that fateful interaction, there had been "bad blood" between the Washingtons and Opelousases.[24] Was this a classic love triangle gone awry?

The authorities seemed to think so, though they conceded that the evidence against the Washingtons was "purely circumstantial."[25] In fact, less than a week after the Opelousases had been murdered, a man by the name of Houston Goodwill was arrested in New Iberia and brought to Crowley, the Acadia Parish seat.[26] It appeared that he, too, had problems with the family. According to the local newspaper, Houston was actually Edna's brother-in-law. Up until roughly a week before Edna and her children were murdered, Houston and his wife had been living in the very outhouse where the crime occurred. This small structure was on the same plot of land as the Opelousases' main house, likely not more than a couple yards away. It was in this larger cottage with her parents where Edna had originally lived with her children. Yet, she and her sister were not the Opelousases' only children, so conceivably quarters were a little tight.

When Houston supposedly got violent with his wife and threatened her life sometime in early November 1909, everyone heard it. Out of an abundance of caution, the family decided to swap living arrangements: Edna's sister and her children would move into the main house and Edna and *her* children would move into the smaller cabin. Houston, meanwhile, had been "driven from the place," leaving for parts unknown.[27] Roughly a week later, however, it seemed that he had come back, intending to make good on his threat to kill his wife. Against the darkness of the Louisiana sky, Houston reportedly got to work, hacking at the female form asleep in the outhouse. According to the authorities' theory, it was too late when the wannabe wife killer realized his mistake: he'd slain his sister-in-law and her children had started to stir. In a moment of panic, he axed them, too. Then he ran.

As in the case of the Washingtons, the evidence against Houston Goodwill was "purely circumstantial," though Sheriff Fontenot considered it "strong enough" to detain Houston for additional questioning.[28] But the authorities' theory about Houston's involvement seems hasty at best. Although it's possible that Houston killed his sister-in-law and her children in a fatal case of mistaken identity, his supposedly frenzied realization doesn't align with the two-implement violence that marked the victims' bodies. Why would someone unnerved by such a mistake suddenly switch from using an ax to using a knife? How would they have had the collected demeanor, let alone the time?

And here's where the paper trail starts to thin. As much as the authorities arrested people "on suspicion," they tended to release them without fanfare. Whatever evidence had brought Edna's brother-in-law and most of the Washington family into custody wasn't enough to keep them there. Houston, George, America, and Estelle eventually walked out of jail, though the details of when and how are unknown. It seemed at the time that whoever had killed the Opelousas family had gotten away with murder.

/ / /

About a month after the Opelousas family was brutally murdered in their home, a massive blizzard pummeled the South during the holiday season.[29] It was one of those once-in-a-lifetime kinds of storms that plunged the region into an early winter, bringing biting cold and nipping winds to towns ill-prepared to handle heavy rain, let alone snow and ice. But bad weather wasn't enough to stop the Southern Pacific Railroad's trains from chugging along, bringing people and goods across the southern states. From Rayne, hopping any one of the four passenger lines headed west, Crowley would be the first stop—followed by a series of tiny towns—and then, before long, Lake Charles.[30]

It was the rapid expansion of the railroads—the Southern Pacific and its competitors—that brought cheap and convenient labor to the rice belt region. From the early 1880s to the mid 1910s, the number of miles of tracks crisscrossing the United States more than doubled. This massive infrastructure project required significant manpower—men to lay rails, drive spikes, haul equipment, and dig troughs. In 1910 Lake Charles, Richard Lee was just the man for the job. Early that year, in the aftermath of the must-see blizzard, Richard was working as a section hand for the Kansas City Southern Railroad and needed a place to stay for roughly a month.[31]

Elijah and Minnie Hodge agreed to take in Richard as a temporary boarder. This arrangement wouldn't have been out of the ordinary for Black families at this time; it was another mouth to feed, but the person would pay for board and help make ends meet. The Hodges had a toddler son, so the extra income would be welcome.[32]

It was within this context that the three adults and one young child resided in a simple frame house near the intersection of Jackson and Rock Streets on the northern side of the city, just one block north and east of where the Southern Pacific's tracks bisected Lake Charles. Even though the family and their tenant lived within a dozen blocks of five different lumber and milling companies, there was no guarantee of work so close to home.[33] It seems that Richard's gig had the potential to take him far out of town, wherever the next section of tracks needed to be laid. Elijah, on the other hand, had to make the lengthy journey north for his job at the "Albert Goos' mill at Goos Ferry," one of a handful of sawmills that dotted the meandering Calcasieu River.[34] Likely, the seven-mile one-way trip meant that sometimes Elijah would stay up north for a night or two—probably boarding with a local family or camping out near the mill.[35] Then he'd come back, check on his family, and return to work. This was a fairly common situation for working-class Black men whose employment opportunities were constrained by Jim Crow policies. After all, the Hodge family had taken in a boarder of their own. As long as Elijah's lodging costs were less than the money Richard paid the couple, they stood to make a small profit.

On Thursday, February 10, Minnie made her husband, Elijah, a cup of coffee before he left for work.[36] When Elijah returned home on Friday morning, he presumably expected to be greeted by his wife and baby boy. Instead, he found Minnie's head split open and his young son's face crushed.[37] One paper inferred that Minnie had been "hacked at . . . time after time," suggesting extreme brute force was used to extinguish her life.[38] Another put it plainly: the bodies had been "chopped almost to pieces."[39] However their bodies were cut, whatever mutilation rendered them lifeless, Minnie and her son were now lying in a bed, covered in congealed black blood. And their husband and father had discovered them.

He sounded the alarm.[40] Calcasieu Parish Sheriff David J. Reid and four deputies arrived on the scene and made a troubling discovery: two weapons had been employed to commit the murders.[41] An ax hacked and smoothing irons bashed. A disorderly house indicated that something had gone terribly awry after Elijah left for work. Although the murderous implements were located—including the ax beneath a vacant house nearby—the authorities did not have any definitive leads as to who would have wanted the Hodges dead.

Even the five-man coroner's jury was dumbfounded and rendered an unsettling verdict: "death at the hands of parties unknown."[42]

The violence was almost unfathomable. It seemed so horrible, so grotesque, that people had to get a glimpse for themselves. Convening around the house, white and Black bystanders curiously peeked and probed, trying to see anything.[43] They wanted to understand how *this* could have happened *here*. Established in 1861 as Charleston, Lake Charles wasn't huge, but, with a population of over 11,000 residents, it was certainly a city by early 1900s standards.[44] Now, as the region trended upward for its abundant lumber, rice, and turpentine, it seemed that an untraceable assassin was in their midst.

Initially, however, Sheriff Reid and Coroner William L. Fisher suspected someone much closer to home had killed the Hodges: Elijah Hodge himself.[45] According to the coroner's assessment, the coldness of the bodies suggested that they had been dead "quite a while," perhaps as early as Wednesday night.[46] If this timeline were true, then it meant that Elijah had killed his family before he headed to work, fleeing quickly to create an alibi.[47] Not surprisingly, he was arrested and lodged in the Calcasieu Parish jail. A coworker and friend, Abraham Potter, who'd been invited by Elijah to join him on the sojourn home, was also detained.[48]

Just as quickly as he was arrested, Abraham was released.[49] Elijah, however, was not so lucky. Sullen behind bars, he continually professed his innocence, going so far as to name a potential assailant: Richard Lee.[50] Elijah suspected that the family's boarder had turned into a cold-blooded killer. Neighbors of the Hodges corroborated his statements, commenting to the police that the tenant had suddenly disappeared.

Apparently the arrangement with Richard hadn't exactly gone to plan. Minnie said he hadn't paid $1.50 for his board (just over $50 in 2025).[51] He claimed he didn't owe it. When Richard left under less-than-amicable terms, Elijah had solid reason to name him as a suspect who could have wanted the Hodges dead. About a week after the family was found murdered in their home, Richard Lee was arrested in Woodlawn, roughly twenty miles east of Lake Charles. Sheriff Reid and one of his deputies put him in the Calcasieu Parish jail. Somewhere in these developments, the authorities came more and more to believe Elijah was telling the truth and Richard was lying. The former man was released while the state worked to build a case against the latter.

Minnie and son had been murdered in February. Richard Lee's trial started on July 29, 1910, months after he had been officially charged with murder. If found guilty, he risked life behind bars. It didn't exactly instill confidence that the presiding judge, Winston Overton, asked the all-white jurors to "relieve their minds" of any presumptions that the court was biased in favor of the prosecution.[52] Equally concerning, this was the first case for one of Richard's state-appointed attorneys.[53]

When the state presented its argument, witness after witness was called. The gist of their case was that, supposedly, on Wednesday night Minnie had told Richard he needed to pay up or get out. On Thursday morning he headed to work on the railroad. Afterward, he visited an unknown Black woman until the sun set. Then he went to visit *another* woman until 9:15 p.m., give or take fifteen minutes. No earlier than 10:30 p.m., he showed up at Robert Williams's house and spent the night. The next morning, bright and early, he told the section foreman that he would come back to work if he managed to find a new boarding house. The implication, of course, was that Richard had done *something* that precluded him from returning to the Hodge home. Instead of locating a new residence, however, it seems that Richard visited one of the two women from the previous evening before heading to Iowa, Louisiana, around noon. There, he worked on the railroad for a few days under a different boss. Then he got a job on a rice farm. At no point did he go back to the original foreman to collect his pay. Insinuated in the prosecution's argument was that Richard kept trying to get farther and farther away from the murder scene, literally putting distance between himself and the violence.[54]

Despite trying to avoid any association with the crime, there was some compelling evidence against Richard, according to the prosecution. His trousers and coat were found in the same room where Minnie and her son were murdered. The articles were covered in blood. The prosecution surmised that the roughly one-hour window between visiting woman-number-two and Robert Williams was the perfect opportunity to attack Minnie and son while still appearing to have alibis for the evening. Then, still trying to not implicate himself in the madness, Richard hightailed it out of town. He was a man on the run, they claimed.

When Richard took the stand, he denied everything. But he was a Black man being tried before an all-white jury. His attorneys attempted a last-ditch effort to save their client by claiming that the "court was aiding the prosecution" because the judge had asked questions of witnesses that evidently worked in the state's favor.[55] Annoyed, Judge Overton chided the lawyers and emphasized the jury's exclusive power. At 10:15 p.m., the twelve-member jury received its instructions.[56] Before the clock struck 11:00 p.m. they returned their verdict: "guilty without capital punishment."[57] Richard Lee was sentenced to hard labor "for the period of his natural life" at the Louisiana State Penitentiary.[58]

Richard's attorneys appealed the sentence. It seemed that there was a messier story present than what the lower court had heard. As Richard's case was snaking its way to the Louisiana Supreme Court, testimony from neighbors, friends, and others painted a complicated picture of the domestic affairs of the Hodge family. Minnie Hodge was, at least legally, Minnie *Jackson*. Her estranged husband, Monroe Jackson, had confronted her on more than one occasion regarding the paternity of her child—the same child who lay murdered in cold blood in February 1910.[59] According to various witnesses, Monroe threatened Minnie, claiming that she needed to dispose of the child before he returned, lest he "tend to her."[60] By the time the Hodge-Jackson-Lee saga reached its appeal in the Louisiana Supreme Court, it was believed that a single left-handed person committed the murders, despite the variety of implements used. From all available evidence gathered, it seems Richard Lee was right-handed.[61] But this was Jim Crow America, and Judge Overton refused Richard a new trial. He conceded that the "state rested on circumstantial evidence," but that was good enough to render a Black man guilty.[62] The verdict was affirmed: Richard was going to prison for life.[63]

What if, however, Monroe Jackson was actually involved in the murder of his wife and nonbiological son? This is not to suggest Monroe was definitively the culprit, but that the authorities had offered up two individuals who both had seemingly logical reasons to want the Hodge duo dead. If Richard Lee did not kill Minnie due to a lack of payment, there were at least two possible explanations: he was a hitman for hire or he was in the wrong place at the wrong time. In the first scenario, Monroe could have paid Richard to murder the former's wife and child. Whether he would have done this *because* Richard was a boarder in the Hodge household or if the scheme involved getting access to the house's occupants by posing as a boarder is hard to say, but it's not a far-fetched idea. Of course, the question of the killer's dominant hand still lingers. In the second scenario, Monroe could have returned himself to "tend" to Minnie and her son. Then, he could have slipped away undetected, and Richard could have taken the fall as an innocent man. The Jim Crow criminal justice system did not go to great lengths to differentiate between the guilty and the innocent when Black men were involved.[64] This investigative blindness, steeped in both racism and stereotypes, allowed the authorities to fixate on socially constructed suspects rather than embrace the plethora of possibilities permitted by the evidence (or the lack thereof). By understanding how lawmen assumed Black male criminality in circumstantial cases like this one, the prospect of either a serial or Black female offender was ignored.

Although Monroe Jackson and/or Richard Lee could have been involved in the deaths of Minnie Hodge and her son, it is also theoretically possible that this was a typical case of a vengeful husband. Elijah could have murdered his wife and child after having learned that there was a chance that neither was his. If this was the case, he would have had every reason to point fingers at Richard: it would take the heat off his own back and make him appear to be a cooperative witness. Of course, it would also probably make sense for Elijah to point to Monroe, too, especially if he believed *this* man was actually his dead wife's legal husband and dead child's biological father.

Then again, whoever killed the Hodges could have been someone else entirely, someone who was not related to the family and did not know anything about their convoluted personal affairs. That the authorities did not consider this possibility—and that this case has generally not appeared in works on the Louisiana-Texas ax murders—highlights the ways stereotypes about Black men's criminality have precluded—and continue to preclude—sincere investigations into other potential assailants.[65] Imagining that the killer could have been *anyone* else broadens conceptualizations of who has committed murder in the past, and who is capable of murder in the present.

If, in fact, the Hodges were slain by a stranger, then an unknown killer remained at large while Monroe and Richard were implicated in a violent murder they knew nothing about. In fact, this secret slayer could have snuck into the house, believing it to be occupied by Minnie, Elijah, and their little boy on that fateful night. Perhaps the assailant intended to attack the entire family, but realized somewhere in the commotion that Elijah wasn't home. At that point, there would have been nothing left to do but leave. If a stranger killed the Hodges, they had covered their tracks to render themselves untraceable.

/ / /

The Opelousases were killed in mid-November 1909 in Rayne. The Hodges met their end in mid-February 1910 in Lake Charles. The murders occurred in two towns sixty miles and three months apart. This chasm of time and space meant that people in the rice belt region did not link the crimes. Why would they? In both cases, viable suspects emerged. Black men and women who were personally connected to the victims were implicated in the killings, and the evidence against them was compelling. Perhaps the Washington family's feud with the Opelousases had turned fatal. Maybe Houston Goodwill's attempt to murder his wife resulted in the death of his sister-in-law instead. Possibly Richard Lee had decided to slaughter Minnie Hodge rather than settle his debt. Then again, Monroe Jackson could have slain the woman to do just that—right a perceived wrong. Elijah Hodge could have taken away the lives of his loved ones when he sensed they were being taken from him. At the time, no one knew what to think.

Critically, however, there was no consideration of whether somebody wanted *these* families dead. The authorities in Rayne and Lake Charles approached each crime as a tragic but isolated incident, the outcome of interpersonal problems gone terribly awry. As such, the media coverage of both was relatively sparse. The local papers followed the stories, and other outlets in Louisiana and Texas offered abbreviated synopses. Occasionally, far-off newspapers in the Midwest and South reported on the killings, but none attempted to speculate about a potential killer beyond the suspects already discussed.[66] In aggregate, then, print media described these crimes, but it did not offer commentary on what had transpired. For all that the residents of the rice belt knew, two random Black families had been independently killed with an ax. Black communities in Rayne and Lake Charles grieved the loss of their own, but they did not associate their mourning with what was happening elsewhere in the region.

Yet, in recounting the similarities between the murders here, it seems there might have been a thread of more-than-coincidence to consider. Both the Opelousases and the Hodges lived within half a mile of the Southern Pacific Railroad's line from New Orleans to San Francisco. Both Edna and Minnie were home alone with their children on the fateful night of their deaths, which was not necessarily a guarantee given their respective living arrangements. Both were Black women with children under the age of ten. Both were slaughtered with an ax and secondary weapons, including a knife and smoothing irons. In both cases, all of the weapons were recovered. From newspaper reports at the time, it seems reasonable to surmise that both women endured overkill—the infliction of injuries significantly beyond what is needed to fatally wound a victim—while their children were not harmed as egregiously.

These kinds of consistencies between the cases are not airtight proof that the same individual had killed the Opelousases and the Hodges. People at the time did not associate the crimes, and the tenuous yet compelling evidence that links the two is pure speculation. Indeed, historical omnipotence constructs such connections in the first place. But, for a singular messy narrative to emerge in this saga, there must be some kind of logical progression. By default, however, the initial actions of a serial killer do not make sense. The crimes appear random until, quite simply, they don't. In the early 1900s, it was not easy to shift from the senseless to the possible and then to the likely. Maybe the murders of the Opelousas and Hodge families were not committed by the same killer. Then again, perhaps they were.

/ / /

If both lawmen and layfolk did not immediately connect the deaths of the Opelousases and the Hodges, the same could not be said for the murders of the Byers and Andrus families in early 1911. In these two cases, a clear divide emerged between how the authorities understood the crimes and how Black communities interpreted the violence, even as their insights were filtered through the white press. The contexts of Crowley and Lafayette, respectively, highlight the different ways these killings were discussed.

Though Rayne had been labeled the "commercial centre" of Acadia Parish in the late nineteenth century, it was supplanted in the twentieth by its westerly neighbor, Crowley.[67] The seat of the parish, Crowley went from sparse railroad stop to urban hub in a short span of time. In 1890, less than five hundred people called the town home.[68] Only one decade later, the population had multiplied ten-fold.[69] That level of growth brought with it a dizzying balance of good and not-so-good. Determined to be the "rice capital of the country," Crowley boasted mill after mill mere steps from the railroad tracks, capitalizing on proximity to both marshy rice paddies and grain-hungry consumers across the United States.[70] With industry came people—people to run the mills and people to run the people running the mills. That is to say, businessmen demanded modernization in Crowley, and laborers made it a reality. Beautiful entertainment venues, dazzling restaurants, a stately train station, concrete sidewalks, and a bustling downtown made Crowley *the* place to be in Acadia Parish by 1910.[71]

Modern Crowley was also segregated Crowley. While most Black folks were relegated to the essential but invisible work of making the city run, a handful of Black proprietors established businesses of their own. In 1902, the People's Investment Company opened to serve as a financial institution for its own community. A barbershop, skating rink, coffee stand, retail store, and more gave Crowley's Black community places to shop and unwind away from the view of prying white eyes.[72] But separate was never equal: in mid-May 1909, the city council joined national crusades against uncontrolled prostitution and other vices by proposing the establishment of a red-light district in the predominately Black neighborhoods known as "Coontown" and the "Promised Land."[73]

Almost as soon as the ordinance was passed, Black residents and local white women launched discrete protests against the presence of "such a den of crime and immorality" anywhere in Crowley.[74] Nearly three dozen Black citizens had held a meeting to organize their thoughts, arguing that the district was "a cancer to the life and progress" of their community.[75] More than 250 white women signed a petition to repeal the ordinance.[76] Even so, the objections failed to change the minds of the city council. Legalized sins like prostitution, gambling, and drinking were all to be located in a tidy rectangle bounded by Hutchinson Avenue, Western Avenue, Fourth Street, and Avenue "P."[77]

Although Crowley's Black residents had insisted that the red-light district not be located near their community, the city's white institutions passed the ordinance anyway. The financial and (perhaps) personal benefits of such seedy activities trumped any claims of increased immorality for city leaders.[78] As a result, Black citizens were forced into a geographically and socially vulnerable position that reinforced Jim Crow ideologies and confirmed that white authorities were not genuinely concerned with the well-being of *everyone* in their city. For Crowley's Black community, the legal establishment of the red-light district literally "across the street" from the recently built school for their children was undoubtedly a slap in the face.[79]

One day at the end of January 1911, a young girl—likely a pupil at that very school—headed to the home of a local family: the Byerses.[80] Walter Byers worked at the U.S. Rice Milling Company, located between two of the three railroads with tracks in town: the Southern Pacific to the north and the Opelousas, Gulf & Northeastern to the south.[81] From the family's home at 605 Western Avenue, one block north of the "Negro Public School" and just on the outskirts of the red-light district, an "industrious and reputable" Walter would have regularly walked approximately one mile southeast to the mill.[82] Both he and his wife, Silvina, were officers at Morning Star Baptist Church.[83] The couple had a child who was roughly six years old. By all accounts, it seemed that the Byers family was living a peaceful and productive life on Crowley's west side.

Yet, on that fateful Thursday afternoon, the little girl with the nondescript errand noticed something was amiss at the Byerses' home. First, the doors were locked. Then, she got a whiff of the smell. It was, according to city's newspaper, "dreadful."[84] She undoubtedly panicked, and it wasn't long before the authorities were on scene.

Walter had never made it to work that Thursday. Nor, for that matter, had he been there on Wednesday.[85] A close neighbor claimed to have last seen Silvina on Tuesday evening, corroborating Coroner Hines C. Webb's assessment that the victims had been dead for roughly thirty-six hours before the bodies were discovered. Perhaps most troubling was the fact that not only had Walter and Silvina been killed, but so, too, had their young child. Western Avenue was a main thoroughfare and densely populated. Who could have possibly had the motive *and* the audacity to kill the Byerses?

Someone had entered the house through a window and taken an ax to the heads of the unsuspecting family members. Forceful blows extinguished their lives as blood soaked into the single bed occupied by all three victims. Although the authorities initially surmised the family had been sound asleep when they were killed, officers later concluded that Silvina was "killed on the floor and then laid on the bed" by her slayer.[86] They believed she may have refused to go with her attacker, ultimately resulting in her death and posthumous positioning.

While newspapers reported the disturbing prospect that investigators had no clues in the case, there was evidence—besides the bodies themselves—that had been left at the scene. Bloody footprints were found on the floor. On a washstand in the bedroom, a washbowl with "bloody water" implied the killer had washed their hands at some point during or after the ordeal.[87] Beneath the washstand, "a basin half filled with blood" served as a grotesque testament to the violence that had occurred.[88] The murder weapon itself—a bloodstained ax—was located at the head of the bed.

With this scene in mind, both parish and city officials probed into the Byers family's personal affairs. It turned out that things were not quite as peaceful as they appeared. Walter had recently had some altercations. The local paper noted that he had made "several bitter enemies" at church and had a "row" at the mill with a coworker less than a week before he was killed.[89] Said workmate was apparently fired because of the quarrel. Reportedly, the two men eventually "made up," but losing one's livelihood would certainly make anyone upset.[90] Upset enough, the authorities wondered, to commit murder?

But it wasn't just people at church and the mill who raised eyebrows. Ed Jackson, a Black man who had been "mixed up with the family for some time," was the first individual arrested in connection with the murders.[91] Although it is unclear exactly what the issue was between Ed and the Byerses, it seems that it was serious enough to cause Silvina to "leave her home" a few weeks before the family was killed.[92] Still, the evidence against Ed was circumstantial at best. The authorities were not convinced he alone was the killer.

Within a few days of Ed Jackson's arrest, another suspect was placed behind bars: Walter Jackson, a local barber and Ed's brother.[93] Whatever information the police had against the Jackson siblings was held close to the vest. Despite reports that they had gathered evidence that was almost "sufficient to convict," the actual connection between the two families remained shrouded in mystery.[94]

The day after the crimes were discovered, the Byers family was eulogized at the very same church where they had been devoted—if recently confrontational—members.[95] Morning Star Baptist had just undergone its own transition after the death of its beloved pastor, Reverend Joe Barker, mere months before.[96] Now, Henry Clay Ross, educator-turned-pastor, would have to guide his flock and Crowley's broader Black community through their unimaginable grief.[97] That "all the colored people" had reportedly turned out for the morning funeral suggests the murders had a profound impact.[98] Although the Byerses represented a single family, their deaths symbolized an assault on Black Crowley. Just as the community had banded together to resist—albeit unsuccessfully—the establishment of the red-light district adjacent to their neighborhoods, the collective response to this individual event acknowledged the interconnected plight of Black folks in the city.

Quickly, then, Reverend Ross sprang into action, leading Black residents to organize a mass meeting at the church just hours after the homegoing service.[99] There, representatives of the Black community adopted various resolutions that promised to assist the authorities in bringing the killer or killers to justice, representing a form of interracial cooperation between law enforcement and Black locals.[100] At the same time, Black leaders recognized that not everyone in the community might want to help the police; Reverend Ross implored attendees to "tell what they knew" and "stand for law and order."[101]

After all, three of their own had been slaughtered in cold blood and, despite the arrest of the Jackson brothers, it seemed that the real slayer was still at large. If this was true, perhaps nobody was safe. In some ways, then, the mass meeting represented a formal effort at self-defense and a public display of indignation at the atrocity. Crowley's Black community had united in response to tragedy, highlighting how the unsolvable crimes—and their unknowable assailant—compelled a communal reaction.

Less than a month after the Byers family was killed, the authorities headed to Lake Charles "on business" related to the case.[102] Since the crime had taken place in Acadia Parish, Sheriff Louis Fontenot was one of the men traveling to the western part of the state. It was curious that the same mustachioed officer who had investigated the death of Edna Opelousas and her children was now going to the site of the Hodge crime to learn about the Byers one. There is always the possibility that the investigative trip to Lake Charles was nothing more than a historical coincidence. But maybe, just maybe, Sheriff Fontenot and his associates had discussed the other ax murders in the region. If that was the case, their conversation wasn't over yet.

/ / /

Around the same time the Acadia Parish officials headed to Lake Charles, their colleagues in neighboring Lafayette Parish were dealing with a problem of their own. John Thomas, the superintendent of the Louisiana Hospital for the Insane, had notified the authorities in Lafayette that, after supper one night, an inmate named Gaston Godfrey had escaped from their Pineville facility and was likely headed south.[103] Unfortunately, it seemed that "his mania was murder."[104]

When the twenty-some-year-old runaway was found near Maurice, roughly twenty miles south of Lafayette, the authorities had questions for him.[105] From his escape on Thursday, February 23, 1911, to his capture two days later, Gaston's whereabouts needed to be confirmed. Something horrible had happened.

According to the local newspaper, it was 7:00 a.m. on Saturday morning when Lezime Felix made a shocking discovery.[106] His sister, brother-in-law, niece, and nephew were dead in their home in the Trahan and Doucet Addition. Sandwiched between Avenue A (Vermillion Street) and Refinery Street, with the railroad defining its southwestern boundary, the neighborhood was then considered a suburb of Lafayette.[107]

Perhaps Lezime had been the unnamed man described in a New Orleans paper who sought to deliver some meat at the Andrus family's home, but then realized something was awry when no one stirred.[108] The unfortunate discoverer of this brutal scene "gave the alarm," and Lafayette Parish Sheriff Louis Lacoste—flanked by additional officers and the deputy coroner—immediately headed to the neighborhood.[109]

What they found was gut wrenching. Alexander Andrus and Mamie Andrus, both parents in their thirties, had been murdered with an ax, their heads crushed.[110] Two of their children, three-year-old Joachim and baby girl Agnes, had been slaughtered as well.[111] Coroner Dr. Lambert O. Clark "detected warmth in the bodies" and surmised the family had been killed sometime after midnight.[112]

As investigators probed the scene, observing the "brains spattered over the walls and floors," they came to an even more unnerving conclusion: the Andruses had been posthumously moved.[113] Whoever had killed the family had taken the time to reposition their bodies, suggesting a calculated intent. Although reports confirm that Mamie and Alexander were killed *in* bed, their corpses were found in a supplicant position, kneeling *over* the bed as if in prayer. Supposedly, Mamie's arm had been staged to rest on her husband's shoulder.[114] Joachim's body was discovered face down on the bed. Baby Agnes's lifeless form had been moved from her bloodied cradle to her mother's side. Once the murderer had staged this perversely prayerful scene, they fled out the kitchen door and into the darkness.

Excluding the positioning of the bodies, evidence in the house was meager. Reportedly, a makeshift shade—created from the family's own bedding—had been placed in the front window, obscuring the view from passersby. The ultimate clue—the ax—was found in the vicinity of the bed.[115] Not surprisingly, the coroner's jury rendered a verdict of death by an unknown party.[116]

Despite this official assessment, Sheriff Lacoste and the officers believed they knew who had killed the Andruses: Gaston Godfrey.[117] The timing was unnerving. Gaston had left the Louisiana Hospital for the Insane two days before the family was killed. Moreover, his mother, Rose Square, seemed to know more about the situation than she was letting on. Not only did she live near the Andruses, but the authorities suspected she had helped her son escape from Pineville.[118] She had apparently visited him just a week before he fled and, in the aftermath of the crime, deceived the police as to her son's whereabouts. Detained by Sheriff Lacoste, Rose eventually cracked and outed Gaston's location near Maurice, upon which she was released.

When the authorities finally got Gaston in custody, it seemed he had a solid alibi: he'd been working on a farm, and the folks with whom he had been staying testified he "slept at home" on the night in question.[119] Plus, the officers conceded that they hadn't found any evidence linking Gaston with the murder. Still, they didn't care for his attitude when questioned. He laughed and joked, though he also emphatically denied knowing anything about the crimes. Not surprisingly, the deputies hauled Gaston from Maurice to Lafayette and put him in jail until he could be returned to Pineville.[120] This was probably for the best: public fears were high, and one newspaper intimated that if the killer wasn't apprehended by the authorities, they'd be lynched by local citizens.[121]

The death of the Andrus family less than one month after the killing of the Byers family meant it was impossible to ignore the similarities between the two. As one paper noted, "the methods employed were identical."[122] Not to mention, Lafayette and Crowley were less than thirty miles apart, and news traveled fast. Therefore, when the authorities arrested Gaston in connection with the recent slaying, they also tried to implicate him in the earlier one. Yet, if that were the case, then there was a glaring hole in their timeline: the runaway had only been on the lam for a few days, not weeks. Why, then, was it reported that Gaston had been seen in Lafayette on the very day the Byerses were killed, getting "a supply of clothing" from his mother, no less?[123]

Theoretically, Gaston could have been a free man in January 1911 and detained at some point after the Byers family was murdered and before the Andruses were axed. Curiously, however, the *Town Talk*, Alexandria's daily paper, offered a more vexing possibility. According to their report, Gaston Godfrey had not escaped on February 23, but rather on January 8.[124] What's more, Alexandria was literally just across the Red River from Pineville, making the local newspaper's account of what had transpired the closest in proximity to the source. If the *Town Talk* was correct, Gaston would have certainly had time to kill both families. But if he really did escape early in the new year, it seems odd that coverage of his flight didn't appear until the Andrus family was slaughtered. It is equally perplexing that Gaston's mother's timeline contradicted this report. The closest explanation therefore also appears to be the least credible.

Roughly a week after the Andruses had been murdered, Sheriff Lacoste and his deputies had decided that the "dangerous character" who'd run away was not responsible.[125] The killer was still on the loose, and there was no denying that this crime looked a whole lot like the one in Crowley back in January.[126] And the local Lafayette paper had reached an even more disturbing conclusion: these two recent ax murders *also* resembled the slaying of the Opelousas family in Rayne over a year earlier. For the first time, the media reported not that two crimes were related, but *three*. Possibly, the paper speculated, they were all committed by the "same terrible monster."[127]

If the killings had been perpetrated by a single offender, the arrest of Sosthene Guidry, a Black man, for the murder of Edna Opelousas and her children more than sixteen months after their deaths was an illogical maneuver. The authorities suspected him of this particular homicide while simultaneously admitting that there were "no new developments" in the Byers family case.[128] Nor were there updates in the deaths of the Andruses. Acadia Parish Sheriff Louis Fontenot had been present at two of the three crime scenes in question. He was one of the authorities who traveled to Lake Charles for further investigation following the Crowley murder. But police training in early 1900s America simply did not cover anything close to what would today be considered serial murder.[129] So, Sheriff Fontenot did the only thing he knew to do: arrest people associated with *this* crime and *that* crime. That's how the uneventful apprehension of Sosthene occurred. Newspapers did not cover what the authorities found that connected him to the Rayne crime, instead reminding readers of the bountiful similarities between the murders, tacitly hinting that he wasn't the guilty party.[130]

/ / /

The murders of the Byers and Andrus families were different from those of the Opelousas and Hodge families in one distinct way: husbands were killed alongside their wives. Much of what transpired in these four cases was eerily comparable, however. Crowley, Lafayette, Rayne, and Lake Charles all sat on the Southern Pacific Railroad's southernmost line, the Sunset Route. Within these cities and towns, the victims all lived within a mile of the tracks. In the Opelousas and Hodge cases, secondary weapons were used, including a knife and smoothing irons. In the Byers and Andrus instances, calculation appeared with the bloodied washbowl and postmortem staging.

More than proximity to the railroad and deliberate action connected these atrocities. Entire families were slaughtered. All of the victims were Black. The ax was found in every case. Plus, while the first two crimes had occurred sixty miles and two months apart, the next two were separated by half that distance and half that time. Whoever was axing Black families along the Southern Pacific Railroad seemed to be ramping up the frequency of violence, recognized now as a common component of serial murder.

As much as there were similarities between the murders, there were also similarities in how they were investigated: as discrete homicides. Every slaughter until this point had been examined as an isolated incident in which the authorities sought to understand why someone wanted a particular family dead. They focused on interpersonal dynamics to find the assailant, operating under a sort of linkage blindness that allowed them to hypothesize that something was oddly serial about the killings without actually doing anything different in their investigations. Unsurprisingly, therefore, except for Richard Lee, all of the named suspects ended up being released.

Yet, while the authorities were reticent to approach these murders from a more interrelated angle, print media played a significant role in shaping public opinion that a pattern had started to emerge. Three different parishes—Acadia, Calcasieu, and Lafayette—had experienced the axing of more than a dozen Black people in their jurisdictions in fifteen months. All but two of those individuals were killed within twenty-five miles of each other. More than half of them had been slaughtered in a single month. Sheriffs Fontenot, Reid, and Lacoste had to face what the press reported by the early spring of 1911: the crimes were probably committed by the "same person who no doubt is insane, or affected with some fiendish mania against the negro race."[131]

Although it would be easy to interpret this conclusion by the white media as evidence of a desire to sensationalize these murders in the interest of selling more newspapers, the press could have reflected Black folks' localized knowledge about the crimes. White authorities' repeated assumptions of interpersonal motives to explain the deaths of the Opelousas, Hodge, Byers, and Andrus families discounted the possibility that these crimes could have been related. Stereotypes about Black criminality prevented investigators from seeing a pattern of carnage, yet the region's Black communities believed there were too many commonalities to be coincidences. While the white press might have been the first place that publicly implied a serial killer had come to the rice belt, this declaration was likely a reflection of Black folks' speculations laid bare for readers.

2

Unlikable Suspects

William McWilliams and Raymond Barnabet

Roughly four weeks had passed since the Andruses were killed in Lafayette. It would take another six months before Lafayette Parish Sheriff Louis Lacoste was able to make an arrest in connection with their murders. Before that could happen, however, another Black family would be axed under the cover of darkness. Finally, the assailant crossed state lines.

Not only was the first San Antonio murder unique, but the apprehension of a seemingly unlikely suspect—an aged white man—further complicated the crime. Moreover, the outcome of the case against William McWilliams stands in stark contrast to the case against Raymond Barnabet, Clementine Barnabet's father, who was detained for the Lafayette crime. Although the evidence against the former was circumstantial albeit compelling, the proof against the latter was contradictory and personal. Still, William was likely released while Raymond was condemned to die. In aggregate, these men's interactions with the rice belt's criminal justice systems reveal a nuanced portrait of social expectations combined with linkage blindness.

/ / /

While Sheriff Lacoste and others contemplated what happened to the Andrus family, residents of another town along the Southern Pacific Railroad went about their day-to-day lives, thus far unsuspecting of the chaos that had befallen their Louisiana neighbors. From the lowlands of the rice country to the sugared hills of Houston and the cotton-studded landscape of central Texas, the chasm between Lafayette and San Antonio was both geographic and cultural. Still, locals in the Alamo City had a fateful connection to their eastern counterparts: an ornate train station with twinkling lights and charming architecture located near downtown. This depot was known as Sunset Station.

In San Antonio, Elizabeth Castelow had probably heard about Sunset Station. Her life there was a far cry from her teenage years in Hays County, where she had been raised by a single father in the early 1880s.[1] As a young woman, Lizzie had married a man by the name of Samuel R. Lane.[2] In a matter of months, however, he had abandoned his wife for the call of the open frontier, styling himself a "cowboy" and traveling northward all the way to Indian Territory.[3]

Elizabeth had moved to San Antonio and built a new life for herself as a seamstress. It wasn't long before she met Alfred Louis Casaway. Originally from New Orleans, Louis, as he was known, had migrated westward decades earlier, landing in San Antonio and building a strong reputation for himself, first as a janitor at City Hall and then at a local school.[4] He had even served as bailiff of the grand jury. Lizzie liked the way Louis treated her, and the duo decided to make things official after her divorce was granted.[5] There was just one barrier to their marriage: Elizabeth Castelow was a white woman and Louis Casaway was a Black man.

In Jim Crow America, their marriage was illegal, so they headed across the U.S.-Mexico border to Ciudad Porfirio Díaz (today Piedras Negras). When they returned to San Antonio, they were charged with "violating the law of miscegenation," but the grand jury never filed an indictment.[6] The two settled down to raise a family: first came a daughter, Josie, followed by another, Louise, a few years later, and then a baby boy, Alfred Carlyle.

Residing on San Antonio's east side in a racially diverse neighborhood, the Casaways navigated Jim Crow norms from the vantage point of Blackness. Some speculated that Lizzie was "very fair of complexion" but had "a trace of negro blood."[7] Although there is no evidence to indicate Elizabeth wasn't white, the construction of stories regarding her racial identity highlights the stakes of the couple's decision to marry and procreate across the color line.[8]

By the early spring of 1911, the Casaways had built a seemingly supportive community near their North Olive Street home. Richard and Delia Campbell, their neighbors, were also family: one local paper said the wife was Louis Casaway's sister. Richard, meanwhile, was a lawyer, which meant the Campbells' was likely one of the only homes on the block, Black or white, to have a personal telephone. When a call came in on the morning of March 22, a boarder in the Campbell home, Bessie Drake, picked up the receiver.[9] It was Principal

Tarver from the Grant School—the Black schoolhouse where Louis worked. It seemed the "always prompt" janitor hadn't shown up that morning and therefore hadn't unlocked the building.[10]

Bessie immediately tried to establish contact with the Casaways. When she didn't get a reply, she alerted Delia Campbell, who sensed something was wrong. The *San Antonio Express* reported it was Delia who "peered into the bedroom" and, upon seeing her brother dead, ran home in a panic to contact the authorities.[11] The *San Antonio Light* claimed it was Richard Campbell who "forced the window screen up" and saw Louis's lifeless body.[12] Although the local papers disagreed as to who exactly discovered the horrific scene, both agreed that one of the Campbells had been the unfortunate observer and that the husband and father was the first victim sighted.

It didn't take long for Bexar County Sheriff John Wallace Tobin and other law enforcement officials to arrive onsite. Someone had accessed the Casaway property from the rear, stopping at the woodshed out back to grab an ax. Then they stepped onto the back porch and headed into the kitchen via the unlocked door, weapon in hand. From there, the assailant entered the bedroom occupied by Louis Casaway, who was presumably sleeping on his stomach with his face on the pillow. The slayer raised the ax high and slammed it forcibly into the back of Louis's skull, crushing his head with such force that his brain was exposed and blood splattered onto the wall.[13]

The killer then headed into the room where Lizzie was sleeping. "The most disfigured of the family," Elizabeth had been attacked so savagely that from her neck up was "an unrecognizable mass."[14] The slayer likely then axed little Alfred Carlyle; the young baby lay mutilated right beside his mother. Six-year-old Josie, having retired to the same room, was then slaughtered in bed, the ax being used to crush her head, too. It seemed the murderer then picked up the young girl's limp form and threw her toward the bottom of the bed, leaving her contorted body "resting on her mother's feet."[15]

What was unclear was when three-year-old Louise had been killed. According to the *Express*, the prevailing theory was that she was slain right after her father, the two sharing a bed.[16] The *Light* had a different take on what had transpired, suggesting that she wasn't murdered second, but last. In the paper's estimation, which was reported as "the theory of the officers," the intruder retraced their steps, perhaps realizing in all of the commotion that the last member of the Casaway family—Louise—had awakened beside her father.[17] It appeared the little girl started to get out of bed and was in an upright position when the killer struck. Her skull was immediately fractured, and the back part of her head crushed. Near the bed where Louise was killed, a doll was found covered in blood. The ax, "dripping with the blood of the once happy family," was found resting against one of the two beds where the Casaways met their untimely end.[18]

Only the family's dog survived.[19]

/ / /

Born and bred in Texas, Sheriff John Tobin had been a militiaman before trying his hand at more mainstream law and order, and his commitment to his hometown ran deep. Serving as the chief of San Antonio's fire department and treasurer of Bexar County, Tobin's transition to county lawman was a natural progression of his dedication to public service.[20] Known as the "gunless sheriff," Tobin's approach to law enforcement was markedly different from many of his contemporaries.[21] Upon his death, many commented that "no one ever loved or worked for the welfare of the people of San Antonio more than John Tobin."[22] His belief in San Antonio—as a city and as a community—was steadfast.

Therefore, when Sheriff Tobin, Coroner Ben S. Fisk, and other officials showed up to investigate the crime scene, it wasn't just a cursory look to check off some list. It was spearheaded by someone who wanted answers. Moreover, it was led by an individual who knew both Casaways directly: Lizzie had been employed in the sheriff's home as a seamstress and Louis had once been the grand jury bailiff.[23] This was both political *and* personal for John Tobin. Arguably, it was these connections between the sheriff and the victims—not to mention Elizabeth's status as a white woman—that enabled this crime to be investigated more thoroughly than its predecessors.

At the scene, the crimson ax offered a curious clue: from the saturation of the blood and the presence of Elizabeth's dark brown hair on the implement, it seemed the Casaways had all been killed with the flat end of the ax-head, not the blade.[24] This meant that whomever had murdered the family had used excessive force to batter, pummel, and beat their skulls. Investigators were perplexed that "no bloody finger marks" were found in the house, implying that the ax was long enough to make contact without getting too close.[25]

Already theorizing that the killer had no sense of urgency in the commission of this act, the officers learned that pillows and a bedspread had been placed in at least two windows of the home, presumably blocking any passersby from witnessing the carnage.[26] Whoever had murdered the family had clearly wanted to be undisturbed. In the house, proof that the killing wasn't a robbery gone awry abounded. Dresser drawers were undamaged, clothes with money in the pockets were left in plain sight, Louis's gold watch had been readily located, and the general state of the home was "neat and clean," minus the blood spatter.[27]

There were footprints leading *away* from the back porch of the house, not toward it, suggesting that the killer had entered the residence before it started raining that night, but didn't leave until after the ground was soaked.[28] A lack of mud inside the home supported this theory. That particular stretch of North Olive Street was known for characteristically "black mud" that clung to shoes and made traceable impressions—ones that would be analyzed via "minute investigation."[29] Lawmen were able to identify a "No. 6" shoeprint in the Casaway family's yard, but the tracks quickly disappeared, having been washed away by the rain.[30]

The unlocked door and no evidence of forced entry caused reporters to note that Louis must have forgotten to close the thumb latch before heading to bed.[31] Unless, of course, the Casaways had invited their would-be slayer over, unaware of the fate that would befall them. It was this theory that was peddled two days after the murder as the authorities continued to probe the scene. They learned that Louis Casaway had gone to a local saloon and purchased a "bucket of beer."[32] This was an odd choice given that neither Louis nor Lizzie drank on a regular basis. Perhaps this meant the family was having a visitor that night. If so, the detectives believed this guest must have slipped something in the alcohol, coaxed the couple to drink, and then waited nearby until the family had retired for the night before returning to carry out the crime. Yet, no sooner had the beer bucket story emerged than it was determined to be a false lead. None of the neighborhood saloons had sold Louis anything to drink that night.[33]

The fact that such a narrative emerged in the first place shouldn't have been a surprise to investigators, however. The *Express* probably exaggerated when it reported that "at least 1000" people had flocked to the crime scene once news of the murder was known.[34] Meanwhile, the *Light*'s front-page photograph of a sizable crowd watching "the removal of the five bodies" confirms a throng of bystanders.[35] Surely some of these individuals plied the police with information they'd heard first-, second-, or third-hand about the Casaways, offering numerous rumors regarding how the family met their demise, but the authorities concluded "it was all mere gossip," while at the same time following up on potential tips.[36] An interracial couple and their children had been bludgeoned with an ax, and both Black and white San Antonians wanted to know why.

The morning the Casaways were found dead in their San Antonio home, their bodies were taken to the Williamson and Sinclair undertaking establishment until the quintuple funeral could be held at nearby St. Paul's Church two days later.[37] The entire Black community turned out for the three-hearse procession.[38] As had been the case with the other ax murders, mourning and grieving became communal acts that declared public dismay at the tragedy that had transpired. Regardless of one's personal relationship to the Casaways, the collective experience of anguish linked Black San Antonians to one another.

The family members were placed in three caskets: Louis in one, Elizabeth and baby Alfred Carlyle in another, and sisters Josie and Louise in the last.[39] Buried in City Cemetery No. 3 mere blocks from where they were murdered, the Casaways' final resting place was three graves dug side by side. A succinct word on their burial permits tried to encapsulate everything that could not be described: "murder."[40] Indeed, as the funeral emphasized the community's loss, neighbors were "wrought up to a high pitch" at the reminder of what had transpired.[41]

The same day the Casaways were buried, a perplexing sighting reportedly occurred at their now-vacant North Olive Street home. Around the same time of night that the victims had been slain three days earlier, the family's dog began howling. A group of folks in a house nearby heard the creature and looked across the street. Suddenly, a blue light appeared in the windows. It disappeared, only to reappear in a moment. The watchers grew frightened, and word spread about the mysterious glow shining dimly in the Casaways' home. For thirty minutes the light appeared before going out for good. No one approached the house to investigate its cause. One man who'd watched the light was certain he'd heard "a sound like a blow, followed by a sharp cry."[42] The dog, meanwhile, appeared to mourn the loss of its family. It sat on the back stairs and watched the door expectantly for a meal that did not come.[43]

/ / /

Although detectives had been scouring the crime scene for evidence as to who might have killed the Casaways, they had no strong leads. The coroner ruled that they met their deaths at the hands of parties unknown.[44] Sheriff Tobin, however, had developed a theory not about *who* had murdered the family, but *why.* He suspected they had been killed *because* they were an interracial family.[45] As such, he sent letters to his counterparts across Texas, hoping to learn more information about Lizzie Casaway. In a matter of days, the sheriff of Hays County had written back, corroborating details about her early life, including her marriage to Sam Lane.[46] Less than a week after the Casaways were murdered, investigators hypothesized that a white man—or perhaps white *men*—had committed the crime.[47]

A grand jury was assembled and their "principal matter" was to "bring the guilty ones to justice."[48] In trying to find witnesses to testify before the jurymen, Sheriff Tobin and his officers located two of Lizzie's brothers in the seats of Llano and Travis counties.[49] Even though it seemed like the detectives were making progress, the sheriff had his doubts, going so far as to state that he didn't expect interviewing the siblings to be of much use and had resigned himself to the fact that "the solution may never be obtained."[50] His officers, on the other hand, said they had sufficient evidence "for several persons" to appear before the grand jury.[51] None of the leads panned out, so when the grand jury presented its report to the judge at the end of the month, none of the fifty-four bills returned were related to the murder case that had swept the city.[52]

While the grand jury was investigating the murder, news of the crime had reached the ears of Texas Governor Oscar Colquitt. He offered a $250 reward (over $8,400 in 2025) for the capture and conviction of the Casaway family's killer.[53] This was the first time in any of the Louisiana-Texas ax murder cases that the state had offered a financial incentive to solve the crime. Whether Governor Colquitt genuinely cared about the plight of the Casaway family is hard to say, but Sheriff Tobin had put pressure on anyone who would listen that the deaths represented an unacceptable blemish upon his record of public service. Plus, one of the local San Antonio papers had written that Tobin's first remark upon investigating the crime scene was: "How a human being could commit such a crime is beyond my comprehension. I will pay $250 for a clue that may lead to the apprehension of the murderer."[54] Even if he had simply said these words rather than acted upon them, the fact remained that a public official had declared a monetary stake in the case. For the governor not to at least acknowledge the crime and match the contribution, whether real or imaginary, would have been a political blunder. That available evidence suggests Sheriff Tobin did indeed put money behind his words confirms the strategic importance of the governor's involvement.[55]

By offering a reward, Governor Colquitt tacitly acknowledged that the Casaway case had taken on importance *beyond* San Antonio's Black community. Whether this interest stemmed from Sheriff Tobin's investigative clout, the fact that Lizzie Casaway was a white woman, or some other curious detail about the crime is unknown. Undeniably, the governor's incentive elevated the significance of community in the resolution of this case. Offering money to catch the killer implicitly acknowledged that group cohesion was an essential part of solving this crime.

Although the San Antonio Police Department, the Bexar County Sheriff's Department, and now the governor of Texas had all rallied—albeit in different ways—to catch the Casaways' slayer, neighbors and members of the city's Black community did not simply wallow in their grief. They organized. Gathering at Benevolent Hall or the Almeda Hall on March 31, source depending, residents held a mass meeting to raise additional funds for the capture of the killer.[56] According to various reports, their goal was to solicit $500, double the governor's reward.[57] The city's German newspaper published the actual total: $345.[58] Although it was less than what Black San Antonians had hoped, the funds nonetheless represented a significant statement of support. Moreover, it also suggested that the Casaways' community was not content to let white authorities drive engagement with this case. Black Texans claimed their right to advocate on behalf of their own, aware that the victims represented not a random family brutally slain, but known members of San Antonio's Black community. After all, justice would not come from the governor's mansion in Austin.

As the grand jury investigated the case and different entities put money on the line—totaling $845 (over $27,000 in 2025) by early April 1911—Sheriff Tobin wondered if he and his investigators were on the right path at all.[59] So far, they had no leads. Interviews had gone nowhere, evidence in the house was inconclusive, and rumors had never been substantiated. Even the city's police captain had reportedly remarked that his men had "not the slightest kind of clue" to follow.[60] There was also one sticky piece to the puzzle. Supposedly, the family's dog did not bark or make any sort of noticeable outcry the night the murders happened. According to investigators, this meant one of two things: the dog had been drugged (alongside the family) or the murderer was familiar to the animal.[61] If the latter was true, the Casaways had been killed by someone they knew.

/ / /

More than two months had passed since the Casaway family had been murdered in their home when, seemingly out of the blue, Sheriff Tobin received a letter. According to one of the local papers, it read:

> San Antonio, Tex., May, 1911.—To Sheriff of Bexar County, and also to R. A. Campbell, lawyer—I understand that you all are in search for the man that killed the Louis Casaway family. Well, I am the man, and I am going to give you trouble in catching me, and whenever you run across me there will be trouble on your hands.
>
> I am no negro. I am a full-blood white man, and again, I never wrote this. I had it done by a man that is today about three hundred miles from here, and I am in the city of San Antonio now. So catch me if you can and there will be trouble on your hands, because I am in a dangerous place and I mean to kill the first one that tackles me about this matter, so you can all pop your whip and get busy. I am ready to die at any time, so look out.
>
> I had a right to kill that family, and if you ever catch me I will explain it to you.[62]

And just like that, Sheriff Tobin had a new lead. But he wavered as to whether it was "some crank" who wanted to insert himself into the investigation, or if the actual killer had finally grown a conscience and decided to relieve his "troubled mind."[63] Either way, the writer had taunted the authorities, implying that they would be unable to catch him. More ominously, he implied that he was ready to kill *and* ready to be killed.

Three months after the sheriff received the anonymous letter, the authorities arrested William McWilliams, an elderly white man who lived on San Antonio's east side.[64] City directories for 1910–1912 list a William McWilliams who was married and retired living on a street named Gravel—either in the 400 block or near South Palmetto—in the east end.[65] Curiously, however, the Sanborn Fire Insurance Map for San Antonio for 1912 suggests that addresses on Gravel stopped in the 200s and that no dwellings were located near where the road narrowed at Palmetto.[66] What is clear, however, is that it was not simply William's geographic proximity to the victims that raised suspicions.

It seemed that William had been involved in a discussion about race fairly recently and mentioned that "he had sent five negroes to the cemetery," adding that "three of them were put in one hole."[67] Although technically the Casaways were buried in three plots and at most two members of the family were in a single casket, the sentiment behind the statements was obvious enough.

Investigators visited the seventy-nine-year-old man at his house and convinced him to go with them to the sheriff's office, where they questioned him for two hours.[68] William would soon claim he had been "tricked" into going with the lawmen.[69] Moreover, he denied that he was the one who had killed the Casaways, but claimed that he knew who committed the crimes.[70] The real murderer, he said, was a man of "influence and wealth."[71] The authorities weren't buying his story. At some point in this ordeal William began to recognize the severity of his situation. He asked to be allowed bond but was informed that the charges against him were not bailable. He was led to the county jail to await his fate. With the assistance of his lawyer, William filed a writ of habeas corpus and claimed he was being "illegally restrained of his liberty."[72]

During his habeas corpus hearing, the evidence against William was damning, albeit circumstantial. There was the conversation he had supposedly had about putting—or "planting"—multiple bodies in the same hole.[73] In that same discussion William mentioned that Sheriff Tobin was looking for a man named "Mack Hamilton" as the guilty party, while implying that he and Hamilton were one and the same.[74] More convincingly, the authorities had found a letter in William's house the day of his arrest that was written on similar paper to the note received by Sheriff Tobin in May. The state went so far as to argue that the handwriting in both letters was "done by the same person," linking William to the written confession.[75]

Unfortunately for the defendant, he didn't need the state to put him at the Casaway house around the time of the murder. He willingly admitted he'd been there. Apparently, William McWilliams had a quasi-personal relationship to Elizabeth. He'd been raised by the Hamilton family, relatives of Lizzie's, who lived in an area known as Perry Hill. William had served in the Confederate military, moved to San Antonio, and lost contact with his foster family. One day, a descendant reached out to him and, during a visit to the city, dropped what must have been bombshell news: Elizabeth was "married to a negro."[76]

It seems that William did not believe the accusation, at least not initially. He decided to get proof for himself by visiting the Casaways. On March 21, 1911, the almost-octogenarian reportedly stood at the family's front gate on North Olive Street, chatting with Elizabeth to learn more about her apparently uncouth marriage. While talking, William looked through a window and observed one of the Casaway children playing with a toy. According to the district attorney, this was the same blood-soaked doll that was located near Josie's body the very next day.[77]

Clearly, the state's evidence suggested William McWilliams slaughtered the Casaways because he had been alerted to the fact that the couple had crossed the color line. It did not help that a day or two before the family was killed, Elizabeth had reportedly told a local woman that she "had been urged to leave her husband and children," but refused to do so.[78] Two days before the murder, Louis had supposedly "had a quarrel with a white man."[79] Whether either of these incidents actually referred to unpleasant interactions with William remains pure speculation, but the timing is compelling.

The state had concocted a circumstantial yet cohesive story that seemed to confirm William McWilliam's involvement in the murder of the Casaway family. He had the trifecta of guilt: means, motive, and opportunity. Not to mention the fact that on the first day of his habeas corpus hearing, William continually laughed.

By day two, however, his tone had changed. His demeanor was stoic as his attorney sought to defend him. His lawyer's argument followed two threads: much of the evidence against his client should have been procedurally inadmissible and the defendant had an imaginative—but not insane—mind. According to the defense, the statements William made during his two-hour questioning at the sheriff's office could not be used as evidence against him because they were made while his client was "under restraint."[80] William, however, had voluntarily spoken with the authorities.

It seems the defense did not claim that William McWilliams had never made incriminating statements—to a wide variety of people, it turned out. Instead, the attorney implied that his client liked to talk, but that the state had not produced concrete evidence of his guilt. Moreover, he argued, William was too old to be a significant flight risk.[81] If—and that was a big if—the district attorney managed to find enough actual proof of his involvement, he could easily be located again and could then be taken into custody.

After two days the habeas corpus hearing was finally over.[82] The judge's decision was rendered the following morning: unless he could pay the $1,000 bond ($33,000 in 2025) for each of the five charges of murder in the killing of the Casaway family, William McWilliams would remain behind bars until the grand jury began in two months.[83] He was "visibly affected" by the pronouncement.[84]

Although local and regional papers stated that the McWilliams case would be taken up by the jurymen in October, there is no evidence to suggest anything further proceeded with this investigation.[85] The San Antonio press does not appear to have covered the jury's findings related to the death of the Casaways, nor is there any proof the charges against William resulted in a trial.[86] Given that the grand jury had returned 113 indictments by the end of the month, it seems an intentional choice to avoid coverage of the McWilliams story, as other sensational outcomes were regularly discussed.[87] Moreover, less than a year after the habeas corpus hearing, various reports claimed that "no clue" had ever been found toward identifying the family's slayer.[88] While this assertion undoubtedly has an air of amnesia, it seems that, despite the state's findings, William McWilliam was never tried for this crime.

To explain this conundrum, there is at least one speculative possibility. A "William McWilliams" from the early 1910s is listed in a Bexar County probate index with "lunacy" beside his name.[89] Perhaps the reason additional information about his case was not publicized is because there wasn't a case at all: he was declared legally unfit to stand trial. Although this theory is hypothetical, it offers one explanation for the murky what-ifs in the William McWilliams saga.

/ / /

There is no denying that the death of the Casaway family rattled San Antonio. In the days following the crime, news coverage traveled from the city's east side across the United States, reaching all the way from Long Beach, California, to Charleston, South Carolina.[90] Details of the murder even reached international audiences when the *Manitoba Free Press* published an article explaining miscegenation as the motive.[91] Evidence suggests that print media coverage of the Casaway crime exceeded that of the Opelousas, Hodge, Byers, and Andrus killings combined. Perhaps this significant uptick in exposure was due to Elizabeth's status as a white woman. Then again, it could have been caused by the crime's location: San Antonio was the most populous city in the state at the time, edging out Dallas by a few thousand inhabitants. Either way, the Casaway murder represents the first large wave of media attention paid to one of the alarmingly similar ax murders.

In Lafayette and Crowley, the death of the Casaways raised concerns. Within a week of the crime, the Lafayette press reprinted a piece that supposedly had run in the Crowley paper. The story mentioned ax murders of Black families in Rayne, Crowley, Lafayette, *and San Antonio.* It noted the similarities between the killing of the Andruses and the Casaways, stating that Lafayette Parish Sheriff Louis Lacoste had even reached out to his Texas counterparts to assist in their investigation. Perhaps most tantalizingly, the article concluded that the crimes had likely "been perpetuated [*sic*] by the same person."[92] If the Casaways had been killed by the same individual who'd also killed the Opelousases, Byerses, and Andruses, then the motive behind the fatal attack wasn't miscegenation.

The newspapers in Lafayette and Crowley were able to publish such a speculative story because their towns had already lived through the chaos of families being axed to death under the cover of night. They could draw the kinds of perplexing connections that only make sense if a similar situation had already occurred. This is why it was reporters in *these* particular towns—and not in Texas or elsewhere—who were first able to recognize the stakes: a serial killer was on the loose *and had crossed state lines.*

Indeed, the ability to draw this conclusion was based on the communal aspect of the ax murders themselves. Although individual families were killed, the crimes impacted Black communities, and their aftermaths were covered by the local presses. Newspapermen visited crime scenes, interviewed residents, and offered speculations. Thus, though white papers published the vast majority of articles about these crimes, they did so by implicitly privileging Black folks' knowledge. This is not to suggest that the media was unbiased or that Jim Crow ideologies did not cloud their assessments, but that the dynamic which emerged between the local presses and the Black communities in their orbit allowed public consensuses about the murders to be reached well before the authorities arrived at similar conclusions.

In Lafayette and Crowley, Black residents and newspapermen knew that the assailant had visited Rayne, Lake Charles, and San Antonio, in addition to their own two cities. They knew that, at each location, a Black family had been murdered with an ax and the weapon was always recovered from the scene. Importantly, however, they also knew that, in each case, local authorities focused on an individual motive for killing a single family. This linkage blindness meant that Black Louisianians and, by extension, the regional media figured out something the white authorities had not: an interstate serial killer was operating in the rice belt.

/ / /

Although local Black communities and the region's white press had concluded the ax murders were related, white lawmen continued to hunt for individual suspects who wanted specific families dead. That's how the six-month stall in progress on the Andrus case came to an end: Lafayette Parish Sheriff Louis Lacoste got a clue. A man by the name of Raymond Barnabet was suspected of killing the family. Raymond, for better or worse, was considered an unpleasant fixture in his community.[93] It did not help that he was known for having a violent temper and did not get along well with neighbors. In fact, the entire Barnabet family—comprised of two parents and nine children—was considered less than ideal.[94] Yet, whether the Barnabets actually were problematic or whether the rumor mill unfairly labeled them as such is hard to say. What is known is that Raymond and his common-law wife, Dinah Porter, had apparently gotten into some kind of altercation. Fed up with her husband, Dinah reportedly told a friend about Raymond's "responsibility for the crime."[95] Her friend contacted the authorities.

Of course, it would be easy to dismiss Dinah's claims as those of a revenge-seeking wife. But it was known that Raymond didn't exactly get along with the Andrus family. He had once worked with Alexander in the Southern Pacific coal chutes, and the two had "bad blood" between them.[96] The local Lafayette paper opined that the motive for the murder was jealousy.[97] A New Orleans daily added that Raymond had reportedly "threatened revenge" against the Andrus family.[98] So, while it seems there was no physical evidence connecting Raymond to the crime, there were circumstantial threads that had the potential to weave a damning web.

Located in a cotton field between Rayne and Crowley, Raymond was apprehended by Sheriff Lacoste and his officers.[99] When he was detained, however, he was told he was wanted for "wife desertion."[100] Raymond went willingly with the investigators, seemingly oblivious to the true nature of the crimes attributed to him.

Sheriff Lacoste lodged the suspect not in the Lafayette Parish jail, as would have been customary, but in the Acadia Parish jail in nearby Crowley.[101] It was only upon his arrival in this adjacent town that Raymond learned of the real charges against him: murder. Simultaneously, a local judge signed a jarring affidavit concretizing the prisoner's plight: "one Raymond Bernabet did unlawfully, willfully, feloniously and of his malice afterthought did kill and murder one Mamie Andrus."[102] Multiplied by four, it seemed Raymond was in a great deal of trouble.

It turned out, Sheriff Lacoste had more than a tip and hearsay supposedly linking Raymond to the deaths of the Andruses. At least five witnesses had been detained by the authorities to confirm his guilt.[103] These individuals were placed in the Lafayette jail, geographically separated from the man they planned to testify against. Finally, someone would stand trial for the crime that had terrorized the region for months.

At his arraignment, Raymond Barnabet pleaded not guilty.[104] His trial date was set for mid-October, and the court appointed multiple attorneys to defend him. Although none of the three visited their client in jail, they did file a motion for continuance. They argued that the names of the witnesses—those individuals who'd been jailed in Lafayette by Sheriff Lacoste—were deliberately missing from the indictments.[105] The claim was that Raymond's lawyers hadn't been allowed to prepare for trial properly because they had no idea what they were up against. The defense's appeal for a fifteen-day delay was denied. Raymond would be tried immediately.

/ / /

On October 19, 1911, Raymond Barnabet stood in a Lafayette courtroom, charged with the murder of the Andrus family back in February. If found guilty, he would be executed. Although Raymond had been indicted for killing the entire family, he was being tried specifically for the death of baby Agnes Andrus. The trial was split into two parts: the state would make most of its arguments in the morning, court would adjourn at 1:00 p.m. for a brief break, and then would reconvene at 2:00 p.m. to wrap up and move on to the defense counsel's arguments.[106]

Unbeknownst to Raymond (and apparently his attorneys), the star witnesses for the prosecution were Dinah Porter, Clementine Barnabet, and Zepherin Barnabet. In an unpredictable turn of events, Raymond's own family—his common-law wife and two of his children—would offer damning testimony that had the potential to send him to the gallows. Despite the discrepancies in their accounts, the gist was provocative: Raymond had disappeared from their house on the night of the murders and his whereabouts were unknown. No wonder the witnesses' names had not appeared on the indictment: their testimony was designed to be the ultimate surprise . . . and perhaps betrayal.

According to Dinah, Raymond left around 7:00 p.m. on February 24, commenting that he was headed to the neighboring town of Broussard on the freight train. When he returned, it seemed he was grumpy and irritable, perhaps covered in bloodstained clothing, perhaps not. Dinah recalled him storming in at some early morning hour (likely around 1:00 a.m. or 2:00 a.m.), upset that she had not saved him supper and frustrated that he had lost his pipe after being kicked off the train. She said Raymond angrily headed to bed, swearing all the while because he was hungry and smokeless. In Dinah's recollection, he was dressed in the same attire he had worn the previous evening, though she would later notice a small bloodstain on his right sleeve after he was caught scratching his back with a knife. In her estimation, this uncomfortable strategy for pain relief explained the blood's origin, not some gruesome murder scene.[107]

Clementine, on the other hand, remembered Raymond arriving home around daybreak, pipe pursed between his lips, blue jumper or shirt covered in "blood and brains."[108] She claimed he asked her to wash the evidence, to which she obliged by using the communal facilities shared by the Stevens family, who lived on the other side of the garret. According to her, one of the Stevens girls let her into their side of the property, where she hung up the now clean garments to air dry. Apparently, Raymond ordered that Clementine bring him some supper, boasting that he had committed a heinous act "with an ax back of town."[109]

To further complicate the story, Zepherin said Raymond got home in the morning (after daybreak), face splattered with blood, wearing only trousers and an undershirt. His blue jumper had gone missing. According to Zepherin, Raymond "cursed him [Zepherin] for a S. of a B. and ordered him in a loud voice to go and get his pipe out of that damn woman," who was presumably Dinah.[110] While both Clementine and Zepherin claimed their father commented about having participated in the murder of a "whole family of negroes," Dinah never corroborated such a story, despite her being the one who told her friend about Raymond's supposed involvement in the first place.[111] She conceded, however, that Raymond had attempted to kill her with an ax the previous month, suggesting that perhaps a violent streak was not outside of his nature. Back then, Raymond had warned her to "be careful how she fooled with other men" and that he was "through with her for good."[112]

If the testimonies of Clementine and Zepherin are to be believed, they were not only risking Raymond's life by taking the stand—they were also risking their own. According to the siblings, Raymond "threatened to kill his whole family" if they told anyone that their father was a murderer.[113] Yet, as much as their accounts suggested Raymond was a killer, the discrepancies between the two did not build a foolproof case in favor of the state. Moreover, Dinah's contradictory testimony exonerated her husband—she admitted he was temperamental, but she vehemently denied that he was a murderer, retracting the very accusation that had started this ordeal.

While the state's star witnesses agreed on a general outline of events—namely Raymond's absence from the family's home on the same night the Andruses were murdered—the specifics of each of their testimonies offered plentiful contradictions. They couldn't agree on what time he arrived home, what he was wearing, or the location of his pipe. Still, Raymond was a Black man on trial for his life in Louisiana in the early 1900s. Perhaps the white male jury would ignore these inconsistencies in favor of a Jim Crow version of justice.

By the time the district attorney rested his case in the afternoon, the evidence against Raymond was circumstantial at best. Even so, the prosecution's strategy had likely shaken the man. For hours, he had heard the opposing side try to convince the jury that he had deliberately and fiendishly murdered the Andruses. His own family—his wife and children—were turning against him, working to seal a verdict that would have their husband and father executed. When the court rested for lunch, it was clear what the state was trying to do. What Raymond had already heard—and what he no doubt suspected was coming—likely filled him with dread. He was "anxious to testify" and probably ready to refute the convoluted stories his family had told.[114] But first he needed to calm his nerves.

Although the court took a break for lunch, Raymond did not eat. Instead, he slipped a handful of coins to one of his jail mates, Augustin Dugas, to purchase something strong. Before long, Raymond had downed an entire bottle of "sporting wine."[115]

By the time the sheriff escorted him back to the courtroom at 2:00 p.m., Raymond Barnabet was a different man. According to one of his attorneys, he appeared to be under the influence of "some opiate or alcoholic liquor."[116] His eyes were bloodshot, his behavior was erratic, his commentary was egregious, and his faculties were, well, nonexistent. His lawyers believed he chose to get drunk to drown the pain of watching his children "take the stand to swear his life away."[117] As the defense finally took control of the courtroom, it was clear that any strategy to put Raymond on the stand would now be pointless. Perhaps the counselors thought they had a relatively easy case until their client started muttering. Regrettably for Raymond, the jury overheard him say "mon foutu," a Louisiana Creole phrase that, in this context, roughly translates to "I am screwed" or "I am damned."[118] The jurors were intrigued by this statement and, perhaps unwilling to recognize that the defendant before them was inebriated, wondered if it wasn't an unintentional admission of guilt.[119]

It was within this context that the Stevenses—the Barnabets' neighbors—were called to testify. The Stevenses, considered a respectable but poor Black family who happened to be ensnared in the Barnabets' drama due to proximity, asserted that all was quiet on their neighbors' side of the property the morning the murders were discovered. Adelle Stevens, the family's daughter, stated that she rose after daylight, noticed no noise coming from the Barnabets' quarters, and assumed they were all asleep. In either a sincere gesture or ironic twist of fate, she claimed to have knocked on her neighbors' door to alert them to the heinous crime. No one seemed pleased to learn this news. If Raymond had murdered the Andrus family, it seemed the Stevenses were not privy to such information.

According to Adelle, Clementine never asked permission to hang clothing on their side, nor did any members of the Barnabet family enter the Stevenses' abode that night (or the following morning). The Barnabets—including Clementine and Zepherin—had a "bad reputation," and thus the Stevenses attempted to distance themselves from this troubling family.[120] Even so, it seemed that the Stevenses' accounts could work to the advantage of the defense by permitting doubt to seep in regarding Raymond's confession-by-proxy.

Unfortunately for Raymond, his counsel's strategy did not work. He was found guilty of murder.[121] According to Louisiana law, the punishment for such a final crime was fitting: death.[122] But the sentence could only be carried out if the defendant was of sound mind and able to understand the finiteness of execution. Raymond, meanwhile, couldn't even understand where he was. His afternoon antics in court gave his lawyers an opportunity to refute the validity of the entire trial, claiming that he "was incapable of understanding the nature of the proceedings against him."[123] His presumed guilt was predicated on a series of missteps that almost cost him his life. In a matter of days, Raymond's attorneys filed a motion for a new trial. For it to be granted, there would be a hearing before the month's end.

Meanwhile, news of Raymond Barnabet's conviction had reached the public. The reaction was not good. In reporting on recent events in other parts of the state, the *Daily Picayune* (New Orleans) updated readers on the verdict and explained that folks had expected either a modified verdict or a mistrial.

The paper opined: "The evidence outside an alleged confession was all circumstantial and not very strong."[124] It seemed that even though Raymond was not a likeable fixture of Lafayette, residents of the Crescent City believed he had been given a farce of a trial.

The sentiment against Raymond's verdict was so strong that Lafayette's district attorney wrote a public article to the *Picayune*'s editor trying to defend the state's actions. He claimed that no one was actually surprised by the verdict (except Raymond, presumably), and that the evidence he had presented was "most positive and convincing."[125] Toward the end of his rebuttal, the prosecutor cleared his conscience by stating: "I reiterate that I concur with the jury that the verdict is just; that it is the only verdict that could have been brought in under the evidence, and that I am willing to assume the responsibilities for the execution of an innocent man if I am mistaken in my conclusions."[126] Clearly, the state's attorney had decided that Raymond's drunken episode had not endangered the validity of his trial.

It turned out, it wasn't just the district attorney who got scrutinized for the outcome of the case. The jurymen were so angered by the *Picayune*'s reporting of the trial that they gathered to draft their own protestation. They felt the article had unfairly represented them as careless jurors who had condemned a man to death with insufficient evidence.[127] In truth, they claimed, their verdict was based on both facts and proof. That the decision would result in a man's execution was simply a byproduct of doing their citizenly duty.

Likely, then, the district attorney and the jurymen were angered when they learned that the motion for a new trial was granted, based on sworn testimony heard by the court on October 27, 1911.[128] At this hearing, Raymond's attorneys hinged their argument on two main claims: the evidence against their client was pathetically weak, and their client had been pitifully drunk for a significant portion of his trial. Various witnesses were called, including a now-sober Raymond and some of his jail mates. When the defendant took the stand, he confessed to having drank so much that he was unable to participate in his own defense. In fact, all he remembered from the previous week's trial were three people who'd testified against him: Dinah, Zepherin, and Clementine.[129]

While seeking a new trial for their client, Raymond's attorneys did more than poke loopholes in the prosecution's threadbare theory. The defendant, it seemed, had shared some curious new information. A reliable source told Raymond that a man by the name of Albert Mitchell had a frightening encounter the night the Andrus family was killed. Albert was approached on the street by "several armed men" and told to show them where the Andruses lived. He did so and was then ordered to "get away from the neighborhood at once."[130] Had a random passerby come face-to-face with the family's killer?

Raymond's lawyers thought the lead was worth exploring, or at least leveraging to ensure their client got a new trial. At the end of October 1911, Raymond was whisked away to the Lafayette jail to await the next session of the district court. A year later, he would be freed, not because of a retrial, but because of his daughter's courtroom confession.[131]

/ / /

In February 1911, the four-member Andrus family had been violently slaughtered in their Lafayette, Louisiana home. Four weeks later and four hundred miles to the west, the Casaway family of five met an equally brutal fate. This latter crime, distinguished both by its Alamo City location and the presence of a white woman among its victims, was eventually connected to an aged white man purportedly motivated by an antimiscegenation crusade. The arrest of William McWilliams for murdering the Casaways, followed by the apprehension of Raymond Barnabet for the killing of the Andruses, highlighted the way lawmen investigated these cases as individual homicides. William's lack of a trial, despite compelling evidence of his guilt, stands in stark contrast to Raymond's condemnation to die, despite contradictory witness testimony. Most important, however, is the fact that both men's motives were imagined as specific and isolated.

For almost two years, the authorities had been investigating a variety of ax murders in the rice belt region as discrete crimes. Although this strategy resulted in numerous arrests, more and more families were being slaughtered. Following the Casaway crime, this discrepancy led Black communities and white newspaper outlets to recognize something the police had not: a serial killer was in their midst. It would not be long before the murderer had a name.

3

Arresting Clementine

Tortured Admission and a Media Maneuver

The apprehension and prosecution of Raymond Barnabet for the Andrus family murder presented a fascinating conundrum for Lafayette's Black community: they were relieved someone was behind bars for that crime while acknowledging that the killer of the Byerses was "never apprehended."[1] That Black folks had already established the likelihood that the Opelousas, Byers, Andrus, and Casaway families were murdered by the same person presumably meant that they either believed Raymond was a prolific serial killer or doubted whether he was even guilty of the crime for which he'd been charged and convicted. Roughly a month after his trial, they would have an uncomfortable answer: Raymond Barnabet was either entirely innocent or an accomplice to murder. No matter what, however, he was not the lone perpetrator. His daughter, Clementine, had quite the story to tell, and it contradicted what she'd said under oath just a few weeks before.

Clementine Barnabet's first confession followed the next crime in this saga. The young woman's response to the Randall family murder explains how she became ensnared in Louisiana's criminal justice system and what her entanglement suggests about her potential culpability. Indeed, law enforcement officials and nameless reporters concocted narratives of guilt and innocence to accomplish specific agendas. Then, when another murder happened *after* Clementine's confession, people struggled to reconcile the idea that her admission had not stymied the violence blanketing the region.

/ / /

As Raymond Barnabet started the 1911 holiday season behind bars, others in Lafayette carried on with their festivities. The murders seemed to have abated, the region was experiencing its usual mild weather, and local shops were peddling wares ready to adorn mantles and dinner tables alike.[2] On November 26, the Sunday before Thanksgiving, Black and white citizens of Lafayette filed into their respective churches. Around 7:00 a.m. on Monday morning, a young girl named Devine headed home after spending the night at her uncle's house.[3] As rain poured from the sky, the child, who was around ten years old, noticed that the kitchen door was open. Peering inside, she saw her entire family lying in their own blood. She "gave the alarm," calling out for any individual nearby to summon help.[4] Law enforcement officers—including Lafayette Parish Sheriff Louis Lacoste—arrived at the home of the Randall family, located between Lafayette and Madison Streets a few blocks south of the cotton oil mill.[5] The three-room cabin was also less than one mile south of the Southern Pacific Railroad. The scene that investigators found could only be described as "one of the most cold-blooded murders ever committed in Southwest Louisiana," according to a local newspaper.[6]

Inside, Norbert, his wife, Azema, and their baby daughter, Agnes, were found lying in one bed.[7] In another bed in the same room, the couple's six-year-old son, Rene; five-year-old son, Norbert Jr.; and an eight-year-old overnight visitor named Albert Scythe had been posthumously stacked, their child-sized corpses crowded toward the foot of the bed.[8] From the position of the bodies found at the scene—not to mention a bent mosquito net over the couple's bed—detectives surmised that the husband had been slain first while sleeping, and his wife was targeted next. Though reports agreed that all of the family members had been brutalized with an "ordinary pole ax," some also surmised that Norbert Randall had been shot *before* being mutilated, leaving a depression in his pillow.[9] Piecing together the order of weapon usage, however, was a complicated undertaking. Similarly, while it appears that the children likely stirred in all of the commotion, reports disagree about whether or not one (or more) of them tried to physically run away, as a little footprint was identified beside the second bed.[10]

As much as discrepancies abounded regarding *some* aspects of the crime, others were eerily familiar. The assailant apparently entered the house through a door, which was later found open by the detectives. An ax was used to slaughter the victims, and, like the wounds found on the Casaways, the mutilations left on the Randall family members' bodies implied that "blunt end blows" had terminated their lives.[11] As in the Andrus case, some of the bodies were staged—stacked—after the victims had been killed. Whoever had attacked the Randall family had taken care to wash the ax of bloodstains, highlighting "the remarkable coolness and deliberation" behind this extraordinarily violent rampage.[12] Like all of the other crimes so far, the ax was found at the scene.

Although the murder weapon was readily recovered, the bullet that had passed through Norbert's head was nowhere to be found.[13] Nor, for that, matter was the gun recovered.[14] An "electric arc light" on the street had illuminated the room in the nighttime, providing the perpetrator "full view" of the sleeping family before they had time to react.[15] Plus, it had rained profusely that very night, so "any outside trace" of the assailant had been washed away.[16] Physical clues leading to the killer were in short supply.

So too were any theories of motive. Norbert Randall worked for Dr. Lambert O. Clark—the same physician who had investigated the Andrus scene as deputy coroner some months earlier and had been a founding member of the Lafayette Sanitarium, a state-of-the-art hospital that had just opened to visitors the week before the Randalls were killed.[17] Dr. Clark now had the unenviable task of trying to determine how his employee of "most excellent character" met his unfortunate demise.[18] Meanwhile, the authorities wondered if the family was killed because Azema had attended a "religious meeting" mere hours before she was murdered.[19] Apparently, this was no mainstream faith community, but one described as "peculiar" and known as the Sacrifice Church. Still, the investigators didn't think the gathering had anything to do with the crime. At least three regional newspapers offered a tantalizing justification for murder—the Randall and Andrus families were supposedly related, with the husband of the former and the wife of the latter being siblings.[20] It was within this broader context that the coroner's jury rendered an unsettling verdict: the Randalls came to their death "by the hand of a party or parties unknown."[21]

/ / /

When the Randalls were hacked to death in their Lafayette home at the end of November 1911, they joined an ever-growing list of Black families slaughtered by ax under the cover of darkness in southwestern Louisiana and southeastern Texas. What had happened before happened again: people flocked to the scene of the crime, morbidly curious to get a glimpse of the carnage.[22] Throughout the morning, passersby visited the home, perhaps chatting among themselves about the horrific atrocity. Then, around noon, one of those bystanders caught Lafayette Parish Sheriff Louis Lacoste's eye. Her name was Clementine Barnabet.[23]

Whether Sheriff Lacoste found Clementine suspicious because her father had recently been tried for a similar crime remains hard to say. Roughly a month earlier, Raymond Barnabet had been convicted of killing the Andrus family—albeit on flimsy evidence—and had been subsequently granted a new trial after getting flagrantly drunk at his first one. His wife, daughter, and son had all testified against him. Now the very same daughter was acting questionably—perhaps snickering and chuckling—in the aftermath of the Randall crime.[24]

Sheriff Lacoste's men headed to the nearby James Guidry residence, where Clementine worked—presumably as a live-in domestic—and arrested her.[25] Her reaction was anything but expected: she laughed. She insisted she had nothing to do with the crime, but the evidence was already damning.[26] In Clementine's room were blood-soaked clothes, saturated in such a way that the officers surmised she had picked up the dead children and then stained her dress and underwear.[27] Worse, there were crimson fingerprints on the latch string of the Guidry home.[28] And, if that wasn't enough, the United Press wired a story that reported witnesses had seen Clementine in the vicinity of the Randall house late on Sunday night.[29] If just one of these pieces of evidence had appeared, it would have been alarming. The trifecta of clues, however, made the detectives confident they had the right slayer.

Yet, as assured as the authorities were of Clementine's guilt, they weren't convinced she was the only culprit. They assumed she must have had at least one Black male accomplice, which was a frequent allegation Black women faced in the early 1900s. After all, Clementine was roughly five feet, four inches tall and supposedly weighed 152 pounds.[30] Plus, she was only about nineteen years old. The detectives didn't think a young Black woman of such stature could have physically wielded an ax with the force and precision needed to have dispatched an entire family. If the investigators had considered the fact that there were myriad young Black women incarcerated throughout the country for violent and ferocious crimes, they might not have assumed an accomplice was necessary.[31] Moreover, if they had pondered the strength Black women needed to engage in arduous domestic labor—including chopping wood, hauling water, scrubbing floors, stirring clothes, and more—they might not have questioned Clementine's ability. Instead, their inability to recognize the full spectrum of Black women's (criminal) behaviors meant that they not only denied Clementine's potential true culpability, but they implicitly rendered Black men murderous based on stereotypes rather than evidence.

Sheriff Lacoste thus took three Black men into custody alongside Clementine: Edwin Charles, Gregory Porter, and her own brother, Zepherin Barnabet.[32] Zepherin, the same sibling who had also testified against his father a month earlier, was now being held for a disturbingly similar crime. The ax murders in Lafayette had turned into a family affair. The authorities started to wonder if maybe all three Barnabets—father, son, and daughter—were involved in the two local crimes.[33] They wanted to get to the bottom of this convoluted situation once and for all. Clementine had not been in the Lafayette jail for long before being transported to New Orleans for additional questioning, presumably with Sheriff Lacoste at her side.[34]

The New Orleans Police Department was an experienced detective bureau known for a type of lawlessness that got results.[35] Sometimes obtaining those results required a special kind "third degree" examination.[36] The third degree was, quite simply, a euphemism for torture.[37] Routinely employed by lawmen to get information from suspects—regardless of the validity of said information—the third degree was a widespread practice that represented yet another form of racialized violence Black Americans experienced in Jim Crow society. That Clementine was a young woman would not have spared her from this treatment—her race increased the likelihood that she would suffer police brutality. From the perspective of the New Orleans officers, the goal was clear: solicit a confession by any means necessary.

Newspapers reported that Clementine experienced a third-degree examination. The two threads of this torture—psychological harm and physical suffering—could have rattled the young woman's sense of self. She could have been intentionally deprived of sleep and food.[38] Accompanied by incessant and increasingly agitated questioning, she may have grown panicked by the prolonged noise and lack of rest. If she refused to speak, the police could have tossed her in an isolated cell far removed from other prisoners without so much as a bed or chair.[39] Her space could have had no light or sound, creating sensory deprivation that was disorienting and terrifying. Then again, the detectives could have restrained Clementine securely before transporting her to the middle of nowhere at some early morning hour, using distance from the city and the power dynamics of white men versus a young Black woman to scare her witless.[40] In these scenarios, Clementine might have escaped a literal assault, but she would have still endured significant trauma.

Then again, the authorities could have approached her third-degree interrogation with physical pain at the fore. Perhaps they simply beat her with a "rubber hose, clubs, or fists," taking care to land the hardest attacks on parts of the body that could be covered with clothing.[41] Those same attacks might have intentionally been aimed at vital organs.[42] They might have held her head under water, put lit cigars against her body, forced her to stand still for hours upon hours, or shone a blinding light directly at her face.[43] If they maimed Clementine, the officers could have broken or fractured bones, punctured a lung, caused internal bleeding, or knocked out her teeth. She also would have faced the very real threat of sexual assault.

In a third-degree examination, nothing was off limits. The detectives could carry out their most sadistic fantasies under the guise of helping a criminal investigation. The police could have threatened to kill Clementine. Then again, they also could have tried.[44] Whatever they did to her got the results they wanted: Clementine talked.

/ / /

As the year's final month dawned, Clementine had a confession to make. She killed the Randall family.[45] In a matter of days, newspapers across the country published the sensational account.

Clementine was apparently a deaconess in the "Church of Sacrifice," the same Sacrifice Church that had appeared in the investigation into the Randalls' murder.[46] As a "very religious" devotee, she was prepared to do whatever her faith required of her, even if that meant killing someone.[47] When she purportedly received "messages from God" to slaughter an entire family, she listened.[48]

Supposedly, she stashed an ax in the folds of her clothes. Then, creeping up to the Randall family's cabin, Clementine claimed she bludgeoned Norbert and Azema in their sleep before turning her ax on the then-crying children. A handful of blows was all that was needed to hack the young bodies, leaving them "scattered in bits" all over the room.[49] The Randalls, according to Clementine, had "refused to obey 'church orders'" and needed to be handled.[50] Proudly, she boasted that she slaughtered the family "without assistance."[51]

In a poignant moment of strategy, remorse, chicanery—or all of the above—Clementine supposedly remarked, "'An' judge, thet [*sic*] ain't all, either.'"[52] She then detailed how she struck down the Andrus family the previous February.

Like the Randalls, the Andruses refused to "obey the message from God," and Clementine, with her father's assistance, sought to personally rectify the situation.[53] She admitted to "hacking the sleeping members" of the family before performing a "blood orgie [*sic*] with wierd [*sic*] prayers and incantations."[54]

Throughout the entirety of her confession, it was not just Clementine's words that stunned listeners. She laughed hysterically, supposedly rocking back and forth before rolling her eyes into the back of her head, rendering her pupils nearly invisible.[55] No wonder some papers reported that "an inquiry into her sanity" was pending.[56]

Yet, if Clementine had murdered the Andruses, then she had omitted her involvement under oath when she nearly sent her father to the gallows in October. But if she had nothing to do with the Andrus family deaths, however, Clementine had become a scapegoat for a larger plot—one that could involve the elusive Sacrifice Church, the Lafayette and New Orleans Police Departments, or another unknown entity altogether.

/ / /

Arguably, there *was* a larger plot involved in Clementine's confession. The way news of her admission circulated reveals a fascinating conundrum. From Washington, D.C., to Keokuk, Iowa, dozens of newspapers across the country published damning accounts of Clementine's guilt.[57] Even the Canadian press covered her confession.[58] Yet, there is no evidence that local papers immediately reported on this turn of events. They mentioned that Clementine had been accused of murder, but they never commented on her chilling revelation.[59] The *Lafayette Advertiser* made no note of Clementine's confession. Neither did papers in Rayne, Crowley, New Iberia, or Baton Rouge. In fact, the *Times-Democrat* of New Orleans ran a story entitled "No Confession from Negro Girl" the exact same day the *Belleville News Democrat*—a small-town Illinois paper—ran a short piece with an obvious headline: "Girl Admits Killing Ten."[60]

The closest paper to Lafayette that printed the confession may have been in Lake Charles, seventy-five miles to the west.[61] What's instructive about this article is not necessarily its contents, but the inconspicuous text that reads "United Press" in parentheses just below the sub-headline. What this reveals is that the story came from a relatively new newswire that had emerged on the national print media scene in 1907. It seems papers subscribed to the U.P. wire service had access to this sensational declaration.

Yet, it wasn't just the United Press that carried the story of Clementine's confession. The National News Association and the National Telegraph Service also reported her supposed guilt.[62] The Associated Press, meanwhile, was suspiciously mute. Although it ran a piece that Clementine professed her innocence before her third-degree examination, it seems the next article the A.P. published about the case simply confirmed the charges against her.[63] Why would the national news wires print such contradictory stories?

My contention is that, although news of Clementine's guilt was carried by the United Press, the National News Association, and the National Telegraph Service, it wasn't *supposed* to be published at all. Likely, someone close to the case was trying to control its media coverage, perhaps because local authorities wavered in their belief that Clementine could have acted alone.[64] If she had accomplices, tipping them off with an astonishing confession in local papers surely wouldn't bode well for the investigation. While Clementine *did* confess in late November 1911, Lafayette police likely didn't want the public to know what had transpired. Somewhere along the chain of command, someone didn't relay the message to not print the story in myriad papers that participated in the smaller newswires. Whether those snafus were accidental or deliberate remains hard to say, but the result was that a segment of the population woke up at the end 1911 to learn that a young Black woman had confessed to murdering two families in cold blood because they hadn't obeyed church orders. Those in Clementine's community, however, believed for the time being that she had never confessed.

/ / /

Given the severity of what Clementine Barnabet supposedly said and the conditions under which she said it, it is worth exploring the possibility that her admission was simply untrue. Newspapers reported that the confession had been obtained after she had been tortured, the young woman was only a teenager, she had grown up in a seemingly volatile home, and questions about her mental health already circulated in the public consciousness. If she had offered a false confession, she would have been in company with everyone from women during the Salem witch trials to the Central Park Five, saying what the white men in authority told her they wanted to hear.

Even without torture, police interrogations intentionally create anxiety and despair.[65] Investigators are allowed to use a variety of ethically dubious tactics to extract information. Lying to subjects about incriminating evidence, promising a lesser punishment with no ability to enforce said deal, asking hypothetical questions about potentially committing the suspected crime, and more can be used by the authorities during an interrogation. In the context of Clementine's ordeal, the addition of torture presumably heightened feelings of panic and helplessness. As such, she could have made one of three types of false confessions: coerced-compliant, coerced-internalized, or coerced-reactive.[66] The difference in the types of false confessions is less about the untruth of the admission, and more about the psychology and decision-making processes that go into rationalizing such a potentially life-altering falsehood.

If Clementine had made a coerced-compliant confession, she would have simply caved to social pressure.[67] The police might have fed her bits of information gathered from the crime scene, scared her straight after some kind of physical and/or psychological harm, and then emerged with a tidy confession that seemed like it could have only come from a guilty party.

Similarly, if Clementine had made a coerced-internalized confession, she would have caved to social pressure, but she would *also* have come to believe that she committed the Randall family murder (and perhaps the Andrus family killing too). In this type of admission, the suspect develops "a profound distrust of their own memory," becoming susceptible to a plethora of external sources.[68] Again, Clementine could have been told information that the authorities already knew, but rather than going along with their ploy, she might have earnestly begun to question her innocence. In so doing, false memories could have been implanted into her mind and Clementine could have convinced herself that somehow, someway, she had axed the Randalls.

On the opposite side, Clementine could have made a coerced-reactive confession in which she knew she did not commit the crime but admitted guilt to protect someone else (or potentially herself). In this scenario, Clementine would have had to believe that either there was some person who represented a bigger threat to her safety than those with whom she would presumably be detained, or, that she deserved to take the fall for the real killer due to her relationship with said individual. If Clementine was behind bars, for example, Raymond couldn't make good on his supposed threat to kill her for having testified against him roughly a month earlier.[69]

Although it would be easy to argue that Clementine's confession—whether coerced-compliant, coerced-internalized, or coerced-reactive—was potentially false due to the questionable methods used to obtain it, there are two additional risk factors that ought to be considered: age and mental health. Modern studies have repeatedly shown that juveniles are particularly susceptible to false confessions.[70] Quite simply, their brains aren't as fully developed as those of adults, causing younger suspects to seek out short-term rewards (i.e., being released from the interrogation room) without fully grasping the long-term consequences (i.e., twenty-five years in prison). When Clementine was taken to New Orleans, she was likely an older teenager. At her father's trial, she testified that she was "about 19," which is the age accepted in this study.[71] However, since Louisiana didn't require birth certificates until 1912, census takers were notoriously wrong at listing ages, and individuals sometimes didn't even know their own exact birthdate, it's impossible to precisely confirm Clementine's age. What is consistent with all available records, however, is that she was significantly younger than her mid-twenties, the age range now believed to represent complete brain maturation.[72] This suggests that the young woman was unable to make the kinds of informed decisions expected of a mature adult in a similar situation. Like other younger Black women ensnared in the criminal justice system in the early twentieth century, Clementine's experience was generally interpreted through the lens of adulthood even though she was still in late adolescence.[73]

In a similar vein, though brief murmurings related to Clementine's mental health appeared in November 1911, she was presumed to be rational, sane, and competent. Yet, scant details about her upbringing suggest a difficult childhood in a tumultuous home. Though little is known about her youth, Clementine was born sometime in the late 1880s, likely the middle child out of nine and one of two daughters. Between the censuses of 1900 and 1910, the eleven-member Barnabet family is recorded with a series of phonetically similar names, although no girl by the name of Clementine appears. Knowing that turn-of-the-century census takers were not necessarily diligent in their record-keeping practices, and many subscribed to the racial ideologies that permeated the country at the time, the absence of the young woman's exact name is not alarming. Her known siblings, including Zepherin and Noah, and her stepmother, Dinah, confirm the accuracy of her family. Plus, it seems the Barnabets were known for having nicknames, as Raymond referred to Zepherin as Ferran (Pherin) during his trial, and the former is listed as Antoine in the censuses.[74]

From the sparsely available information, Clementine's parents were believed to have a turbulent—possibly abusive—relationship.[75] Reportedly, they were both born in the early 1860s in Louisiana, possibly enslaved as young children. By the end of the century, Clementine's brother Zepherin recounted having to step between their parents to quell altercations, especially when Raymond started drinking.[76] To complicate matters further, Dinah was often referred to as Raymond's girlfriend or mistress, rather than legal wife. Even Clementine identified her as her stepmother rather than her biological parent.[77] On more than one occasion she was identified as Dinah Porter and had supposedly separated from Raymond at some point in the early 1910s.

If in fact Clementine lived at home during the spring of 1911, based on her testimony during her dad's trial, she appears to have moved into her employer's residence by the fall. Reportedly, she labored as a domestic servant for white households in the Lafayette area, though she was never able to keep a job for very long.[78] Newspapers opined it was because of her "worthless character."[79] Maybe the fact that she was a teenager placed her in challenging predicaments as she sought to earn a paltry wage in a system designed to keep her, and people who looked like her, at the very bottom. Likely, the realities of Black women's vulnerabilities within the frameworks of Jim Crow ideologies contributed to Clementine's haphazard employment record.[80] After all, being a young Black woman in the New South did not give her many places to turn to for safety.

While not every child who grows up under less-than-ideal circumstances develops mental illness, discussions of the prospect of such within Black women's history are long overdue. So, although there is no definitive proof that Clementine suffered from any kind of mental disorder, there also isn't any proof that she didn't. Acknowledging that she could have been psychologically unwell—perhaps from a mental illness or perhaps from the daily trauma she might have endured—offers a step toward these uncomfortable conversations. If in fact she had suffered from something akin to battered woman or battered child syndrome, or had an unknown mental illness, her decision to confess was not exclusively a response to the torture she reportedly endured. Yet, the fact that the authorities interpreted Clementine's confession as evidence of her guilt highlights the reality that, throughout American history, Black men and women—as well as boys and girls—have been more likely to be presumed criminal rather than mentally ill. This trend not only reinforces stereotypes about Black criminality, but permits psychological disorders to go underdiagnosed in Black communities.

/ / /

Post-confession, it seemed the Lafayette Police Department had a three-pronged approach to try to prove Clementine's guilt. Up first: keep her in police custody so that "an inquiry into her sanity" could be undertaken.[81] Second: send her bloodstained clothes to the state chemist in New Orleans for additional processing.[82] And third: keep the criminalized Barnabets apart from one another. Raymond was transferred from the Lafayette Parish jail to one in Crowley because the authorities wanted to prevent him from communicating with his daughter.[83] Clementine was held in Lafayette and "placed in a strong steel cell."[84]

As Christmastime gave way to the new year, communities along the Southern Pacific Railroad were cautiously optimistic that not just one—but two—deranged killers were in police custody. It seemed that the mayhem that had become synonymous with the last name Barnabet had come to an end. In fact, things became even more certain when, on Wednesday, January 17, 1912, Louisiana's state chemist, Dr. Abraham Metz, called the district attorney for Lafayette Parish with some news: Clementine's ensanguined clothes tested positive for human blood.[85] She had claimed the stains were from her own menstruation, but turn-of-the-century chemical technology supposedly matched the blood on Clementine's "white and blue shirtwaists" with that which had soaked into the pillowcases at the murder scene.[86] Dr. Metz determined that the "blood and brain" found on Clementine's belongings had come from "wounds inflicted on living persons."[87] That was damning evidence by the day's technological advancements.[88] The prosecutor could start to develop an ironclad case against Clementine in the Randall family slayings. With enough evidence, maybe he'd be able to argue she was involved in the Andrus family killings, too.

News of Chemist Metz's findings sent waves of relief through the local communities. Lafayette Parish Sheriff Louis Lacoste was "highly pleased" with the chemical findings.[89] Yet, Black communities in the region struggled to reconcile the fact that, although two Barnabets had been detained for the local ax murders, similar crimes that had occurred in nearby Rayne and Crowley still had no good suspects, not to mention the lack of resolutions in the San Antonio and Lake Charles cases. Although Dr. Metz's account alleviated some concerns, many Black folks continued the precautionary measures they had undertaken following the previous crimes: securing windows, barring doors, and posting a guard throughout the night.[90] It was better to be safe than sorry.

Two days after Dr. Metz told the district attorney about his findings, Harriet Crane found something far worse. On Friday, January 19, shortly before noon, she'd called over to her daughter's house on the western side of Crowley. Known as the "Promised Land," this all-Black neighborhood was less than a mile from where Raymond was incarcerated and less than a mile from the Southern Pacific Railroad tracks. It was also roughly two blocks from where the Byerses had been murdered in January 1911—almost exactly one year earlier. When Harriet got no response, she asked a neighbor about Marie's whereabouts. He didn't know. The pair walked over to her two-room cabin and noticed the back door was ajar.[91]

They asked a passerby to cautiously enter the home. He encountered a ghastly scene: the "mangled remains" of four individuals piled onto a bed in the front room.[92] Harriet Crane's daughter and three grandchildren had been murdered.

Marie Warner, her nine-year-old daughter, Pearl; her seven-year-old son, Garry; and her five-year-old daughter, Harriet, had all been brutally axed in their sleep. Acadia Parish Sheriff Louis Fontenot and his officers surmised that the assailant had entered the house from the back door and then proceeded to hack at the family. Footprints in the backyard implied that maybe more than one person had attacked the Warners, so the authorities sent for bloodhounds to follow the tracks.

Investigators deduced that the killer had posthumously moved some of the bleeding corpses, dragging them from the back room, where they had been axed, to the front room, where they were discovered. All four bodies were found "lying across the bed, face downward," as if they had been deliberately staged.[93] Nearby, the "blood-stained axe" served as telltale evidence left at the scene.[94]

Within hours of the discovery of the Warner family murder, the deputy coroner empaneled a jury of inquest and the authorities started looking for the perpetrator. Unsuccessfully, they tried to guard the house, hoping to preserve the scene for clues. Onlookers flocked, however, compromising whatever semblance of an investigation they attempted to conduct. The bloodhounds couldn't pick up a single path, as too many people had trampled the ground around the residence.[95] So, although the detectives were pondering the prospect of multiple killers, they had lost the main clue that pointed them in that direction.

As officers worked the angle of physical evidence left at the scene, they also attempted to figure out why anyone would have wanted the Warners dead. Marie was probably in her late twenties or early thirties. In 1910, she'd worked as a laundress in a white household.[96] She'd been separated from her husband for approximately four years, and he reportedly lived in Beaumont, Texas.[97] Her death certificate said she was a twenty-four-year-old divorced housekeeper.[98] There was nothing immediately obvious in her past or present that suggested she would be a likely murder victim. Perhaps the only tenuous thread was the literal proximity between the Warner and Byers homes, though reporters did not make anything of this fact. Instead, the press focused on the method of murder, linking it to the previous crime in Crowley, the two in Lafayette, and the one in Rayne.[99] Being axed to death was the defining feature of the slaughters.

Yet, if there was a general belief that the various ax murders were all related, then there was also an uncomfortable reality: neither Clementine nor Raymond Barnabet could have physically killed the Warners because they were both sitting in jail. As much as the Barnabets were reasonable suspects for their respective crimes, they were horrible guesses for this one.[100]

Two days after the Warners were murdered, the authorities believed they finally had a lead: a friend of the family and a local Baptist preacher were arrested.[101] Eliza Richards and Reverend Joseph Wilkins were detained in separate local jails, the former being moved from the Crowley facility and taken to Lake Charles and the latter incarcerated in Lafayette.[102] Now, the jails of three parishes were actively holding suspects believed to be implicated in several ax murders that had occurred in the rice belt over the last couple of years.

Although newspapers implied the evidence against both Eliza and Joseph was "strong," they were generally mute about the specifics that prompted the arrests.[103] Curiously, it was reported that both Eliza and Joseph were originally from the small town of Arnaudville, but had moved to Crowley a few years earlier. And while reporters suggested that Eliza's arrest was because she was "intimate friends" with Marie Warner, Joseph was described simply as a pastor of St. Joseph's Baptist Church.[104] Amid the horror of Black families being murdered with impunity, it seemed that one's relationship to the victims and employment status as a clergyman were suspicious enough to warrant apprehension.

Reportedly, Zepherin Barnabet was also rearrested in the aftermath of the Warner family murder.[105] Though he had established an alibi on the night the

Randalls were killed in Lafayette back in November, parish authorities were taking no chances after this latest crime. It seems that Edwin Charles, one of the men who'd been arrested, released, and rearrested following the Randall family slaying, had likely remained behind bars since December.

Two other Black men—Daniel Pratters and M. J. Snipe—were arrested in Glenmora, more than sixty miles north of Crowley, over a week after the Warners were murdered.[106] The latter was technically Reverend Snipe, reportedly a preacher of the African Methodist Church in Crowley.[107] Apparently, the duo had fled the Acadia Parish town in the aftermath of the latest killing and were discovered at a turpentine camp before being hauled to jail. Perhaps the fact that a regional news outlet claimed Marie Warner belonged to a church that preached "the necessity of a blood sacrifice for sin" added more fodder to the detectives' theory that a deviant faith community was behind the crimes.[108] After all, Clementine had implied that the Randalls and Andruses had sinned by refusing to "obey the message from God."[109] Not surprisingly then, another Black pastor was detained in connection with the ax murders, highlighting the consequences of labeling religion as a potential motive.

The apprehension of eight different individuals—Raymond Barnabet, Clementine Barnabet, Zepherin Barnabet, Edwin Charles, Eliza Richards, Joseph Wilkins, Daniel Pratters, and M. J. Snipe—related to three different murders in two different parishes did little to quell the panic of Black residents in the region. It seemed that no matter who was arrested, the crimes continued. Raymond had been behind bars when the Randalls were killed in Lafayette. Then he, his daughter Clementine, and Edwin Charles were in jail when the Warners were slaughtered in Crowley. Now, Eliza, Daniel, and the Reverends Wilkins and Snipe had been arrested, plus Zepherin had been rearrested, but that didn't mean the violence would stop. If anything, the precedent suggested precisely the opposite: the madness would continue. Black folks *knew* a serial killer had come to the rice belt.

Understandably, Black communities in the region responded to this latest horror with fear and dread. Few folks could be found out on the streets after dark, and adult family members held shifts watching their homes and loved ones at night, worried that the murderer would strike them next. Lights burned brightly in Black neighborhoods, offering a modicum of reassurance that perhaps the killer wouldn't attack a home where the occupants might be awake. The local newspaper likely exaggerated the situation when it mentioned that "unless something is done to stop the murders, it is predicted that Coontown will soon be depopulated," but maybe some families did move from the area, leveraging whatever means they had to put literal distance between themselves and the sites of the crimes.[110] In Crowley, without a viable lead as to why the Byerses and Warners had been killed, no one knew if they were safe.

It wasn't just Black residents who reacted to the Warner family murder. The governor of Louisiana, Jared Young Sanders, authorized a reward of $500 (over $16,400 in 2025) for the "arrest and conviction of the parties" who had killed the Warners.[111] It had taken the deaths of six Black families—comprising twenty-three individuals—in Louisiana for the state to finally get financially involved, and that was after Black residents of Crowley had pleaded for this appropriation.[112] Meanwhile, when the Casaways had been killed in Texas back in March 1911, Governor Colquitt had readily offered $250 from the treasury to find their murderer, likely immediately putting up a reward because Elizabeth Casaway was a white woman and the local sheriff had intimated he'd also give $250.[113] This disparity in how rewards were offered by the two states involved in the ax murder chaos highlights the monetary consequences of Jim Crow America—Black life was literally valued less than its white counterpart.

/ / /

The aftermath of Clementine Barnabet's confession—whether real of fabricated—was that a particular motive entered the public consciousness that had never appeared in this saga until this point: religious fanaticism.[114] Each prior murder had been considered as a standalone case, but Clementine's confession provided the first potential rationale that could be used to explain *all* of the crimes that had occurred until now. It is within this context of religious fanaticism as a plausible motive that the arrest of Reverend Joseph Wilkins is significant. He appears to have been the first man of the cloth implicated in the ax murders, but he was by no means the last. The authorities were now on the hunt for deviant religions and their leaders.

Sheriff Louis Lacoste—the same Lafayette Parish lawman who'd had Clementine arrested back in November—came to believe that religious fanaticism was indeed the motive for the ax slayings. He declared the Sacrifice Church "a new sect" that was responsible for the recent spate of crimes occurring in towns buttressing the Southern Pacific Railroad.[115] Yet, the official police interpretation was twinged with the racist undertones of Jim Crow America: authorities believed "that the negroes are so intensely moved and impressed by the teaching of the testament [of] sacrificial ideas and ceremonies that they are incited to commit atrocious crimes."[116] This statement implied that emotion—and perhaps perceived ignorance—drove Black folks *in particular* to engage in violent actions. Thus, not only were Black residents of the rice belt the targets of the elusive ax murderer, but they were also targets of racist ideologies promulgated by white authorities. This dual imagery permitted a perverse sort of victim-blaming that flattened the diversity of experiences within the region's Black communities, suggesting that these crimes were intraracial due to communal pathologies. If the killer was *of* the community, then perhaps this was not a case of a deranged individual, but of a community-wide deficiency. In reality, however, Sheriff Lacoste and his officers *wanted* to see religious deviance in their investigation. They were predisposed to doing so through a racial lens that further pathologized Black Louisianians.

With Clementine in jail and another murder having occurred in an adjacent parish, Sheriff Lacoste needed to find the Sacrifice Church and identify its adherents. He claimed that the group had a meeting somewhere relatively close to the Randall family house on the very same night they were murdered.[117] It was this same meeting that Azema Randall apparently attended before she was killed.[118] Where Sheriff Lacoste got that information is unknown, though it was reported that the investigator had been keeping tabs on members of the Sacrifice Church. A nearby paper claimed that a number of folks had been "under surveillance" since that fateful November night.[119] The article stated that Sheriff Lacoste had a hunch back then but not enough evidence to support his feelings. If this was true, however, parish officials had kept this speculation to themselves for two months, perhaps secreting away valuable information that might have led to the arrest of the assailant(s) before the Warners were slaughtered.

/ / /

For the first two years that Black families along the Southern Pacific Railroad had been axed indiscriminately, law enforcement officials had proposed unsophisticated rationales that produced viable yet often unconvincing suspects. Detectives in three Louisiana parishes and one Texas county struggled to balance the specifics of the crime(s) in their jurisdiction with the reality that their counterparts down the tracks were grappling with eerily similar homicides. Linkage blindness clouded their investigations, as much the result of turn-of-the-century police techniques as of stereotypes and Jim Crow ideologies. Finally, however, they had been given a motive that was not exclusive to a specific murder. It did not matter if it was true or not—it provided an uncomfortable answer that had the potential to break the cases wide open. That the answer had come from a young Black woman should not be ignored.

The 1911 confession of Clementine Barnabet to the murder of the Randall and Andrus families in Lafayette represented a turning point in the ax murder saga. Whether Clementine had actually committed the crimes she claimed remains a matter of speculation. Even excluding the newspaper reports that she was tortured by New Orleans detectives, there are ample reasons to believe her confession could have been false. She was a young Black woman who'd been put in a vulnerable position both literally and figuratively. If she had simply told the authorities what they wanted to hear, perhaps she had prioritized self-preservation over everything else. Then again, she could have been suffering from some kind of undiagnosed mental health issue and not comprehended the gravity of her situation.

On the other hand, however, recent movements to believe Black women offer an avenue to consider Clementine's statements as genuine—her truth. Available evidence suggests that nothing she said to the police contradicted their findings. Though the authorities could have fed her details of the crime that she then incorporated into a fictitious or internalized confession, it is also entirely possible that the reason she knew such specifics is because she was guilty. The discovery of "blood and brains" on her clothing—as well as the bloody latch on her employer's gate—represented additional damning clues.[120] If Clementine Barnabet had murdered the Randalls and Andruses, she had just confessed to being a serial killer.

4

Inevitable Crimes

Religious Fanaticism and the Axman

The start of a new year had not brought a clean slate to the rice belt. Instead, another Black family had been axed in their own home, even as the most likely suspects were locked away in jail. The day after the Warners were found mutilated in Crowley, the Broussards were discovered slaughtered in Lake Charles. Neither Clementine Barnabet nor her father could have physically wielded the ax that killed either family. The murderer was still on the loose, and both local communities and lawmen were at a loss.

Exploring the deaths of the Broussard and Dove families in early 1912 emphasizes how two distinct but overlapping narratives emerged regarding the seemingly inevitable violence permeating the rice belt region. On one hand, Clementine's declaration of religion as a motive gained credibility when biblical text was found at the Broussards' home after they were slain. On the other hand, the "axman" moniker only appeared after the Doves were killed, suggesting that modus operandi was more important than motive in identifying the perpetrator. Combined, these two crimes—and the varied responses to them—led to the further criminalization of Black faith practices and increasingly publicized stories about how Black communities made sense of a serial killer in their midst.

/ / /

The Northern family lived on Rock Street in Lake Charles with the Southern Pacific Railroad's tracks visible from their front door.[1] Their property was a veritable fortress, surrounded by a tall wire fence with a keyed "heavy bolt" securing the entrance gate.[2] On January 20, 1912—Saturday night—Victoria Northern was home cooking. As the sun started to set, she noticed the Broussards, her neighbors to the north, had lit a lamp in their three-room cabin. Although the family had reportedly lived in Lake Charles for years, they hadn't lived on Rock Street for long, having just moved into their house the previous fall. Perhaps Victoria was still learning the habits of the Broussards and therefore observed the light with a little more attention than usual. Then again, she was likely aware that families were using lamps to thwart the threat of an ax murderer on the loose—plus, the slaughter of the Warner family in Crowley fifty-odd miles to the east had just been discovered the day before. Of course, Victoria could have been so absorbed in her cooking that the glow barely registered. After all, she did not finish up in the kitchen until after 1:00 a.m.[3]

In the morning, Victoria realized that the Broussards' back door was open, but it seemed no one was moving about inside the house. She asked her husband, Elijah, to check on the new neighbors. He knocked on the door. No one answered. Though he offered to go inside the house, Victoria insisted he should get an officer instead. Meanwhile another neighbor—Julia Thibodeaux—stopped by to get some milk from Victoria.[4] The two women chatted about the alarming situation and, when Julia returned home, she alerted her husband, Jacob, and advised him to call the authorities. Instead, Jacob headed over to the Broussard home and glanced into the space where the door was ajar. He thought he saw "a child's leg sticking out of the bed."[5] Gathering two local men as reinforcements, Jacob entered the house, passing through the kitchen and into the children's bedroom. With a simple glance, the trio had seen enough. The men immediately summoned the police *and* the coroner.

Calcasieu Parish Sheriff David J. Reid and Coroner William L. Fisher—officials who had also worked the Hodge family murder roughly two years earlier—headed to the crime scene.[6] Maybe these investigators noted the parallels between the two slaughters as they walked through the house. It appeared the killer entered the residence via a kitchen window and then stealthily moved to the southwestern room where Felix Broussard and his wife, Matilda, were sleeping soundly. With the "blunt edge" of an ax, the assailant struck Felix, inflicting blows that mangled the man's face.[7] Possibly the noise awakened Matilda, who threw up her arm in self-defense. The effort was for naught: the murderer used the same ax to crush her head into a horrific pulp. Around the room, blood covered nearly every surface, including the walls and bedding. Crimson pools soiled the floor as the victims' wounds dripped steadily.

Likely, the slayer then crossed into the northwestern room, where the

Broussards' three young children—Margaret, Alberta, and Louis—were sleeping. Aged eight, six, and three, respectively, the kids were not spared from the carnage. Instead, the killer dispatched each youngster with one or two "powerful blows," again using the ax to batter their heads and extinguish all signs of life.[8] Found in bed as though sleeping, with the covers over their feet, none of the children appeared to have awakened before being murdered. Officers theorized that the intruder then exited the home through the kitchen door, leaving the telltale ax to be discovered in the morning.

As news of the crime traveled through Lake Charles, Black and white residents flocked to Rock Street. According to one New Orleans paper, the bystanders numbered "several thousand," both at the house and the mortuary.[9] For investigators, the next logical step was empaneling a coroner's jury. The five men questioned several witnesses, but they learned nothing useful. Rather than declare that the family had met their demise at the hands of parties unknown, however, Coroner Fisher decided to leave the investigation open.[10] This seemingly small shift subtly hinted that the authorities were not only conceding that they were stumped, but that they believed time might help them uncover more clues. After more than two years of Black families being axed along the Southern Pacific Railroad, it appeared detectives were finally prepared to change their approach to solving the crimes. Leaving the coroner's inquest open meant the deaths of the Broussards could be *formally* linked to another homicide if the evidence supported such a conclusion.

/ / /

It did not take long for the biggest—and most puzzling—piece of evidence to become publicly known. From across the street of the Broussard home, a general outline of text was visible on the front door. Written in strong, bold lead pencil in horizontal lines was an inscription: "When He maketh inquisition for blood He forgetteth not the cry of the humble."[11] Not surprisingly, the discovery of this message seemed to confirm what many already suspected—the Broussards were killed in the name of religious fanaticism.

At the time of the murders, it was assumed that the inscription was a permutation of the King James Version of Psalm 9:12. In the Western Judeo-Christian tradition, there are 150 psalms that address a range of topics, from thankfulness for God's blessings to lamentations for problems, followed by pleas for divine assistance and anticipation of God's help. Psalm 9 specifically offers a contrast of ideas: God's righteousness as enduring and perpetual, which is in opposition to human wickedness and evil. In the King James Version, verse 12 reads: "When he maketh inquisition for blood, *he remembereth them:* he forgetteth not the cry of the humble" (emphasis added). Alongside the rest of the psalm, the text offers an ominous tone of fear of eternal damnation unless one knows God earnestly and praises Him despite opposition. If the person who left the inscription on the family's door was drawing from this psalm to make their point, perhaps they accomplished their goal.

That the writing on the door was not a verbatim transcript of the verse did not matter to folks in the rice belt.[12] According to local reports, the inscription came from the Bible, even if it was a little off. There is an easy explanation behind this discrepancy: the inscriber could have written what they *heard* was Psalm 9:12, regardless of whether they'd ever laid eyes on the scripture itself. Verbally recounting stories, especially religious ones, had emerged as a key feature of the spread of Christianity among Black adherents when slavery prohibited them from reading.[13] It is possible that the inscription was written by someone who was literate in the sense of knowing the mechanics of reading and writing, but who was also deeply steeped in the oral traditions essential to Black religious life in turn-of-the-century Louisiana. A minister who observed the text was not fazed by the incomplete wording and speculated that perhaps the killer identified with "the humble" and believed it was their "duty to take human life."[14]

Although the permutation of Psalm 9:12 was by far the largest and most pronounced writing left on the Broussard family door, it wasn't the only text. The local paper explained that beside the scripture was the phrase "Human 5" (sometimes written as "Human Five").[15] Some reports speculated the expression was actually a signature—a disturbing way for someone to take credit for the carnage.[16] Both inscriptions had each word underscored, adding heft to the declarative nature of the inscrutable messages. It seemed the killer had provided more clues than ever before, but their significance was (and remains) baffling.

/ / /

Although murmurs of religion as a motive for the ax murders of Black families in the rice belt region had circulated before the Broussards were killed—in part thanks to Clementine Barnabet's November 1911 confession—cries of religious fanaticism exploded in the aftermath of this crime. While the Lake Charles press initially offered two potential assailants—a "band of fanatic negroes" or "an insane white man"—reporters in the city did not extrapolate much beyond these general outlines.[17] Outside of southwestern Louisiana, however, the death of the Broussards finally linked the Sacrifice Church to the region's ax murders via a damning declaration: the group was a cult hellbent on human sacrifice.[18] Not only did the cult theory demonize Black religious expression via racist tropes and fetishization, but it contextualized Clementine as deviant and powerful—someone to fear.[19]

For the first time since the ax crimes had started more than two years earlier, print media across the United States introduced the rhetoric of a cult to explain what otherwise seemed unexplainable. By this point in American history, utopian separatists—often labeled as cults—had been in existence for more than sixty years and groups like the Oneida Community and the Israelite House of David had managed to put down roots and live relatively unmolested, though they were looked at with odd fascination. On the other hand, more troublemaking or preposterous groups like the Bride of Christ Church and the Koreshan Unity were readily condemned, mocked, and vilified. Closer to the location of the ax murders, New Orleans's own Council of God had been seemingly destroyed by the authorities in the early 1900s.[20] Thus, although few could agree on a single definition of a cult or its composition, the lay public did have a working understanding of these entities.

The word "cult" carried a negative connotation, and people who were described using this term were typically perceived to be religiously deviant, meaning that they did not conform to America's Protestant Christian norms.[21] Just as important as the beliefs held by the group was the grasp they held on members. Cults were thought to have charismatic leaders who convinced followers—often described as weak-minded, ignorant, and impressionable—to carry out their wildest whims. If said whims included violent crimes like murder, then it was possible that the assailant was being manipulated by someone higher up in the organization.

Perhaps the Sacrifice Church that Clementine Barnabet had named was not simply a figment of her imagination or a fringe faith community. If it was a cult, and she was a deaconess—as had been reported back in the fall—then there were potentially others in positions of power above her *and* minions in positions of obedience below her. If the group really was a cult, then it theoretically should have earned that name based on its structure *and* its beliefs. This would mean that Clementine's own culpability should be called into question as she could have been brainwashed into acting in the interest of the group's leader.[22] If the group wasn't a cult—if adherents could freely leave the organization without any consequences—then multiple people willingly accepted murder as an important tenet of their faith.

Thus, the authorities needed to find the Sacrifice Church. If they could locate its headquarters, talk to its followers, interrogate its leaders, and discern its beliefs, then perhaps detectives would finally be able to solve the ax murders. Far-flung newspapers reported on white investigators' strategies as they questioned Black residents using "every known method" at their disposal.[23] One of the most popular ones was to get men drunk and *then* interview them. Try as they might, however, the authorities couldn't make any progress. They concluded that "the negroes simply will not talk," and one veteran Crowley detective said that the ax murders represented "one of those cases the law cannot cover," in part because the witnesses weren't cooperative.[24]

It'd be easy to conclude that folks were so scared of the Sacrifice Church that they refused to speak up. Perhaps their silence was further proof of the crippling fear this elusive organization instilled in Black communities from Lafayette to Lake Charles and beyond. Truthfully, they *were* scared. But said fear might have been two-fold: a fear of the ax murderer *and* a fear of the authorities. Both of these concerns were legitimate. In the Jim Crow South, the devaluation of Black life meant that law enforcement agencies were not trustworthy entities to Black communities. Opening up about the Sacrifice Church had the potential to leave folks vulnerable *and* without protection. Black residents of the rice belt continually navigated these two distinct pressures: potential death from an unknown killer and potential persecution from known authorities.

Black folks knew there was something dangerous about white men in relatively powerful positions probing into the social and cultural fabrics of their lives. It's probably accurate to say there *was* local knowledge about the Sacrifice Church, but no one was willing to share information with the police.[25] The result of this de facto closed-lip policy is a frustrating conundrum for modern-day researchers: all evidence suggests that the lore of the Sacrifice Church had been circulating for months at this point, and still, like the killer, the community seemingly left no trace—except, perhaps, for the sacrificed bodies.

Likely, then, one of the most tentative ways to understand the Sacrifice Church is not as a religion, per se, but as a reflection of what white society thought about Black faith expression, particularly that which deviated from "Black Christian social respectability."[26] In other words, the Sacrifice Church represented white anxieties regarding Black religious engagement that challenged social norms and appropriated fear and violence toward inscrutable ends.

/ / /

Detectives in Louisiana clearly believed the Sacrifice Church was real, hidden, and dangerous. It was within this context that the authorities in the rice belt began scrutinizing Black preachers, starting when Lafayette Parish Sheriff Louis Lacoste contacted his counterparts in nearby Jennings to arrest a man by the name of Reverend King Harris.[27]

What was known about Reverend Harris versus what was said about him is hard to distinguish. After his apprehension, for example, he confessed to having been in Lafayette the night the Randall family was killed.[28] The authorities surmised this meant he was there for religiously murderous reasons, though there was no proof to corroborate this suspicion.[29] Moreover, Reverend Harris was believed to be "high up in church circles" in his faith community: the Sacrifice Church.[30] Some reports even claimed he was the group's leader.[31]

Yet, Reverend Harris categorically denied that he belonged to the Sacrifice Church, let alone that his teachings ever compelled parishioners to kill. He stated that his congregation was part of the "Christ Sanctified Holy Church" or "Christ Sanctified Church"—source depending—and that it had been established in the area for ten years.[32] Christ's Sanctified Holy Church was (and still is) a legitimate Pentecostal denomination that emerged in the late 1800s, while Christ Holy Sanctified Church of America, Inc., emerged in the early 1900s, meaning there were at least two documented denominations that could have been the root of Harris's religious practice.[33] Meanwhile, observable proof of the Sacrifice Church was lacking. It seems plausible that white authorities, in their haste to pin the ax murders on somebody, had not been diligent about learning the differences between Black faith traditions and communities. Not only did this implicitly criminalize many Black religious groups, but it discouraged Black folks from speaking out about the Sacrifice Church. If *presumed* association with the deviant community could lead to scrutiny and arrest, then outright discussion of its existence could be interpreted as guilt.

Apparently, some of the ideas promoted by Reverend Harris were a cause for concern. He said that he preached the "gospel of the New Testament" and "baptism by fire."[34] Indeed, Sanctified churches emphasize spirit baptisms and scriptural teachings.[35] While there is nothing particularly alarming about these concepts in and of themselves, the authorities latched onto such euphemistic rhetoric in their attempt to curtail what they thought was literal human sacrifice occurring in their jurisdictions. They ascertained that King Harris was prone to "extremes in matters religious," but had to concede that, for all his excesses, he didn't seem to know about the Sacrifice Church.[36]

There is at least one more possibility worth considering. Maybe the reason the authorities were unable to recover information about the faith community is because it simply didn't exist. Far beyond the detectives mislabeling Black religious diversity, perhaps Clementine Barnabet concocted a religious motive to justify her crimes, defend someone else's, or regurgitate for the investigators exactly what they wanted to hear.

/ / /

The day after the mangled bodies of Marie Warner and her children were found in their Crowley home, the bloodied remains of five members of the Broussard family were discovered in their three-room Lake Charles cabin. Investigators did not hesitate to link these two crimes: both families had been brutally axed in the middle of the night and their houses were within walking distance of the Southern Pacific Railroad's southernmost tracks. The white press then expanded the commonalities to many of the earlier murders, including those at Rayne and Lafayette, and drew on stereotypes about Black faith communities when describing the Sacrifice Church. White authorities played into those same typecasts, criminalizing Black faiths in the process. Crowley's *Daily Signal* captured the gravity of the situation by detailing the "series of awful butcheries" of Black families.[37] Indeed, in that singular phrase the reporter summarized a phenomenon that was not yet known by name: serial murder. Religious fanaticism had been offered as a potential motive for the crimes, but underneath such speculation was the terrifying knowledge that a serial killer was prowling the rice belt.

By January 1912, eight Black families had been murdered from Lafayette, Louisiana, to San Antonio, Texas. In total, twenty-nine individuals, the majority of them children under the age of ten, had been violently slaughtered with an ax. Although some of the crime scenes had unique features—like the use of secondary weapons, the posthumous positioning of the bodies, and an interracial family among the slain—significant commonalities suggested the killings were related. The victims all lived within a mile of the SPRR's Sunset Route, the telltale ax was readily located at the scene, the families were never robbed, and a mother plus her child or children were always counted among the deceased.

The authorities developed a working theory that the deaths were being caused by religious fanaticism promoted by the elusive Sacrifice Church. Not only did this hunch align with Clementine's confession, but it gained additional support when a biblical inscription was found on the Broussard family's front door in the aftermath of their killing. This led to rampant stories and assumptions labeling the Sacrifice Church a cult. As lawmen attempted to locate the Sacrifice Church, they also turned heightened attention to Black religious leaders, aware of the possibility that someone could have been deploying malleable minions to do their bidding.

Although Black residents of Lake Charles undoubtedly made the connection between the death of the Broussards and the various other ax murders that had happened in the region over the years, they were also focused on the perceived immediate threat. An unknown assassin had targeted their neighbors in the middle of the night, slaughtering all of the occupants of the home without regard for age or gender. It seemed the Broussards had been murdered at random, and the arrest of various parties for prior crimes had not thwarted this one. For all intents and purposes, then, that meant *any* Black family living within a mile of the Southern Pacific Railroad could be axed to death. No one was safe.

If no one was safe, then a sobering reality emerged: white authorities were not just ineffective—they were potentially exacerbating an already horrific situation. Developing a theory of religious fanaticism could *theoretically* explain the previous murders, but it also could do nothing to prevent another one. Thus, while lawmen attempted to find the Sacrifice Church, they conceded they were at a loss to stop the ax attacks. Black communities would have to protect themselves by broadening their understanding of what kinds of crimes could be included in this series of assaults. Although religion was certainly a viable rationale, Black folks would come to view the use of an ax as *the* telltale signature of the unknowable assailant. In so doing, the potential scope of the killer's rampage would reach a feverish pitch in a matter of months.

/ / /

As much as Clementine Barnabet's 1911 confession represented a turning point in how investigators conceptualized the rice belt ax murders that started in 1909, the death of the Broussard family in Lake Charles, Louisiana, in January 1912 shifted how print media discussed the crimes. Until this point, pieces published about the slaughters attempted to stick roughly to the known facts. On occasion some bit of information would be fudged—the name of a victim, the location of the weapon, the placement of the bodies—but the gist of the articles aligned with whatever had been reported by the local press. Then, when Reverend King Harris was arrested and the Broussards were found murdered with a biblical inscription scrawled on their front door, reporters ran with creative license to craft narratives of religious fanaticism that extended well beyond the detectives' investigative scope, eventually concluding the Sacrifice Church was a ghoulish cult. In so doing, not only did they manipulate the facts of the crime scenes themselves, but they disseminated stereotypes about Black Louisianans and Voodoo that were damagingly hyperbolic compared to folks' on-the-ground experiences.

Newspapers regularly commented on the ignorant, primitive, and superstitious character of Black residents of the rice belt. Arguing that the region's progress lagged behind its more cosmopolitan cousin, New Orleans, a widely reprinted article implied that the ax murders were the unfortunate byproduct of a misguided belief in "blood atonement."[38] This creed apparently required human sacrifices as compensation for sins, leading to the recent surge in crimes. Another highly popular article likewise claimed that, though Black churches in the area might have borne Christian crosses, such symbols represented the "fateful figure five," a nod to the infamous "Human 5" inscription left on the Broussards' door, and the unsubstantiated theory that the elusive Sacrifice Church aimed to kill precisely five people at a time, despite the fact that most of the murders did not have five victims.[39] In these cases, writers latched onto mainstream Christian norms, including atonement for one's sins and the iconography of a cross, and suggested they had been perverted into a "barbarous belief" that culminated in murder.[40] This perversion, it was reported, stemmed from the fact that most Black Louisianans in rural parts of the state were "incredibly superstitious."[41] Yet, even those who were considered "fairly well educated" were also terrified of the ax murders.[42] That the white press published these stereotypes at all says more about the way the public and the state sought to demonize and imagine a Black religious other that was "unrestrained," fanatical, and, ultimately, murderous.[43]

In the rice belt in early 1912, Black folks did not have time to ponder the falsehoods being spread about their panic-inducing predicament. While faraway news wires published attention-grabbing stories linking the recent murders to the Sacrifice Church via Voodoo, criminalizing Black religious expression in the process, local residents were trying to pick up the pieces of their broken communities. The deaths of the Warner and Broussard families in Crowley and Lake Charles, respectively, had happened so close to one another that it was impossible to ignore their similarities. Although a handful of people had been arrested after the Crowley crime—including Reverends Joseph Wilkins and King Harris, as well as Eliza Richards—the immediate discovery of an identical murder fifty-some miles to the west quashed any hope that one of the detainees was the guilty party.

This disconnect between what was actually happening in the rice belt and what far-flung presses were reporting was happening likely contributed to a growing distrust of outsider white journalists by the region's Black communities. Black religious diversity had been stereotyped and criminalized in the name of sellable stories. At the same time, local Black folks had already developed concern over the ineffectiveness of white lawmen in the area. Presumed Black religious deviance had narrowed authorities' foci without thwarting future attacks. Combined, these experiences forced Black residents to turn inward, requiring them to navigate the unknowable while facing additional threats steeped in Jim Crow ideologies and investigative blindness. Religion had become a way to explain—but not end—the madness.

Not surprisingly, after the Broussards were killed, yet another Black preacher was apprehended. Reverend Abraham Nelson was arrested in Jennings—like his counterpart, King Harris—and brought to Lake Charles.[44] Both men were also supposedly Sanctified preachers, though law enforcement officials had already conflated Sanctified churches and the Sacrifice Church in the aftermath of the Broussards' death. Reportedly, Reverend Nelson had recently taken to breaking into families' homes after midnight and, when discovered, quoting biblical passages. Damningly, he had also apparently done hard time in the penitentiary before becoming a man of the cloth. The authorities, operating from stereotypes of racialized criminality and violence, concluded he must be associated with the religiously motivated ax murders.

Pentecostal preachers like Harris and Nelson were of particular interest to lawmen, even though it seemed that their detention never got the detectives closer to solving the crimes. By mid-February 1912, there was an uncomfortable cycle in the rice belt: a Black family would be murdered, Black men (and a few women) would be arrested, another family would be killed, more folks would be rounded up, and all the while the violence would continue unabated. So far, butcheries in Rayne, Lafayette, Crowley, and Lake Charles had put communities on edge. The death of the Casaways in San Antonio in the spring of 1911 was a fuzzy memory—separated from its Louisiana parallels due to distance and distinctiveness.[45] Since that crime, however, the ax murders had been confined to Louisiana.

/ / /

Likely, then, when Hattie Dove and her children moved more than one hundred miles south from the small town of San Augustine, Texas, to the big city of Beaumont, concern related to the unsolved homicides in the neighboring state never crossed their minds.[46] Hattie's husband, John, had gotten a good job in Nacogdoches as a cotton packer, and the couple's eldest daughter, eighteen-year-old Jessie, had recently married a man named Andrew Quirk.[47] Unfortunately, the union between the two was not looked upon favorably by Jessie's parents. Her mother was "opposed to him," and her father claimed he was a "low down, no account negro."[48] Still, the family devised a plan: have John go to Nacogdoches to earn a living and have Hattie and the three children move to Beaumont to help support Andrew's aspirations of "going into business."[49] When the cotton packing season was over, John would presumably join the rest of his loved ones.

By February 1912, the Doves had only been living in Beaumont for roughly four months, and already things were bad. Jessie had written her father a distressing letter that arguably confirmed her parents' worries: Andrew had turned out to be a "worthless fellow" and had deserted the family.[50] Between his abandonment and a wave of sickness that had swept through the household, the situation was dire. As strangers in a new city, the Doves did not have a robust social network to support them in this time of need. One of the children had tried to ameliorate their condition by selling perfume and "toilet preparations" in their community.[51] This job was a marked contrast from what the youngest kids really wanted to do—go to school.

It seemed that even the presence of a boarder—John Smith—in the Dove household did not alleviate the family's problems.[52] He worked at a column factory and had been on night duty on February 18. A neighbor heard the front gate of the Doves' Cable Street home open and close around 9:30 p.m., but thought no more of the sound. Perhaps it had simply been John leaving for his shift.

The next morning, a different neighbor went to the Doves' house and knocked on the window. No one answered. He managed to open a pane and was greeted with a horrific sight. Hattie and her teenage son, Ernest, had been slaughtered in their sleep, their lifeless bodies bloodied from a single fatal blow to the head of each. According to one local paper, overturned furniture, scattered bed linens, and blood-soaked surfaces in an adjacent room told the story of a violent struggle. It seemed Jessie and her younger sister, Ethel, had awakened due to the horrible sounds and tried to fight the intruder. Despite their efforts, the girls were overtaken by the assailant, and their heads pummeled nearly to a pulp.[53] Another local report opined that all of the Doves had been slain in their sleep, the only difference between the manner of death being whether the blade or butt of the ax had been used—and where exactly on the head the victim had been struck. The crime had undoubtedly occurred many hours before it was discovered, as the bodies were stiff and the blood congealed.[54]

In the immediate aftermath of the Dove family murder, the white authorities followed their usual approach: the criminalization—and subsequent arrest—of a number of Black men. As had been the case in nearly every previous crime, Black men with personal, tangential, and inscrutable relationships to the victims were presumed criminal. First to be detained was John Smith, the renter, but his alibi proved sufficient. Then there was an unnamed man apprehended in the nearby sawmill community of Voth.[55] Next were Wade Guidry and Kenney Valley, both detained for their generic "mysterious actions."[56] Yet, by the time John Dove arrived in Beaumont a few days after the crime was discovered, it was clear that he had a specific suspect in mind: Andrew Quirk.[57] Andrew, it seemed, had been sighted on West Forsythe Street a few days before the murder and perhaps even the morning of, but his visit to Beaumont had not struck anyone as abnormal at that time.[58] Now that his wife, siblings-in-law, and mother-in-law had been slaughtered in cold blood, his recent appearance became suspicious.

As John Dove pledged to help officers capture his family's killer, he narrowed his sights on his son-in-law. He learned that Andrew had been seen in Orange, thirty miles to the east, on the same day the bodies were discovered, so he headed to the neighboring town to search.[59] Another rumor circulated that Andrew had continued east to Lake Charles. At least one regional paper claimed that John's disdain for Andrew wasn't just personal. The man was supposedly a "voodoo doctor" and bore a "hard reputation" among Black folks.[60] Clearly, John had reason to believe that the murder of his entire family had been the product of an unhealthy and desperate domestic situation.

Meanwhile, Beaumont investigators sought to follow up on another lead. A local paper reported that a Black boy had been sent on an errand to deliver a note to the Dove household the evening before the family was murdered.[61] Being unable to read, the messenger simply stated that he would be able to recognize the man who had retained his services, but did not know about the contents of the note. Once it had been received, however, he relayed an inscrutable response: "it would be all right."[62] Although it seems the message was never recovered by the authorities, that didn't stop local folks from speculating as to its substance. Perhaps it had been a note from Andrew Quirk. He could have asked to visit, either earnestly or under some ruse to gain entry into the home. The message, whether sent by Andrew or someone else, likely did not alert the family that their hours were numbered.

But even the local white press couldn't deny the obvious: the crime was so eerily similar to the serial slayings in Louisiana that there was "no doubt but that all the murders were committed by the same person."[63] Beaumont, it turned out, was located along the Southern Pacific Railroad. The Doves lived at 1428 Cable Street, between Catalpa and Gladys Avenues. Less than a mile due west were two rail lines: the Southern Pacific's Sunset Route and the Santa Fe Railroad.[64] It seemed that the Doves had unknowingly relocated along the precise path of an elusive assassin.

Yet, more than proximity to the railroad linked the Beaumont slaughter to its eastern counterparts. The telltale ax was found inside the Dove family's home.[65] The discovery of the murder weapon offered a curious puzzle: the ax had been stolen from the yard of a nearby house, and in its stead was placed a *different* ax with a "badly warped handle."[66] Although the owner of the first implement was easy to identify, the second one was unknown.

Understandably, the numerous similarities between the Doves' murder and those that had previously occurred in Louisiana enabled regional presses to reach the logical conclusion that religious fanaticism was behind the latest killing.[67] The editor of the *Lake Charles Daily Times* phoned his colleague at the *Beaumont Journal* to explain that the residents of the Calcasieu Parish city thought the Dove family had been murdered by the same person who had slaughtered the Broussards less than a month earlier.[68] If that were true, however, then Lake Charles locals believed that the killer had also slain the Warners in Crowley. It was reported that the chain continued backward with the Randalls and Andruses in Lafayette, the Byerses again in Crowley, and the Opelousases in Rayne.[69] Of course, the Casaways in San Antonio and the Hodges in Lake Charles should have also been included in this victim roster, but newspapers did not readily connect those crimes, in part because the Casaway murder had been the only Texas killing until this point and seemed to have a distinct motive, and in part because the Hodge slaughter was never linked to the ax madness, perhaps due to the interpersonal drama that seemed to explain its cause.

There was, however, one notable difference between this murder and all of the others: the Dove children were older than those found at every other crime scene. Censuses and newspapers rarely agreed on ages for folks in this era, but the ranges presented in this case versus the others suggest the victims included two different groups of children. Reportedly, the Dove children were all older than twelve. In the other crimes, the slain children were under ten. This indicates that, regardless of the imprecision of the numbers, prepubescent kids were killed in the earlier slayings while adolescents were found in this case.

Of course, this alteration to the age range of the victims could have been a subtle clue that the Doves had been murdered by a copycat killer. If so, hiding behind the ax madness would have allowed an individual to exact a personal grievance upon this specific family without being detected. The scene could have been staged to, at least superficially, resemble the other slayings dotting the landscape, throwing investigators into a frenzy as they searched for manufactured connections. However, it seems the authorities never delved into this possibility.

The terrifying prospect that a single person had massacred Black families from Lafayette all the way to San Antonio—leveraging the Southern Pacific Railroad to wreak havoc on unsuspecting communities—ushered in the first reports that offered a deceptively simple moniker that captured the region's murderous monster: the "axman."[70] Naming the boogeyman admitted two rather fatalistic realities. First was the fact that the authorities were stumped. In a matter of months, law enforcement agencies had gone from speculating about whether the Randall and Andrus family murders were related to *assum-*

ing that any Black family axed along the railroad had been killed by the same perpetrator. Following the thread of religious fanaticism had done nothing to stop the slaughters. That the killer hadn't been caught yet did not bode well for any town that fell victim to the madness. It was within this context that the second tragic admission appeared: if detectives couldn't figure out who killed the Doves, they now *expected* that the murders would continue.[71] In roughly one month, the authorities had finally reached the conclusion that local Black communities had already known: they—white lawmen—were powerless to stop the murders.

/ / /

By naming the axman, it seemed that the authorities were prepared to shift the nature of their investigation. Although the recent murders in Lake Charles and Crowley had solidified religious fanaticism as a viable motive for the crimes and led to the arrest of a number of Black preachers, investigators continued to work the cases that appeared in their jurisdiction, dumbfounded when yet another massacre would occur in a nearby city or town. Following the deaths of the Dove family, however, reports that interstate collaboration was taking place suggested a conceptual adjustment in how the murders were being pursued.

Officials from Lafayette, Crowley, and Lake Charles planned to visit their counterparts in Beaumont to learn more about the recent killing.[72] Representatives from the various sheriffs' and police departments convened to plan a "systematic course of investigation" that would allow the different agencies to work together effectively to apprehend the elusive axman.[73] Mere days after information about this interstate conference was published, however, at least one regional newspaper attempted to backpedal on the claims, insisting that there had been no joint meeting to compare notes or develop a "combined effort" to capture the axman.[74] Thus, it seems that individual jurisdictions understood collaboration was essential to solving these crimes, but the extent to which they acted on this belief is difficult to determine.

Law enforcement officials were not the only individuals concerned with ferreting out the axman's identity. Black folks in Beaumont and beyond took matters into their own hands. As "thousands upon thousands" of people filed past the Doves' bodies at Broussard and Little's undertaking establishment, they prayed to God to be spared the axman's wrath, certain that "a curse had fallen upon the race."[75] Yet, Black residents of the city did more than just offer up supplications: they organized a collection for a burial fund and established a subscription to raise $500 for the "arrest and conviction" of the family's killer.[76] Again, a local Black community deeply impacted by this unfathomable chaos rallied together to support their own. That the Doves were newer transplants to Beaumont did not lessen the impact of—nor the response to—their violent death.

Likely, the facts that the Doves did not have strong ties to the area and that the motive of religious fanaticism permeated public consciousness meant that people shifted their speculations from *why* the Doves were killed to *how* they were murdered. Not surprisingly, then, theirs appears to be the first crime in which newspapers covered a piece of regional knowledge that had surfaced: the Doves had been chloroformed.[77] While investigators had questioned whether the Casaways had been poisoned in the spring of 1911, chloroform was never specifically mentioned by the press, and the theory of the family having been "doped" does not seem to have been adopted by Black San Antonians.[78] In the aftermath of the Dove murders, however, Black folks throughout the region—including those in cities heretofore spared from the axman's wrath—concluded that the most logical explanation for how the slaughter was accomplished had to be chloroform-included stupefaction.

After ascertaining that the victims had most likely been drugged, Black residents of southwestern Louisiana and southeastern Texas developed methods they believed would protect themselves from a similar fate. One popular technique involved placing multiple vessels of water in a room to "destroy the effects of chloroform."[79] Perhaps news reports did not exaggerate when claiming that glasses, buckets, tubs, and containers could be found all over homes in Black communities, placed strategically under windowsills and near entryways.[80] A riff on this approach required "wet towels and cloths" to be wrapped around door knobs, shoved in keyholes, and jammed into windows.[81] Whether rags or basins, it seems clear that Black folks devised and executed plans to keep chloroform out of their homes.

For months, these strategies proliferated in the rice belt, fueled by the belief that the only way the killer could dispatch an entire family without alerting other occupants of the house or nearby neighbors was to have mitigated any chance of resistance from within. Yet, the likelihood that the assailant used chloroform specifically—or that water would effectively neutralize its impact—is incredibly low. Still, the fact that this information persisted is an indication that the community was taking their protection into their own hands. By invoking this self-defense approach, Black communities privileged their own local knowledge while implying that the white establishment could not be trusted to keep them safe. To Black folks, the fact that the authorities had not publicized speculations about stupefaction did not mean such poisoning had not occurred, but simply that lawmen did not care enough to share their theories with impacted communities.

There was one problem with the drugging hypothesis, however. The image of a rogue assailant holding a chloroform-soaked cloth to a victim's nose and mouth for a brief moment, thereby bringing about rapid insensibility, was incredibly popular by the early 1900s. It was also wrong. To cause unconsciousness, a high concentration of the narcotic must be administered for a relatively long period of time—likely at least five minutes.[82] Although chemists and physicians had been well aware of this reality since the compound's discovery in the 1830s, that did not stop the press or the rumor mill from crafting a frightening narrative of sudden unconsciousness.

/ / /

Roughly a week after the Dove family had been discovered slaughtered in their Beaumont home—days after the axman moniker had been coined and unsubstantiated fears of chloroform permeated the region—Acadia Parish Sheriff Louis Fontenot received a tantalizing letter that offered to shine light on the ax murders. The author, purportedly an unnamed Black man from nearby St. Martinville, said he knew all about the murder at Rayne and "who the guilty persons are."[83] The letter writer's admission of knowledge about one of the crimes likely represented the first publicized moment, excluding Clementine's confession, when a member of the region's Black community willfully and individually inserted himself into the authorities' investigation. Until this point, white lawmen had repeatedly bemoaned the fact that Black folks in the rice belt were tight-lipped about their knowledge regarding the murders. Now, however, it seemed that someone was ready to talk.

The author argued that the Rayne crime was committed by a "clique of religious fanatics," and he was willing to speak now because he feared for his life.[84] For someone who supposedly knew all about one of the crimes, the writer then backtracked to make sure the authorities knew he was not involved in the faith community but came to know about the murders "through confidences placed in him by one of the accomplices."[85] He positioned himself as knowledgeable enough to be useful, but not enough to be suspicious.

Who this man was and why he decided to come forward with this information at this specific point in the axman saga is impossible to determine. Since he had written the letter, he was presumed literate, likely legitimating his claims to the authorities. But he also said he was from St. Martinville. This tiny town—the seat of St. Martin Parish—was approximately fifteen miles from the closest crime scene in Lafayette and roughly double that distance from Rayne, making it feasible the informant did have useful information. And Clementine Barnabet, too, would claim that she was from St. Martinville.[86]

On February 26, 1912, Sheriff Fontenot headed to meet with the letter writer. Though news of Sheriff Fontenot's case-breaking trip to St. Martinville was publicized broadly, its outcome was kept under wraps. Whatever he learned—if he learned anything at all—wasn't published. Thus, the St. Martinville letter must be viewed with healthy skepticism; perhaps the author simply wanted to become a part of this newsworthy story. If this was the case, then the appearance of this letter could represent the beginnings of community fragmentation within the axman madness. Until this point, Black folks in the region had generally presented a unified front, collectively condemning the crimes, calling for lawfulness, and refusing to provide fodder for white authorities' criminalization of their faith practices. Now, however, diversity of Black thought regarding the crimes had entered public consciousness. It would only be a matter of time before diversity of Black *responses* to the axman shifted local dynamics from cohesive to contentious.

/ / /

The murder of the Dove family in Beaumont, Texas, represented the third ax murder in the rice belt in roughly a month, coming on the heels of the Warner slaughter in Crowley and the Broussard crime in Lake Charles in late January 1912. While the death of the Broussards thrust the motive of religious fanaticism to the fore, the massacre of the Doves introduced a seemingly contradictory assailant via the elusive axman. As local communities coped with this fatalistic madness, misinformation about the killings circulated in the public consciousness nationwide. Damning articles sensationalizing the murders as human sacrifices linked to Voodoo demonized an already ostracized religion, and erroneous claims that the Sacrifice Church was a Sanctified church further criminalized Black preachers.

In the rice belt, Black communities tried to make sense of *how*—as opposed to *why*—families were killed. This approach led not only to the adoption of the axman moniker, but to the belief that chloroform had been used to stupefy victims before they were murdered. That this latter conclusion was false does not negate the fact that the Black communities impacted by these murders were coming together for protection and solace when they couldn't get either from white authorities. Still, the publication of a tipster's letter by the local white press suggested that Black thought regarding these crimes was neither uniform nor monolithic. As much as Black folks knew they had to defend themselves against the axman, they did not necessarily agree on what that process should entail. After all, rice belt communities had been on edge for months and every clue so far had turned out to be a dead end. Would the murders ever stop?

5

Self-Defense Strategies

The Axman Strikes Again

By the end of February 1912, it was obvious that something was very wrong in southwestern Louisiana and southeastern Texas. Dozens of Black folks had been murdered with an ax, arresting suspects did nothing to stop the violence, and the authorities were convinced that religious fanatics were to blame. On the ground, Black residents of affected towns developed self-defense strategies to counter the unknowable threat. These techniques ranged from making formal appeals to law enforcement officials and organizing local neighborhood patrols to purchasing guns and fleeing from the rice belt. Examining how these approaches functioned—and the varied consequences they produced—provides a more concrete glimpse into the day-to-day experiences of living under sustained terror. It also highlights an important shift that occurred in this murderous saga from winter to spring 1912: the axman came to exist as both a legitimate threat and a figment of folks' collective imagination.

The self-defense approaches developed by Black communities during the first few months of 1912 were not limited to folks residing in cities and towns that had been visited by the axman; those in areas heretofore not struck by the violent killer responded to the unknowable. While it would be easy to label these panics as unjustifiable and excessive, they offer strong evidence of just how terrifying it was to live through the madness and how much people spread information they considered vital to protecting themselves and other Black communities.

Try as they might to defend themselves from the axman, the discovery of the Monroe family's bloodied bodies in Glidden, Texas, at the end of March 1912 confirmed to Black communities that the rampage was far from over. Examining how this latest crime fit into the broader context of the region's serial murders reveals how local Black folks' belief in the axman contradicted white authorities' theory of a named suspect. While Glidden's lawmen attempted to prosecute Jim Fields for the death of the Monroes, the Black community *knew* who had killed the family: the axman. Not only had the crimes become inevitable, but they had also become unsolvable.

/ / /

In the immediate aftermath of the Warner and Broussard family murders, Black residents of the rice belt made large-scale, formal attempts to quell the madness. In Crowley, Reverend Henry Clay Ross—the same leader who had organized resolutions following the death of the Byerses in February 1911—again stood before members of the Black community at Morning Star Baptist Church a year later to call for "bringing to justice" the perpetrator of the city's most recent crime.[1] Agreeing to work alongside law enforcement to apprehend the assailant, attendees planned to draft additional resolutions related to this latest offense. In nearby Lafayette, roughly 150 Black citizens gathered at Good Hope Baptist Church and passed declarations of their own.[2] One of their resolutions captured the sentiment of others published throughout the region: "Be it further resolved, that we pledge ourselves to furnish to the authorities and officers any information we may have that would lend to the ferreting out of these crimes and we further pledge ourselves to be used in any capacity by the authorities of our city in helping them to bring about the desired results in reference to the crimes committed in Lafayette, Rayne, Crowley and Lake Charles."[3] Although Black folks in impacted cities and towns focused on the immediate dangers in their neighborhoods, they also connected their plight to that of their kinfolk throughout the region. Additional mass meetings in Beaumont and Lake Charles sought not only to assist law enforcement personnel, but to raise funds to catch the assailant.[4] These public displays of solidarity served a dual function: they allowed some Black citizens to distance themselves from the murderer and they presented a seemingly unified front to the white establishment. Both outcomes had implicit undercurrents. First, they created an us-versus-them optic that demonized those who may have been unwilling to help the authorities. Second, they flattened diversity of thought within local Black communities by having a representative few stand in for the masses. Last, they suggested that formal institutions—like the police and sheriffs' departments—were potentially capable of catching the axman. Given the tenuous relationship between Black folks and law enforcement harkening all the way back to slavery, these visible declarations of support for and trust in the officers were politically strategic pleas.[5] It was not necessarily that Black communities had suddenly come to believe in white authorities, but that they recognized the importance of appearing to do so. Self-defense could only be made scrutable if those in charge firmly thought there was a threat worth defending oneself against. Thus, appealing to lawmen helped legitimate Black communities' own protection mechanisms.

While Black residents of the rice belt sometimes leveraged formal government apparatuses to address the axman madness, the most common forms of self-defense they employed came from within their communities. Although they expressed solidarity with law enforcement to ferret out the killer, they also confirmed their doubts in those same authorities via the acquisition of weapons. They needed to be "prepared for trouble."[6] In Crowley, Alexandria, Lake Charles, and elsewhere, news of Black gun ownership following the Dove family murder coincided with reports regarding heightened panic in the area.[7] Across the state line, Black folks in Beaumont, Galveston, and beyond also armed themselves, readying their homes for a visit from the axman.[8] By early 1912, then, there was evidence that communities that had never been directly impacted by the ax murders were responding tangibly to the unknowable nature of the crimes. Alexandria, Louisiana, and Galveston, Texas, were both more than seventy miles from the closest slaughters, yet the uncertainty about the killer's motives or identity meant their residents did not feel immune.

That Black folks throughout southwestern Louisiana and southeastern Texas armed themselves en masse during the winter and spring of 1912 was not met without concern. By the end of January, one paper opined that "the black man with a shotgun or a pistol, in a community where the whites are in a minority, is a menace."[9] A month later, however, it was reported that white residents of the rice belt had agreed to "let them arm themselves now," and, as result, nearly every Black man supposedly had a shotgun or revolver close at hand.[10] In reality, white sentiment regarding the widespread acquisition of guns by Black residents was likely more nuanced than these out-of-town papers claimed. A regional outlet perhaps captured the tension by expressing concern that "the reckless use of firearms" by those who feared the axman was getting out of control.[11] Indeed, distress about expansive Black gun ownership was less about the literal possession of the weapons and more about the ease with which individuals were willing to fire them.

To be fair, the crimes that occurred in early 1912 did spark the first identifiable cases of axman victims by proxy. The day after the Dove family was discovered murdered, an informal watch group in Beaumont attempted to organize their shifts. Horace Alexander, a twenty-one-year-old sawmill laborer, reportedly visited the home of Adam Bobinaux that afternoon and offered to take a turn guarding the house that night.[12] Adam agreed, and his brother Ben (who also lived in the house) joined Horace in protecting the residence from the axman. The duo "sat up until midnight" before switching shifts.[13] Ben and Horace retired to bed inside the three-room cottage and Adam became the lone sentry. There he was, a solitary man defending his own home, knowing that a local family had been discovered brutally murdered in *their* own home just a couple days prior. Around 2:00 a.m., when Adam saw someone approach the rear door of his house, he earnestly thought the axman was trying to gain entry and wasted no time in opening fire with his double-barreled shotgun. The prowler was shot in the lungs, killing him instantly. The intruder, however, was Horace Alexander. Both tragic and ironic, the young man's death at the hands of a known party while trying to protect folks from an unknown one drives home just how terrified Black residents of the rice belt had become by February 1912.

Just over a week after this fatal shooting in Beaumont, Black folks in Lake Charles experienced another axman victim by proxy. This time, however, the death was not caused by a member of the local community, but by the police. A Black man named A. E. Johnson appeared in Black neighborhoods in the city eight weeks after the Broussards had been murdered, claiming he could protect folks from the axman using charms and wires.[14] Instead, his unfamiliarity and drunken state caused locals to contact the authorities, who arrived on scene and attempted to apprehend the self-professed protector. In a matter of minutes, the situation escalated and A. E.'s refusal to go to jail led to his death. Following the coroner's inquest, the offending officer was absolved from blame in the altercation. It was declared self-defense.[15]

In the aftermath of this shooting, the police rummaged through A. E.'s belongings and reportedly found letters elucidating clues regarding the axman murders, though the specific contents were never published and presumably amounted to nothing. What was printed were the contents of his suitcase: "minor electrical appurtenances," two insurance policies made out to his mother, and some clothes.[16] In his pocket was found $18.44 (roughly $600 in 2025).[17] These findings enabled the authorities to reach a fascinating conclusion: A. E. Johnson was either a Voodoo or hoodoo doctor.

Labeling an otherwise unremarkable Black man as a practitioner of Voodoo or hoodoo at this particular moment in the ax murder saga is instructive because it not only shows how white authorities and local presses conflated these two distinct practices, it also emphasizes how the axman myth was made.[18] As such, it doesn't matter if there was any truth to these claims. If A. E. wasn't involved in Voodoo, the association between this faith community and these ax murders had gained so much strength that disentangling the two was a hopeless task. Voodoo became the mechanism by which many Black and white people came to process the crimes, forcing causal arguments onto things that weren't correlated. Meanwhile, if A. E. was a Voodoo practitioner, then his intentions to protect Black Lake Charles residents from the ax murders were irrelevant. Public opinion had decided that Voodoo was dangerous. Public opinion had also decided that strangers were dangerous. When an out-of-town Black man said he could protect local folks from the axman, he was immediately met with suspicion.

/ / /

Although the case of A. E. Johnson shows how religion was regularly demonized in the context of the axman murders, it was also deployed by local communities in the name of self-defense. Faith functioned in complicated ways at the height of these crimes: as the supposed fanatical motive, as Clementine Barnabet's claimed rationale, as a method of community coherence, and as an individual person's safeguard against the unknowable. It is not a coincidence, for example, that most mass meetings in Black neighborhoods were held in local churches. Religious leaders shepherded their frightened flocks through the chaos caused by the axman. At the exact same time, men of the cloth—including Reverends King Harris, Joseph Wilkins, M. J. Snipe, and Abraham Nelson—had been arrested for their potential involvement in the crimes. In this process, certain faith communities were lambasted, the Sacrifice Church was construed as the murderous party, and Voodoo became a social ill to those ignorant of the rice belt's religious culture.

One of the most common displays of faith that newspapers mentioned was prayer. For example, a report from Vermont commented that Black churches throughout the rice belt were "thronged with weeping and praying" congregants.[19] That such a faraway news outlet captured the status of Black faith communities in the aftermath of yet another ax murder is telling. As much as religion was supposedly at the root of the madness, it was also a visible sign of communal response. Closer to the scene of the crimes, references to prayer meetings in early 1912 emphasized how local people grieved collectively.[20] While mainstream Christian churches no doubt served many Black residents of the rice belt during this trying time, there were also those who questioned if "the Lord had deserted them" as the murders continued unabated.[21] Perhaps some felt that there were limits to what mainstream religion could do and therefore turned to additional measures to protect themselves and their loved ones.

While far-flung reports likely conflated the syncretic practices Black folks in the rice belt employed to stave off the axman, there was no denying that people were willing to try *anything* to get the madness to end. Were Voodoo practitioners actually selling "hundreds of charms" to panicked residents?[22] Maybe, but confirming such would be difficult. The idea that laypeople were prepared to believe in the power of amulets over the police, however, was reasonable. After all, it was argued that local authorities were "powerless to prevent" another murder.[23] If this was true—and it certainly seemed to be—then leveraging a plethora of tools in the name of self-defense was a logical decision. That Black residents of the Lake Charles neighborhood where the Broussards were murdered had taken to purchasing "rabbit feet" was a rational response to the unknowable nature of the crimes.[24] So, while religion certainly seemed to be a viable motive for the axman slaughters, it also offered an avenue for salvation and a means of collective community support.

/ / /

Before anyone had been killed with an ax in 1912, Black communities in the rice belt were already taking "extraordinary precautions" to ward off the axman.[25] In the aftermath of the Warner family murder, however, it was reported that every hardware store in Crowley had "sold its entire stock of door bolts and window fasteners," primarily to Black folks who were readying their homes against unwanted invaders.[26] When the Broussards were killed in Lake Charles, people barred doors and bolted windows out of precaution, going so far as to literally nail down the openings.[27] Following the slaughter of the Dove family, Beaumont residents immediately boarded up all potential entrances to their houses, building barricades to keep the axman out.[28] Even in Baton Rouge, where the axman had yet to strike, Black citizens "shut tight" their abodes and appealed to the authorities for help.[29] It was likely not an exaggeration to claim that houses in Black neighborhoods became "veritable arsensal[s]" almost overnight in response to the region's latest killing.[30] Between the mass acquisition of weapons and the fortification of their dwellings, it seemed that Black communities in the rice belt were effectively preparing for war with an unknowable enemy.

In order to fight this war, however, soldiers needed to be deployed. By early 1912—and likely even earlier than that—Black folks established watch groups and patrols, often sleeping in "relay fashion" so that a given home was never without surveillance.[31] This meant that people's regular sleep patterns were disturbed, presumably leading to fatigue, grogginess, irritability, and more.[32] The situation was so dire that even a local paper noted that "few adults among them sleep," referring to the continual panic felt—but also the attempt at collective community support—in Black neighborhoods.[33]

Families would cram into a single home to maximize the number of men available to rotate on the patrol.[34] Then, throughout the night, the residents would keep a light burning and try to sleep, though it seems many were unsuccessful at truly managing to rest.[35] Their communities were under siege, and no one seemed to know why or when the axman would strike again. Until the threat could be confirmed to be something else, it had to be treated as the actual assailant.

Not surprisingly, then, the white press reported on would-be axman incidents that turned out to be false alarms. While standing guard, Black men shot at inanimate objects, wayward animals, and even one another—sometimes fatally so.[36] This pattern of flawed actions highlights the depth of community care circulating in the rice belt at this time, more than it serves as evidence of how fear of the unknowable led to rash judgments and erroneous conclusions. Black men and women were so dedicated to protecting their loved ones and their broader communities that they often evinced a utilitarian approach to self-defense: target a single threat to save the masses. Being mistaken about the severity of said threat was far less deadly than assuming it *couldn't* be the axman.

/ / /

The vast majority of self-defense techniques Black communities employed at the height of the axman madness represented a fight response: pass resolutions, acquire weapons, establish guards, and pray for salvation. By early 1912, however, there were murmurs of another approach some folks had embraced: flight from the region. At the end of January, a number of far-flung newspapers claimed "thrifty and prosperous negros are preparing to emigrate" in response to the unceasing ax murders.[37] Just over a month later, reports expanded the list of folks who were leaving the region to include devoted "old family servants" with "scant belongings."[38] Concern about a Black exodus was likely exaggerated, as many people did not have the resources to move, thanks to the legacies of slavery, sharecropping, and Jim Crow. Yet, the prospect that people might leave—and that awareness of this possibility was real enough to be discussed in white print media—is incredibly instructive. It shows the lengths some people were willing to go to put literal distance between themselves and the danger. It also highlights fears about migration to other communities and the impact such flight could have on the region's economy.

To be clear, had Black communities left the rice belt en masse to flee the ax murders, they would have been joining a robust migration history from Louisiana, Texas, Mississippi, and Tennessee that started in the late 1870s. After Reconstruction, "rooted in faith and in fear," thousands of Black folks moved to Kansas, spurred by alarming political machinations that threatened people's livelihoods and sense of safety.[39] That a singular event—the state's constitutional convention—compelled Black Louisianians to move provides a parallel to the hyperlocal factors that affected regional migration in the early 1910s. However, what made flight distinctive in the axman case was that the fear came from within Black communities rather than from without.

Still, any sizeable departure of laborers would have had a noticeable effect on the profitability of the season's rice crop.[40] Black men and women comprised the backbone of the Louisiana rice industry, employed by mills that relied on the Southern Pacific Railroad to ship their goods to markets throughout the United States. Thus, when Black residents decided to leave the area, their absence was noticeable. Arguably, a couple of years before World War I propelled the first large-scale wave of the Great Migration, the axman murders offered temporally and geographically specific push factors that compelled some people to leave.[41] It was the literal movement of laborers from the rice belt region that shifted the national conversation about the murders from their religious overtones to their economic consequences.

The fear that Black out-migration would cripple the rice industry—and snowball to other staple grain industries—led to the first known article about the axman crimes written in the *New York Times*.[42] Although the *Times* did not represent the pinnacle of print journalism in terms of circulation, the paper's insistence on avoiding sensationalism and promoting facts over fiction meant its coverage of the murders—whether as a reprint or original piece—offered some heft to the otherwise seemingly outlandish claims reported elsewhere.

While the axman piece was necessarily hyperbolic in some respects, it likely wasn't too far off in stating that, between recent excessive rain and the flight of Black laborers from the region, Louisiana's 1912 rice crop would be worth half of its 1911 value. Another paper offered that the effects of this depleted crop would require the United States to "import 310,000,000 pounds more of rice than usual," further leading to an international imbalance with disastrous consequences.[43] Likely, both of these articles—and others about the economic impact of the murders—exaggerated the certainty with which they discussed Black migration.[44] Nonetheless, they inadvertently confirmed just how essential Black labor was to the rice belt region. In so doing, they ultimately raised the stakes of the killings, placing the violence into national consciousness in a way that caught the attention of wealthy white Americans: the bottom line was now under attack. If there was any possibility that the murders could have a negative impact on white society, either through changes in quality of life or through upending the established social order, then perhaps a larger national awareness of the crimes would take *seriously* the religious fanaticism ostensibly sweeping through southwestern Louisiana and southeastern Texas. Fear of economic collapse—no matter its actual likelihood—revealed that these murders were affecting everyone, whether they knew it or not.

The beginning of 1912 ushered in a wave of self-defense strategies that Black folks used to combat the unknowable threat of the axman. Because it was impossible to know which dangers were legitimate, this period also represented the beginning of efforts to prey upon the heightened sense of terror permeating the area. Hoaxes and pranks emerged, typically in the form of cryptic letters written to terrify an otherwise unsuspecting family.[45] Although there is no evidence the axman wrote warning missives to victims, that didn't stop local Black communities from panicking when news of such notes appeared. That they can now be seen as hoaxes and pranks should not undermine how seriously they were taken by those who lived through the madness. Indeed, Black communities' efforts to engage in self-defense strategies throughout the first three months of 1912 were well warranted, despite the proliferation of threatening letters. After all, the axman had killed the Warners in Crowley, the Broussards in Lake Charles, and the Doves in Beaumont. Before the end of March, another family would join the victim roster alongside nine others.

/ / /

In the midst of the axman madness, life continued, however hesitantly. On March 6, 1912, Jim Fields and Ida Booker married in Columbus, Texas, just under two hundred miles west of Beaumont.[46] Ida was a young woman, roughly twenty years old, and the eldest child of seven.[47] Working beside her family members, she was listed as a "farm laborer" in the 1910 census, likely engaging in backbreaking manual tasks like plowing, seeding, aerating, and harvesting. Her husband was perhaps the same Jim Fields listed in the 1880 census in a single-mother household, the second youngest of four children.[48] By the time the duo wed, he would have been significantly older than his bride, dwarfing her age by at least a decade. Whether the match between Jim and Ida was rooted in love or practicality—or both—is impossible to determine, but what is known is that their early life together was tumultuous to say the least.

After the two married, Jim set out to earn a living, securing a job in Buckholts, a town about a hundred miles north of Columbus. He left his new bride at her parents' house and planned to return to get her once his employment was settled. Jim arrived to retrieve his wife and they headed to neighboring Glidden. Functioning as a giant railroad pit stop for the Galveston, Harrisburg, & San Antonio Railway—a company that maintained intertwined interests with the Southern Pacific Railroad starting in the late nineteenth century—Glidden's entire economy revolved around those noisy locomotives chugging into town. It was precisely the power of the rails that the Fieldses were counting on that late March night. The plan was to catch the train to nearby Flatonia, where they'd then be able to head to Buckholts.

The Fieldses did not have to navigate Glidden alone in the dark: Jim's brother Charlie lived in the area.[49] Along with Charlie's wife, the group started for the rail depot early in the morning—perhaps as early as midnight—via a wagon. Upon learning that the night train would not stop in Glidden, however, they presumably left the station and headed back toward Charlie's house.[50] The Fieldses never made it back to the train station. Instead, Colorado County Sheriff Ethelbert B. Mayes and his bloodhounds greeted them.[51] The dogs had picked up a scent that started at the Monroe residence and ended at the newlyweds' location a mile or two away.

Apparently, around 7:00 a.m. on March 27, 1912, Parthenia Monroe, the eldest child of Ellen and John Monroe, headed over to her mother's house to check on her family.[52] It seemed that John had separated from his wife a number of years earlier and moved to Yoakum some fifty miles away, while Parthenia moved in with her elderly grandmother, who had been widowed. Ellen, meanwhile, had taken in a boarder named Lyle Finucane, who had lodged with the Monroes for years. So, when Parthenia went to the Monroe residence that Wednesday morning, she likely expected to be greeted by her mother, her four youngest siblings, and their renter. Instead, she found a bloodbath. Everyone was dead.

When Sheriff Mayes and his officers arrived on the scene, they tried to figure out what had happened. Although regional reports differed as to whether the assailant entered through a window or a rear door, they agreed that the adults were attacked first.[53] In the room where Lyle and Ellen had been sleeping, the killer raised the fatal weapon—the family's own woodpile ax—and slammed it into the man's head, pulverizing his face so that the only recognizable feature was his lower right jaw with part of his moustache still attached. Slivers of his skull and parts of his brain splattered about the room, covering the walls and floor. In the commotion, Lyle either fell to the floor or was dragged off the bed. Next, Ellen was struck with the ax over her right ear. Although that blow was undoubtedly excruciating, it was not immediately fatal. The woman got out of bed and headed for the door, perhaps trying to save her children or herself. Instead, a "stream of blood" evinced her short-lived steps, as her mangled body was found on the floor about a yard away from where she had first been assaulted.[54]

The murderer then went across the hall to another bedroom, where the four young Monroes were sleeping. The three littlest—thirteen-year-old Dewey Lee, twelve-year-old Jessie, and eight-year-old Alberta—were slaughtered in a single bed, the ax being used to crush their temples. Stepping to the cot where sixteen-year-old Willie lay peacefully asleep, the intruder pummeled the teenager's face, extinguishing the last sign of life in the small house.[55] None of the children awakened in the madness. The killer reportedly "wiped or washed" the bloody ax, leaving it beside Willie's bed to be discovered in the morning.[56] The assailant washed their hands in a tin basin at the back of the house and then presumably left the scene.[57]

When the authorities reached the Monroe residence, the bodies were still warm.[58] Coupled with the facts that Lyle had been working at the railroad roundhouse until midnight and Willie had been sighted at a wedding also around that hour, officials concluded the occupants must have been killed between 12:00 a.m. and 7:00 a.m. While investigators quickly established this generous timeline, they had a harder time ascertaining a potential motive.

Reportedly, Lyle and Ellen were closer than landlord and tenant. Newspapers opined that they were "leading an immoral life," both technically being married to other people, but having been separated from their respective spouses for years.[59] Lyle was described as "an octoroon of considerable intelligence," while Ellen became a "black negress."[60] Still, the local press conceded they were "harmless and inoffensive," implying that the nature of their relationship should not have precipitated their demise.[61] So, if the Monroes weren't killed because of some perceived transgression, why were they lying in cold blood?

/ / /

According to news outlets nationwide, the Glidden ax murder represented the inevitable: the continuation of the "reign of terror" promulgated by religious fanaticism in the rice belt.[62] Even regional presses acknowledged the similarities between this crime and those that had occurred earlier in the year.[63] The Doves had been murdered in Beaumont the month before, while the Broussards and Warners had been slaughtered in Lake Charles and Crowley, respectively, in January. Now, at the end of March, it appeared that a fourth family had been added to the axman's ever-growing roster in 1912 alone. Added to the victim list stretching all the way back to November 1909, it seemed that forty-two lives had been claimed in this panic-inducing rampage.

The day after the Monroes were found dead in their home, the arrival of detectives from Beaumont was likely not a surprise to Sheriff Mayes and his officers. Jefferson County Sheriff Jake Giles wanted to make a "special study" of the latest killing, aware that what had just happened in Colorado County closely resembled the still-unsolved homicide in his jurisdiction.[64] That another sheriff's department was interested in the Glidden crime conceptually fueled the shift toward interagency collaboration, but that did not stop local officers from trying to determine who wanted the Monroes—and just the Monroes—dead. In fact, the Beaumont officials quickly came to a perplexing conclusion: the most recent crime had "no connection" to its eastern counterparts.[65] As had been the case so many times in the past, the authorities simply did not have the skill set to investigate the slaughter as anything other than an individual murder, even though ample evidence implied it was one in an expansive series.[66]

There may have been some merit to the Texas investigators' approach, however. Unlike at every other crime scene attributed to the axman, it seemed that "articles of value" were missing from the Monroe residence, offering robbery as a potential motive.[67] Contradictorily, however, at least one regional report also claimed that Ellen's body was discovered with "laces and tawdry jewelry," perhaps odd items to leave if the killer had raided the home for valuables.[68] Thus, it is unclear whether the Monroe home was actually burglarized, or if this theory had emerged as an effort to explain the seemingly unexplainable.

In the aftermath of the crime, what was incontrovertible was the fact that Sheriff Mayes's bloodhounds picked up a scent that led to the house where Jim and Ida Fields had spent the night. There, the newlyweds, Charlie Fields and his wife, a man known as "Uncle Fink" Washington, and an unnamed boy were located.[69] Although everyone in the house was arrested and placed in jail, it seems the authorities were particularly interested in Jim and Ida. Apparently, tread impressions resembling those of a man and a woman were found in the yard of the Monroe residence. When Sheriff Mayes placed shoes belonging to the couple into the tracks, "they corresponded exactly."[70]

Mere days after Jim and Ida Fields were arrested, Ida had something to tell the authorities. If it was true, it was one hell of a story. She said that on the night Charlie had taken the couple to the train depot, they hadn't gone straight back to her brother-in-law's home. Instead, she asked Jim about a residence they were passing. He identified it as "the house where Lyle Finucane and Ellen Monroe live."[71] Ida said Jim then asked his brother to stop the wagon so he and his new bride could get out. Upon exiting the vehicle, Jim reportedly asked Ida if she would stand by him no matter what, and she replied that she would, as long as it was "right."[72] Ida stated that Jim disappeared for about twenty minutes behind the house, she heard something that "sounded like licks," and then he reemerged asking the same question of her fidelity and loyalty.[73] Likely the couple then retraced their steps back to Charlie's, ostensibly to wait for the next train. Instead, the police intercepted them before they could leave.

Given the similarities between the Monroe family murder and those attributed to the axman, Ida Fields's revelation should be viewed with a healthy dose of skepticism. It seemed conveniently incriminating against a single person: her new husband. While she placed herself in literal proximity to the crime, she had basically argued that Jim targeted the Monroes on a whim while returning from the train station—a return trip that only happened because the night train hadn't stopped in Glidden.

For all of Ida's description of that fateful night, it seems that one crucial bit of information was missing from her story. At no point in her statement did she claim Jim killed the Monroes—she merely placed him at the scene at the time in which *someone* slaughtered the family. But locating Jim at the scene was enough for the authorities—after all, the axman had come to Glidden. Blaming Jim Fields was undeniably convenient, even if it didn't seem terribly consistent.

Ida's testimony led to her release on bail while Jim remained in custody in nearby Columbus. Likely the other four individuals arrested the morning after the crime were released for lack of evidence. Meanwhile, the justice of the peace who conducted an inquest into the murders became convinced of Jim's guilt.[74] Justice Aubrey A. Gregory filed his report stating that the deceased came to their deaths "from the effect of many wounds, beats[,] and bruises inflicted upon their heads with an axe, at the hands of Jim Fields."[75]

For the next six months Jim was ensnared in a legal battle to prove his innocence.[76] A special May term of the grand jury was summoned to try him for the murder of Lyle Finucane. Even the instructions written to the jurymen admitted that "the State relies wholly upon circumstantial evidence."[77] In May, Jim was indicted on six counts of murder, his trial beginning at the end of the month.[78] Despite being in the Jim Crow South, the jury, after a brief deliberation, returned a verdict of "not guilty" in June.[79] One Texas paper explained the outcome by noting that "the jury did not have sufficient evidence upon which to convict Fields."[80] In the courtroom, Black spectators cheered at the trial's outcome.[81] While folks were absolutely terrified of the axman, it seems they did not think Jim Fields was the region's killer. The remaining charges against him were dismissed on September 23, 1912, and he was released. Six months of Jim's life had been spent trying to undo the damage of that singular night.

Upon his release, he didn't try to rekindle his relationship with Ida. In 1915, she filed for divorce, citing abandonment as the reason.[82] According to Ida, she'd been deserted since March 27, 1912: the day the Monroe family had been discovered slaughtered in their beds. It was the same day Jim Fields, her new husband, was arrested on suspicion of murder. It seems the axman destroyed families and communities in more ways than one.

/ / /

During the first three months of 1912, Black communities in the rice belt responded to the axman madness in concrete ways that were intertwined with day-to-day life. In fact, there was a regionwide shift in how people navigated their world, ranging from formal declarations of support for law enforcement officials to being so anxious about the crimes that they were unable to sleep. These responses allowed folks to craft a variety of survival strategies that suited their specific needs. Many people armed themselves with guns and reinforced their homes, determined to fight off any would-be intruder. Still others reacted in community, holding prayer meetings and establishing watch groups to patrol their neighborhoods. A smaller number fled the region, sparking nationwide panic that a depletion of Black labor from the local rice paddies would snowball with dire economic consequences.

Because the self-defense tactics Black residents employed were rooted in fear of the unknowable, they sometimes resulted in unforeseen outcomes. Unfamiliar individuals—including people like A. E. Johnson—became highly suspicious, and locals sought assistance to expel strangers from their communities. Even known acquaintances like Horace Alexander found themselves on the wrong end of a weapon when jittery sentinels had to make split-second decisions to protect their loved ones. That some of these encounters turned fatal suggests the axman had collateral victims too—people slaughtered not by the elusive assailant directly, but as a result of the sustained terror left in their wake.

In aggregate, living under perpetual dread fundamentally changed how Black folks engaged with the axman as both a potential killer and a shorthand for certain death. Since November 1909, someone had been violently murdering Black families in the rice belt, stringing together an expansive chain of crimes linked by a cruel ax, proximity to the Southern Pacific Railroad, the complete annihilation of the home's occupants, and the lack useable evidence in the aftermath. By March 1912, then, local communities had been under siege for twenty-eight months and the crimes had significantly picked up in intensity since the start of the year. From November 1909 to

March 1911—sixteen months—four families had been murdered with an ax. From January to March 1912—just three months—another four families were slaughtered by the axman. Black communities throughout southwestern Louisiana and southeastern Texas had rational reasons to panic. Theirs was a legitimate response to an unknowable and increasingly destructive threat.

The death of the Monroe family in Glidden, Texas, at the end of March 1912 thus presented a fascinating conundrum. Although regional sentiment was that the axman had struck yet again—and even law enforcement officials acknowledged such a possibility—detectives did not have the ability to investigate the murder as anything other than an individual homicide. Thus, when the sheriff used bloodhounds to eventually arrest Jim Fields and his new wife, Ida, there was no discussion of the couple potentially being involved in any of the other axman killings.

The Fieldses' interlude into the axman saga ought to be considered within the larger context of the previous crimes. In many of the other cases, the authorities sought to understand who wanted a *particular* family dead, relying on interpersonal relationships to build theories of guilt. The authorities *typically* named individuals who knew the victims on a personal level as the potential killer, implying that someone with a specific connection to a specific family would be the culprit. Yet, there is no evidence Jim Fields knew the Monroes other than in passing. Ida Fields seemed to learn of their existence the night they were murdered. The seemingly random nature of this crime permitted local Black folks to assume the axman had come to town *and* exculpate a potential suspect. The lack of a logical assailant—despite white lawmen's beliefs—enabled Glidden's Black community to reinforce collective solidarity. They may not have known who the axman was, but they knew who he wasn't: Jim Fields. In less than a week, Black folks throughout the region would learn that the ax*man* was really the ax*woman.*

The site of the ax murders in Glidden, Texas. This photograph was taken in March 1912, mere days after the Monroe family was killed in their home. (Nesbitt Memorial Library Archives, Columbus, Texas)

Dave McKinney, La Grange, Texas, April 1912. News of "the ex-slave with [his] musket ready for action" made the local paper ("Ready for the Ax-Man," *La Grange Weekly Journal,* April 25, 1912). (Fayette Heritage Museum and Archives, La Grange, Texas)

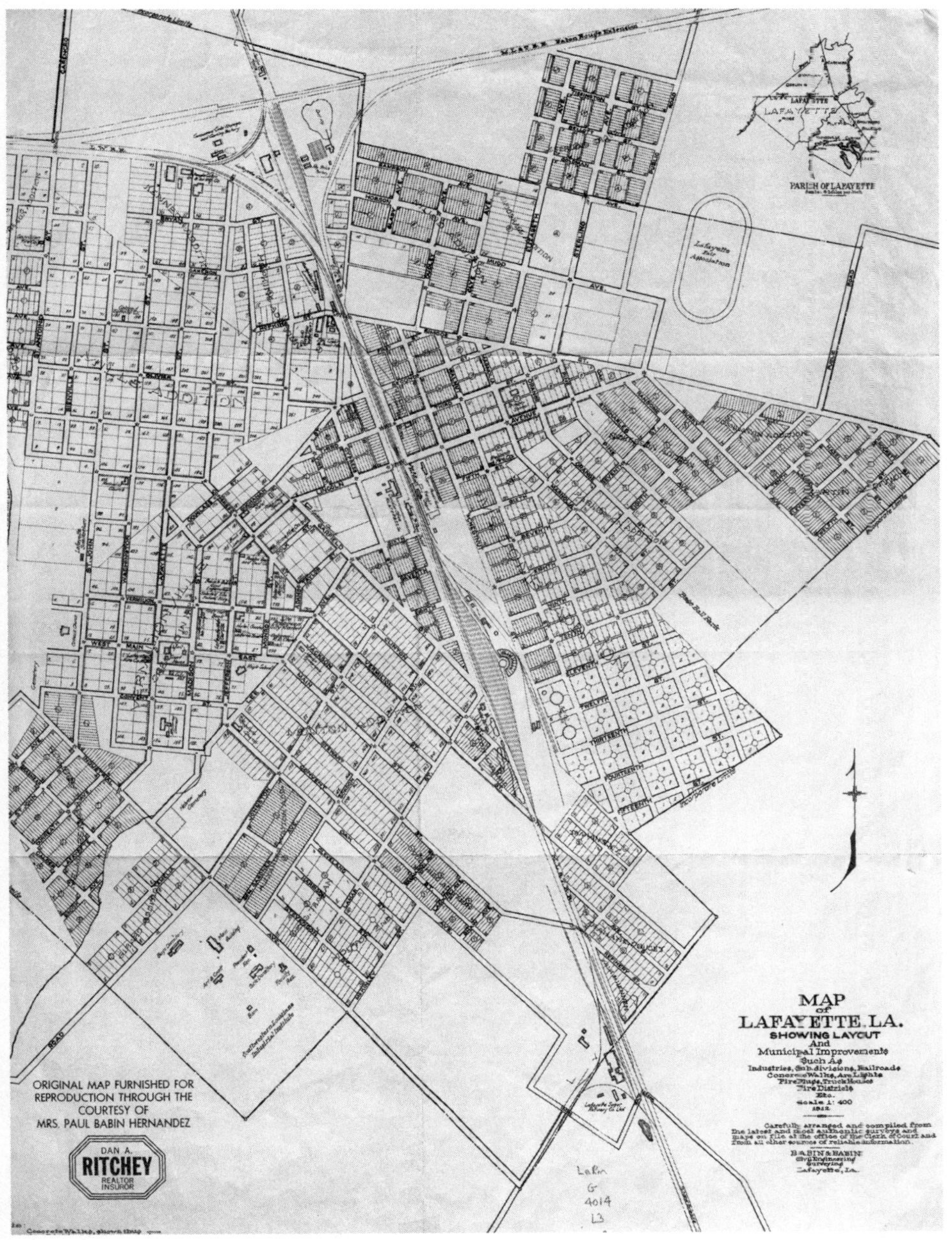

Map of Lafayette, Louisiana, in 1912. The Trahan and Doucet addition, where the Andrus family was murdered in February 1911, is adjacent to the railroad tracks near the bottom righthand side. (Map of Lafayette, La., Drawer 7, Folder 1, Louisiana Collection, Special Collections, Edith Garland Dupre Library, University of Louisiana at Lafayette)

Voodoo's Horrors Break Out Again.

"Here all the horrors of Voodooism are revived and little children go to their deaths, a sacrifice to the serpent."

A Typical Group of Louisiana Rice Pickers from Whom the Victims of the "Sect of Sacrifice" Are Taken.

How the Cruel and Gruesome Murders of Africa's Wicked Serpent Worship Have Been Revived in Louisiana by a Fanatic "Sect of Sacrifice"

How the Dead Fingers of the Baby Victims Are Spread Apart with Pieces of Wood After They Are Sacrificed!

Here Is the Way You Will Get Your Valentines in the Future

Aerial Mail-Carriers Who Will Shoot the Mail-Bags from the Sky Into Receiving Stations on Land

The New Mail-Aeroplane, Showing How the Mail-Matter Enclosed in a Shell-Like Contrivance Is Sent Through the Air Into Basket-Like Receiving Stations.

During the first few months of 1912, a highly sensationalized article circulated nationwide regarding the Louisiana-Texas ax murders. This image comes from the February 18, 1912, issue of the *San Francisco Examiner.* (Newspapers.com)

Few newspapers printed the only known picture of Clementine Barnabet, despite the international recognition her case garnered. This image comes from the April 6, 1912, issue of the *Times-Democrat* of New Orleans.

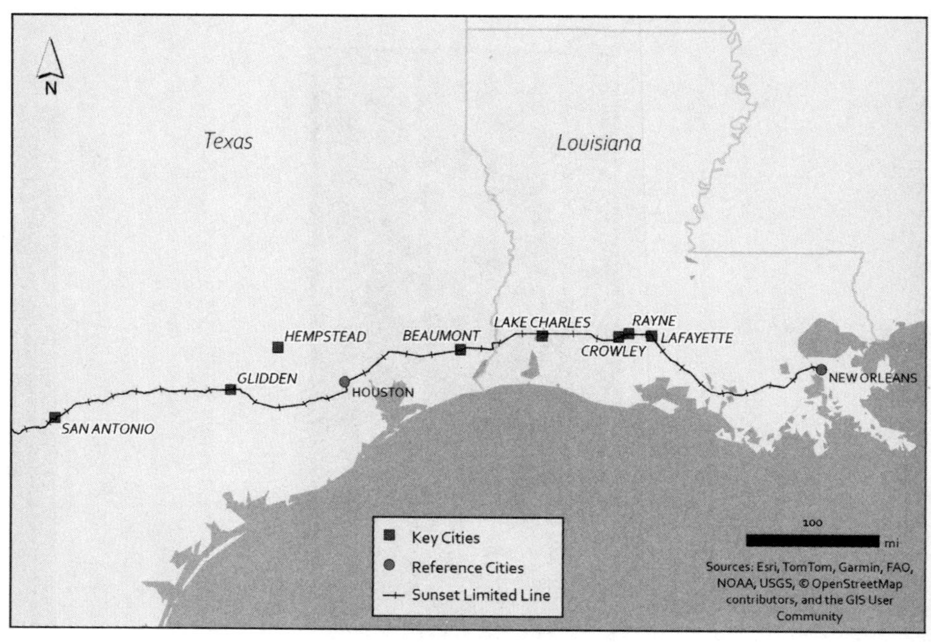

Camp-D, the women's quarters at the Louisiana State Penitentiary, during the early 1900s. (Henry L. Fuqua Jr., Lytle Photograph Collection and Papers, Mss. 1898, Louisiana and Lower Mississippi Valley Collections, LSU Libraries, Baton Rouge, La.)

PART II

Post-Confession

6

Clementine's Confession

A Black Female Serial Killer Is Made

For the first two weeks of April 1912, newspapers in every corner of the United States—and others in far-flung places like Australia and the United Kingdom—printed a riveting narrative that sounded as terrifying as it was tantalizing: Clementine Barnabet had confessed to the axman murders.[1] The Black press, as had been the case throughout the murderous saga, was generally mute. Although Clementine had taken credit for two of the crimes in November 1911, that declaration was not circulated evenly, likely due to a botched attempt by the Lafayette authorities to control media coverage of their prime suspect as they searched for accomplices.

By the spring of 1912, then, her latest admission of guilt was effectively her *first* confession in the areas most impacted by the axman crimes. In a matter of days, Clementine Barnabet had gone from an unknown young Black woman incarcerated in a random southwestern Louisiana city to a household name synonymous with religiously motivated ax murder. Even though she could not have physically wielded the weapon that killed the Warners, Broussards, Doves, or Monroes, the white press readily implicated her in all of the axman crimes. Quite literally overnight, regional and national print media made Clementine into a *prolific* serial killer. That reporters could do so at all was the product of an unnerving acknowledgment: Clementine had made herself into a serial killer first.

Considering Clementine's publicized confession—using her reported words to ascertain who she said she killed, what she said she did, and why she said she did it—reveals how she was made into a murderer. Exploring how Lafayette authorities responded to her statements offers concrete evidence of Clementine's entanglement with the local criminal justice system. Likewise, her confession highlights the stakes of white men believing—or not—

the words of a young Black woman in Jim Crow America. Turning to how print media made Clementine into a prolific serial killer focuses on how the press sensationalized her victim count, religion, appearance, and age, affording her a level of subversive power that belied the statements she made to the authorities. Finally, speculation about Clementine's worldview—not who she projected herself to be or who the media wanted her to be—offers tentative insights into her situation. As a young Black woman who had confessed to multiple murders, she had no refuge: white society castigated her, the local Black community threatened to lynch her, and her family had been implicated in the crimes, too. Yet, by vilifying herself, Clementine Barnabet was imbued with a nearly mythical amount of power thanks to the white press.

/ / /

To appreciate the scale of Clementine's confession—both in terms of how widely it was disseminated and how distorted it became—it is worth reprinting, in full, the first-person account that was published in the *New Orleans Item,* a regional newspaper that had sent a reporter named R. H. Broussard (no relation to the murder victims) to visit Clementine in jail.[2]

To be clear, this is not to suggest that what the *Item* printed was actually a verbatim transcript of her confession. There is no way to determine how the author might have manipulated Clementine's words, nor to ascertain how the young woman might have misrepresented herself and her reality. Still, the *Item*'s article is the longest known document that purports to embody Clementine's voice. Its merits are considered later, but for now, here is Clementine's confession exactly as it was published, including the reporter's interjections and subtitles:

> *My name is Clementine Barnabat and I was born and partly raised near the town of St. Martinville (La.) and moved to Lafayette about three years ago, when I began to lead a life of degradation. I have never been married. It was while in the company of two other women and two men, while in New Iberia (La.) that we met an old negro who told us that he could sell us 'candjas' meaning by that hoodoos, with which we could do as we pleased and we would never be detected and would be protected from the hands of the law by the mere fact of these 'candjas' being in our possession.*
>
> *We bought them and paid $3 each for them and left New Iberia the same night, returning to Lafayette, when we began to plan our actions. We had not yet*

decided on committing any murders, but it was while we were discussing our future plans that the question came up as to whether we could kill and be protected by the hoodoos. One of the gang was instructed to go to New Iberia and interview the hoodoo man, who said we were safe in any and all actions which we might do. Our lives would at all times be fully protected by the power of the hoodoos.

Drew Lot for First Murder.

It was sometime during the year 1910, I believe in the fall, and I went to Rayne with my companions, and we drew lots to know who would make the first attempt of the hoodoos in committing murder. The lot fell to me, and accordingly, I set to work that night. I went to my sister, who lived at Rayne, near the O. G. railroad depot, and later during the night went up town, disguised as a man, and securing an ax in a yard near the cabin where I killed the mother and four children.

When asked how she gained admission into the house she said that the house was lighted.

I saw that the light was burning and by t[h]at I could easily see inside. I saw the mother sleeping in her bed, then I decided that I would enter that house and there begin the work which we had planned.

On entering the house I struck the woman on the right temple and killed her instantly. One of the children was awakened by the noise, and before he could raise his head from the pillow I struck him a blow somewhere near the left ear, then I struck the other two. I left the man['s] clothes which I wore in the house and left the house in woman's clothes, returned to my sister's house and later during the same night I boarded a night train for Lafayette, arriving here about midnight. It was about 9 when I killed them.

Reported Deed to Others.

On my return to Lafayette I reported the matter to the other members of the 'gang,' and we watched the developments in the case with great interest. When we saw that we had not been detected we decided that the hoodoos had done their part and that we were safe.

She then told us how they had killed the family at Crowley, explaining every detail. How they left Crowley the same night, one of the women going to Rayne and the others coming to Lafayette.

In Crowley, she said, *I entered the house with one of the women, while the other kept watch, and as I had the ax in my hand I committed the murders. I struck the man first and just as I did so the woman woke up. I struck her a blow in the face with the butt end of the ax and felled her. I then struck her once or twice to be sure she was dead. Once this was done it was an easy matter to get rid of the two small children. We thought it better to kill them than to leave orphans, as they would suffer.*

Laid Plans for New Crime.

From Crowley we came back as far as Rayne together, one of the three stopping in Rayne and the other two, myself and another, came to Lafayette. Later we were joined by the third, who told us how the officers had searched for the murderers all around her. We never spoke of committing any more murders until sometime in February. The night before an election, when we knew that all officers would be busy 'politic[k]ing,' we went to the refinery and there we laid our plans, not knowing who would be the victim or victims.

When we reached the railroad crossing we saw light burning in a cabin near Ramagosa's store. We decided that that was a good place, so we went there; myself and one of the women entered the house and I struck Timi, the man, first, and then his wife and afterward his two small children, one of whom was an infant in a cradle near the bed. We had overlooked him until he woke up and began to cry. I turned around and struck him in the forehead, killing him instantly.

We took the man and woman and placed them in a kneeling position and left the house. I was near the house the next morning when Timi's brother came to the house and called them, and not getting any answers he looked through the window and saw them dead. He began crying and I was one of the first to go to him and asked him what had happened. He told me and I went to notify their parents, who lived nearby. I helped to wash them and prepare them for burial.

Fourth and Last Murder.

When asked to tell how the last murder had been committed, she said:

It was on a Sunday night. We were out for a frolic, and we went to the meeting of the 'God Sacrifice Church.' After we left there we secured an ax and wrapped it in a bundle with old clothes which we carried with us. We met two of the night officers, and when we saw them coming we hid the ax in the grass until the officers had passed us and went back to get it. We went a little way up the street and saw someone coming. I laid the ax behind a tree and when we saw who it was, it was King Harrison, the minister of the God Sacrifice Church[,] we told him that there had been two men fighting up the street and it would be better for him to go by the other street, as the officers would see him around there and arrest him. He did as we told him, and went around.

This left us all alone in the street, so we crawled to the house and entered from behind and killed them. Once we had killed them I took a pistol, which I had hidden under my dress, and shot at Norbert Randall, the man I had killed. I struck him somewhere in the breast or body. I got the pistol from my brother's house during the afternoon and returned it the same night, so as not to be seen with it should the officers catch me.

After this we went up to town to talk the matter over. I returned home about 2 o'clock in the morning and went to bed, where I stayed until I was awakened by the man I worked for the next morning about 5. I worked around the house until I was arrested by Mr. Peck, about 10 in the morning.

When asked if there had been any agreement made not to tell on one another, she said that there had been such an agreement made, but she wanted to tell her own part of it so as to clear her conscience.[3]

On a basic level, Clementine's confession implied several facts related to her involvement in the murders. First was the claim that she axed four families—one in Rayne, one in Crowley, and two in Lafayette. Second was the statement that conjures procured from a hoodoo doctor enabled her to murder without being caught. Third was the admission that she had four accomplices—two men and two women—but that she was barred from naming them. Last, her confession offered no substantive motive for the crimes, though she would elaborate the very next day that religion had indeed driven her to kill.[4] According to this subsequent admission, Clementine was a member of the Sacrifice Church. Initially, however, she wavered as to whether this particular faith community compelled her to kill or if she acted of her own volition while belonging to a fringe religion. Each of these facts offered Clementine a type of power that allowed the white press to elevate her supposed culpability while embracing racist beliefs in Black faith expression and Black criminality. Clementine Barnabet had confessed to a reporter—in essence, publicly—to being a serial killer.

///

As soon as Clementine Barnabet admitted to killing four Black families along the Southern Pacific Railroad, the temporary Lafayette Parish district attorney, Howard E. Bruner, sought to charge her with murder and a grand jury was impaneled.[5] While the jurymen debated what charges, if any, could be brought against Clementine, parish authorities followed the leads mentioned in her confession narrative.

Up first was figuring out which families she was taking credit for killing. While select newspapers explained that she had previously admitted to slaughtering the Andruses and Randalls in Lafayette following her third-degree examination by the New Orleans Police Department, she now claimed two additional crimes. The Rayne murder she described coincides with that of the Opelousas family in November 1909. Similarly, the Crowley homicide aligns with that of the Byerses in January 1911. In both cases, however, Clementine misidentified the number of victims, stating that a "mother and four children" were killed in Rayne and "two small children" were axed alongside their parents in Crowley.[6] Sometimes, she offered the wrong gender for a given victim, perhaps an outcome of the murders having been committed in darkness. Odder still was the fact that she erroneously dated the Rayne crime to 1910, though she was correct that it had taken place in the fall. Given these inconsistencies, it would be easy to dismiss Clementine's confession as false.

Possibly, however, she was mistaken when remembering the details. After all, she had described the circumstances of all four murders with alarming accuracy. For example, when Edna Opelousas and her children were slaughtered in Rayne, her sister recalled seeing "a man entering the place."[7] Clementine had confessed that she had been "disguised as a man" when she ostensibly committed the crime.[8] She also knew that the Andruses were posthumously moved, Norbert Randall had been shot, and Silvina Byers had awakened in the commotion. All of this, coupled with claims that she "cannot and does not read the newspapers," made Clementine's confession very damning indeed.[9]

So, if Clementine's details were fuzzy, but the gist reliable, then she took credit for killing the Opelousases in Rayne in November 1909, the Byerses in Crowley in January 1911, the Andruses in Lafayette in February 1911, and the Randalls also in Lafayette in November 1911. In total, she professed that seventeen people had been slaughtered by her hand, ten of them children under the age of ten. And though the axman slaughters had spanned four hundred miles from Lafayette to San Antonio, Clementine claimed a subset that crossed a mere twenty-five-mile section of the Southern Pacific Railroad. She declared that she had planned a murder in New Orleans—near a railroad station no less—but abandoned those intentions due to busyness near the targeted house.[10] She also suggested that she and her accomplices had talked about axing families in the smaller railroad towns of Scott, Duson, Broussard, and Cades, but decided these places were too tiny for them to escape undetected.[11] Whether Clementine had actually tried to expand her murderous rampage or if she was engaging in a perverse form of criminal bravado remains hard to say. The killings she'd admitted to were horrific on their own accord; there was no need to embellish her heinousness.

As the authorities pieced together the murders Clementine claimed, they sought to understand what initially started the killings: the mysterious "candjas" she and her accomplices had acquired from a "hoodoo man" in New Iberia.[12] A staple of southern Black cultures, particularly in Louisiana, conjures historically were handmade artifacts imbued with special powers that benefited the holder.[13] For believers, hoodoo—and the conjures associated with the practice—granted access to the supernatural via worldly elements. Comprised of ingredients and objects selected for particular purposes, conjures were typically made-to-order by specialists who had either learned the trade or acquired it as a gift. These specialists, often labeled as hoodoo "doctors," tended to be local practitioners with knowledge of mixing herbs/plants, harnessing attributes of colors, fabrics, words, and liquors, and leveraging Black folkways toward directed ends. Conjures could cure illness, manipulate romance, protect loved ones, and attract good luck. Yet, conjures could also be nefarious, harming enemies and bringing misfortune to unsuspecting victims. Thus, conjures represented powerful tools that people could use to influence the trajectory of their lives—or the lives of others. Of course, the power of conjures was rooted in belief in both the object and its creator, as well as its user and target(s). At times, charlatans exploited believers' faith, typically for financial gain.

Investigators sought to identify Clementine's conjure and the specialist who had sold it. Apparently, Clementine's charm was comprised of "two crossed needles, bound with thread and wrapped with red flannel and a few old rags."[14] Sometimes referred to as a "bag" or "outfit," Clementine's conjure was designed to protect her from "all harm."[15] The problem, it seemed, was that Clementine had lost her original conjure. Although she had tried to make a faithful replica, she had been unable to put the same "spell" on it as the hoodoo man.[16] She claimed it was the loss of her beloved charm—and the power it held—that had led to her November 1911 arrest, not the suspicious behaviors the authorities noted following the Randall family murder.

If Clementine believed in her charm, then it seems she also believed in its seller: Joseph Thibodeaux.[17] Detained in New Iberia and brought to the Lafayette Parish jail, Joseph was identified by Clementine as the hoodoo doctor who had sold her the conjure. She reportedly said to him, "you said I wouldn't be arrested, but you see here I am in jail," accusing him of her plight.[18] Yet, while she was convinced the deputy had arrested the right guy, Joseph protested that he had never seen Clementine before and was entirely innocent. In fact, he said he was a simple farmer and a member of the Catholic Church—hardly someone engaged in "witchcraft."[19]

Try as he might to distance himself from Clementine Barnabet, Joseph Thibodeaux had made some incriminating statements, though they weren't specific to the ax murders. According to the regional media, Joseph had "grown rich" selling "remedies" to residents of the rice belt.[20] Apparently, he'd sold a preparation of nails and white powder to a local white man for $40 (approximately $1,300 in 2025), providing instructions that would protect the client's property from arson. Joseph's "love potions" were supposedly popular among Black folks in the area, and he was known as a man of "considerable means."[21] Plus, he was said to have a "shrewd countenance" and was a successful property owner, perhaps further proof that he was more than just a farmer.[22]

The authorities took no chances with Joseph Thibodeaux, who quickly realized the "serious nature" of his situation.[23] He would not be released until the hullabaloo related to the ax murders died down. When detectives asked him why he had been unable to thwart his own arrest with his "magic arrangements," he had no response.[24] Their likely disparaging question implied everything they thought about hoodoo: it was fraudulent mischief that complicated solving these crimes. In reality, hoodoo practitioners were typically respected—if feared—members of their communities, sometimes rivaling Christian preachers in terms of power and importance.[25]

Although finding the famed hoodoo doctor was part of the detectives' strategy, they also wanted to locate Clementine's accomplices. She had confessed that two men and two women helped carry out her diabolical deeds, though she oscillated as to whether anyone else physically wielded an ax. But when the authorities solicited names, she was reticent to divulge any. Clementine intentionally manipulated the kinds of information she revealed to white lawmen, aware that confessing to murder had empowered her as a gatekeeper of knowledge, regardless of its credibility. For the detectives to potentially solve the axman crimes, they had to listen to—but not necessarily believe—a young Black woman. In Jim Crow America, this kind of dynamic was rarely considered useful or indispensable. The terror that had gripped the rice belt, however, required white men in positions of power to at least acknowledge their predicament.

Eventually, Clementine identified Mary Cochon and Irene—no last name—as her female co-collaborators. She claimed the duo visited her in jail and confessed to killing Black families in Lake Charles and Beaumont.[26] If this was true, then the Broussards and Doves had met their demises at the hands of Clementine's accomplices. Even the regional press pondered how Clementine could have learned of these 1912 murders without some direct knowledge, as she'd been physically behind bars when the crimes happened. Given the hysteria surrounding the axman—not to mention the sheer volume of people who had been arrested and released in connection with the madness—Clementine may have heard about subsequent slaughters through the grapevine.

Clementine did not make it easy for investigators to find Mary and Irene. Even after the lawmen subjected her to "sweating"—reminiscent of her third-degree examination in November—they were never confident they'd arrested the right women.[27] An Irene Duce, a Mary Parkerson, and a Valena Mabry were all detained by the Lafayette authorities, but how or if they were related to Clementine was convoluted. Irene Duce apparently wasn't even the "Irene" Clementine had named—that was actually Valena Mabry. The arrested Irene was known as a "bad character" and one of Clementine's associates.[28] Mary, meanwhile, matched the description Clementine had provided, but was picked up on a charge of forgery, not murder. It seems the authorities came to believe Valena didn't even know Clementine at all, but that the confessed murderer had intentionally offered a "false identification" to thwart detectives.[29] Of course, there is technically the possibility that all of the women knew Clementine and were connected to the ax murders. Clementine was manipulating the investigators, leveraging "cunning duplicity" to keep them guessing.[30]

While Clementine had sent officers "chasing jack o-lanterns" to find her female accomplices, she was initially mute about the men in her company.[31] The authorities would have to find them themselves. One of the first men arrested was a Black preacher and refinery fireman named William, Tom, or George Thompson, depending on the source.[32] Like so many of the other pastors detained in this saga, Reverend Thompson claimed affiliation with a Baptist church, which then morphed into a Sanctified church, whereby the investigators quickly connected him to the elusive Sacrifice Church. At some point in this hubbub, Clementine's brother Tatite was arrested, likely because she had mentioned borrowing his gun to shoot Norbert Randall.[33] Before long, her brother Zepherin was also apprehended.[34] Next came the detention of Pauline Barnabet, a half-sister of Clementine's who reportedly lived in Rayne but regularly traveled to Lafayette and Crowley.[35] Within a few days of Clementine's confession, then, four Barnabet siblings were behind bars, the two brothers suspected of "knowing more" about the crimes for which their sister had taken credit.[36] Their father, Raymond Barnabet, had been languishing in jail since the previous October after having been granted a retrial. The axman murders had again become a Barnabet family affair.

After Zepherin was arrested, he identified a man by the name of Ute Thomas as having "assisted" in the commission of the crimes.[37] A few days later, Ute's son, Darman, was also apprehended, then transported from Ville Platte to Lafayette for questioning.[38] Although Zepherin had initially claimed he, his father, his sister, Ute Thomas, the no-last-name Irene, and an unknown person had murdered the Andrus family, with the arrest of Darman he changed his story.[39] Now, Zepherin removed himself as an accomplice and named five killers: Clementine and Raymond Barnabet, Ute and Darman Thomas, and Irene.[40]

Newspapers ran with the five motif that seemed to cloud both Zepherin's and Clementine's statements, harkening back to the elusive "Human Five" signature found on the Broussard family's front door in the aftermath of their February 1912 murder. That the siblings identified five assailants—albeit in different ratios of men to women—supposedly aligned with a "secret oath" taken by the killers.[41] Plus, five ostensibly represented the number of victims found at the Andrus home, further evidence of the "voodoo charm of the talisman."[42] It seems no one stopped to check if such an assertion was right; after all, only four Andruses were murdered that night. And even if Zepherin's confession had merit—and that's a stretch—it didn't solve the glaring issue: he only explained who killed one family, not the other nine.

Clearly, the quest to find Clementine's accomplices was muddled. By the end of April 1912, the detention of various Barnabet family members, a Sanctified preacher, and several seemingly random other people suggested lawmen were not nearly as confident in their investigation as they wanted folks to believe. When Sheriff Lacoste claimed that he had "all five [suspects] in jail," this was wishful thinking.[43] The ax murders had persisted long after Raymond and Clementine Barnabet had been incarcerated, and the Barnabet siblings had proven themselves to be unreliable witnesses when they testified against their father back in October. Why would they suddenly decide to tell the truth?

/ / /

With various individuals ensnared in Clementine's web of murder, it's not surprising that the authorities still wanted to understand the *why* of it all. At first, it appeared that Clementine and her accomplices had simply wanted to test the legitimacy of their conjures. The group discussed whether they could kill undetected and, after confirming with Joseph Thibodeaux that they'd be protected, decided to act on this rather shallow idea.[44] Within two days, however, Clementine had changed her tune, claiming that she murdered the families so that she could "fondle the dead babies."[45] She was emphatic that neither jealousy nor robbery motivated the crimes, but a "strong passion" to embrace dead bodies.[46] More specifically, she was restless until "she had killed an infant and pressed its form to her breast."[47] Not surprisingly, this admission led the district attorney to label Clementine a "moral pervert."[48] In the parlance of the time, moral perversion was considered a deficiency of moral decency, often couched in the language of sexual gratification achieved through non-normative means.[49]

If Clementine was indeed a moral pervert, then the implication was that she derived sexual satisfaction from her crimes, perhaps not dissimilar to what is now known about many serial killers today.[50] That there are few examples of sexually motivated female serial killers does not mean they don't exist, but that they are less frequently identified. Perhaps Clementine Barnabet should be added to this list, or perhaps she was lying, as had ostensibly been the case before. Her testimony against her father was inconsistent, she'd taken credit for a crime she had once attributed to him, and she was frustratingly coy when naming accomplices. It was not a far stretch to conclude that the motive she'd given was intentionally misleading.

Killing to test her conjure was one theory. Murdering for sexual pleasure was another. And then there was the original rationale that Clementine had given during her first confession: religious duty. It seems that although she recirculated this idea—while sometimes trying to separate herself from the Sacrifice Church—the authorities were split regarding its legitimacy. Some thought that Clementine and her accomplices had "weakened brains [that] were easily affected by the exhortations they had heard" in the Sacrifice Church, ultimately compelling them to commit murder.[51] Others were confident Clementine was insane, erroneously implicated in horrific crimes that had nothing to do with her.[52] Whatever people thought of Clementine's potential involvement, getting to the bottom of the Sacrifice Church was necessary, just in case there was a connection.

Although months had passed since the authorities first hypothesized that the Sacrifice Church was involved in these killings, they hadn't learned much more. The highly publicized arrest of Reverend King Harris in January 1912 had caused a dangerous slippage between the elusive Sacrifice Church and Pentecostal Sanctified churches that led to the apprehension of numerous Black preachers throughout the winter and early spring.[53] Now, however, more murders had happened, a young Black woman had confessed, and detectives were working every conceivable angle to solve these crimes and stop others from occurring.

Perhaps, then, when the *New Orleans Item* ran an article entitled "Sanctified Sect Teachings Now Revealed" in early April 1912, there was an opportunity to clear up any confusion between sanctification and sacrifice. That members of a given Sanctified church had intentionally waited until someone was arrested for and publicly confessed to the ax murders before speaking to the media highlights not only how much they tried to distance themselves from the crimes, but also how aware they were of reporters' sloppiness. Even with such cautiousness, however, the *Item* could not help but draw potentially damning parallels. For example, the piece harped on passages that were supposedly marked in Reverend Thompson's Bible that talked about "the use of an axe," with a particular interest in Matthew 3:10.[54] The specific scripture in the preacher's Bible read: "And now also the axe is laid unto the root of the trees, therefore every tree which bringeth forth not good fruit is hewn down and cast into the fire."[55] It did not take much deductive reasoning to conclude that this passage could be interpreted to condone selective murder. Thus, while Reverend Thompson aligned himself with the Baptist denomination, the journalistic flair of the text implied that he was actually acquainted with whatever Sanctified church—and thereby Sacrifice Church—was behind the Louisiana-Texas ax murders. Released from custody on the promise of providing names of his congregants, the preacher now had his faith community put under the microscope.[56] When he failed to turn over any names, the clergyman remained "under surveillance" by Lafayette authorities, though at some point he presumably ceased to be a person of interest.[57]

Try as they might, it seemed investigators never found the Sacrifice Church, despite arresting numerous ministers and having heard the appalling if contradictory confession of Clementine Barnabet. Instead, they conflated Pentecostal communities with a potentially murderous one, wavered as to the power of this elusive group, and questioned whether a religious motive for serial killing was even a legitimate prospect. Their quest to out this organization either pushed it further underground or imitated a dog chasing its tail. That is to say, maybe local Black communities protected their own or maybe Clementine fabricated an entire organization. In either case, folks in the rice belt had to accept that the truth about the Sacrifice Church would likely forever remain a mystery.

/ / /

Although the press generally treated Clementine's confession as legitimate, not everyone shared this assessment. Some folks in Lafayette thought she had concocted her involvement in the crimes, but others countered that there was no way for her to know the details of each murder if she was illiterate, as was reported.[58] Given her misleading testimony against her father in October 1911, however, people surmised Clementine was insane and therefore untruthful.[59] Still others questioned whether her accomplices had more to do with the crimes than she implied.[60] Curiously, some hypothesized that Clementine was actually the "ignorant tool of a white man" hellbent on exterminating Black families.[61] What was not considered in questioning the validity of her confession was whether investigators could have fed her information related to the killings.

Regional detectives wavered regarding Clementine's credibility. Acadia Parish Sheriff Louis Fontenot thought she was "not at all reliable," conceding that, although she could have killed the Randalls in Lafayette, she had nothing to do with any of the other crimes.[62] Meanwhile, Lafayette Parish Sheriff Louis Lacoste was convinced Clementine was "the guilty person" and that her confession was both rational and true (save the intentionally misleading parts).[63] That the sheriffs reached such opposing conclusions regarding Clementine's culpability confirms the divisiveness of her case. Many simply could not believe she was capable of such heinousness and therefore assumed she was mouthing falsehoods. Others opined that she was "a degenerate" but responsible, evidence of the "lowest scale of humanity."[64] That such deductions were reached despite Clementine's public confession suggests the young Black woman's self-reported responsibility was contested by white authorities. To accept her statements at face value would have acknowledged her power in crippling the region and outsmarting dozens if not hundreds of white men. It would have recognized her deft skill in plotting unfathomable violence and avoiding detection, effectively undermining assumptions that Black criminality was primitive and unsophisticated. Thus, when officials and reporters questioned Clementine's capacity to kill, they not only challenged Black women's professed experiences, they embraced white superiority.

/ / /

The legitimacy of Clementine's confession—or lack thereof—invited a flurry of news reports in an incredibly short span of time that thrust this unknown young Black woman into the national and international limelight. This expansive media coverage manufactured an identity for Clementine that did not align with what local investigators had come to believe. Outside of the rice belt, in the eyes of the media and the public, she had become the leader of a cult that demanded human sacrifice to gain immortality. Clementine's role in this entire saga was exaggerated, leading to a plethora of claims that all coalesced around a simple idea: she was a prolific serial killer and criminal mastermind.

From Washington, D.C., to Washington state, story after story claimed Clementine "led a mysterious negro cult," despite there being no evidence in her printed confession that she self-identified with any sort of leadership position.[65] If Clementine was indeed the "directing head" of the Sacrifice Church, she had seemingly withheld this information from local authorities while spewing a bunch of other details that obfuscated her true role.[66] Why, then, would this fact suddenly become public outside of the rice belt but not within it?

Likely, the white press wanted to craft Clementine into a cult leader because it offered a sellable narrative: a young Black woman had orchestrated numerous religiously motivated murders. The International News Service, for example, published an expansive article that claimed Clementine "directed the slaughter" and named "many" who participated in the "bloody orgy" that followed each murder.[67] Similarly, the Associated Press ran a story that identified Clementine as "high priestess of a negro cult" and claimed that she knew other families would "pay the sacrifice" after having been selected to be killed.[68] Articles like these demonized Clementine while embellishing upon her confession, eventually building a perverse leaderboard that continually increased her victim count from seventeen to twenty to thirty-five to forty.[69] As the fictitious roster grew, so too did Clementine's perceived depravity. After all, if she was the leader of a cult, she likely had "a certain intelligence and cunning."[70] For a Black teenager to wield such power—whether over her followers or public consciousness—was no small feat in Jim Crow America.

That Clementine Barnabet became associated with the belief that "by life sacrifice alone may a person gain immortality" added to the tantalizing nature of her confession.[71] Not only was she the supposed leader of a murderous cult, but the group's rationale was rooted in immortality. At the same time, newspapers claimed Clementine was a "Voodoo Priestess," offering a convoluted hodgepodge of problematic beliefs to make sense of the senseless.[72] Clementine never intimated immortality was her motivation, nor did she practice Voodoo. While she might have occasionally claimed the Sacrifice Church (and *also* the Catholic Church), she emphasized that God had compelled her to kill.[73] That Voodoo does not worship the Christian God should have been an obvious sign she was not involved in that diasporic faith community. Instead, the national press ran with such a half-baked story because it helped fuel a particular image of Clementine as abhorrent and deviant in multiple ways. After all, the axman crimes had been attributed to Voodoo by January 1912 in the aftermath of the Broussard family murder. The leap from the religion as a motive to Clementine as a Voodoo leader was a small one.

Commenting on Clementine Barnabet as a cult leader who promoted human sacrifice was not enough to make her into a serial killer in the eyes of the media: she needed to become a literal monster. Thus, descriptions of Clementine's appearance alternated between her as an unhinged killer and an everyday Black woman. This duality meant that part of what made her terrifying was the fact that she was indistinguishable from everyone else. The regional press could not help but discuss her frequent smiles and laughs, implying that this emotional response was inappropriate to the situation at hand. When expounding on her confession, for example, she reportedly gave "a laugh and a smile indicating intense satisfaction."[74] The next day, she smiled "with devilish delight" that rendered her "practically insane."[75] Meanwhile, papers readily admitted that Clementine had labored as a domestic servant for "many Lafayette families" and had lived her whole life in the region.[76] Although she apparently was not always a satisfactory employee, that she managed to hold jobs at all suggested she could not have been as terrifying as journalists now claimed. The forced intimacy of domestic labor required Black women and girls to coexist with their white employers in vulnerable positions that sometimes extended in both directions across the power imbalance.[77]

To be fair, Clementine's behaviors at work led some to label her a "worthless character."[78] Perhaps part of this description came from a seemingly fascinating attribute she possessed: a "sphinxlike attitude."[79] It would be months before the significance of this behavior was printed publicly, but when it was, the implication was that Clementine's clandestine movements were ideal for committing murder. The press would report that "her tread is stealthy and catlike, and families for whom she worked say that she would often come into a room entirely unnoticed, and then chuckle at the surprise created."[80] Even a descendant of a family that purportedly employed Clementine has confirmed this unique trait, so perhaps there is merit to her soft steps.[81] That this peculiarity would eventually become evidence of her murderous mania indicates how thoroughly the media attempted to distinguish Clementine from everyday people while conceding that she wasn't that different after all. She was a domestic servant just like many Black women in Jim Crow America. If she could commit murder undetected, what stopped other Black women from doing the same?

While the press debated Clementine's mannerisms, trying to ascertain if she truly was as heinous as she claimed, they also offered instructive descriptions of her body. When she'd first confessed back in the fall, a far-flung paper labeled her "a Louisiana creole, 18, tall, straight limbed and only one-eighth negro."[82] By the following spring, however, she was a "half-blood negress."[83] She was also "a mulatto."[84] At the same time, the regional media told readers she looked like "an ordinary negro servant" with "copper-colored skin."[85] These depictions of Clementine's racial composition suggest a preoccupation with determining her ancestry. If she was "mixed race" *and* had committed these violent murders, antimiscegenation advocates could use her case as proof that racial blending resulted in moral degeneracy.[86] Similarly, labeling her as "Creole" afforded a shorthand for the social and cultural problem of the mixing of the races, specifically in Louisiana.[87] Thus, Clementine's color—

the literal shade of her skin—became a point of fixation for journalists who sought to explain what went wrong to cause her to kill.

Yet, it wasn't just Clementine's complexion that was discussed, but also her size. Hundreds of articles around the United States claimed that the young woman was "strong and robust," implying that she was physically capable of inflicting significant harm on her victims.[88] This description accompanied assessments of her height. One of the New Orleans outlets opined that Clementine was roughly five feet, six inches, or five feet, seven inches—taller than the average woman at this time.[89] Evidence suggests she was not actually this tall—probably more like five feet, four inches, or average height—but making her literally larger than life contributed to the monstrous image the press sought to create.[90] Perhaps A. M. Dickinson's piece in Utica's *Saturday Globe* most colorfully captured Clementine's presence by noting: "She is a large negress and looks as though she might make Goliath hesitate."[91] Corporally constructing Clementine Barnabet to be a killer was part of a larger media strategy that rendered Black female offenders—whether guilty or innocent—Amazonian and therefore threatening.[92] By no means would she have been the first Black woman to be vilified by reporters in early 1900s America, but she would have likely been one of the most well-known.

Against the backdrop of Clementine's shocking depiction as an inhuman Black female serial killer and cult leader who promoted human sacrifice to gain immortality was a glaring acknowledgment: she was only a teenager. Her youthfulness contributed to her perceived monstrousness as people struggled to rationalize how someone so young could take credit for crimes that were so abhorrent. Through subtle references like mentioning that Clementine was "only about 18 years old," the media made clear that her age did not align with their expectations of who was capable of such depravity.[93] Regularly labeled as "young" and a "girl," Clementine's status as a teenager presented a conundrum in understanding the scale of her crimes.[94]

Thus, to explain Clementine's culpability alongside her age, at least one regional paper suggested that she had been "frequently arrested for street walking and loitering," implying that a criminal history preceded this latest turn to murder.[95] Another reported that the young woman had always caused her father "much trouble," perhaps insinuating that she had a habit of butting heads with authority.[96] While most serial killers do have a record of petty crimes that occurred before (or sometimes concurrently with) their fatal offenses, this fact is muddied by the biases in Jim Crow policing that rendered Blackness a crime in and of itself. So, whether Clementine actually had a rap sheet is a moot point; her assumed criminality was used to contradict reservations about her ability to murder entire families based on her age.

By the time news of Clementine Barnabet's confession had reached audiences across the ocean, a single paragraph reprinted throughout the British empire summarized everything the U.S. media had constructed:

> Barnabet has a strain of white blood which dates back to the days of the plantation slaves. She has not the thick lips and crinkly hair of the negress, but has a fine, tall, robust, good figure, and is handsome. In her eyes there is the look of a hunted creature. She does not appear to be demented, and is rather more intelligent than the average girl of her class. Moreover, she knows the Bible, and can quote readily in support of blood sacrifice as practised in olden times. "Blood initiation, blood atonement" are words constantly on her lips, and as she talks her eyes glare like those of a tigress.[97]

Just like that, Clementine became an amalgamation of perceived social ills: racial mixture, religious perversion, deviant intelligence, youthful corruption, and fatal attractiveness. What she had confessed to detectives and newspapermen in that Lafayette jail cell had taken on a life of its own, morphing into a narrative that said far more about society's fears than about the young woman's actual actions. Whether Clementine slaughtered any of the seventeen people she'd claimed was irrelevant. White media wanted—arguably needed—her to be a murderer. She was proof of the most damning consequences of "The Negro Problem": a pathological criminal whose very identity rendered her inconceivably ordinary and aberrant. With the stroke of a pen and the clack of a typewriter, journalistic flair artfully crafted Clementine Barnabet into a cult-leading, sacrifice-promoting, religion-manipulating serial killer.

/ / /

Far beyond the bars of her jail cell, print media had constructed Clementine Barnabet to be an inhuman fiend full of depravity and perversion. Report after report lambasted her with labels like "human butcher" and "negress murderess."[98] Yet, within these sensational articles are minute glimpses into Clementine's worldview. A New Orleans paper offered a brief statement that Clementine had accepted that she would be given the death penalty, "and so asked to see her mother."[99] This unknown parent—not her stepmother, Dinah—perhaps represents one of the few people in Clementine's world that she trusted. Another reporter commented that Clementine was "more like a child in her ignorance," noting how excited the young woman was to have her photograph taken for the newspaper.[100] Brief mentions like these highlight Clementine's youthfulness against the backdrop of the uncertainty she faced. After all, she was but a teenager who had spent almost half a year in jail after being tortured into confessing to murder. Seeking out her mother and delighting in a seemingly vain pleasure were exactly the kinds of behavior a nineteen-year-old might display. Photography was neither cheap nor readily accessible to most Black families in the early 1900s South, so Clementine's interest in sitting for a picture might have been a genuine response to a new experience. Her tumultuous home life with her father and stepmother perhaps meant her biological mother's comfort would have eased some worries and provided some reassurance. Thus, though the press certainly constructed Clementine as a monster, journalists also subtly revealed her humanity.

So, while the grand jury was debating indicting Clementine on six counts of murder, it should not come as a surprise that she reportedly sang two of the most popular hymns of the day: "Nearer My God to Thee" and "Lead, Kindly Light."[101] The latter of these included the following lyrics:

> The night is dark, and I am far from home—
> Lead Thou me on!
> Keep Thou my feet; I do not ask to see
> The distant scene,—one step enough for me.[102]

To anyone watching, the lyrics might have seemed ironic. Here was a confessed murderer singing about seeking her God in a time of need, being led by Him, following His will, looking for Him, recognizing His power, and being compelled to go forward. Maybe she believed that was precisely what she was doing. Perhaps she thought she had been a faithful adherent. A devoted disciple. Then again, perhaps she was simply nervous and sang to herself to calm her spirits and steady her breath.

The grand jury returned a "true bill," indicting Clementine with six counts of murder, all relating to the deaths of the Randall family and their overnight guest, Albert Scythe.[103] Six pieces of paper reiterated the same charge, the wording altered only to account for the different names of the victims:

"That one Clementine Barnabet, at the parish aforesaid; on the 27th day of November A.D. 1911, did unlawfully, willfully, feloniously, and of her malice aforethought kill and murder" a given member of the Randall household.[104] Again. And again. And again, again, again.

Although Clementine confessed to the murders of three other families, likely the decision to only indict her on six charges was a product of two simple considerations. First, her father was still behind bars, waiting to be retried for the deaths of the Andrus family in Lafayette in February 1911. If she was actually responsible for their deaths, however, then Raymond would theoretically be released. Second, although both Rayne and Crowley were within the jurisdiction of the Eighteenth District Court, the state might have wanted to focus their efforts on the one case they believed they stood the strongest chance of winning: that of the deaths of the Randall family, to which Clementine had already confessed—twice.

Local Black folks would have been fine with another option: lynching Clementine.[105] In the days following her confession, the Associated Press explained that Black residents in the Lafayette area had descended on the parish jail, "silently gazing" at the spot where Clementine was supposedly held.[106] According to newspapers nationwide, if she were to be released, the local Black community would have killed her. If that had occurred, Clementine would have likely been the fifty-first Black woman to have been lynched between 1889 and 1918, according to the NAACP.[107] Still, such an account would not have accurately captured the uniqueness of Clementine's plight. After all, less than 2 percent of Black lynching victims documented by the NAACP were women. Of that subset, the organization did not—and perhaps would not—differentiate between white-on-Black and Black-on-Black extralegal violence.

Although intraracial lynchings were relatively rare in the Jim Crow South, they did occur. One calculation reports that between 1882 and 1930, for example, eighteen Black-on-Black lynchings occurred in Louisiana, half of which were clustered in the northwestern corner of the state and one in the Lafayette area.[108] Thus, the prospect of exacting vigilante justice on Clementine did have precedent. However, the fact that Clementine was a Black woman represented an anomaly even to intraracial lynch mobs.[109] Scholars have explored the ways gender and race inform both the study and memory of lynching, yet there is more work to be done on the numerous conceivable configurations of these extralegal proceedings.[110] That Lafayette's Black community was willing to lynch one of their own—and a young woman at that—offers compelling evidence that intraracial intergender mob violence was possible, if improbable.

That such an action never came to fruition may also have been the product of a curious decision by Lafayette officials to place a detective—posing as a prisoner—in Clementine's jail cell. This observer was supposed to "keep a careful record of every word spoken and every movement made by her."[111] Implicitly, however, the inclusion of an additional lawman in close proximity to Clementine may have helped thwart any attempt to exact vigilante justice, though it seems this was not the intent behind the undercover operation.

If America's crooked criminal justice system was allowed to play out, then Clementine was supposed to be arraigned one week after she confessed to murdering seventeen people.[112] Instead, the authorities delayed the arraignment in the hopes of talking her into divulging more incriminating information.[113] Meanwhile, it seems Clementine took the news of her indictment with indifference, simply shrugging her shoulders in response.[114] According to the Associated Press reporter, however, her reaction was far more animated. When asked about the likely outcome of her upcoming trial, Clementine supposedly "smiled and with her fingers described a noose about her neck."[115] Either the young Black woman who'd captivated the nation knew how to manipulate her audience, or the white press desperately wanted to believe she did. In both cases, the power afforded to Clementine—whether through her self-presentation or the media—reverberated well beyond the rice belt.

/ / /

In early April 1912, Clementine Barnabet became a household name across the United States as she boldly confessed to dastardly deeds: the violent murders of seventeen individuals in southwestern Louisiana. Recounting how she'd slain the Opelousas, Byers, Andrus, and Randall families with an ax, she evinced no remorse for the terror, grief, and panic her actions caused. Her statements to police implied that her accomplices—sometimes believed to be her followers—continued the killing spree without her physical presence. Although she would eventually name some of her co-conspirators, the authorities questioned if Clementine was being truthful. Between her leads and their sleuthing, a plethora of Barnabets and a handful of others were jailed by the end of the month. Finally, it seemed that the crimes that had plagued the rice belt for roughly two and a half years were over.

While Clementine's confession gave the local authorities tangible clues to pursue, it gave national and international media a litany of information from which to construct this otherwise obscure young Black woman into a prolific serial killer. In newspapers far removed from her supposed killing fields, Clementine was given an incredible amount of power as a cult leader and Voodoo priestess, touted as the mastermind behind dozens of murders carried out as human sacrifices. These crimes, it was reported, were believed by the cult's followers to offer them immortality. A nineteen-year-old Black woman, it seemed, had organized this entire operation.

Yet, what news outlets printed about Clementine's confession did not align with the already convoluted story she'd told investigators in Lafayette. Apparently, the fact that she'd admitted to killing seventeen people "with her own hands" was not sensational enough for the country's largest news wires.[116] Instead, Clementine had to become a monstrous murderer, deliberately crafted to be both fiendishly atypical and alarmingly ordinary. In addition to her behaviors, her race, her size, and her age were scrutinized and deployed to directed ends, leading to a manufactured image of Clementine that terrified and tantalized an entire country.

Although the press fashioned a version of Clementine Barnabet that encapsulated a variety of fears that seemed to extend far beyond statements attributed to the young woman, there was one sticking point in this entire ordeal: the state chemist had proven that her clothes contained "the same blood as was found on the bed clothes of the Randall family" from when they were killed in November 1911.[117] This evidence was supposedly so strong that the authorities believed they could convict Clementine "even outside of her own confession."[118] At the same time, however, regional authorities had been piecing together a multitown theory of a bloodthirsty axman targeting Black families living in close proximity to the Southern Pacific Railroad's Sunset Route. If these murders were all connected *and* Clementine was involved, then her admission to four of the crimes was not the full story. She was either the mastermind of an incredible killing spree or the devoted tool of an elusive puppeteer.[119] Perhaps the Associated Press was right to run an article that claimed Clementine had offered a damning warning: "the killings would continue."[120]

7

Clementine's Prediction

The Axman's Reign of Terror in Texas

In a matter of days, Clementine Barnabet's prediction that the killings would continue came true. Either she knew how to weave one hell of a tale and got lucky, or she knew *something* about the axman crimes. She had implied to the authorities that her incarceration would not stop the madness, as others would "carry out the work of extermination all along the Southern Pacific Railroad from New Orleans to San Francisco."[1] Now, mere days after her confession, the Burton family had been slaughtered with an ax in their San Antonio home. Before long, the Marshalls would be attacked in Hempstead, Texas. And then, by summer's end, the Dashiells would be assaulted back in the Alamo City. Yet, these last two crimes were generally nonfatal, complicating what had become a defining feature of the axman: certain death.

These latest crimes occurred *after* Clementine Barnabet's confession, reinforcing the fact that she could not have physically killed these families (or any of the 1912 victims). Yet, the continuation of the axman crimes after the axwoman admitted guilt necessarily caused widespread panic in and beyond the rice belt. The self-defense strategies that were employed by Black communities following Clementine's springtime confession evinced increasingly jumpy, paranoid, and distrustful responses to the unknowable threat. Likewise, it was only in the aftermath of the Burton family murder that fractures appeared among white authorities regarding how best to address this uncertainty. In short, the timing of subsequent axman attacks contributed to the splintering of affected communities, as the killer had finally pushed both Black *and* white folks to their limit.

/ / /

On April 11, 1912—a Thursday—Betty Evers visited her nineteen-year-old daughter in San Antonio, Texas.[2] Carrie Burton, one of Betty's children, lived but a few houses away on North Center Street. Perhaps Betty had gone to see her grandchildren—three-year-old Naomi and one-year-old Edward, nicknamed Sonny—or perhaps she hoped to catch her son, Leon, who was staying with his sister and her family. Betty likely knew she would not get to talk with her son-in-law, William, because he wouldn't get off work as a bar porter at Sommers' Garden, a local saloon, until roughly 11 p.m.[3] By then, Betty would be long gone. What Betty didn't know—what she couldn't have known—was that that fateful night was the last time she'd see her family alive.

Between midnight and daybreak—well after William Burton had returned—Carrie was startled awake. It sounded like someone was in her home. She started toward the sound and instead came face to face with the intruder. The unknown assailant slammed an ax into Carrie's face, cleaving her skull and ripping away her forehead and features.[4] Presumably her body crumpled in a moment, falling to the floor. Blood began to pool.

In the adjoining room, Carrie's attacker had likely encountered Leon first, crushing his skull with the ax before turning the weapon on the little children. Naomi's head had been "fearfully mutilated," her lifeless form found on the floor near the stove.[5] Baby Edward was reportedly spared the grotesque overkill, but a well-placed blow had ended his life in an instant. His tiny body was placed on the bed beside Leon's. Back in the front room, William was struck "as if hit by a steam hammer," the ax obliterating his frontal lobe in the process.[6] At some point in the carnage, a butcher knife was thrust into Carrie's back and a pocketknife plunged into Leon's. William suffered the same fate.

Around 7:15 a.m. that morning, Callie Burse, a North Center Street neighbor, attempted a delivery to the Burtons' home.[7] She knocked on the front door and got no response. She went to a window on the side of the house and realized something was wrong: the curtains were soaked in blood. Immediately, San Antonio city and Bexar County officials were summoned.

Inside the Burton home, all of the adult bodies were found lying face down, with the men on beds and Carrie on the floor. One local paper reported that a bucket of water was found in the room with the children, its contents bloodied by the assassin.[8] Another claimed that the "mud print of a shoe" was found in the damp ground around the house, perhaps a clue to the killer's tracks.[9] The lack of missing articles implied the family wasn't robbed, and the fact that the doors and windows were locked, perhaps with a single exception, stumped the detectives. Regional outlets commented on the "blood and brains" strewn about the home and on the fact that it seemed "more than usual malice" had motivated the murder.[10] Curiously, in the immediate aftermath of the crime, the local press didn't mention whether the telltale ax was found at the scene. The lack of this once crucial piece of evidence did not stop hundreds of newspapers from making the obvious connection: the axman had come to San Antonio.[11]

Based on Clementine's recent confession, the previous killings, and the hysteria that had been permeating the rice belt for years, it's no wonder people also thought "religious fanatics" via the Sacrifice Church had come to the Alamo City.[12] To have reached any other conclusions would have belied how the ax murders had shaped public consciousness for months on end. That both a mysterious axman and an elusive group of religious extremists could have slaughtered the Burtons was not out of the realm of speculation in the spring of 1912: the sustained terror that captivated southwestern Louisiana and southeastern Texas permitted—arguably required—uncertainties and contradictions. If anything, Clementine's confession perhaps nudged the public to believe that a cult had descended on the region.

The similarities were unmistakable—a Black family had been axed to death within a mile of the Sunset Route, and a handful of victims had been found, fueling the belief that the number five had significance to the killer. Yet, not only did none of the families Clementine Barnabet supposedly murdered contain five members at the time of their death, but she only took *personal* credit for crimes between Lafayette and Crowley, Louisiana. San Antonio was four hundred miles away. Although she had reportedly implied the killings would continue, she had provided so much conflicting information to the authorities that it was impossible to ascertain the truth.

Until this point, the other San Antonio crime—the March 1911 murder of the Casaway family—had only briefly been associated with the axman crimes in southwestern Louisiana. Now, in the aftermath of the Burton attack, it was clear there were more linkages between the Burtons and the Casaways than the way they were killed. The families lived less than three blocks apart. Both families had young children who were murdered, including a three-year-old girl and a baby boy. Plus, both families were transplants to San Antonio, with Louis Casaway moving from New Orleans, his wife coming from Hays County, and the Burtons relocating from Fayette County. While the Casaway parents were quite a bit older than the Burton adults, conceivably they at least knew of each other, given the proximity between their houses and the similarities in their lives.

According to the authorities, however, there was one huge commonality between the families: the belief that the wife was a white woman. In the Casaway case, there was reliable proof to support this claim, as Elizabeth and Louis had married in Mexico, Sheriff Tobin knew both adults personally, and Lizzie's family members assisted in the investigation into her death. Although some local folks insisted Elizabeth had a "trace of negro blood," there is substantial evidence she was indeed white.[13] In the case of the Burton family, it appears the opposite was true: Carrie was "a light mulatto who was sometimes mistaken for a white woman."[14] While Carrie might have been "fair-skinned," available evidence supports the idea that she was a Black woman who had married a Black man and was raising Black children until the family was brutally murdered.[15]

The Sunday after the Burtons were found dead in their home, a large choir sang for their funeral.[16] As was the case with the Casaway family, the five victims were buried in three caskets in City Cemetery No. 3. While the Burtons were put to rest, Black communities in San Antonio were restless. As people debated whether the family was killed specifically or indiscriminately, they employed many of the self-defense strategies that had been fixtures of the rice belt for months. They barred windows and doors, brought dogs inside to serve as noisy sentinels, stockpiled weapons, and created rotating guards to protect their loved ones.[17] Like their counterparts in Louisiana, they questioned whether the Burtons could have been chloroformed.[18] They were taking no risks; they wanted to be prepared for anything. If the axman—or some other unknown evil—had already visited the city twice, what was to say they wouldn't strike again?

/ / /

The same morning Black residents in San Antonio prepared to say their final farewells to the Burton family, Black folks in Hempstead awoke to a nightmare: the axman had come to Waller County, Texas. In a few short days, it seemed the killer had traveled roughly two hundred miles east and a touch north, landing in the modest railroad town that moved goods and people from the Gulf Coast to the Texas interior.[19] A couple thousand people called Hempstead home in the early twentieth century as cotton and oil industries sprang up in the region. Yet, early on that fateful April morning, the axman headed for a singular destination: the Marshall family's residence, just one block east of the town's courthouse.[20]

Although newspapers reported that there were six people in the home on that particular day, censuses suggest the Marshall domicile was extensive and multigenerational. In 1910, for example, Ed Marshall was listed as the head of the household, followed by his wife, Alice. Four of her siblings, her father, and two of her nephews also lived in the house.[21] It seemed that Alice's aging father, Isaac "Ike" Burney, had been widowed, one of her sisters had been divorced (with two young boys in tow), and her remaining siblings—two brothers and a sister—were all older teenagers. By 1912, perhaps not all of these individuals still resided in the household, as Alice's siblings could have married or charted out on their own. Certainly, the presence of Eva Jones, a young Black woman who was there that April morning, was not captured in the census. So, *at minimum* there were six people in the home that day. The media claimed the unfortunate half dozen were Alice Marshall, her sister Carrie Burney, their father Ike Burney, Eva Jones, and two young boys, likely Alice's nephews.

Sometime in the early darkness of April 14, someone entered the Marshalls' home—probably through a door—and attacked Ike with an ax.[22] Then, crossing into an adjacent room where Alice, Carrie, and Eva were sleeping, the killer struck the first two women violently. In the commotion, Eva awoke. The assailant took aim at her, but only managed to slightly wound her hand. Thinking quickly, she rolled beneath the bed, out of her attacker's immediate reach. She screamed—and likely screamed some more—and the killer fled.

Unlike at the previous crime scenes, no one needed to discover the bodies. However painful and traumatic the attack had been, Ike and Carrie clung tenuously to their lives. Eva was alive, though undoubtedly terrified. The two little boys were physically unscathed but probably psychologically scarred. The only person who died instantly from the attack was Alice Marshall. In fact, her death certificate stated she was "killed by the axeman."[23]

Doctors who examined the victims reported that there was "no hope for the recovery" of either Carrie or Ike.[24] They were alive, but barely. Ike Burney died at 10:00 p.m. on April 17, 1912, just three days after one of his daughters was killed. His cause of death was only slightly more speculative than Alice's: "struck on head by the axman or some unknown party."[25] Carrie, on the other hand, died in 1938 of pellagra according to her death certificate, meaning she recovered (at least partially) from the attack.[26]

That only one person was killed outright wasn't the only unique feature of the violence wrought on the Marshall family home. At least two anomalies highlight how expectations about serial murder can't always map neatly onto reality. The Waller County sheriff's office surmised that, although the weapon used the in the assault was an ax, it wasn't the same kind of ax that was found in the other fatal crimes. It was smaller—perhaps "a hatchet or small hand-axe."[27] While other implements or their aftermaths were identified at previous crime scenes—smoothing irons when the Hodge family was killed, a gunshot wound in Norbert Randall's head, and knives stuck in the bodies of members of the Burton family—*all* of these tools were supplementary. Each of the families slain between November 1909 and April 1912 had been *primarily* brutalized with a standard ax. The implement was almost always found at the crime scene, though its location was not reported in the Burton family case.

While it would be easy to label the Marshall family attack a crude copycat of the axman due to the obvious difference in both weapon selection and body count, that conclusion does not allow for known behavioral shifts regarding certain types of serial killers. On one hand, if the attack was committed by a singular axman who'd spent nearly the last two and a half years turning the rice belt into a hellish nightmare for Black families, perhaps there simply wasn't a standard ax nearby. Given that the weapon in many of the other crime scenes was later discovered to have come from the immediate vicinity, any sort of improvisation would have reflected the implements that were in physical proximity to the Marshall home. On the other hand, if the assault was rooted in the Sacrifice Church's directives, using a small hatchet versus a common ax likely did not undermine the faith community's sacrificial mandates. So, although the weapon of choice in this crime was certainly a curious one, the circumstances were similar enough for everyday folks to add the Marshall family to the ever-growing victim roster.

Similarly, the lack of additional victims could have reflected a common trajectory for serial killers who effectively "burn out" of their crimes.[28] In these cases, an individual engages in murders until a point when the fantasy that drives their compulsion to kill becomes unsatisfying. Sometimes, in a quest to recreate that initial euphoria, these killers grow reckless. This spiral can coincide with overconfidence, which can cause perpetrators to make mistakes. Perhaps, then, the axman had either misjudged the force needed to wield that smaller weapon with fatal intent or miscalculated the number of people in the house—or both. It would have taken precision to overpower four grown adults with a hatchet, especially if the killer was used to a tool with more heft. Thus, the assailant could have realized this mistake mid-attack and strategically tried to stun everyone in the house before finishing off the victims. The job would be significantly easier to pull off if all occupants were writhing in pain; otherwise, continually hacking away at one person would give others in the house time to confront their attacker or escape. Yet, in such a scenario, an almost-victim screaming or moaning would surely attract attention. Thus, Eva's wails could have interrupted the plan to return to Ike and Carrie, leaving them in unfathomable agony as the assailant slipped away, fantasy incomplete. Perhaps her screams had been enough to not only save her life, but the lives of Carrie Burney and those two young boys.

/ / /

Although modern readers can theorize about why the nonfatal Hempstead attack should be included in the axman saga using established research into criminal profiling and psychology, investigators in early 1900s America did not even have the vocabulary of serial killing to explain what was happening in the rice belt. Instead, they relied on their own detective techniques that involved trained bloodhounds, selective coroners' juries, imprecise evidence collection, and rudimentary blood testing. Not surprisingly, then, in the aftermath of the assault on the Marshall family residence, lawmen looked for artifacts the killer might have left in the house or surrounding area. While they initially believed there were no clues at the crime scene, in a matter of days a "bundle of rags" was supposedly found about a block away.[29] The "shape and condition" of the pile caused the authorities to speculate that a single killer had wrapped their feet with the fabric, effectively silencing their movements.[30] Perhaps the murderer had indeed tiptoed around the house, using muffled steps to gain a marginal and short-lived advantage over the occupants. Then again, the intruder may not have bothered to conceal the sounds of impending death but simply wiped their feet on the scraps at some point during or after the violent ordeal. Maybe the rags were simply in the wrong place at the right time—a random heap that had nothing to do with the attack, but got roped in nonetheless because the alternative of no physical evidence whatsoever seemed far too unsettling.

Besides the curious bundle of rags, it was reported that the assailant left behind a shoe—a man's shoe—while fleeing the scene.[31] This seemed to confirm various suspicions that the axman was indeed a man. Yet, the image of a one-shoed murderer hobbling unevenly around Hempstead under the cover of darkness raises a whole lot more questions than it answers. Why go through the process of silencing one's feet to leave behind a shoe? Even if the rags were misplaced, why leave one shoe behind and, presumably, not the other?

In general, leaving physical evidence behind—like a shoe or a bundle of rags—did not automatically give the authorities the kind of advantage modern forensics would afford today. Finding a generic men's shoe would simply have resulted in a basic analysis of the treads, an attempt by bloodhounds to pick up the owner's scent, and interviews of neighbors, friends, and "suspicious characters" to see if someone knew something about the shoe's mysterious origins.[32] Perhaps, then, the discovery of this clue contributed to the unsatisfactory arrest of two Black men the day after the Marshall family attack.[33] A regional newspaper reported that one of the men was Alice Marshall's own husband.[34] Not surprisingly, he was released in time to attend his wife's funeral. The apprehension—and release—of these suspects thus did not negate what public consciousness knew: the axman had come to Hempstead. It seemed the murders were inevitable, and it would be months before any additional named suspects were arrested.[35] By that point, fear of the elusive killer had ensured this attack was squarely aligned with a pantheon of others.

That people apparently did not make much of a potential discrepancy between this crime and its predecessors is telling. The Marshalls lived within a few blocks of the train tracks, but it wasn't the Sunset Route of the Southern Pacific Railroad. Their home was near the Sunset-Central lines of the Houston & Texas Central Railroad.[36] Technically, however, the H&TC had been under Southern Pacific control since 1883, though it operated independently until the 1920s.[37] Whether a layperson—or a determined assassin—knew the intricacies of turn-of-the-century railroad business is difficult to say. What is clear is that Hempstead was not located along the east-west line that linked all of the previous ax murders. Had the killer actually come to Waller County, or was the attack on the Marshalls staged to resemble the axman's crimes?

Admittedly, there is strong evidence that the Marshall family was not assaulted by the axman. Not only was the crime scene not located along the Southern Pacific Railroad, but the presence of survivors may indicate an inexperienced wannabe murderer rather than an increasingly dissatisfied serial killer. Moreover, the weapon of choice—a hatchet—was dissimilar to every other axman attack. The discovery of the shoe and bundle of rags also represent anomalies compared to the previous crimes.

All of these discrepancies can be explained in ways that don't undermine linkages to the earlier ax murders in the rice belt, however. If anything, the differences between this attack and the prior ones could align with observed serial killer behavior and/or shifts in investigative strategies. The most compelling rationale for including the Marshall family attack in the axman canon is simple: people at the time firmly believed this crime was connected to the others. Evidentiary inconsistencies did not mean—and *could not mean*—that the Marshalls were assaulted by anyone other than the axman.

/ / /

In early April 1912, Clementine Barnabet had confessed to murdering four families with an ax between Lafayette and Crowley, Louisiana. While she may not have taken credit for any of the crimes that occurred outside of Acadia and Lafayette parishes, Clementine's terrifying prediction and manipulative responses enabled national media to lay blame for all of the axman murders on this young Black woman. In so doing, Clementine's self-presentation swirled with journalists' interpretations to construct a powerful, if contradictory, image of a Black female serial killer.

Then, less than two weeks later, the Burtons were murdered in San Antonio in the early morning hours of Friday, the 12th. On Sunday, the Marshall family home was attacked in Hempstead, leaving one dead at the scene, another dying, and others scarred and traumatized. Had Clementine guessed correctly about the axman's incessant rampage? Or had she orchestrated these latest crimes? Obviously, she could not have physically slaughtered either family (or any of the families killed in 1912, for that matter). Yet, Clementine could have masterminded their deaths. She could have been part of a religiously motivated killing ring. She could have been a scapegoat. She could have murdered exactly four families, as she said, or she could have killed no one at all.

It is also possible that Clementine Barnabet and the axman were entirely unrelated. Perhaps an ax-wielding serial killer was targeting Black families along the Southern Pacific Railroad. Maybe this assailant had committed all of the crimes; maybe they had done some of them. Then again, perhaps a copycat killer was emulating either Clementine or the axman, acting on the belief that their murders would be linked to someone else. Or, despite the overwhelming evidence of uncanny similarities between the murders, the crimes could have been eerily coincidental but otherwise unrelated. In the spring of 1912, any of these prospects could have been *the* truth.

It was precisely the many truths swirling about in the late spring and early summer of 1912 that had folks on edge. People had followed Clementine's saga and they knew her name. It had been traded on lips pursed with disdain and fear. The dizzying rumors—about her as a scapegoat-turned-comrade-turned-mastermind-turned-copycat-killer-turned-anything-imaginable—kept everyone talking about this mysterious young woman who was currently sitting behind bars in a local jail in Lafayette. Yet, her confinement didn't square neatly with the Burtons being murdered and the Marshalls being attacked. People knew there was a disconnect, but they didn't definitively understand what was disconnected.

By this point, the axman—and (possibly) Clementine Barnabet—had wrought havoc on the rice belt for more than two years. So, when she confessed *and* her prediction came true in under a fortnight, the fear that had blanketed communities for months on end exploded into unrestrained panic. The nightmare people had been living through had suddenly become even more ghoulish.

In Hempstead, where the Marshalls had just been attacked, the Black community gathered at local churches and stayed up at night "with lights burning brightly."[38] Families posted guards at their homes while refusing to sleep. Presumably they were armed. Reportedly, some even left the area, moving away for safety.[39] Likewise, in San Antonio, where the Burtons had been murdered, Black residents gathered their weapons and became nighttime sentinels.[40] They brought their dogs indoors, raised curtains, and burned lights perpetually, attempting to give the illusion that their residence was a beehive of activity at all hours.[41] People were willing to do anything—*everything*—to prevent themselves and their loved ones from becoming the next victims of the axman.

But it wasn't just Black communities in Hempstead and San Antonio that responded to the latest assaults. The rice belt had been under siege for years. The most recent crimes incited Black residents of the entire region and beyond. Thus, when the *El Paso Herald* reported that "nobody cares . . . that the ax man is mighty busy exterminating whole families in Central Texas," the newspaper meant that white folks were indifferent to the recent murders.

In reality, the race-specific concerns were more muddied. According to one regional outlet, both Black and white communities in Waller County were "badly frightened" following the Hempstead attack.[42] Another implied there was nothing for white folks in the rice belt to worry about because the slaughters had been "confined to the colored race."[43] And yet another suggested white Louisianans were "wrought up" over the murders because they'd supposedly led to an increase in *other* crimes in the area.[44] Thus, in the aftermath of Clementine's confession, the regional response to the axman crimes varied depending on one's proximity—geographic, racial, economic, etc.—to the madness.

Black communities in the rice belt felt the axman madness—and Clementine's implied power—most acutely. Understandably, these were the neighborhoods directly impacted by the crimes, where families, friends, employers, church members, and more learned of the untimely demise of folks just like them. Yet, Clementine's springtime confession granted her power within more than her own community. Fear of the axman—and, by extension, the axwoman—permeated regions of Louisiana and Texas heretofore unscathed by the fatal violence. This meant that Clementine wielded an imagined power over both Black *and* white Americans far beyond the scope of the crimes she claimed to have committed. Black folks feared what she would do to their communities; white folks feared what she represented. Although these forms of terror were different—one actionable and one conceptual—they embodied types of power that belied evidentiary support. Her ability to manipulate the press—and the press's ability to manipulate her—had coalesced around the perfect storm: the construction of a powerful Black female serial killer.

/ / /

The attacks on the Burton and Marshall families in April 1912, coming on the heels of Clementine Barnabet's attention-grabbing confession earlier that month, led to a flurry of efforts by Black communities within and beyond the rice belt to protect themselves from the unknowable. From town to town, people not only engaged in self-defense strategies as they had before, but the seemingly unceasing nature of the chaos meant that folks were increasingly terrified, distrustful, and jumpy. This shift in people's emotional and physiological responses to the axman led to complicated and sometimes contradictory efforts at community care. Genuine self-defense strategies intersected with earnest mistakes, intentional mischief, selfish desires, fatal accidents, and more. Black communities united and splintered, evidence of how failures to not only solve the axman crimes, but of white society to take them seriously in the first place, drove Black residents to "work out among themselves their own salvation or damnation."[45] Black folks' panic was the result of fear of the unknowable *and* fear that white authorities' indifference and ineffectiveness could cost them their lives.

In Columbus, Texas, for example, Black men and women rotated nighttime sentinels by bunking multiple families in the same house.[46] Concern regarding overcrowding and poor ventilation was so prevalent that the authorities cautioned the frightened about unwittingly subjecting their loved ones to another killer: tuberculosis. White officials chided Black Texans for addressing one problem and creating another, revealing how race and class created a chasm of experiences in how people responded to the axman. Yet, even the regional press conceded that folks would not be opening windows to let in fresh air—the axman was lurking.

In Beaumont, a family reported someone trying to pry open a window to their house, located only one and a half blocks from where the Dove family had been murdered two months before.[47] In Diana, a map dot just north of the oil city, a "mad" Black man was captured and restrained by local residents who feared two things: the axman and the police. Rather than turn him over to the authorities, his "friends" kept a watchful eye on him.[48] These kinds of incidents highlighted how Black communities negotiated two kinds of fear: that of the unknowable (the axman) and that of the knowable (white lawmen). The arrival of the axman pushed Black communities to their breaking points, but it did not permit them to disregard their understandings of Jim Crow society.

In Brenham, twenty miles to the east of Hempstead, where the Marshalls had recently been attacked, Black folks were apparently so scared of the axman that they were stealing cartridges from local stores to load their weapons.[49] The city marshal was fed up with the fact that they had been "discharging guns and pistols" with increasing frequency and threatened to begin making arrests to quell the "senseless alarm."[50] Clearly, the officer could not empathize with how the unknowable nature of the crimes meant that any assumption of sensibility could also prove deadly. Yet again, race and class shaped how people in the same area experienced the axman: Black folks understood their situation as urgent, terrifying, and possible, while white residents believed the threat was nebulous and hyperbolic.

In Smithville, a Black boy named Ernest Smothers was unable to sleep one mid-April night. He got up and moved around, perhaps trying to ease his restlessness. Occupants of the house grew anxious and, with their "nerves tautened" by the exhaustive watch groups the community had organized, surmised the axman had come to town.[51] Ernest was shot and killed by West Duvall, one of the makeshift neighborhood guards, who mistook him for the elusive killer.[52] Then, hearing the gunshot, another neighbor, Max Warren, ran toward the residence to provide assistance. Realizing there was no significant threat, he headed back to his home. *Other* watchmen, likely equally harried from trying to know the unknowable, assumed the axman was making his getaway. In a moment, Max Warren was also dead, having been shot by his own neighbors. In a town roughly fifty miles from the closest ax murders—a town nowhere near the Sunset Route—there were two more victims, not of the axman *precisely,* but of what the axman came to represent. That's how irrational fear of the unknowable had to function; any assumption of safety could (and sometimes did) turn naively fatal in an instant. White society's indifference to or indignation at the axman panic was a stark contrast to the real and deadly consequences Black communities experienced while protecting themselves from an unknowable threat against which the authorities could not (or would not) provide security.

In Navasota, a Black woman woke up screaming in the middle of the night, convinced that the axman had "sprinkled some fluid" on the beds of her sleeping family members, presumably preparing to murder them all.[53] A couple days later, a Black man in the same town took aim through his front door at the sound of a "stealthy step" trying to enter.[54] In an instant, he shot and killed his dog. The rapid sale of "weapons and ammunition" to Black folks in Navasota in an incredibly short span of time also led to the speedy use of said firearms. The shooting was so bad that the local paper opined it "rivaled the siege of Vicksburg."[55] While this statement was likely inflated, there was no denying that Black people were not taking chances on being the next victim of the axman, nor on white authorities protecting them. That white Texans viewed Black folks' preparedness as over-the-top reflected not the reality of the unsolvable crimes, but of people's presumed proximity to the madness. The white press could proclaim that "the colored people need have no greater fear of danger here than elsewhere" without understanding that the local Black community's fear wasn't greater in Navasota than elsewhere: Black folks *throughout* the region were absolutely terrified.[56] Fear of the axman was totalizing to southern Black communities in a way that white society could not understand.

In Gonzales, a mysterious anonymous Black woman was run out of town by Black residents after claiming to be a member of the "Church of Sacrifice."[57] Who knows if she was telling the truth. Something similar happened in Lockhart, where the police were summoned when a Black woman's "dress and mysterious actions" raised suspicions among local residents.[58] Apparently her explanations weren't satisfactory, she was placed in jail, and then forced out of town on the first train the following morning. In Bartlett, an older Black woman adorned with "fake hair," multiple skirts, and "various trinkets" was believed to be a Voodoo practitioner *and* "an 'ax' woman."[59] After she was arrested, local Black folks told the police that they would kill her if she was released into their custody. In Belton, *another* Black woman clad in a purple skirt, a large hat, and a "black veil with white cloth tied over her mouth" professed that she was "half crazy and half ax-man."[60] The local Black community panicked. Clearly, outsiders—and those dressed like outsiders—were not welcome in many towns at the height of the axman chaos. They were unknown, the killer was unknowable, and the risk was simply too great.

That these communities summoned the authorities need not be interpreted as evidence of amicable relationships between lawmen and Black Texans. Jim Crow ideologies meant Black folks knew the risks they incurred by inviting armed white men into their neighborhoods to resolve their problems. Soliciting the police thus reveals the extent to which Black communities were willing to trade one kind of possible violence for another during the axman madness. The police represented the lesser of two evils, not a guaranteed form of protection.

Sometimes, however, people leveraged the uncertainty of the ax murders to their own benefit. In Marshall, a Black man was arrested in connection with a grocery store robbery. After a bit of a skirmish, he was released by the authorities. They said he "had out-talked the officers, saying that he was sure that the dreaded 'axe man' had come for him."[61] He was able to avoid criminal charges by saying that his actions were related to self-defense from the axman. *That* is the kind of convoluted way this madness functioned. A criminalized Black man convinced white lawmen that, though he'd engaged in illegal behaviors, his actions were justified because of a real but unknowable threat.

These examples don't even begin to cover the growing list of small Texas towns—Cuero, Huntsville, Hearne, Eden, Taylor, Martin, and Wharton—where Black residents braced themselves for the ax murderer by organizing nighttime vigilance committees and refusing to leave home after sunset.[62] Nor, for that matter, do they cover the state's large cities that also feared the axman. Perhaps Houston summed up the approach many Black communities in the rice belt had adopted by April 1912: "shoot first" and ask questions later.[63]

Meanwhile, Louisiana had its own chaos to deal with. In DeSoto Parish, rumors and fear allowed a domestic dispute between a Black man and a Black woman to be interpreted as a nocturnal visit of the axman.[64] In Donaldsonville, Black residents linked the axman and the "glass man," a silent killer who supposedly snuck shards of glass into people's food in a likely excruciating attempt to murder them.[65] In Junction City, concern that an "itinerant preacher" was really the axman caused Black residents of the town to threaten the newcomer with such ferocity that local police took the Black man into custody "for safe keeping."[66] He hightailed it out of town as soon as he was released. In Algiers, a Black woman pleaded with the authorities for protection after she found a "can of dynamite" under her house and a cryptic note with the same Bible verse that had been seen on the Broussard family's front door when they were murdered in Lake Charles back in January. Although the officers thought the case wasn't serious, Bessie Jones lived in "mortal fear" that she would be killed by the axman.[67] That dynamite had not been used in any of the crimes so far was irrelevant to her. So much about the madness was unknowable that it was better to be safe than sorry.

All the way in Mississippi, a state previously immune to the ax murders, reports of several notices posted on Black folks' homes claiming that the axman had come to Gloster to slaughter two families as an act of salvation excited fears and produced panic. According to one regional paper, the missive read:

> Notice—To the colored people of my race: I am now among you and you have been warned to stop your sinful ways and you won't listen. Now in two weeks I am going to destroy two families to save you all.
>
> THE AX MAN.[68]

It didn't help that there *was* a Louisiana connection: a "strange man" who claimed to be from Baton Rouge reportedly was traveling through the area fixing timepieces and umbrellas. And there was an equally suspicious woman with him. But he supposedly didn't have any watch-repairing tools on his person. Instead, he had a Bible. The authorities were called and both outsiders were whisked away to jail.

Towns that had never been visited by the elusive assassin and places that were not located on the presumed murder route from New Orleans to San Francisco sincerely believed they were in imminent danger. While local Black communities had employed a variety of self-defense techniques in early 1912, by the late spring their strategies had grown more desperate. This shift was partially prompted by the unsettling reality that Clementine had predicted the continuation of the crimes. It was also fueled by time itself. Indeed, the hallmark of serial murder is also the most unnerving aspect: a series of violence has to take place. That the rice belt was still under attack after more than two years—and that the authorities appeared to be no closer to cracking the case—meant that communities had reached their breaking point.

During the first few months of 1912, media outlets had bemoaned the regional economic consequences of Black flight from the rice belt in the wake of the axman murders.[69] Back then, they had likely over-exaggerated the certainty with which Black outmigration was a given response to the crimes. By mid-April, however, local responses to the unknowable nature of the killings were having an undeniable physical impact on Black laborers in the region. Multiple white newspapers in southwestern Louisiana and southeastern Texas deplored the fact that Black residents were apparently so dedicated to their self-defense strategies that they were falling asleep on the job in the daytime.[70] Via the Associated Press, readers across the country learned that fear from the axman was so severe in the rice belt that some Black people had even stopped working altogether, "making the labor problem serious."[71] While it would be easy to argue these stories were couched in racist stereotypes and therefore should be considered unreliable, the texts are proof that the region's Black communities experienced physical symptoms of sustained terror. And, if Black people's bodies had to cope with the stress of fitful sleep, chronic worry, perpetual anxiety, and continual dread, then it is reasonable to believe that their white employers also felt the effects of the axman. It did not matter that all but one of the murder victims were Black; by the spring of 1912 the killer had implicitly targeted a large swath of the Jim Crow South.

/ / /

It wasn't just Black communities that responded to the chaos that enveloped the rice belt by mid-April 1912. Regional authorities were baffled about the crimes in their jurisdictions. At this particular moment in the axman saga, it was Bexar County Sheriff John Tobin who embraced some of the most telling strategies. If any lawman was genuinely impacted by what was going on—so much so that he was willing to risk his livelihood over it—it was Sheriff Tobin. He had investigated the murder of the Casaway family back in March 1911, eventually building what appeared to be a strong case against William McWilliams. Just over a year later, he returned to that same east side neighborhood and learned of the slaughter of the Burtons. In the intervening months, the officer had kept up with the latest axman news, eventually relying on his knowledge of the scope of the problem to try to protect his city.

This is why, for example, it was not surprising that Sheriff Tobin had a "full and complete account" of the latest San Antonio murder sent to his counterparts in Glidden, Hempstead, Beaumont, and Lake Charles.[72] In the aftermath of the murder of the Burton family, the lawman had arrested two "voodoo doctors" as suspects.[73] When the Marshalls were attacked a few days later, he then reached the conclusion that one of the men he'd apprehended was "the companion" of the Hempstead assailant.[74] Like so many of his counterparts in law enforcement, the Bexar County investigator had followed the implicit theory that the axman was Black. Although he wavered as to whether the motive was religious, racial, or both, Sheriff Tobin paid close attention to suspects who "expressed an antipathy for mulattoes."[75] Apparently, he was swayed by various arguments that the axman targeted families with at least one "light-colored" member.[76] Yet, if the officer sincerely thought the crimes in his city were connected to those elsewhere in the rice belt, then it seems there was a major flaw in narrowing in on an antimiscegenation angle. After all, it was only in the Alamo City cases where explicit conversations about the potentially interracial composition of the families occurred. Elsewhere in the region, those slain were simply Black.

Still, Sheriff Tobin got a boost to this theory with a fascinating letter he received roughly a week after the Burtons were murdered. Reportedly, the note read:

> Dear Sir: I want all of you at the city hall and court house to understand that we are not negroes that are going around killing negroes who [are] married to half white women. We are sure white men and you will be surprised to know

> who we are. All negroes married to half or full white women shall be murdered. We have lots of money to back us. We go from city to city.
>
> We are white men like you, but find us if you can. Yours very truly.[77]

Despite the contents of the letter, Sheriff Tobin was convinced it was written by "a negro religious crank."[78] Perhaps he held this thought because it was easier to relate to the other ax murders. Or perhaps he had fallen victim to his own biases—likely reinforced by Jim Crow society—and therefore *wanted* the axman to be Black. Yet, if Sheriff Tobin was wrong—if the killers actually turned out to be multiple white men with financial support and an antimiscegenation mission—then he wasn't the only investigator who had devoted significant resources looking in the wrong direction. Plus, it would mean that Black communities that feared the wrath of one of their own were misguided. Although this curious letter offered an entirely new way to conceptualize the axman murders in theory, regional authorities continued to look for Black assailants.

As Sheriff Tobin worked his own leads, he recognized that Black San Antonians were petrified, and his officers simply could not provide them with the assurances they needed. In the aftermath of the Burton family murder, some Black men appealed to the authorities for "permits to carry weapons," while others decided to forgo the formal process and arm themselves anyway.[79] Members of the community also asked the city police department to assign more officers to patrol their neighborhoods, but they were told no more deputies could be appointed. Sheriff Tobin, as a representative of all of Bexar County, circumvented the efforts of the city authorities by commissioning a number of Black men as "deputy sheriffs."[80] Evidence suggests some of these individuals were appointed within days of the murder of the Burton family.[81] In response, San Antonio police officers began arresting the recently commissioned deputies for "unlawfully carrying arms."[82] They were fined $100 each (over $3,300 in 2025).[83] A clash between the county sheriff's office and the city's police department ensued, mere months before a local election could possibly cost John Tobin his job.[84]

According to the city officials, Sheriff Tobin had the audacity to deputize "nearly two hundred negroes."[85] Worse, those men now believed they had the right to carry all kinds of weapons, including revolvers. This shift in power in San Antonio not only threatened the lives of the city's police force, they argued, but it was also a gross overreach of the laws of the state. Meanwhile, Sheriff Tobin acknowledged deputizing some men, but it was no more than dozen and possibly just six. Angry at the seemingly preposterous outrage over his decision, John Tobin did not mince words when he commented: "That the police department should view the arming of these negroes with alarm is rather absurd to my mind. The appointments were made solely because of the unrest created in the negro resident districts following the murders committed by the 'axman.' In these districts the protection afforded by the city police is practically null, and I received many applications for deputy appointments."[86] In those three sentences Sheriff Tobin captured the stakes of the recent crimes, the staying power of the axman trope, the limits of white law enforcement to effectively protect *all* members of the local community, and the right of Black residents to engage in communal- and self-defense. For all the ways he might have relied on certain assumptions while conducting his own investigations into the axman, it seems the Bexar County officer did genuinely have the welfare of Black San Antonians on his mind in the spring of 1912. It also seems that Sheriff Tobin's approach to this situation was unique. While he believed that the city's Black community had the right to protect itself, other white authorities had declared Black armed self-defense not just unconscionable, but illegal. Powerful white men disagreed not only about the legitimacy of the threat of the axman, but about their own counterparts' ability to respond.

Sheriff Tobin's explanation of his decision did not sit well with city officials, despite him being the highest lawman in the county. A grand jury was summoned to investigate the sheriff's own investigation into the axman cases.[87] The presiding judge expressed sorrow that the ax murderer had returned to San Antonio, but advised the jurymen to "see that pistol-toting is stopped" and to address the fact that "no officer should be allowed to deputize more deputies than the law allows."[88] Although the sheriff had not overstepped his role, the judge's assessment implied that the city's policing institutions needed to consolidate their own power rather than outsource it to Black men. In this way, the authorities prioritized themselves in the face of incontrovertible evidence that Black San Antonians were in danger—whether due to the axman or *fear* of the axman.

Efforts to punish Sheriff Tobin via the grand jury for appointing "the most reputable" Black men as temporary deputies were a response to the optics of the entire ordeal.[89] A white man—the highest-ranking member of the county's law enforcement apparatus no less—had publicly cast his support behind San Antonio's Black community. His willingness to overrule the city police department's authority was a de facto indictment of the agency's ability—or lack thereof—to protect some of its taxpayers. That the city would respond with a public shaming of its own was both an explicit indictment of John Tobin and an implicit snub at Black San Antonians. Just because one powerful white man supported them did not mean they would be any safer from the axman.

Before summer's end, the axman returned to San Antonio. One fateful mid-August day, the Dashiells made the innocent decision to leave a window slightly open for "a little air."[90] Although they'd had an axman scare back in June, the family presumably weighed the likelihood of another attack against a miserable night's fitful sleep and decided to take their chances.[91] Around 4:00 a.m., Lula Dashiell awoke to "the blow of the ax" on her arm and started screaming as she tried to shield her fifteen-year-old daughter, Harriet, from the attack.[92] Hearing the commotion, James Dashiell, the husband and father of the Gibbs Street residence, grabbed a gun and took aim at the intruder.[93] His son did too. According to the press, they missed. According to the family, they didn't.[94] The Dashiells survived, and the prevailing narrative implied the axman got away. An alternative narrative—one that has survived over one hundred years via oral tradition in the Dashiell family—is shared in appendix B.

As people tried to speculate as to who would have possibly wanted to harm the Dashiell family, San Antonio's Black community knew this latest assault was not a coincidence: the Dashiells lived just one block away from the Burtons, the family that had been murdered back in April. Moreover, the Dashiells *also* lived within a few blocks of the Casaways—the family that was axed in March 1911—*and* the two families were best friends. Plus, all three families were believed to have transgressed the color line in some way. James Dashiell, once identified as "a mulatto," was the son of an enslaved woman and her owner, a prosperous Texas rancher.[95] Carrie Burton was mistaken for a white woman, while Elizabeth Casaway was confirmed to be one. In aggregate, Black San Antonians *knew* these crimes were the work of a single perpetrator: the axman. That Clementine Barnabet had confessed to some—but not all—of the region's ax murders did not change the local knowledge Black folks constructed. The axman *had* to be the guilty party.[96]

/ / /

The assaults on the Burtons and Dashiells in San Antonio not only implied that Clementine's prediction had been correct, but that the killing of the Casaway family back in March 1911 likely wasn't as isolated as the authorities had once believed. The same week the Burton family was murdered, the Marshalls were attacked in Hempstead over two hundred miles away. For the first time ever, people had come face-to-face with the axman and survived. This reality was repeated in August 1912 with the attack on the Dashiell family, and they would privately identify the assailants—plural—as being white men. Publicly, they were "unable to furnish any description of the man."[97]

These assaults—the fatal slaughter of the Burtons and the generally non-fatal attacks on the Marshalls and Dashiells—fueled widespread panic in the rice belt and beyond. Quite obviously, the one person who'd confessed to *any* of the axman crimes could not have physically wielded the weapon that maimed these families—or any of the 1912 families. But Clementine had warned that the murders would continue, and indeed they had. Perhaps she knew more than she was saying. Or perhaps she had successfully bluffed. Or perhaps she had guessed correctly about a crime spree in which she was not involved.

Although Black communities had been engaging in self-defense techniques at least since the early months of 1912, their approach to protecting themselves and their loved ones reached a fever pitch following Clementine's confession. Her admission of guilt followed immediately by more crimes meant the axman—or at least *an* axman—was still on the loose. Plus, the murders had developed a sense of inevitability since late February. Combined, these realities forced local Black folks to respond to a sort of fatalism that was anxiety-producing and community-breaking. Outsiders *and* neighbors became suspects. Family members became foes. Creativity became condemnation. Assistance became assault. And simply being outside in the dark became a dangerous activity.[98] Responding to the unknowable threat of the axman had fundamentally reshaped life in the rice belt. In so doing, it had finally impacted white society via economic consequences. No longer was there exaggerated concern about the region's agricultural output; worries about Black folks' labor locally highlighted just how much the axman was driving their decision-making. For all of these anxieties, however, Black communities' armed self-defense was still an unsettling and highly politicized undercurrent of this moment. White society was annoyed by the financial fallout of the axman, but still far removed from the physiological stressors caused by the unknowable. As such, it was easy to bemoan challenges with Black laborers while simultaneously disregarding the legitimacy of their desire for (armed) self-defense.

The unknown killer had power over not only Black communities in southwestern Louisiana and southeastern Texas, but also over local white politics. Bexar County Sheriff John Tobin had investigated his second axman crime by April 1912 and had kept abreast of the murders that had dotted the area since at least March 1911. Thus, when he controversially deputized no more than a dozen Black men to patrol their neighborhoods following the Burton family slaughter, he did so with broad knowledge that police across the region had proven ineffective, that evidence suggested the murders would continue, and that Black residents of the rice belt were teetering on the brink of hysteria. Yet, what he viewed as a public safety need was seen as an implied critique of the city's police department, dragging the axman saga into the realm of local politics. Sheriff Tobin won reelection that year, but not before his judgment and credibility were called into question. That a white sheriff defended Black folks' right to *armed* self-defense publicly and unapologetically showcases the stakes of the elusive axman: the sheer panic the killer had created had the power to bend—but not break—Jim Crow expectations.

8

Clementine's Trial

Mental Illness versus Moral Perversion

When Clementine Barnabet confessed to a series of murders in April 1912, she had been in jail in Lafayette, Louisiana, since the previous November. She sat in her cell while additional crimes were committed in the spring and summer, awaiting her fate within the state's criminal justice system. In October, the young Black woman would finally get her day in court.

During her highly publicized trial, three different—though overlapping—versions of Clementine emerged. Up first was the picture her court-appointed attorneys sought to paint. Next was the image the state sought to create. Finally, there was Clementine's presentation of herself when she addressed the court. Although no trial transcripts have been located, other records can be used to cobble together a narrative of what likely transpired over those tense October weeks. In the end, both the verdict and Clementine's reaction to it demonstrated just how atypical this saga had become.

/ / /

Judge William Campbell presided over an inaugural meeting to select a grand jury to review the 175-case docket for the October 1912 term of the Eighteenth District Court of Louisiana.[1] Campbell, a Lafayette native in his mid-fifties who had served as the city's mayor in the early 1900s, was well acquainted with not only the parish's legal apparatus, but also the culture of southwestern Louisiana.[2] In the Jim Crow South, both grand and petit juries tended to look a whole lot more like Campbell than the peers of the defendants. White men decided the fate of Black men and women.

It's hard to say whether the grand jury's members actually deliberated Clementine's case. She had confessed to killing people, which was illegal. Her confession probably sped her case into the "trial necessary" category without much fanfare. Moreover, reporters noted a cold statement Clementine made as she awaited the grand jury's decision. Supposedly—although this is a tenuous attribution—she said: "I do not care what they do with me—they can hang me if they wish."[3]

When Clementine finally stood before the grand jury, she was informed of the charges against her and that a true bill was returned.[4] Then she "stood mute."[5] Was Clementine apathetic toward her fate, or did she believe her faith would save her from a mortal end? Was she a sphinxlike killer who relished in cryptic confessions and defiance in the face of death?[6] Or was she a scared young Black woman who put up a protective front to shield herself from probing eyes?

Although it is impossible to know the answers to these questions, what was undeniably true was that Clementine Barnabet was about to become the center of national and international attention yet again. Hundreds of news outlets followed her sensational trial, boomeranging the young Black woman into the limelight roughly six months after she had first become a household name. Once more, print media empowered Clementine.

/ / /

The young Black woman's trio of public defenders was a mismatched crew of white men with varied legal experience. George P. Lessley, a Church Point native, graduated from Louisiana State University's law school sometime in the early 1910s.[7] Jean Jacques Fournet, a St. Martinville native, was sworn in as a "practicing attorney" by Louisiana's Supreme Court in 1910.[8] John L. Kennedy, born in Lafayette but raised in New Orleans, had earned his law degree from Tulane University in 1892.[9]

By the time Clementine's case headed for trial, it was widely publicized that the state intended to convict her "independent of her repeated confessions of guilt."[10] Meanwhile, her attorneys were banking on the convoluted nature of her statements. It was true that she had confessed, but that alone didn't mean she did what she said she did. If anything, it might mean she was insane, which was precisely what Clementine's lawyers intended to argue.

Labeling Clementine crazy was different from trying to prove her mental faculties were legally deficit. For that her attorneys petitioned the court to appoint a "lunacy commission" to ascertain the young woman's state of mind.[11] In their request, they explained that they wanted experts to determine Clementine's "consequent moral and legal accountability or non-accountability for her acts," and that such findings were paramount due to the stakes of the case: if convicted, she could be executed.[12] That Clementine's counsel framed her mental health around both moral *and* legal responsibility was a curious choice, especially because it was the latter angle that would determine her fate.

By law, the commission would be comprised of the parish coroner and the superintendents of the state's two public asylums.[13] Clementine's lawyers, meanwhile, had requested that a specialist "in the study and treatment of mental disease" be included.[14] If they found that Clementine was insane—either at the present moment or when she had ostensibly murdered the Randalls—she would be committed to the asylum at Pineville or Jackson.[15] If they found her sane, there was technically one more chance for her to be determined insane—by the judge or jury—and be committed.[16] If no one found Clementine insane, however, then she would be tried for murder. If found guilty, the law said she'd be executed.[17]

That Clementine's attorneys filed such a petition in the first place did not sit well with District Attorney Percy T. Ogden. He wanted to go to trial and was prepared to fight tooth and nail for the chance.[18] Presumably, then, the prosecutor was even more bothered when Judge Campbell appointed the lunacy commission.[19] The court selected Dr. Edward M. Hummel from New Orleans as the specialist.[20] Dr. Robert D. Voorhies, the physician for Southwestern Industrial Institute in Lafayette (today the University of Louisiana at Lafayette), was also named to serve.[21] Dr. John Tolson, a Lafayette resident, rounded out the appointments. On October 18, Lafayette Parish Deputy Sheriff Saul Broussard served the court's orders to the two local doctors.[22] Once the message reached New Orleans, the men would have fewer than three days to determine whether Clementine Barnabet was sane.

On October 20—the day before the trial was slated to begin—Dr. Hummel arrived in Lafayette and the commission's proceedings began. That evening, the three men questioned Clementine in the parish jail, examining her mental status.[23] Although the kinds of tests administered and the way they approached her are unknown, the context was the Jim Crow South. It is likely that the men harbored racial prejudice or had been trained to interpret certain behaviors through racialized and gendered lenses. To be clear, this is not suggesting that they were explicitly racist (though not precluding that possibility either), but that the world in which they functioned was racist. These doctors, well-to-do white men, were expected to be experts in their fields, and yet those very disciplines espoused problematic understandings of both Black folks and young women.[24] And here was Clementine, a young Black woman who was purported to be the epitome of evil, already renowned thanks to her own publicized confession and the speculations of the media. No matter what she did, it would be interpreted through a biased framework.

Reportedly, the lunacy commission completed two "long and thorough examinations" of Clementine and traced her family history, specifically looking at her father, her stepmother, and her brother. No evidence of "hereditary insanity" was identified.[25] Given all of the drama that had ensued with the Barnabets over the previous year, not to mention the family's negative reputation in the area, this finding might have come as a surprise. Raymond, Clementine's father, had supposedly left home once "after beating his wife."[26] Her brother Zepherin was already ensnared in the axman madness—having been arrested and released multiple times—and developed quite the reputation in the process. Another brother, Noah, had been convicted of bestiality five years earlier.[27] Dinah, meanwhile, was likely not Clementine's biological mother, so any examination of her offered a false genetic connection to the accused. That the commission pondered Clementine's familial history and then came to such a benign conclusion is perhaps evidence of their desire to render her responsible for these crimes rather than any definitive proof that her closest relatives did not suffer from mental illness.

The examinations of Clementine herself, and how the commissioners understood the subject they encountered, were the most informative. Dr. Hummel, for example, tried to use "hypnotic suggestion" to ascertain the truth from Clementine, and she, recognizing his intention, reportedly "balked" and then covered her face to avoid his tactics.[28] He also attempted to learn more about her accomplices, but the people she named were supposedly preposterous: either entirely fabricated or "too well known," a slight shift from those she'd implicated back in April.[29] The experts asked Clementine about her feelings regarding the death penalty, trying to get her to understand the gravity of the situation. In response, she apparently shrugged her shoulders and declared: "They can only kill me once."[30] This echoed a comment she had ostensibly made a few days earlier, stating: "I shall have at least this satisfaction when I go, that I sent a number ahead of me."[31] Whether Clementine's callous responses were a deliberate shielding or an honest admission is impossible to determine, but they certainly contributed to the commission's image of her as morally inferior and ignorant.

According to the doctors, Clementine's seemingly evasive comments were not proof that she suffered from either hallucinations or delusions, but that she did indeed know "right from wrong."[32] Apparently, one of the "wrong" characteristics she displayed was an overpowering desire for "gratification of her low sensual nature," implying that Clementine's professed crimes came from perverse sexual need.[33] Clementine had confessed to fondling dead bodies back in April, but even then the legitimacy of her claim had been questionable. Perhaps the consistency of this narrative made it more believable, so the doctors used it—alongside other observations—to reach a telling conclusion: Clementine was "nearer the brute than mankind."[34] In a single day, three white men criminalized and animalized a young Black woman under the guise of assessing her mental health. Then they presented their findings to the court:

> We, the undersigned physicians, appointed by your Honorable Court to inquire into the mental condition of one Clementine Barnabet now confined in the Parish jail under charge of murder, beg to report that we have conducted such an inquiry, carefully examining the subject, mentally and physically, and now offer the following conclusions:
>
> That we have found the subject to be morally depraved, unusually ignorant and of a low grade mentality, but not deficient in such a manner as to constitute her imbecile or idiotic. We found in the case no sign of an acquired insanity.
>
> It is, therefore, our joint opinion that the said Clementine Barnabet is sane in a legal sense of the word.[35]

With that, the lunacy commission determined that Clementine Barnabet was sane enough to stand trial.[36] The rhetoric of their findings played into stereotypes about Black criminality, drawing as much from Cesare Lombroso's theories of biological criminality as from early sociologists' assertions that Black criminality was proof of Black inferiority.[37] According to the commission, Clementine might have been "morally depraved" and "unusually ignorant," but not "[an] imbecile."[38]

The terms the commissioners used were not particularly offensive adjectives at this point in American history. Instead, these were scientific vocabularies denoting particular kinds of mental faculties (though not everyone agreed on their definitions). Charles Davenport, a famed eugenicist of the early 1900s, stated that "imbecility is due to the absence of some definite simple factor" that was inherited from one's parents.[39] Reverend James H. F. Peile favored a different take on the issue: "moral imbecile" was code for "habitual criminal," while physical imbecile was "the so-called unemployable."[40] Meanwhile, a popular textbook of the day defined insanity as "a general name for a great variety of conditions of mental lack of balance."[41] All of these ostensibly scientific terms weren't objective, let alone accurate. Plus, the metrics used to measure intelligence said a whole lot more about what mainstream society valued than the individual test-taker's knowledge or capacity. All of this is to say that finding Clementine semi-deficient was not fact, at least according to today's standards. It was convenient, but not conclusive, despite being presented as such.

In 1912 America, "acquired insanity"—as opposed to "congenital insanity" or "hereditary insanity"—was the result of a healthy brain having "suffered from morbid processes" that led to both physical and mental symptoms.[42] Further broken down into subcategories like "mania" and "katatonia," "acquired insanity" was believed to manifest in physical changes like weight loss, hallucinations (and delusions), incontinence, and a general impairment of judgment.[43] But these markers were just as subjective as those that ranked intelligence, and they were imbued with racial, gender, age, and class assumptions about whose behaviors were criminalized and whose were rewarded. It is not surprising that, based on the commission's findings, Clementine *did not* exhibit known characteristics of acquired insanity. She was a young Black woman from southwestern Louisiana who grew up in a working-class family during the Jim Crow era *and she had confessed to murder.* Arguably, the politics of the time meant Clementine had to be sane in order to stand trial, but also incompetent enough to fit stereotypes of Black criminality.[44]

Clementine's defense had taken a serious blow. Now it seemed that the best her attorneys could hope for was a bit of leeway regarding the terms of Clementine's sentence. They were betting on a "qualified verdict," which could leverage the commission's report and her "low standard of morality" to prevent capital punishment from being invoked.[45] In all probability, Lessley, Fournet, and Kennedy did not believe they stood a chance at exonerating their client. The evidence was compelling, and the commission's findings thwarted their original strategy.

Before the lunacy commission found that Clementine did not suffer from acquired insanity, newspapers reported that her lawyers had intended to argue specifically for *religious* insanity.[46] Whether this was journalistic flair added to a generic insanity case is impossible to determine, but it offers a fascinating defense worth unpacking. Given how much religious uncertainty circulated around the confessed axwoman, her attorneys may have been developing this novel angle. Yet, the commission's findings thwarted their plans. Just as a racial and gendered lens was used to find Clementine sane, albeit inferior, so too could a religious lens have been used to confirm her culpability. To have made a successful argument that Clementine was religiously insane would have required the deftest defense possible—a nimble threading of evidence that could have fundamentally shaken how the United States defined religious freedom for years to come. While this might sound hyperbolic, the broader context of such a defense reveals the dangerous slippages it could create.

The question centers around whether the beliefs Clementine practiced qualified as a religion as understood by society during the early twentieth century. If they did not, the question was whether her own worldview could be classified as insane. According to her lawyers, however, the question should have been whether Clementine Barnabet was so devoutly religious that she was certifiably insane. Yet, this line of logic was fundamentally too tricky to pursue. After all, if this were the case, then the line between fanaticism and craziness could no longer be demarcated. It was in the best interest of the Protestant nation to declare her competent enough to stand trial.

/ / /

On October 21, 1912, the same day the lunacy commission presented its findings, Clementine Barnabet was marched into a Lafayette courtroom to await her fate. Reportedly, as she processed in, she offered a "broad smile, or grin" to the Black observers she recognized.[47] Although the local paper agreed with its New Orleans counterpart that the crowd was comprised of interracial spectators, the Associated Press ran a story that claimed the courtroom was devoid of Black attendees due to a widespread belief that Clementine had the "evil eye" and was "capable of casting a spell upon one."[48] Perhaps the truth was somewhere in the middle: the trial was undoubtedly well-attended, likely by both Black and white spectators, but there may have been some who feared Clementine so much that they refused to be in the same room as her.[49] If that was the case, it seems Clementine Barnabet, even as she faced possible execution, had a significant amount of power as a young Black woman in Jim Crow America. The media had made her into a terrifying killer, and it appears she lived up to that image, regardless of its legitimacy.

Although Clementine stood before Judge William Campbell on that Monday, likely expecting to be tried, District Attorney Ogden filed a motion requesting the trial be postponed to give time for his star witness to arrive.[50] Both the defense *and* prosecution were doing everything in their power to gain the upper hand. If Clementine's lawyers could try to argue for insanity, then the state could rely on what was considered incontrovertible evidence: blood. To do so, however, they needed Dr. Abraham Metz's expertise. He was the "celebrated chemist" who had processed Clementine's bloodstained clothing in the aftermath of the Randall family murder, but he had to travel from New Orleans to Lafayette to testify.[51] The trial was delayed a few days.

On October 24, 1912, Clementine Barnabet again stood in a Lafayette courtroom. By noon, a twelve-person petit jury had been selected, comprised not of the defendant's peers, but exclusively of white men.[52] The judge who would give them instructions, William Campbell, was also a white man. The two lawyers who wanted to send her to the gallows, Percy T. Odgen and Ralph William Elliott, were white men as well. And her three court-appointed attorneys, George P. Lessley, Jean Jacques Fournet, and John L. Kennedy, were indeed also white men. If the descriptions of the crowd bear some truth, then it seems the people in the courtroom who looked like Clementine were also terrified of her. News reports implied they sided with the prosecution: if she were to be acquitted, Lafayette's Black community would lynch her.[53] Thus, Clementine, a young Black woman, faced a hostile environment when she walked into court that Thursday morning. Those representing the justice apparatus looked nothing like her and lived in a world of white male privilege strengthened by Jim Crow ideologies. Those who shared racial solidarity with her felt no allegiance to her as a confessed killer. Effectively, Clementine Barnabet was now alone, despite sitting in a courtroom full of people.

Unsurprisingly, the regional press claimed she regularly displayed "utter unconcern and indifference," accompanied by a "lack of emotion."[54] Maybe journalists minimized a subdued response, or maybe they faithfully reported Clementine's affect. Of course, this behavior could be interpreted as proof that the lunacy commission did not accurately diagnose the young woman's mental state. At the same time, it could be read as evidence of Clementine's participation in a larger culture of dissemblance stretching back to Black women's experiences under slavery.[55] Likely, the young woman did have an emotional response to her situation, but intentionally withheld its display from the prying eyes that had already rendered her fiendish, inhuman, and brutish. By remaining stoic, she could feed into these tropes while shielding herself. Perhaps this strategy was self-preservation.

The trial opened with District Attorney Ogden reading one of the indictments against Clementine—the one that charged her with the murder of Azema Randall.[56] Likely, it was not by happenstance that the defendant was first tried for the death of the wife and mother of the Randall family. Trying Clementine for the death of a woman—even a Black woman—played into subconscious narratives of slain women as innocent. Although Black men and women faced significant criminalization in the postbellum era, victimized Black womanhood—through rape, murder, lynching, and other violent acts—became increasingly more socially legible in print media, both fictional and newsprint, into the twentieth century.[57] In part, this visibility came from the victims themselves and the communities affected.[58] What complicated Clementine's situation, of course, was that both the victim *and* the perpetrator were Black women. Yet, intraracial-intragender violence was not without precedent.[59]

Prosecutor Ogden also knew that if the state could secure a conviction on this first charge, there was theoretically no need to proceed any further—the assumption was that Clementine would be executed. Perhaps that was part of the reason evidence related to the other bodies found at the crime scene was permissible, even though the jurymen were advised to focus on Azema's murder. Not surprisingly, then, after Attorney Odgen read the charge, Judge Campbell instructed the jury "as to the gravity of the case": a *woman's* life was on the line.[60]

The state presented its evidence first. They had issued subpoenas for at least nine people, summoning everybody from Clementine's former employer to the Lafayette coroner.[61] It was the latter, Dr. Louis A. Prejean, who was called as the first witness.[62] On the stand, he described the state of the victims' bloodied bodies found in the small cabin. He commented on the fluids "smeared on the walls."[63] Coroner Prejean surmised the Randall family had been dispatched with a "blunt instrument."[64]

Lafayette Parish Sheriff Louis Lacoste testified that he saw the bodies and an ax in the house. He and his deputies arrested Clementine at James Guidry's home, where she worked as a domestic servant. He noticed a "bloody rope hung on a gate."[65] An otherwise trivial witness, O. P. Guilbeau, confirmed that the rope was indeed *the* rope. Another minor witness, Police Chief Edwin Chargois, verified Clementine's arrest. Both Sheriff Lacoste and Deputy Sheriff

Alphonse Peck concurred that they found "bloody clothes" in Clementine's room and sent those articles to Dr. Abraham Metz for chemical analyses.[66]

Although a portion of Sheriff Lacoste's testimony described the crime scene he encountered that November morning, he also commented on his interactions with Clementine in the aftermath, telling the court that she had made a variety of confessions that were "varying one from another."[67] Two local police officers confirmed Clementine's "rambling stories," building further evidence that she was unreliable and untrustworthy.[68]

Meanwhile, Mrs. James Guidry stated that she could not remember what time Clementine had returned home the night the Randalls were murdered, but recalled that the young woman had been summoned by her husband to begin the next day's work at 4:00 a.m. When news of the killing reached Clementine that day, she reportedly began acting "unusual."[69] Incriminatingly, Mrs. Guidry identified the bloody clothing—presumably the same shirtwaist Dr. Metz had examined in January 1912—as attire given to Clementine.

The three members of the lunacy commission testified, rehashing many of the findings of their written report. They told the court that they had performed both a "mental and physical examination" of the defendant and reached the conclusion that she was sane.[70] Dr. Hummel explained that although Clementine was "legally responsible," she also had "perverted passion" that had presumably produced such murderous results.[71] As medical doctors, there is no doubt that the statements of these men were weighted more strongly than those of some of the other witnesses—and that their credibility would likely be scrutinized more heavily, too.

A similar assessment likely surrounded the much-awaited testimony of state chemist Abraham Metz. According to the Tulane professor, he received at least three key pieces of physical evidence associated with the Randall family murder: Clementine's soiled clothes, a blood-soaked pillowcase from the Randalls' home, and an ax, presumably the one found at the crime scene.[72] He explained to the court how he subjected these artifacts to technical chemical processes and reached a damning conclusion: "the ax handle contained human blood and [the] clothes contained either blood or brain matter."[73] Apparently the weapon's blade was clean.[74] This coincided with the fact that the Randalls had been mutilated with the flat end of an ax-head.[75] He also argued that the blood found on Clementine's garments matched that found on the crime scene pillowcase, presenting strong evidence in support of the prosecution.[76] A renowned chemist had testified that he had used scientific methods to link the defendant's bloody clothes to the location where the bodies were found *and* the weapon that was used to kill them. Whether there was any need for additional witnesses is hard to say.

What is known is that at least three other people did testify, though where exactly they fit in the prosecution's lineup is unclear. The editor of the *New Orleans Item,* the same newspaper that had printed the lengthy first-person account of Clementine's confession, was summoned to the witness stand. R. H. Broussard stated that Clementine "told voluntarily" of her crimes, recounting her April statements.[77] He said she spoke of traveling to New Iberia to meet with Joseph Thibodeaux (the hoodoo practitioner), learning it was possible to kill indiscriminately without detection via the protection of a conjure, and then executing the murders of both the Randall and Andrus families. Reverend King Harris—the same preacher from Jennings who had been arrested as a suspect in the Randall family murders—also took the stand as a prosecutorial witness against Clementine.[78] Both he and Dr. Lambert O. Clark, the deputy coroner for Lafayette Parish, claimed that Clementine had confessed to the murders and was "always smiling [while] narrating the crimes."[79] That District Attorney Ogden had freely admitted he planned to prosecute Clementine without relying on her confessions means that the decision to summon these witnesses—alongside the others who had addressed her incriminating statements—was likely made to reinforce an already strong case.[80]

Newspapers reported that the state summoned fifteen people to the witness stand, yet not everyone who was subpoenaed was included in their coverage. Given that this was a high-profile trial and that minute details about otherwise insignificant witnesses were published, it seems unlikely that the press simply overlooked these testimonies. More likely, either these individuals were unable to attend the trial or the prosecution rested its case early. According to the United Press reporter, this is precisely what happened. Papers across the country printed a telling line: "The testimony was not all in when the state rested, but the prosecution decided that it had presented enough."[81]

When it was the defense's turn to control the courtroom, then, the odds were not in their favor. Although they subpoenaed at least twelve individuals to testify on behalf of their client, half of these witnesses had already been called by the prosecution.[82] The regional press barely covered the cross-examinations or introduction of additional evidence; the state's case had been undeniably critical of Clementine, and it seemed the best her attorneys could do was perform damage control. That's how the *Daily Picayune* (New Orleans) could explain with no fanfare that the testimonies of James Guidry (Clementine's employer), Dinah Porter (Clementine's stepmother), and Raymond Barnabet (Clementine's father) were inconsequential and had "little bearing upon the issues of the case."[83]

Yet, it seemed that not all hope was lost when Attorney John L. Kennedy offered "one of the most magnificent presentations" that had been heard throughout the trial.[84] He argued three points. Up first was the claim that Clementine's "extra judicial confessions" were doubtful at best.[85] Whether he knew the conditions of her November 1911 admission or was referring exclusively to her springtime stories is unclear, but he intended to question the context of her statements. If Clementine had confessed under duress—or in any environment outside of a legal one—her lawyers argued that her words were too tainted to be reliable.

Second was the jarring revelation that the condition of the physical evidence had not been preserved when it was transported from Lafayette to New Orleans for chemical analysis. Instead, Attorney Kennedy argued, the items Professor Metz received were "badly mixed," suggesting that the blood that was apparently shared between Clementine's clothes and the Randalls' pillowcase was not proof of her culpability, but of the investigators' sloppiness.[86] If the artifacts had been "all bundled together," then the core part of the state's argument—including the testimony of its star witness—was based on a faulty premise.[87]

Finally, Clementine's lawyer poked holes in the expertise of the lunacy commission. On cross-examination, Dr. Hummel admitted that "there was no definite line of demarcation between sanity and insanity."[88] He conceded that "individual opinion" often drove the diagnoses within his field, suggesting that the science of mental health was not nearly as objective as the prosecution had implied.[89] Curiously, the defense decided to challenge the very experts they had once called upon to examine their client. If they had not gotten the outcome they wanted from the commission's official report, then questioning its validity still permitted the jury—rather than the doctors—to find Clementine insane.

Despite introducing a significant amount of doubt regarding Clementine's guilt—perhaps enough to entirely exonerate their client—her lawyers did not argue for her release. Instead, they claimed that the evidence presented "should be sufficient justification for confining the prisoner to the insane asylum, but would not warrant the verdict demanded by the state."[90] Thus, Clementine's attorneys were not asking the jury to release her, but simply not to kill her. They probably reached this conclusion based on a rather unusual development in the case.

On October 25, the second day of the trial, Clementine made a demand that practically ended her lawyers' damage control. Against the wishes of her attorneys, she insisted her written confession be placed before the jury, even though she had entered a not guilty plea at her arraignment. Sitting somewhat sequestered in the courtroom, guarded by three deputies, she supposedly shouted: "I am the axe woman of the sacrifice sect. I killed them all, men, women, and babies and I hugged the dead babies to my breast. But I am not guilty of murder."[91]

I killed them all. . . . But I am not guilty of murder.

In Clementine's world, killing in the name of religion was not murder, but dutiful sacrifice. It was a necessary action of faithful devotion. And yet, with that solitary outburst, Clementine Barnabet had sealed her fate. Religious conviction was no match for secular law. The lunacy commission had determined that Clementine was sane. And a sane woman had just admitted to killing men, women, and children. Per the parameters of state law, a sane adult who killed someone, regardless of rationale, had committed murder.[92]

The jury's deliberations were likely only perfunctory. The debate was not whether Clementine was guilty, but whether she should be executed. The prosecution pleaded for "an unqualified verdict" that would result in the defendant's death.[93] Her attorneys, meanwhile, sought to have her institutionalized in an insane asylum. The jury was given their instructions at midnight, and by 9:00 a.m. the next morning they had reached a decision: "guilty without capital punishment."[94] Clementine would not face death, but neither would she be remanded to a mental hospital. Instead, she was condemned to life at the Louisiana State Penitentiary.[95]

The decision not to have Clementine executed was likely two-fold. First, though the lunacy commission found Clementine sane, they did suggest that her mental capacities were "deficient."[96] Her attorneys had portrayed her as the victim of an "unfortunate birth" who had found herself in "degrading environments," offering additional evidence that solicited pity for their client.[97] Perhaps the jurymen agreed with such assessments and believed that execution was not an appropriate outcome for someone in her condition. Second, and more complicated, was the reality that she was a young woman. Although tropes about Black women's criminality in early twentieth-century America often animalized, masculinized, and demonized the supposed perpetrators, the extent to which such characterizations resulted in the state-sanctioned death of the assailant is low.[98] Black women were readily criminalized, but they were not readily executed.[99] The belief that women, both Black and white, were less deserving of such a sentence than men likely contributed to Clementine's life sentence. One paper explained her predicament by noting: "she was a peril to the entire community and probably only the natural dislike of American states to hang a woman saved her from death on the scaffold."[100] Clementine's suffering would be long-lasting.

/ / /

In the aftermath of Clementine's courtroom outburst, it seems she was not pleased with her sentence, as apparently she "expected more severe punishment."[101] If Clementine genuinely thought she should have been executed by the state, newspapers reported that her rationale was not based on regret for the murders included in her confession. Instead, multiple articles claimed she believed she would be "recovered by an angel in a chariot of fire" if she paid the ultimate price.[102] The press quickly latched onto the fact that Clementine, a young Black woman convicted of killing a single person and implicated in many more deaths, had purportedly invoked a direct parallel to Elijah, a biblical figure with a tellingly unique feature: he did not die. In 2 Kings, the description of the prophet's ascent reads: "And it came to pass, as they still went on, and talked, that, behold, there appeared a chariot of fire, and horses of fire, and parted them both asunder; and Elijah went up by a whirlwind into heaven."[103] Perhaps, then, Clementine knew the story of Elijah and fashioned herself in his image, implying that the death penalty would not have the same effect on her as it would a mortal being. Equally likely, however, is the possibility that an overzealous reporter either fabricated this association or took it out of its context. That the narrative originated with the United Press—the same newswire that had printed Clementine's November 1911 confession despite authorities' attempts to control press coverage—suggests an eagerness to break stories, perhaps without due diligence.

Presumably, the U.P. reporter did not liken Clementine to Elijah simply because of his heavenly ascent. For many months newspapers had reported that the young woman was a priestess, cult leader, axwoman, and prophetess. She had come to identify with the Sacrifice Church, despite the authorities never being able to crack the facade of the faith or farce. In the courtroom, she had blended her myriad associations into a damning declaration. If there was any shred of truth in her assertion, particularly regarding her faith, then possibly her devotion extended beyond that of a casual practitioner. Perhaps she had crossed the line from committed follower to convicted prophetess. If so, then publishing a story associating Clementine with Elijah was likely about more than the ability to not die.

In Old Testament scriptures, Elijah did things that suggested he was faithful to God.[104] He raised a widow's child from the dead.[105] He prophesied a drought.[106] He ended the drought.[107] He set a waterlogged altar on fire.[108] These were all miraculous things accomplished through God. When armies were sent to arrest Elijah, he had two of the captains killed with fire.[109] Plus, these were not the only individuals whose deaths came at the hands of this prophet.

Looking at his life in totality, then, not only was Elijah a significant figure in Scripture, but he was depicted as a devoted believer with a penchant for performing miracles. At the same time, he was unapologetic for his faith *and* the actions he undertook to maintain it. In a single article, the United Press offered the possibility that perhaps Clementine had channeled Elijah throughout her convoluted criminal career. He had his enemies killed, and, implicitly, she selected families to be sacrificed. He had an ox slaughtered on a water-soaked altar to prove a point; she, reportedly, had opted to sacrifice people. Elijah had God's word to protect him on his journeys. Clementine had a conjure. He prophesied a drought and the deaths of various people. She prophesied the continuance of the ax murders. Finally, no discussion of Elijah would be complete without mentioning the prediction in the Book of Malachi: Elijah would come back to earth ahead of the return of the Messiah.[110] Given this context, perhaps the U.P. reporter surmised that Clementine believed she, too, would return. If so, the intimation was that she wouldn't have to live out the rest of her life at the Louisiana State Penitentiary.

The United Press's willingness to align Clementine with Elijah did more than embrace scriptural similarities. It also implicitly allowed audiences to imagine her as staking claim to a type of power that was biblical, miraculous, and divine. Heretofore, Clementine's religious convictions had varied between a God-mandated murder in her November 1911 confession to affiliation with the Sacrifice Church in the spring of 1912. Her courtroom outburst had enabled her to claim power as a serial killer. Yet, it was the reporter's invocation of Elijah that elevated Clementine's status from inhumanly depraved to divinely inhuman.

If there was a kernel of truth in the United Press's assessment that Clementine believed she was like Elijah, revisiting her lawyers' initial contention—that she might have been insane—is worthwhile. Diagnosing any potential mental illness or disorder she could have had is beyond the purview of this book, though discussing whether any of her confessions could have come from a rational place is useful. Throughout these pages, logical explanations behind her words and actions have been offered, but that does not necessarily mean they align with how Clementine might have seen the world. While the lunacy commission concluded the young woman was legally sane, their opinion was neither unbiased nor objectively sound. Clementine could have suffered from any number of mental health conditions that ensnared her in a life-altering predicament. Maybe she had a neurocognitive or psychotic disorder that was never diagnosed, perhaps because the very condition itself had not yet been scientifically discovered. If this was the case, then the subject of her responsibility—separate from her confessions—should have weighed heavily on the court.

Questioning Clementine's mental health invites a larger conversation for scholars of Black women's history. So often, these histories privilege respectability, crafting productive narratives about a population that has often been written out of mainstream stories. Black women's historians—including those who study criminality—have often explained "deviant" actions through lenses that support this cause. Where respectability has been challenged, it has been replaced with rationality and resistance, affording historical subjects levels of agency and reason that explain their actions.[111] In both cases, scholars have sought to articulate the *why* of Black women's behaviors in ways that resist stereotypes and demand autonomy. Imbuing historical actors with logic has become a central part of crafting Black women's history, providing evidence of the political stakes of this field.

Consequentially, in Black women's history, privileging respectability *and* rationality has inadvertently ignored those with severe mental illness. It is easy, perhaps even intuitive, to explain Clementine's confessions as strategic maneuvers to accomplish specific aims. It is far more uncomfortable to hypothesize that Clementine could have been mentally unwell and therefore acted purely according to her mind's unique wiring. Yet, this kind of theorizing encourages scholars to push past the frameworks of respectability and rationality to tell a more complete history of Black womanhood (and girlhood) in the United States. If Clementine suffered from some kind of mental illness to such an extent that she should have been declared legally insane, she was certainly not the only Black woman in early 1900s America who was in such a predicament. Reckoning with this more expansive expression of experiences affords a more complicated and therefore realistic portrayal of Black life in the past.

/ / /

Clementine Barnabet had captured national attention twice in her young life—thrice if her November 1911 confession was included. In April 1912, she became a household name after admitting to killing seventeen people in four families along a twenty-five-mile stretch of the Southern Pacific Railroad in southwestern Louisiana. Six months later, the nineteen-year-old Black woman was again splayed across headlines, this time because she had been found guilty of murder and sentenced to the state penitentiary for life. Though she was convicted on just one count of murder and testimony was heard that implicated her in another five deaths, the United Press penned a sensational story that claimed Clementine was a member of a religious organization that had murdered "300 persons in the past six years."[112] The Associated Press joined in on the exaggerations—albeit less egregiously—by claiming Clementine confessed to murdering nineteen people as a follower of the Sacrifice Church.[113] These articles were reprinted throughout the United States and even Canada, once again constructing Clementine to be both a faithful devotee *and* a prolific killer.[114] Just as the "axman" had once dominated news cycles as an unknowable and terrifying murderer, the "axwoman" became an incomprehensible reflection of the dangerous outcome of religious deviance and moral depravity.[115]

Back in Lafayette, meanwhile, there were practical needs to address in the aftermath of Clementine's trial. She might have seemed larger than life in the press, but on the ground she was now a convicted felon who had to be transported to prison. She was one of five individuals who had been given a penitentiary sentence during the October term of court.[116] A sixth prisoner joined the procession to the Louisiana State Penitentiary on Monday, October 28. That day, throngs of people flocked to the Lafayette train station, trying to "get a glimpse of the notorious young murderess."[117] Even without the superfluous flair far-flung journalists had used to embellish Clementine's story, she had become a celebrity in Lafayette and beyond. The parish authorities guarded the inmates as they rode the rails east to Baton Rouge, the capital.[118] There, they would be ingested into the state's expansive penal system.

Meanwhile, the outcome of Clementine's trial meant the release of a number of the individuals she'd ensnared in her web. Irene Duce was freed after having spent roughly six months behind bars.[119] Zepherin Barnabet, Clementine's brother, also walked out of jail. He had been incarcerated on and off since late 1911 for his potential involvement in the ax murders. A week after his release, he was rearrested on three charges: "lying in wait" plus "horse stealing and stabbing with intent to kill."[120] If the local and regional presses are to be believed, Zepherin was not the only Barnabet involved in the most recent fracas—so too were either one or two more Barnabet brothers, including Noah, and perhaps an uncle as well.[121] Not surprisingly, the Barnabets' newest crimes were readily linked to the Sacrifice Church, and Lafayette's Black community feared the return of the axman.[122] Although one regional newspaper opined that Black folks were prepared to lynch the Barnabets if they were caught by a posse rather than the police, the press quickly retracted such a claim and conceded that locals thought the family was "so imbued with the power of 'hoodooism'" that any attack on them would immediately backfire.[123] By association with Clementine, her relatives had also become larger than life.

While Clementine's brothers sparked yet more fear in the region, it seems the release of Raymond Barnabet, her father, did not cause any problems, despite the fact that some believed he was somehow involved in the crimes.[124] Raymond was the only member of the family besides Clementine to actually stand trial for any of the ax murders. And, like his daughter, he had been convicted, though the testimony against him was contradictory and circumstantial. Raymond's attorneys had petitioned for a retrial based on his drunken state during the latter part of the trial. Since October 1911, he had been sitting in jail waiting for his case to come up again. Now, however, he had been released from custody based on his daughter's trial. Her testimony had been part of what had nearly sent him to the gallows; now her confession had set him free.

Reportedly, Raymond Barnabet told Sheriff Lacoste that he "would leave the country forever," fearful that staying in Louisiana would endanger his wellbeing.[125] Both father and daughter would be starting the next chapter of their lives in radically different places than those they'd known. Raymond was disappearing into the wind. Clementine, meanwhile, was about to enter "hell on earth."[126] No chariot of fire could save her now.

9

Clementine's Incarceration

Serving Time at Angola

At just nineteen years old, Clementine Barnabet, a young Black woman, had been convicted of murdering Azema Randall and condemned to spend the rest of her life at the Louisiana State Penitentiary. In reality, she was released after roughly ten years. Piecing together Clementine's incarceration reveals the forced community she experienced behind bars, highlighting the numerous ways she resembled her contemporaries. Yet, Clementine's detention was also unique. Upon her release, however, the infamous axwoman effectively disappeared.

Glimpses into Clementine's imprisonment reveal a different form of empowerment than what she experienced on the outside. As a confessed Black female serial killer, Clementine leveraged her publicity to cultivate a level of power disproportionate to both her position in society and the evidence linking her to additional ax murders. By the end of her incarceration, however, the presumed invisibility of Black womanhood allowed Clementine to vanish from the historical record. The gendered and racialized identity that had rendered her a household name in April 1912 afforded her a phenomenal amount of anonymity ten years later. This sort of unassumed power does not negate the dehumanizing and traumatic experiences she endured in prison, but highlights how assumptions and stereotypes about Black women's capacities ultimately contributed to Clementine's ability to reinvent herself upon her release.

/ / /

When Clementine Barnabet arrived at "The Walls," a processing center from which she could be shipped to any number of carceral institutions throughout Louisiana, she stepped into a deep legacy of blending punishment with profitability. From slavery to convict leasing, the exploitation of Black labor through private enterprise meant that the state had monetized its penal project since its earliest days.[1] When The Walls opened in 1835, the facility was not a processing center but the first penitentiary, a 440-cell structure on the edge of downtown Baton Rouge.[2] There, a twenty-five-foot-high brick barrier wrapped around the grounds, literally containing those society deemed criminal.[3]

By 1844, the passage of *An Act to Provide for the Better Administration of the Louisiana Penitentiary* effectively gave the governor the right to privatize the prison.[4] Within a few months, the state negotiated its first five-year leasing agreement, enabling McHatton, Pratt, and Company to assume unilateral control of the penitentiary—and its 176 prisoners, the majority of whom were enslaved men.[5] When McHatton took over, they defined what it meant to be punished by the state of Louisiana. Throughout their lease term, details of rampant abuses were made public. Inmates were beaten, starved, kicked, trampled, maimed, and even killed. They were expendable bodies tasked with dangerous labor and could simply be replaced. When those first five years were up, the state negotiated another deal with the company. And another. In fact, it was not until the Union occupation of Baton Rouge in 1862—and the forced relocation of inmates to the city workhouse in New Orleans—that the McHatton arrangement was terminated.[6] While the prisoners might have been disposable, so too were the private firms interested in the exploitative possibilities of captive labor. Others lined up to replace McHatton, ever ready to slash expenses in the name of profitability.

In 1869, the acquisition of the lease by James, Buckner, and Company represented a three-decade-long downfall of "brutality and cruelty" that ushered the penitentiary into the twentieth century.[7] When Samuel L. James—the brainchild of the lease and an ex-Confederate officer—purchased a few plantations in West Feliciana Parish in 1880, he consolidated three parcels under the name Angola.[8] Located about fifty miles northwest of Baton Rouge, this now-massive property relied on geographic characteristics to facilitate its own isolation.

The labor was arduous, including everything from picking cotton, driving carts, rolling logs, and firing boilers to erecting structures, building levees, and planting crops.[9] To be clear, not everyone who was imprisoned by the state was sent to James's Angola. The majority of Louisiana's inmates were still either leased out to other industries throughout the state or, if they were considered both white and skilled, simply housed at The Walls. It was those unlucky few sent upriver to Angola who suffered immensely.

One Black woman named Carrie Johnson (alias Annie Williams) was discharged from Angola in June 1887. A week later, she was rearrested and attempted suicide at the New Orleans Central Police Station rather than risk having to return upriver.[10] She told a local reporter that twenty-six male and four female inmates had died due to "exposure and brutal treatment" while she was there.[11] Perhaps she had heard of another Black woman's brutish fate during her stint: Kitty McCoy was forced to pick cotton despite suffering from blood poisoning. She could not keep pace and collapsed. She was beaten mercilessly—given "fully one hundred blows with the thick heavy strap"—and then left in agony.[12] In the morning, Kitty was dead.

Until his death in 1894, James brutalized convicts at Angola and engaged in ever-worsening practices that extended many aspects of slavery's regime by decades.[13] In fact, James's Angola was deemed "the most cynical, profit-oriented, and brutal prison regime in Louisiana history."[14] Although James's son managed the operation after his father's death, the continuation of convict leasing in Louisiana was short lived. The state legislature passed a bill to abolish the arrangement in 1898.[15] The state then purchased Angola from James's estate, reclaiming ownership of its own prison system on January 1, 1901, after more than fifty years of almost continuous convict-for-hire leasing practices.

Although the new legislation gave Louisiana control over *all* correctional facilities in the state, the penitentiary took precedence in terms of scale and depravity. By the end of 1900, on the eve of the state takeover, twenty-eight Black women and three Black men out of 1,014 state prisoners labored at Angola.[16] As the prison grew, so too did the need for laborers: maintaining eight thousand acres of cotton, corn, rice, and sugarcane fields required bodies to work.[17] By 1902, ten years before Clementine arrived at Angola, there were more than five hundred inmates at the remote site.[18] By the end of the decade, the entire population of prisoners in Louisiana had doubled.[19]

/ / /

Clementine Barnabet entered The Walls on October 28, 1912, another victim of the state's turnstile of punishment. She joined women whose fate was now inextricably connected to the state's needs. Whether they would be sent to Angola or another farm—or perhaps stay at The Walls—was determined by those who oversaw Louisiana's penal project.[20] Although the Baton Rouge facility was often overcrowded, poorly ventilated, and generally unpleasant, it was nothing compared to the ghoulish conditions awaiting prisoners in the remote Tunica Hills.[21]

When Clementine arrived at the West Feliciana Parish institution of Angola, she was only about sixty miles northeast from where she'd grown up in Lafayette, but she might as well have been on a different planet. On that northward journey to hell, the flattish marshes of the Atchafalaya basin imperceptibly shifted to rolling, rugged hills. Nestled in the elbow of the state—where Mississippi extends her arm to greet her neighbor—Angola was (and arguably still is) a geographically self-contained operation. To the north, west, and south, the mighty Mississippi River bent in a sweeping C, providing a natural moat against those who might try to flee. To the east, the snake-infested Tunica Hills sealed off the penitentiary from outsiders.

Within the geographic isolation of the prison, the women's quarters, known as Camp-D, were located a mile away from any of the men's camps and near the "Big House," a plantation-style structure that served as the James family home and a daily reminder of the penitentiary's connection to slavery.[22] That the overseers of the female prisoners protested that they had "the hardest time of any of those in charge of convicts" in 1901 perhaps reflected the particularly unnerving situation many incarcerated women faced.[23] Criminalized, guarded with "a sinister looking Winchester rifle," and potentially subjected to "the strap," female convicts were exposed to many of the same indecencies as their male counterparts while also being forced to live in an isolated area near prying white eyes.[24]

While the men were originally housed in three different camps, only one was built for women. It was designed to hold thirty inmates and included "a cell room, storeroom, bathroom, work rooms and housing for the camp captain and guards."[25] Perhaps the "cell room" was similar to those in the men's camps: sleeping quarters with "double-deck iron beds."[26] Just six months after the state took over Angola, there were thirty-eight female inmates—all but one of whom were Black. The overcrowding of the women's quarters would only continue in the years leading up to Clementine's arrival.

In 1908, for example, a scathing report explained that the buildings themselves—some of which were literally "old plantation cabins"—left much to be desired.[27] The women's camp had been damaged by a flood, a continuous problem plaguing a prison built along the banks of the Mississippi River. But mother nature alone couldn't account for the abysmal conditions. A sixty-foot by thirty-foot building housed sixty women, double the original intended occupancy. Although the State responded by renovating the quarters to accommodate sixty inmates, the very next year Camp-D was again over capacity. Additional major improvements would not come to the women's barracks for almost fifty more years.

These were the conditions Clementine Barnabet encountered when she became the newest resident of Camp-D. While she might have heard rumors about the hellish prison, it was also reported that those at Angola had already heard rumors about her. Supposedly, when Clementine first arrived upriver, she "was kept in close confinement," removed from the general population because other prisoners were terrified of her.[28] Given the spatial limits of the women's quarters, however, these claims were possibly exaggerated. Then again, Clementine's springtime confession and fall trial had captivated the nation. Perhaps there was a kernel of truth to the lore of the young woman's arrival—she had instilled fear in folks before, and there was no reason she couldn't do it again.

Despite her reputation, Clementine likely was not treated any differently from other Black women when it came to the value of her labor to the penitentiary.[29] On paper, Angola sought to confine female prisoners to domestic work exclusively. In actuality, racial prejudice and ruthless greed valued Black women's labor more in the fields than in the laundry. Some Black women did toil as cooks and laundresses, while others worked in the dining room or as domestics for specific prison officials, like the warden or chaplain.[30] But these positions typically went to European immigrant women.

So, secluded or not, Clementine presumably started backbreaking work at dawn with everyone else in Camp-D who had been assigned to the fields. The year she arrived at Angola, a boll weevil invasion had ruined the cotton crop, causing the state to switch to sugarcane production on the alluvial grounds.[31] By November 1912, just over two weeks after Clementine was convicted, Angola set a cane-planting record that had "perhaps never been equaled in the state," boasting some twelve hundred acres under cultivation for the season.[32] While the crop might have changed, the expectation of profitable work did not.

Managing labor was only part of the state's approach to punishment. Scant records reveal a litany of corporeal chastisements meted out for various infractions. Although it's impossible to know exactly how many women at Angola were actually given lashes, spent "24 hours in [the] dungeon," or were "blackmarked" for their behaviors, documents confirm these things did happen.[33] Frustratingly, the evidence of the infractions that led to such reprimands is opaque, ranging from "intimidation and impudence" to "disobedience and insolence."[34] Yet, if Kitty McCoy's story is any indication, punishments were violent, merciless, and sometimes deadly.

By the time Clementine Barnabet arrived at the Louisiana State Penitentiary, then, both living and working conditions were abysmal. Yet, for all the information that was recorded about the institution's horrors during the early 1900s, little of it captured the day-to-day drudgery that prisoners endured. Thus, there is a contrast between just how much information was printed about Clementine before she was incarcerated and how little information is available about her time in prison. She had become a household name in April 1912—even her ingest ledger has the moniker "Axe Woman" in chevrons beside her name.[35] Outside of that register, however, only a few newspaper articles have been recovered about Clementine's time at Angola. Perhaps there are records buried somewhere within the state's penal bureaucracy, or perhaps one of the many floods destroyed them decades ago. Either way, the result is an unsatisfactory acknowledgment that tracing Clementine's prison sentence on a granular level is currently a fruitless enterprise.

That is not to suggest, however, that nothing can be said of her time at Angola. Although Clementine was condemned to spend the rest of her life behind bars, the reality is that she served 3,834 days: roughly ten and a half years. During that time, another 348 women found themselves ensnared in the state's penal system, given terms as short as one month and as long as a lifetime.[36] Although it is theoretically possible that not all of these women were sent upriver, the classification system likely meant most of them were at Angola. (Supplementary records confirm 115 were definitely there.) These women represented a sort of forced community, joined by both gender and predicament—the combination of which rendered them unique within the confines of the prison and beyond. Examining how the prison constructed Clementine in comparison with how it described her contemporaries affords a telling conclusion: in Angola, she was just like everyone else.

One way to assess Clementine's typicality is to consider the demographic profile of women at the Louisiana State Penitentiary from October 1912 to April 1923, the exact range of her incarceration. A whopping 92 percent of these women were Black, according to social conventions.[37] Still, Black women comprised less than 3 percent of Angola's overall population during the early 1900s.[38] Listed in ingest ledgers as "griff," "mulatto," "yellow," "brown," and "black"—and with descriptors like "light" and "dark" affixed as well—the racial categorizations of these women were a product of the time in which they lived and the opinions of the individuals who profiled them into the state's penal system. "Griff," after all, was an amorphous shade of brown that was defined at times by assumed lineage and at times by color, reflecting the assigner's own perception.[39] Clementine, for example, was "griff." Yet, newspapers variously described her as "mulatto," "black," "light-skinned," "bright," and "half-blood," socially constructing and reconstructing Clementine's race.[40]

But it wasn't just her race that was made and remade. Clementine's physical body was also a subject of discussion. In the prison's ingest ledger, Clementine was annotated as five feet, four inches tall, weighing 152 pounds, and wearing a size seven shoe.[41] Although of average height, Clementine was about twenty pounds heavier than the typical Black woman at Angola during this time. The standard shoe size was somewhere between a five and a six. Clementine's physical body was thus slightly larger than average, but by no means exceptionally so. Print media *made* her inhumanly incomparable on the outside, but on the inside the literal space Clementine occupied was likely inconspicuous. The metaphorical space she commanded tells a different story.

Whoever ingested Clementine into the belly of the beast recorded her as nineteen years old. Maybe that's accurate. If so, Clementine was typical. Not only did 11 percent of all Black women at Angola during her tenure enter the institution at age nineteen, but 85 percent were reportedly between the ages of sixteen and thirty when they first arrived in prison. Angola's Black female population was overwhelmingly young—at the age of starting families, pursuing relationships, and navigating the challenges of Black womanhood in Jim Crow society as individuals *not* born into slavery. And speaking of relationships, Clementine's status as single put her in respectable company with 44 percent of all Black women at Angola and more than half of those her same age, though 42 percent were also married.[42] If this is starting to sound somewhat banal, that's precisely the point. There was nothing discernable from *looking* at Clementine's prison record that made her different from the other women sentenced to Angola.

Yet, in early 1900s America, people were not convinced that criminality did not have physical signs. Infamous Italian scholar Cesare Lombroso had launched a wave of intellectual discourse in the late nineteenth century that argued certain bodily characteristics were markers of one's criminal nature.[43]

Rooted in sloppy studies, biased results, and questionable premises, Lombroso's findings were heartily and rightfully challenged by the early twentieth century, but not before they had been unleashed onto the world.[44]

Thus, when Clementine Barnabet arrived at Angola, her physical appearance was not simply noted to distinguish her from other Black women incarcerated at the same time. It was a pseudo-scientific reflection of the person who did the screening, couched in the era's criminal anthropology craze.[45] How Clementine would have described herself remains lost, but understanding how she was perceived by others is a worthwhile enterprise. After all, part of what made her so terrifying to her contemporaries was, for a lack of a better term, how "normal"—even "nonthreatening"—she appeared. According to the prison's ledger, Clementine had "small ears, [a] flat pointed nose, [a] scar center forehead[,] edge of hair, [and a] dim splotch scar near right wrist."[46] Perhaps on the surface, this description seems innocuous enough. Only by contextualizing Clementine's physical markers against her 348 contemporaries does evidence emerge detailing *how* Black women were criminalized by the state of Louisiana through commentaries on their corporeality.[47]

Prison officials mentioned teeth, noses, and ears. So too did Lombroso.[48] While he attempted to find biological signs of criminal propensities in a more general population, the employees of the penitentiary already *knew* these women were bad. The state had told them so by sentencing them to hell on earth. Prison employees had an "easier" job than Lombroso: confirm what society *already* believed about these women. Physical descriptors could thus not only help differentiate the women from one another, but help further criminalize those sent to Angola.

Having "good teeth" was noteworthy, but so was having "bad teeth." That 23 percent of women had at least one gold tooth (typically in the front of their mouth) is a fascinating reflection on early twentieth-century oral hygiene, as is the fact that several women were missing teeth. The same can potentially be said of the eight women listed with "blue gums." Although it's possible that such a descriptor was used as a derogatory term related to women with darker complexions, it's also possible that it was an unknowing annotation of oxygen deficiency.[49] Moreover, more than half of the Black women at Angola used tobacco, suggesting it was a commonplace practice and permitted in prison. Given the challenges of dental care in Jim Crow America, that Black women might have experienced oral health complications would not be surprising, criminalized status or not.

Having ears "close to the head" deserved mention, as did having "outstanding" ears. That Clementine had small ears—like 13 percent of women at the penitentiary—did not make her exceptional. Nor, for that matter, did her seemingly contradictory nose: both flat and pointed. Women whose noses comprised either of those adjectives represented 15 percent of the female inmate population during these years. In fact, just under half of the women ingested into the penitentiary had noses worth mentioning: they were round, pug, broad, short, large, and medium. Of those whose noses avoided description, likely similar wording would have been used. To criminalize one's facial features has never been about rigorous anatomical assessment, despite Lombroso's insistence. It has always been about reinforcing the parameters of normalcy.

According to Lombroso, it was not just biological markers that made someone a criminal. So, too, did bodily modifications.[50] That 30 percent of women at the penitentiary during these years had pierced ears might have confirmed Lombroso's theories. That Clementine apparently did not would have challenged them. She was, after all, a confessed murderer. Worse than piercings, in Lombroso's estimation, were tattoos. Lombroso did not believe that permanent ink was a form of art, self-expression, commemoration, experimentation, or even violation. The eight Black women with identified tattoos would have ostensibly confirmed Lombroso's suspicions. In reality, interpreting the women's ink as evidence of criminality erases the legitimate and perhaps complicated reasons such designs ended up on their bodies.

While interpreting the "marks on person" column of various Angola ledgers through a Lombrosian lens is possible, there's more to the story than undermining biological criminality. Interspersed with the artificial characteristics of "the criminal" are glimpses into the difficult, dangerous, and gritty worlds that these women brought with them to the penitentiary. Their bodies became testaments to their pasts—literal reminders of lives otherwise subjected to historical erasure.

Twenty-year-old Nora Simmons was blind in her right eye. Seventeen-year-old Ann Simpson, blind in her left. The former was given a minimum of six years for grand larceny. The latter was given five years for manslaughter. While Nora served four years and two months before she was discharged, Ann died of tuberculosis just over two years into her sentence. Although it's impossible to know from prison ledgers alone whether these young women were born partially blind or developed their disabilities later in life, their conditions informed how they interacted with the world—and how the world interacted with them.

Dora Fobbs, a twenty-nine-year-old laundress from Shreveport, arrived at Angola with her left shoulder broken and disfigured. According to the ingest record, she had been shot in the back. She was charged with manslaughter and given a minimum sentence of ten years. Less than two months into her sentence, she escaped on July 4, 1921.

A decade earlier—on July 1, 1911—Jenny Ann Blair had tried to escape. She was recaptured. Did her disfigured left forearm—which had been broken but presumably never healed properly—jeopardize her ability to flee? That she was in prison for murder meant she had, at least on paper, a lifetime to ponder her failed escape or to try again.

For both Dora and Jenny Ann—as well as the handful of other women whose "crooked" digits and "crippled" limbs remain etched into the record—their maimed bodies reflect the literal fragmentation of Black womanhood in Jim Crow America. Whether born into bodies that society deemed inferior or thrust into them by accident (or on purpose), these individuals embodied physical markers of Black women's vulnerabilities and resilience. Did fingers get crushed under the weight of domestic tasks? Did farm equipment mangle extremities? Did people who called themselves lovers and partners lay hands on those they claimed to care about? Although 85 percent of women in the penitentiary bore scars upon their arrival, the history of these marks remains a matter of speculation.

For example, roughly 13 percent of women incarcerated had "burn scars." Given that, of the available data, 80 percent of women, both Black and white, performed some sort of domestic labor (including laundry, cooking, general housework, etc.), it's possible that at least some of these burn scars were acquired on the job. Washing and ironing clothes was a taxing and potentially hazardous occupation in an era in which the washing machine was one's own arms and heavy flatirons had to be continually heated over a fire or on a stove.[51] Similarly, that at least 13 percent of Black women labored in fields—a manually strenuous job rooted in agricultural productivity—meant they also physically stood in harm's way nearly every day. Yet, even Black women employed as teachers and nurses found themselves sentenced to the penitentiary. Though few, their presence at Angola reveals that more "respectable" occupations did not make Black women immune to criminalization.

If anything, the diversity of demographic, phenotypical, and employment information available about Clementine's contemporaries suggests that women who found themselves toiling away in hell on earth were not "born criminals." Nor, for that matter, were they necessarily guilty of the crimes for which they had been convicted. In fact, many of them may not have considered the things that landed them at Angola to have been crimes at all. For some, they were reclaiming lost wages through property acquisition. For others, acts of self-defense were interpreted as aggression because white society did not deem Black women and girls as defendable in the first place.[52] Whatever the reason, there is no denying that many women at the Louisiana State Penitentiary during these years were criminalized because they were believed to have broken social norms.

In some ways, it is easier to rationalize how women who transgressed the law might have been wronged by society, including those who ended up incarcerated because they were trying to provide for their families or protect themselves. It is fascinating to consider property crimes as assertions of autonomy, or "carnal crimes" to be efforts to reclaim sexual agency and/or pleasure.[53] It is easy to accept that some women were led astray by those with power—whether partners, friends, or employers—and committed crimes not of their own volition.[54] Recognizing that still other women could have suffered from undiagnosed mental illness that governed their actions affords empathy with the plight of society's most vulnerable populations.

Yet, it is much harder to admit that some women of sound mind might have been sentenced to the Louisiana State Penitentiary because they did *precisely* what the court said they did. They genuinely could have been guilty, having acted criminally for no other reason than the fact that they wanted to. For a woman like Clementine, the truth may forever remain shrouded in mystery. To accept this possibility allows for Black women's expressions of violence and harm to be human—messy, inscrutable, and confounding.

/ / /

During the early 1900s, discourse on crime ranged the gamut from Lombrosian defenses of biological criminality to rehabilitative models based on unfortunate plights.[55] Imbued with Jim Crow ideologies—not to mention legislation—which effectively rendered blackness a crime, the criminal justice system in the early twentieth century was a complicated maze that made—and then remade—social norms. Thus, understanding the generic demographics of women sentenced to Angola only tells part of Clementine's story. Understanding how the state of Louisiana defined, managed, and reconciled her contemporaries' punishments contextualizes the meaning of time served at one specific institution over the course of roughly one decade.

Black women found themselves sentenced to the Louisiana State Penitentiary for a variety of felonies. State law categorized crimes under umbrella designations, which were then subdivided. For example, there was the larger category of "carnal crimes," which included rape, prostitution, and seduction.[56] Of the Black women in the prison whose charges are known, 42 percent were convicted of either murder or manslaughter.[57] The difference between the two was motive, at least on paper. In 1910, Louisiana defined murder as "the killing of a human being, with malice aforethought, either express or implied." Manslaughter, on the other hand, was defined as "the unlawful killing of a human being *without* malice, either express or implied" (emphasis added).[58] Just over one quarter of Black women in Angola were charged with theft, burglary, or "kindred offenses." In more common parlance, these were typically property crimes, which included everything from breaking and entering to larceny, embezzlement, robbery, and stealing. Another quarter were charged with "offenses against the person," which were various forms of assault. Specifically, cutting, stabbing, and shooting—or any combination of the three—were common accusations. Less frequent but arguably no less violent was administering poison. In small numbers, Black women were charged with perjury, forgery, arson, concubinage, and violating acts that regulated the sex industry.

Many crimes carried both minimum and maximum sentences. Relatedly, some women were expected to carry out consecutive sentences, often connected to two separate charges, such as burglary and larceny. Regardless of how their time was supposed to be served, the reality is that women typically did not remain incarcerated for the duration of their sentence, minimum or otherwise. Excluding those who were given a life sentence, the average minimum amount of time a Black woman was supposed to have served was 3.7 years, while the average maximum was 4.5 years.[59] In general, her term ended in 1.9 years. The overwhelming majority of these women were discharged from the penitentiary, though three died and another three escaped. While arson and manslaughter carried the longest non-life sentences, Black women charged with cohabitation, concubinage, and perjury were most likely to serve out their full sentences. The same cannot be said of white women. This discrepancy, both by race and by criminal classification, suggests that the state of Louisiana maintained and enforced a disproportionate interest in regulating Black women's sexuality.[60]

The most severe punishments were reserved for women who were found guilty of the most heinous crimes. This logic ostensibly undergirded the terms of one's sentence and meant that certain charges deserved Hammurabian consequences: an eye for an eye, a life for a life. Therefore, the fact that Clementine was given a life sentence did not make her exceptional. She joined thirty-seven other Black women and five white women—or roughly 12 percent of the female population—in being condemned to spend the rest of their lives behind bars. All but one of these women were charged with either murder or murder without capital punishment, a subtle legalese distinction that, when Clementine was sentenced, harkened to Article 57 of the 1910 *Code of Criminal Law of the State of Louisiana:* "Whoever shall have been convicted of murder shall suffer death."[61] In practice, no woman charged with either crime was ever executed during Clementine's tenure. Likely, this departure from the law reflected the way Louisiana adjudicated sentences. Thus, although women could be charged with murder according to the legal code, the correctional code stated that "in all capital cases, the jury *may* qualify its verdict of guilty with the addition of 'without capital punishment'" (emphasis added).[62] That this provision extended to Black women—whose race otherwise barred them from nearly every other protection guaranteed to white women—was a small concession. After all, to *not* be executed meant that, in theory, these women would spend the rest of their mortal lives in an earthly hell.

Arguably, if Clementine's confession—whether forced or factual—to killing more than a dozen people was not troubling enough to earn the death penalty, then the charges brought upon her contemporaries should not be surprising, either. Florida Bryant, a sixteen-year-old Black adolescent, was convicted of murdering Ella Schuerr, and local newspapers reported that she would "probably be the first woman to be hanged in the state penitentiary within the present generation." Similarly, when Nicolina Gebbia, a twenty-seven-year-old first-generation Italian American was charged—alongside her brother and others—with conspiracy to kidnap and murder an Italian boy, newspapers swore that "the death penalty will be inflicted."[63] Instead, both Florida and Nicolina were ingested into Angola with life sentences. And they both got out after ten and a half years.

To modern audiences, it might seem incredulous that individuals with a life sentence could be released from prison after only a decade. In reality, Florida and Nicolina were somewhat exceptional, but in a perplexing way. Excluding those who died or escaped, on average, Black women who were given a life sentence served 9.4 years. For white women, that figure was 9.3 years. Thus, Florida and Nicolina actually served *more* time than many of their peers. Getting out of prison despite being given a life sentence was, well, a given. For all its flaws—of which there are too many to count—Louisiana's early twentieth-century criminal justice system developed a robust system of good time credits, assuming an inmate lived long enough to see said credits accumulate.[64]

When they were released, women typically left the state penitentiary through three legal means: Act 112, Act 160, or Act 293.[65] Act 112 of 1890, which revised an 1886 law, was designed to provide "for commutation of sentences for good behavior of convicts in the penitentiary and in the parish prisons of the State."[66] In practice, the law allowed for escalating good time earned: for sentences over one year, a prisoner earned two months off their sentence for years one and two, three months for years three and four, and four months for all remaining years. If someone was given a life sentence, they were allowed to apply for commutation after serving fifteen years.

Act 160 of 1902 expanded upon the 1890 law in various ways, but two were particularly salient for Clementine's world. First, a "special class" of prisoners was designated as those who "shall be eligible for particularly meritorious service or for highly exemplary conduct."[67] Individuals who were admitted into this class could effectively earn *double* the time outlined in Act 112. Moreover, those who were given life sentences could now be included in this special class. In accordance with the 1902 law, these individuals could have time taken off the fifteen-year benchmark for commutation applications. Act 293 of 1910 was even more generous by allowing second termers the chance to have their sentences commuted, as well as allowing those who attempted to escape to not automatically forfeit their good time credits if they were recaptured.[68] Collectively, prison officials noted that these various laws were "based upon the principle of making the individual work out his own salvation and earn a diminution of his sentence by his own efforts."[69]

Clearly, these three acts fundamentally shaped the prison's ever-rotating composition. The turnstile of punishment continued. Of the 348 other women in the penitentiary during Clementine's tenure for whom such data is available, 303 of them were released while she was incarcerated. If they were all housed at Angola, this means Clementine saw 88 percent of these women leave, whether through legal mechanisms, escape, or death. Clementine witnessed the penitentiary's turnover at a phenomenal rate. In fact, only *one* other woman, Pearly Bonner, effectively served a concurrent sentence with Clementine. During Clementine's stint, Black women typically left hell on earth in less than two years. But in that time—and in that place—the days likely dragged on.

/ / /

As much as Clementine Barnabet was like the hundreds of other women at the Louisiana State Penitentiary during the decade of her incarceration, she was also different from them. Her similarities were the product of two tenets of the American penal system: stripping people of their individuality and enforcing an environment of uniformity. That she was generally demographically average simply added to the illusion that she was typical. Yet, two exceptional things happened to Clementine during her time at Angola that made her unique. Tenuous evidence suggests these events were connected.

Less than a year into her sentence, Clementine did what many could only dream of: she attempted to escape from the penitentiary.[70] How far she fled is unclear, but it seems she didn't cover much ground since she was recaptured by one of the guards the same day. Although Clementine's thwarted flight was exceptional, she was by no means the only individual who sought to brave the unknown rather than stay at the hellish institution. During her tenure, eleven women attempted to abscond. Three of them never returned.

Perhaps Clementine had heard about Annie Bell Brown and Katie Williams, two Black women who did what was considered nearly impossible: they successfully escaped from the Louisiana State Penitentiary in June 1911. While Annie had been incarcerated since September 1906, Katie had just arrived three months earlier.[71] Although they both could have conveniently fled on June 4 independent of one another, they likely worked together to ensure their escape would be a one-way trip. To flee Angola at all, let alone in the brutal humidity and heat of the Louisiana summer, likely meant that their story became one of hushed rumors and hopeful whispers, maybe carried all the way to Clementine's ears over a year later.

Less than a month after Annie and Katie proved it was possible to escape, Beulah Rawling's failed flight reminded prisoners of the true difficulty of such a feat. Not to be deterred, she tried again mere weeks later.[72] Again she was recaptured. Although Beulah's sentence was supposed to be three years for "entering in the daytime with intent to steal," her flawed attempts to flee meant that she served an additional eight months past her original term. Even so, something compelled Beulah to try—and try yet again—to liberate herself from the misery that was the Louisiana State Penitentiary.

Yet, it was more than just stories that likely incentivized Clementine to try to flee. Compared to a "concentration camp" by the Works Progress Administration, Angola in the early twentieth century maintained many of the vestiges of its inhumane convict leasing past.[73] Inmates were beaten mercilessly, deprived of food yet forced to work grueling hours, tortured for the slightest infraction, and housed in crammed quarters that were hardly conducive to survival.

If those abuses weren't bad enough, the threat of sexual assault permeated Angola. Female inmates endured the additional reality that such untoward advances could result in pregnancy. It had happened before—plenty of times, in fact. The history of babies born inside the penitentiary during the nineteenth century confirmed an incriminating legacy of Black women's multiple vulnerabilities at the hands of the state.[74]

So, whether Clementine, Beulah, Katie, and Annie tried to escape from the penitentiary for reasons personal or systemic remains a mystery. What is clear is that they faced legitimate threats while in prison. That they all tried to do something about it—outcomes notwithstanding—provides evidence of Black women's agency under even the most inhospitable of circumstances.

Clementine may have unwittingly joined this community of agentic women for a reason seemingly unique to her: she was subjected to "an operation of the most delicate sort."[75] Given that this procedure happened just one day after her escape attempt, it is possible that the young woman knew it was coming and fled to avoid her fate. Moreover, evidence suggests that Clementine's procedure was rare enough—or her case sensational enough—to deserve mention by the regional press.

In fact, knowledge of this event is only known through two newspaper articles—one published a week after the operation and one printed over seven years later.[76] The limited nature of these sources requires careful consideration of what can be ascertained about Clementine's procedure. Perhaps the only definitive facts about the operation cover who performed it and where. Dr. Lewis Gray Sterling, the penitentiary physician, was assisted by a "Dr."

Wyatt H. Ingram Jr.[77] The latter was actually a prisoner who supposedly had studied medicine while incarcerated and was therefore a "qualified physician and surgeon."[78] In reality, he was a white male inmate who had been given a twelve-year sentence to Angola in 1909 for forgery, but had become a "trustee" of the institution by exhibiting model behavior.[79] Thus, two white men operated on a young Black woman, and one of those men had also been criminalized by the state.

As important as the individuals who performed the procedure was its location: The Walls back in Baton Rouge.[80] The processing center was also known as the place where "serious cases of illness and surgical cases are sent for treatment."[81] This means that Clementine was transported downriver at some point, presumably guarded closely as she returned to central Louisiana. Yet, given the temporal proximity between the operation and Clementine's attempted escape, it seems reasonable to surmise that she tried to flee while in Baton Rouge. The trip between the elbow of Louisiana and the capital city was not exactly fast, and it is unlikely Clementine would have been moved on the same day as the procedure. While she might have heard the stories of other women who risked the snake-infested Tunica Hills, she also likely knew there would be many advantages to absconding in a city, including anonymity, multiple flight paths, and potential assistance from unsuspecting passersby. Despite the benefits to escaping in Baton Rouge, Clementine was unable to successfully execute her plan. She would face the operation anyway.

What procedure was actually performed is muddied by the language of the media in early 1900s America. In the immediate aftermath, the regional press headlined their story with a sensational claim: "Blood Lust Cut Out of Clementine Barnabet."[82] The article followed up with an explanation that Clementine's "desire to slay came from a perversion of the sexual instinct," and the physicians had determined there was a "prospect for the woman's cure."[83] In the later article, Clementine was described as a "pervert" who underwent "an operation that restored her to normal condition."[84] Taken together, these pieces offer little tangible details from which to analyze the procedure. Yet, what seems clear, based both on the veiled word choice and medical knowledge of the time, is that the operation was not performed on Clementine's brain. For starters, prison officials did not think she was mentally ill, nor did the state's lunacy commission find evidence of legal insanity during her trial.[85] Moreover, lobotomies or leucotomies were not regularly performed on patients until the 1930s, and even then they were considered operations to cure mental illness.[86] If authorities had believed Clementine was insane in the 1910s, she likely would have been subjected to experimental psychiatric treatments like electrotherapy and/or hydrotherapy.[87] According to the state of Louisiana, however, Clementine Barnabet was not insane, but sexually perverse.

To cure sexual perversion would have likely meant operating on a person's genitals.[88] Although the information in the articles is too scant to speculate beyond this general observation, the stakes of any procedure of this nature can still be discussed. Clementine Barnabet was roughly twenty years old when two white men—including one prisoner—approached the president of the Board of Control of the State Penitentiary to ask for permission to operate on her.[89] This man, Colonel C. Harrison Parker, was a Confederate veteran, Democratic leader, and well-known dueler. There was no reason to think he genuinely cared about Clementine as a person, let alone as a young Black woman. Instead, he presumably knew the mythology surrounding her supposed crimes and approved Dr. Sterling and his assistant's request to proceed without much hesitation.

That these men asked another white man for his consent to operate on a young Black woman—and did not ask the patient herself—was symptomatic of the era. The humanitarian belief that prisoners had medical rights did not gain much traction in penitentiaries, insane asylums, and other state-run criminalization institutions in the early twentieth century.[90] Nor, for that matter, was it common practice to seek consent from patients who presented before doctors for care. For Black women, however, the politics of racism and sexism often meant that various invasive and often irreversible medical procedures were performed on them in the name of expediency and prejudice.[91] For someone like Clementine, then, her status as a convicted murderer *and* a Black woman meant that when she was placed on that operating table, she was rendered both vulnerable and victimized.

In the immediate aftermath of the procedure, its "success" was lauded with effusively jubilant language. The physicians insisted that Clementine "lost all traces of her old desire to kill" and sang "cheerfully" following the operation.[92] They opined: "the cure is as complete as it is wonderful."[93] Equally ominously, the regional press claimed that post-operation, Clementine was "now one of the mildest prisoners in the penitentiary."[94] This positive narrative of Clementine's suffering likely says more about what prison officials wanted to see as opposed to any demonstrable proof the procedure had worked. While

Clementine's attitude and demeanor were possibly altered after the operation, the rationale for such changes deserves further interrogation.

The doctors wanted to believe the operation worked because they were invested in a particular narrative of the axwoman-turned-model-prisoner. Conversely, Clementine likely wanted the abuses upon her personhood to end, so perhaps she developed strategies to process her imprisonment and to try to avoid additional medical trauma. Maybe she developed a conscious plan to cope with the operation or found herself navigating an unconscious response to bodily trauma (rather than medical successes).[95] It is feasible that she was also traumatized by her experiences at Angola and therefore responded in a manner that was construed as improvement, but was actually a reflection of declining mental health.

After Clementine's operation, she returned to life at the hellish penitentiary. Little is known about her remaining time incarcerated. In 1918, she was "allowed 1 month [as a] cane cutter."[96] That she was allowed to harvest the crop at all is a testament to both the importance of sugar to Angola and the shifting image of the famed axwoman. After the destructive boll weevil forced the penitentiary to abandon cotton for cane in 1911, the state built a massive refinery on site, completing its "model factory."[97] In a few short years, the sugar operation at Angola had become so successful that the penitentiary was lauded as one of the only self-supporting state-run institutions in Louisiana.[98] Yet, the only way the enterprise could be so profitable was if the state extracted as much work as possible from predominately Black bodies.

Thus, Clementine's appointment to cut cane should be viewed as the convergence of the state's greed and her behavior. Likely, if Clementine had still been viewed with the same terror that preceded her arrival at Angola, she would not have been allowed to wield a cane knife—a large, sharp implement that was not a far cry from the infamous ax attributed to her crimes. Similarly, if she had been recalcitrant and insolent, it would have been dangerous to put her in the dense, tall cane fields, where cutters were difficult to spot at all times. That Clementine was allowed to cut cane, which was not a task afforded to every woman at Angola, implies she was not under the same strict supervision as when she first arrived at the prison. Her time behind bars, then, was characterized by predictable if brutal routines and unexpectable moments.

/ / /

On April 28, 1923, Clementine Barnabet was released from the Louisiana State Penitentiary, her sentence commuted by Act 160. According to the law, she had served her time—a decade was enough. Although it seems incredulous that one of America's most notorious killers could be released from prison to no fanfare or news, that appears to be what happened.

She was ostensibly a "free" woman, but to be Black and female in the Jim Crow South meant that freedom was illusionary and fleeting. In many ways, the day Clementine walked out of Angola she also walked out of the historical record. More than a decade had passed while she was in prison, but even time is not enough to heal all wounds. She was a convicted murderer—a *confessed* murderer—and a Black woman in her late twenties or early thirties who had likely aged beyond her years as she toiled in the fields of her own incarceration. On that fateful April day, Clementine became anybody. She knew her past, but she had the blessing of Black womanhood—and the curse of Black womanhood—to keep her past private and to shield her identity from prying eyes. Thus, finding Clementine after she got out of prison is as much an exercise in luck as it is one in creative speculation. So far, luck has not rendered her presence known, so critical fabulation must be used to understand how and why a Black woman as notorious as Clementine could effectively disappear from history.[99]

By the time Clementine emerged from Angola, she likely looked as though she had been through hell. In a lot of ways, she had. After drudging in the baking Louisiana sun cutting cane, her skin was probably weathered and her hands calloused. The stresses of prison could have thinned her hair or wrinkled her eyes, furrowed her brow or hardened her smile. The poor diet could have weakened her bones, and the grueling conditions soured her countenance. The young woman who had entered the penitentiary was released in a body that had seen and felt enough hardship for a lifetime. The scars that Clementine brought with her into the prison were now accompanied by a decade's worth of new, perhaps harsher ones.

It was within this context that Clementine reentered a world that had already belittled and brutalized her on the basis of her race, gender, and class. Now, it could also condemn her as an ex-offender. She was a confessed and convicted killer whose crimes, whether real or imagined, had terrorized the nation for years. Faced with those prospects, Clementine likely tried to distance herself from her past. If this was the case, two seemingly different—but similarly motivated—possibilities emerge: she disappeared back into the community that had feared the mere mention of her name or she put literal distance between herself and her past, migrating elsewhere to start anew.

Unsubstantiated rumors have suggested that, upon her release, Clementine slipped back into Lafayette's Black community. How she could have made herself truly unrecognizable to locals in her hometown remains hard to say, but, with a changed name and aged appearance, it's possible that those most likely to recall her face had their memories blurred by the passage of time. Even if someone made a one-off comment that she reminded them of the infamous axwoman, she could have nervously laughed it off and chalked it up to having a doppelganger. Surely *the* Clementine Barnabet wouldn't have the audacity to show her face around Lafayette again.

And yet, if she *did* return to Lafayette, she likely resumed the kind of work that had been her purview before prison: domestic labor. Doing so would have allowed the woman formerly known as Clementine to remain discreet while slipping into the area's working-class Black community, if desired. So, she could have gotten married or kept to herself. She could have lived in her employer's home or resided somewhere nearby. She could have tried to find her immediate family or deliberately avoid learning of their whereabouts. She could have returned to the very town she'd grown up in and erased all connections to her childhood and adolescence.

Although it is certainly possible Clementine returned to Lafayette, it's worth considering a more tantalizing prospect: she skipped town and reinvented herself somewhere else.[100] Perhaps she managed to board a train—maybe even one on the very Sunset Route that had figured so prominently in her saga—and headed off toward the great unknown. Maybe she purchased a ticket to a city she'd heard of and dreamed about—maybe St. Louis or Chicago or New York or San Francisco. Official stub in hand, she might have crinkled the paper over and over as she fretted about her next move once she departed the train depot. Then again, maybe she stowed away in a cargo hold, jumping off at a random stop because she believed she'd gone far enough, whatever that meant. But it's also possible that she made a pact with someone in prison to meet up on the outside. If this was the case, presumably she traveled with a deliberate sense of purpose as she shed all vestiges of her life in Louisiana. Wherever Clementine ended up, it seems reasonable to conclude that she never regained the notoriety that had shrouded her life as a young woman. Instead, she may have integrated herself into a new Black community, taking on a persona and past that were radically different from the "negress murderess" whose very image haunted a nation.[101] Or maybe, just maybe, she learned from her mistakes, killed again, and was never caught.

Ultimately, no matter where Clementine went when she got out of prison, the country that she encountered was radically different from the one she once knew. While she had been behind bars, more than a decade had passed. The United States had become embroiled in World War I, supplying support, technology, and manpower to the Allied forces. The war had brought temporary prosperity as wartime industries provided much-needed jobs, shaping the nation's demography as Black southerners migrated north and west to urban centers.[102] In the aftermath of the war, however, economic challenges, agricultural misfortunes, and political scandals that emerged after President Harding's unexpected death threatened to send the country into a downward spiral. Indeed, just a few years after Clementine emerged from Angola, the United States experienced its worst economic depression in history. It was not just that prison had changed Clementine, but it had kept her isolated as local, regional, national, and global events continued. If ten years was considered a lifetime at Angola, then a lifetime of changes had also occurred outside of the penitentiary walls.

Epilogue

There is not an easy way to wrap up this saga. Throughout these pages, a single word has captured the complex, contradictory, and confounding: *messy.* This too is messy. Much of this story has oscillated between the knowable and the unknowable, the ordinary and the extraordinary. It has examined the unimaginable fear of the axman and the constructed power of Clementine Barnabet, revealing how Black communities and white lawmen responded to both. It has chronicled how a serial killer was made in early twentieth-century America, decades before the term entered the public lexicon and criminalistics became an established forensic science.

Yet, this book is not simply an account of a series of violent crimes and their aftermaths. The very existence of the axman—and Clementine Barnabet—alongside famous contemporaries like H. H. Holmes, Jack the Ripper, Jane Toppan, Belle Gunness, and Linda Hazzard, confirms that serial killers are a part of America's past (and present), not merely a pop culture obsession. The near erasure of the axman and/or Clementine Barnabet from this history, however, highlights the dangers of stereotyping criminality. In 1912 America, public discourse recognized—and manufactured—the existence of a young Black female serial killer. Today, such celebrity or notoriety seems incongruous with collective assumptions about who gets away with murder more than once.

Perversely, then, the case of Clementine Barnabet reveals an instructive moment in American history when an ordinary Black woman could be anything: a domestic servant, a criminal mastermind, a serial killer, or a cult leader—and perhaps all of these at the same time. This kaleidoscope of possible expressions of Black womanhood afforded Clementine a level of power that reflected who society imagined—and feared—her to be. In the early 1900s, the idea of an ax-wielding, cult-leading, terror-inducing young Black female serial killer was not only possible, but plausible. Clementine's notoriety implied that Black women were capable of covert, methodical, and untraceable violence. That constructed knowledge of this possibility coexisted alongside Jim Crow ideologies about Black inferiority confirms how racial and gendered norms were continually made, remade, and unmade. The combination of Clementine's race, gender, and age may have relegated her to domestic service, but the invisible nature of this work was also ideal for committing murder.

Indeed, Black women's invisibility from certain histories contributes to the messiness of this saga. Clementine Barnabet seemingly walked out of Angola in April 1923 and vanished from historical records. At the same time, there is no evidence to suggest she actually vanished from history. As such, that's one of the challenges with researching this kind of story. Studying everyday Black women requires creative approaches to figuring out what records reveal and what they obscure. In this case, there are additional layers that further complicate the narrative. First is the issue of age, in which trying to find evidence of young Black women and girls compounds the challenges.[1] Second is the problem of locating criminalized young Black women and girls *outside* of the institutions that contained and controlled them.[2] When these obstacles come together, it seems that searching for a convicted young Black woman murderer in the early to mid-twentieth century is as much a process of luck as it is a testament to Black women's historians who embrace the unknowable.

Even so, there's another way to think about why this saga must end in a messy way. The reality is that finding evidence of Clementine's existence—her whereabouts, her livelihood, and even her death—after her release is a fraught, though not impossible, endeavor. If information on Clementine Barnabet's life post-incarceration is to be found, perhaps it will come from word-of-mouth stories passed down in the very communities in which she supposedly blazed a trail of panic and terror. After all, she was likely unrecognizable, and the world had changed tremendously in the decade she spent incarcerated. Perhaps Clementine welcomed these transformations. Perhaps she did not want to be reminded of who she had been—of who the newspapers, authorities, and local communities had created her to be. As one report so succinctly put it: "Clementine knew herself better than those who tried to figure out her motive."[3] That statement is as applicable to her November 1911 confession, her April 1912 confession, and her October 1912 trial as it is to her

April 1923 release from the Louisiana State Penitentiary. There is something empowering in admitting that Clementine knew herself the best. Maybe she knew she simply wanted to start anew—to not be found.

Perhaps she should remain that way.

Appendix A

A Guide to the Axman Crimes

The following table was created to offer a shorthand reference to the various crimes covered in this book. The dates listed are when the bodies were discovered, which may have been different from the date of death. Similarly, some suspects were arrested months after the date of the crime, so even though they are listed under a particular family, their identity may not have been known in the immediate aftermath. Additionally, although most of these suspects were arrested, not everyone was detained. Names of the main suspects—those who figure prominently in more than one crime—are bolded. Finally, the axman is listed in italics to indicate when this moniker first appeared and how it coexisted alongside named suspects.

The "No." column includes two values in parentheses. These represent nonfatal attack victims. This book examines the deaths of forty-nine people and the nonfatal assaults of ten others who were believed to be victims of the Louisiana-Texas axman. Whether all of these crimes should fit under this singular killer is up for debate. This guide is designed to help readers reach their own conclusions.

Below the table are two lists. One names the additional individuals arrested due to Clementine Barnabet's April 1912 confession. Although she implicated and the authorities rounded up a number of people, they were generally not detained specifically for a particular crime. Instead, they were apprehended for their supposed connection—no matter how tenuous—to the confessor. The second list includes the known named victims of the axman who were killed as an indirect result of the crimes.

Year	Month	Day	Location	Family	Victims (w/ approximate ages, if known)	No.	Investigating Sheriff	Named Suspects[a]
1909	Nov.	13	Rayne (LA)	Opelousas	Edna (20s) Three children (ages 4 to 9)	4	Louis Fontenot, Acadia Parish Sheriff	George Washington America Washington Estelle Washington Houston Goodwill Monroe Jackson Sosthene Guidry **Clementine Barnabet**
1910	Feb.	11	Lake Charles (LA)	Hodge	Minnie Unnamed son (age 2)	2	D. J. Reid, Calcasieu Parish Sheriff	Elijah Hodge Abraham Potter Richard Lee
1911	Jan.	26	Crowley (LA)	Byers	Walter Silvina Unnamed child (age 6)	3	Louis Fontenot, Acadia Parish Sheriff	Ed Jackson Walter Jackson **Clementine Barnabet**
1911	Feb.	25	Lafayette (LA)	Andrus	Alexander (30s) Mamie (30s) Joachim (age 3) Agnes (baby)	4	Louis Lacoste, Lafayette Parish Sheriff	**Raymond Barnabet** **Clementine Barnabet** **Zepherin Barnabet**

1911	March	22	San Antonio (TX)	Casaway	Louis (early 50s) Elizabeth (late 30s) Josie (age 6) Louise (age 3) Alfred Carlyle (baby)	5	John Wallace Tobin, Bexar County Sheriff	William McWilliams
1911	Nov.	27	Lafayette (LA)	Randall	Norbert (20s) Azema (20s) Rene (age 6) Norbert Jr. (age 5) Agnes (toddler) Albert Scythe, overnight visitor (age 8)	6	Louis Lacoste, Lafayette Parish Sheriff	**Raymond Barnabet** **Clementine Barnabet** **Zepherin Barnabet** Edwin Charles Gregory Porter Reverend King Harris
1912	Jan.	19	Crowley (LA)	Warner	Marie (mid-20s) Pearl (age 9) Garry (age 7) Harriet (age 5)	4	Louis Fontenot, Acadia Parish Sheriff	Eliza Richards Reverend Joseph Wilkins **Zepherin Barnabet** Daniel Pratters Reverend M. J. Snipe
1912	Jan.	21	Lake Charles (LA)	Broussard	Felix (40s–50s) Mathilda (mid-30s) Margaret (age 8) Alberta (age 6) Louis (age 3)	5	D. J. Reid, Calcasieu Parish Sheriff	Reverend Abraham Nelson

continued

Year	Month	Day	Location	Family	Victims (w/ approximate ages, if known)	No.	Investigating Sheriff	Named Suspects[a]
1912	Feb.	19	Beaumont (TX)	Dove	Hattie (late 30s) Jessie (age 18) Ernest (age 14–16) Ethel (age 12–16)	4	Jake Giles, Jefferson County Sheriff	John Smith Wade Guidry Kenney Valley Andrew Quirk *Axman*
1912	March	27	Glidden (TX)	Monroe	Ellen (early 40s) Dewey Lee (age 13) Jessie (age 12) Alberta (age 8) Lyle Finucane, boarder (mid-30s)	5	Ethelbert B. Mayes, Colorado County Sheriff	Jim Fields Ida Fields Charlie Fields Mrs. Charlie Fields "Uncle Fink" Washington *Axman*
1912	April	12	San Antonio (TX)	Burton	William (late 20s) Carrie (early 20s) Naomi (age 3) Edward (baby) Leon Evers, Carrie's brother (mid-20s)	5	John Wallace Tobin, Bexar County Sheriff	*Axman*

1912	April	14	Hempstead (TX)	Marshall	Alice (34) Isaac Burney, Alice's father (75) Carrie Burney, Alice's sister Eva Jones, boarder Two unnamed boys	2 (4)	J. C. Lipscomb, Waller County Sheriff	*Axman*
1912	Aug.	16	San Antonio (TX)	Dashiell	James (late 40s) Lula (late 30s) John (age 19) James Jr. (age 17) Harriet (age 15) Joseph (age 10)	(6)	John Wallace Tobin, Bexar County Sheriff	*Axman*

[a] There are more named suspects than those included in this table. The table only reflects suspects mentioned in the book, not all of those found in primary source materials.

People suspected as a result of Clementine's April confession:
Pauline Barnabet
Zepherin Barnabet
Mary Cochon
Irene Duce
Valena Mabry
Mary Parkerson
Ella Thebeau
Joseph Thibodeaux
Darman Thomas
Ute Thomas
Reverend Thompson

Named victims-by-proxy:
February 21, 1912: Horace Alexander, Beaumont, Texas
February 29, 1912: A. E. Johnson, Lake Charles, Louisiana
April 17, 1912: Ernest Smothers, Houston, Texas
April 17, 1912: Max Warren, Houston, Texas

Appendix B
The Dashiells' Truth

In chapter 7, two short paragraphs detail the last axman attack: the nonfatal assault on the Dashiell family in San Antonio in August 1912. Yet, this brief mention of what happened on that fateful day ignores the knowledge the Dashiells had—and have passed down via oral history—about what *really* transpired when the axman attacked. That their information does not comport with Clementine Barnabet's confession is irrelevant: their loved ones knew the axman in a way that I cannot begin to comprehend. Within this context I share what the Dashiell family has told me is their truth.

In February 2022, thanks to the fortuitous connection made by another axman researcher, Charles Swenson, I interviewed the children of the youngest child who was in the Dashiell house on that life-changing night. In August 1912, the residents of the home were James and Lula Dashiell, the parents, along with John, James, Harriet, and Joseph, their children. When they were attacked, they believed it was the second time they had been targeted by the axman. Within days, they moved to California.

In San Francisco they rebuilt their lives. The youngest son, Joseph, started a family of his own. It was his children—Joseph Jr., Danielle, Margot, and Merryl—who were generous enough to share their insights with me.

/ / /

The Dashiells had been startled in June by the axman, but the attacker struck again in August. On that fateful night, Lula's arm—resting across her face—sustained the first blow, saving her life but maiming her in the process. Her husband and son shot at the assailant. Newspapers reported they missed. According to the Dashiells, however, there's more to the story.

The move to California might have been coincidental *and* causal. The Dashiell grandchildren mentioned that Lula and James both worked, with the former laboring as a caterer for well-off white families. Apparently, these families had California connections and were able to help the Dashiells line up work. In fact, James had already started to move some belongings out of the house *before* the August attack. So, perhaps there were plans under way, but they ended up being expedited due to that horrifying night. After all, the family hopped the train west within four days of the axman's visit, leaving unfinished business in San Antonio.

Yet, it's what the Dashiells knew about the axman—what their grandchildren know—that is arguably the most fascinating part of this whole saga. And their knowledge starts with a seemingly benign fact: the family had two dogs. Greyhounds, to be exact. A few days before the attack, two men saw Joseph—the youngest son—outside. They reportedly asked, "Whose dogs are these?" He responded that they were his. According to the memory then-ten-year-old Joseph later told his kids, the dogs were found dead the very next morning. A few days after that, the family was attacked.

The Dashiells had—and still have—every reason to believe it was the same two men who killed the dogs that then attempted to murder the family. Moreover, they are certain these two men were white.

But that's not all. According to the family, most newspapers got it wrong when they said James Dashiell and his son missed when they shot at the intruder. The grandchildren were told that their loved ones saw drops of blood on the ground leaving the house. The implication, of course, was that they'd likely hit the axman.

This discrepancy between what was reported by newspapers and what could have *actually* happened has a reasonable explanation. To be Black and have potentially shot a white man in the Jim Crow South was a terrifying prospect. The family knew the repercussions they could face because of this ordeal. They knew what had happened to the Casaways and the Burtons. So, they didn't report what transpired to the police. Instead, they packed up their belongings and moved to California, which is where they were planning to go anyway.

/ / /

The Dashiells' account offers an imprecise but neat bow to wrap up this story. I believe their family was the last to be attacked by the axman between Lafayette and San Antonio. If that's the case, perhaps the Dashiells ended the axman's reign of terror.

Notes

Introduction

1. "Astounding Confession of Negress Solves 17 Murders; Her Own Story of Killings," *New Orleans Item,* April 2, 1912; "Negress Confesses to Killing Twenty Persons," *Arkansas Democrat,* April 2, 1912; "35 Are Slain by Negro Cult," *Asheville Gazette News,* April 2, 1912; "Forty Hideous Murders Charged to Negress, Who Says She Sought to Gain Immortality; Strange Woman Heads 'Church of Sacrifice,'" *Cincinnati Enquirer,* April 3, 1912.

2. "Louisiana Axman Invades Texas and Slaughters a Negro Family of Four," *Daily Picayune* (New Orleans, La.), February 20, 1912; "Beaumont Murders Cause Added Fear in Crowley," *Times-Democrat* (New Orleans, La.), February 21, 1912.

3. There was a second series of ax murders that plagued the Midwest, sprawling from Colorado Springs, Colorado, to Villisca, Iowa, in 1911 and 1912. Some people have tried to connect these crimes to their southern counterparts. For discussions of potential parallels, see: Elliott, *Axes of Evil;* James and James, *The Man from the Train.*

4. Walkowitz, *City of Dreadful Delight;* Halttunen, *Murder Most Foul.*

5. "35 Killed by Negroes," *Santa Fe New Mexican,* April 2, 1912; "Church of Sacrifice," *Daily Argus-Leader* (Sioux Falls, N.D.), April 2, 1912; "Confesses Killing Seventeen Persons," *Harrisburg Telegraph,* April 2, 1912; "A Negress Confesses to the Murder of Seventeen Persons," *Miami Herald,* April 3, 1912.

6. The 1910 census reported just over 1 million Black women working agricultural jobs and roughly 850,000 laboring in domestic roles. Combined, these statistics represent 94.5 percent of gainfully employed Black women in the country. See U.S. Census Bureau, "Bulletin 129 Negroes in the United States," in *Thirteenth Census of the United States* (Government Printing Office, 1915), 32–35.

7. Gross, *Colored Amazons;* Hicks, *Talk with You Like a Woman;* LeFlouria, *Chained in Silence;* Harris, *Sex Workers, Psychics, and Numbers Runners;* Haley, *No Mercy Here;* Gross, *Hannah Mary Tabbs and the Disembodied Torso;* Gross, *Vengeance Feminism.*

8. In addition to the works in footnote 7, consider: Flowe, *Uncontrollable Blackness;* Suddler, *Presumed Criminal.*

9. Taylor, *Brooding over Bloody Revenge;* Gross, *Vengeance Feminism.*

10. For example, see: Bonn, *Why We Love Serial Killers;* James and James, *The Man from the Train;* Larson, *The Devil in the White City;* Schechter, *Depraved;* Vronsky, *Serial Killers;* Wilson and Seaman, *The Serial Killers.*

11. For example, see: Egger, *The Killers Among Us;* Hickey, *Serial Murderers and Their Victims;* Kelleher and Kelleher, *Murder Most Rare;* Ramsland, *Inside the Minds of Serial Killers;* Ressler, Burgess, and Douglas, *Sexual Homicide.*

12. Curtis, *Jack the Ripper and the London Press;* Headley, *The Atlanta Youth Murders and the Politics of Race;* Jenkins, *Using Murder;* McLaren, *A Prescription for Murder;* Leyton, *Hunting Humans;* Seltzer, *Serial Killers;* Schmid, *Natural Born Celebrities.*

13. Branson, "African American Serial Killers," 1–18; Hickey, *Serial Murderers and Their Victims,* 2nd ed.; James and James, *The Man from the Train;* Jenkins, "Serial Murder in the United States 1900–1940," 377–92; Kelleher and Kelleher, *Murder Most Rare;* Schechter and Everitt, *The A-Z Encyclopedia of Serial Killers;* Vronsky, *Female Serial Killers.*

14. Hickey, *Serial Murderers and Their Victims,* 4th ed., 142, 222; Branson, "African American Serial Killers," 1–18; Vronsky, *Female Serial Killers,* 3.

15. Jenkins, *Using Murder;* Kelleher and Kelleher, *Murder Most Rare;* Schmid, *Natural Born Celebrities;* Bonn, *Why We Love Serial Killers.*

16. "Black Amazon's Confession," *Saturday Globe* (Utica, N.Y.), April 6, 1912; "Silly Child Sentenced to Prison for Life," *Chicago Defender,* November 2, 1912.

17. For works on white girlhood, see: Odem, *Delinquent Daughters;* Cahn, *Sexual Reckonings;* Zipf, *Bad Girls at Samarcand.* For works on Black girlhood, see: Hicks, *Talk with You Like a Woman;* Agyepong, *The Criminalization of Black Children;* Jones, "'The Most Unprotected of All Human Beings'"; Henley, "Contested Commitment."

18. Simmons, *Crescent City Girls;* Chatelain, *South Side Girls.*

19. White, "Mining the Forgotten"; Higginbotham, "Beyond the Sound of Silence."

20. Gross, *Hannah Mary Tabbs and the Disembodied Torso,* 5; LeFlouria, *Chained in Silence,* 16; Fuentes, *Dispossessed Lives,* 7.

21. Gross, *Colored Amazons,* 4–5; Harris, *Sex Workers, Psychics, and Numbers Runners,* 10–17.

22. Farmer, "In Search of the Black Women's History Archive," 293; Mitchell, "Silences Broken, Silences Kept," 433–44.

Setting the Scene

1. U.S. Census Bureau, "Irrigation for Rice Growing: Louisiana, Texas, and Arkansas."

2. Throughout this chapter, emphasis is placed on southwestern Louisiana, although the rest of the project analyzes events in southeastern Texas, too. Because the rice belt extends across state borders, there are many cultural similarities between Black communities along the southern Texas-Louisiana state line. San Antonio and Hempstead, which are farther west, are arguably on the outskirts of the rice belt and are known particularly for cotton cultivation. Because these two sites figure into the larger narrative undertaken in this work, however, they are discussed in the context of the Southern Pacific Railroad's impact on the region. The focus on southwestern Louisiana serves as useful background to understand how local communities coped with many of the early ax murders. See Goins and Caldwell, *Historical Atlas of Louisiana.* The uniqueness of Texas is well-documented in Foley, *The White Scourge.*

3. Post, "The Rice Country of Southwestern Louisiana"; Sexton, "Rice Country Revisited"; Wiley, "Salient Changes in Southern Agriculture Since the Civil War," 66.

4. Although rice was grown in French Louisiana as early as 1718, it did not take on a signif-

icant level of commercial importance until after the Civil War. This means that the vast majority of the state's Black rice laborers had never cultivated the grain while enslaved, unlike South Carolina's grain producers. Babineaux, "A History of the Rice Industry."

5. Post, "The Rice Country of Southwestern Louisiana," 582–85.

6. Dethloff, "Rice Revolution in the Southwest," 70.

7. Post, "The Rice Country of Southwestern Louisiana," 580. To avoid confusion and to focus on the role of the railroad in the area's transformation, this chapter does not differentiate between all of the rail lines that eventually came under the purview of the Southern Pacific Railroad. The enterprise bought up dozens of smaller lines throughout the nineteenth and twentieth centuries, sometimes taking them over entirely and sometimes allowing them to continue to operate their own cars and maintain their own tracks. For additional information on the history of the Southern Pacific Railroad as a company, see the comprehensive texts: Hofsommer, *The Southern Pacific;* Orsi, *Sunset Limited.*

8. Howard C. Williams, "History of the Texas and New Orleans Railroad Company," *Handbook of Texas,* https://www.tshaonline.org/handbook/entries/texas-and-new-orleans-railroad, last updated May 14, 2020.

9. Department of the Interior, "Populations of Civil Divisions Less Than Counties—Louisiana," in *Statistics of the Population of the United States at the Tenth Census* (Government Printing Office, 1880).

10. Polk's 1939 *Lafayette City Directory,* page 14, State Library of Louisiana, Baton Rouge.

11. Department of the Interior, "Minor Civil Divisions—Louisiana," in *Census Reports Volume 1, Twelfth Census of the United States Taken in the Year 1900, Population Part 1* (United States Census Office, 1901).

12. U.S. Census Bureau, "Supplement for Louisiana," in *Thirteenth Census of the United States* (Government Printing Office, 1913), 602.

13. The statistic is from Huffard, *Engines of Redemption,* 2; the quote is from Hunter, *To 'Joy My Freedom,* 44.

14. Babineaux, "A History of the Rice Industry"; George C. Werner, "History of the Southern Pacific Transportation Company," *Handbook of Texas,* https://www.tshaonline.org/handbook/entries/southern-pacific-system (published February 1, 1996).

15. Werner, "History of the Southern Pacific Transportation Company," *Handbook of Texas.*

16. Huffard, *Engines of Redemption,* 9; Prince, *The Ballad of Robert Charles,* 30–34.

17. Harris, *Louisiana Products, Resources and Attractions;* Post, "The Rice Country of Southwestern Louisiana"; Sexton, "Rice Country Revisited"; Shanabruch, "The Louisiana Immigration Movement, 1891–1907," 203–26.

18. Harris, *Louisiana Products, Resources and Attractions,* 244.

19. Atakapa translates to "Man-eater" in Choctaw. Goins and Caldwell, *Historical Atlas of Louisiana,* 21; Butler, "The Atakapa Indians," 167–76; Brasseaux, *The Founding of New Acadia.*

20. In 1900, of the Black folks who operated farms in Louisiana, 80 percent were tenants rather than owners; in Texas, the ratio was nearly 70 percent farm tenants. U.S. Census Bureau, "Supplement for Louisiana," in *Thirteenth Census of the United States* (Government Printing Office, 1913), 610; U.S. Census Bureau, "Supplement for Texas," in *Thirteenth Census of the United States* (Government Printing Office, 1913), 668.

21. Du Bois, *Black Reconstruction in America;* Foner, *Reconstruction.*

22. Painter, *Exodusters;* Downs, *Sick from Freedom;* Williams, *Help Me to Find My People.*

23. Note, for example, that of the 488,000 Black residents of Louisiana in 1880, only 80 percent were actually born in the state, suggesting a sizeable level of migration after the Civil War. Department of the Interior, "Table I: Population of the United States by States and Territories" and "Table V: Population by Race, Sex, and Nativity," in *Statistics of the Population of the United States at the Tenth Census* (Government Printing Office, 1880); Foner, *Reconstruction.*

24. Foner, *Reconstruction;* Ross, *The Great New Orleans Kidnapping Case.*

25. Fairclough, *Race and Democracy;* Foner, *Reconstruction;* Woodward, *Origins of the New South.*

26. Huffard, *Engines of Redemption.*

27. Werner, "History of the Southern Pacific Transportation Company," *Handbook of Texas;* Hofsommer, *The Southern Pacific;* White, *Railroaded.*

28. U.S. Census Bureau, "Supplement for Texas," in *Thirteenth Census of the United States* (Government Printing Office, 1913), 593–94.

29. Brasseaux, *The Founding of New Acadia.* This project does not refer to Acadiana in the remaining chapters, as this terminology risks the erasure of African influences in the area. Instead, the terms rice belt region, southwestern Louisiana, and southeastern Texas are employed.

30. Brasseaux, Fontenot, and Oubre, *Creoles of Color in the Bayou Country.*

31. Istre, *Creoles of South Louisiana.*

32. Istre, *Creoles of South Louisiana;* Hall, *Africans in Colonial Louisiana;* Berlin, *Many Thousands Gone.*

33. Le Menestrel, "The Color of Music," 88.

34. U.S. Census Bureau, "Supplement for Louisiana," in *Thirteenth Census of the United States* (Government Printing Office, 1913), 601–2.

35. U.S. Census Bureau, "Supplement for Texas," in *Thirteenth Census of the United States* (Government Printing Office, 1913), 646.

36. U.S. Census Bureau, "Supplement for Texas," in *Thirteenth Census of the United States* (Government Printing Office, 1913), 599; U.S. Census Bureau, "Supplement for Louisiana," in *Thirteenth Census of the United States* (Government Printing Office, 1913), 601.

37. U.S. Census Bureau, "Supplement for Texas," in *Thirteenth Census of the United States* (Government Printing Office, 1913), 650.

38. Long, *Spiritual Merchants;* Anderson, *Conjure in African American Society;* Clark, *Masterless Mistresses;* Dawdy, *Building the Devil's Empire;* Pasquier, "Creole Catholicism Before Black Catholicism," 271–90.

39. Thornton, *Africa and Africans in the Making of the Atlantic World.*

40. Gomez, *Exchanging Our Country Marks.*

41. Du Bois, *The Negro Church;* Blassingame, *The Slave Community;* Raboteau, *Slave Religion;* Long, *Spiritual Merchants;* Anderson, *Conjure in African American Society;* Hazzard-Donald, *Mojo Workin'.*

42. Pinn, *Varieties of African American Religious Experience.*

43. Thompson, *Flash of the Spirit;* Long, *Spiritual Merchants;* Anderson, *Conjure in African American Society.*

44. Murphy, *Working the Spirit.*

45. Montgomery, *Under Their Own Vine and Fig Tree,* 17; Touchstone, "Voodoo in New Orleans," 373–74.

46. Hall, *Africans in Colonial Louisiana;* Chireau, *Black Magic;* Montgomery, *Under Their Own Vine and Fig Tree,* 12–14.

47. Berlin, *Many Thousands Gone;* Thornton, *Africa and Africans in the Making of the Atlantic World;* Gomez, *Exchanging Our Country Marks;* Raboteau, *Slave Religion.*

48. Du Bois, *The Negro Church;* Raboteau, *Slave Religion;* Blassingame, *Slave Community.*

49. Hayes, *Hard, Hard Religion.*

50. Bennett, *Religion and the Rise of Jim Crow in New Orleans;* Burton and Smith, "Slavery in the Colonial Louisiana Backcountry."

51. Hayes, *Hard, Hard, Religion;* Hill, ed., *Varieties of Southern Religious Experience,* 58.

52. Anderson, *Conjure in African American Society,* 25.

53. Long, *Spiritual Merchants,* xvi.

54. Murphy, *Working the Spirit,* 145–75; Pinn, *Varieties of African American Religious Experience.*

55. Montgomery, *Under Their Own Vine and Fig Tree,* 149, 268; Murphy, *Working the Spirit;* Chireau, *Black Magic;* Anderson, *Conjure in African American Society,* 79.

56. Woodward, *The Strange Career of Jim Crow,* xi.

57. Woodward, *The Strange Career of Jim Crow,* 102.

58. Shaler, "The Negro Problem," 707.

59. Gross, *Colored Amazons,* 7; Muhammad, *The Condemnation of Blackness,* 20–21.

60. Muhammad, *The Condemnation of Blackness,* 51.

61. Lombroso-Ferrero, ed., *The Criminal Man.*

62. Flowe, *Uncontrollable Blackness,* 20.

63. Du Bois, *Black Reconstruction in America,* 30.

64. Woodward, *The Strange Career of Jim Crow,* 25.

65. Equal Justice Initiative, *Lynching in America,* 40.

66. Equal Justice Initiative, *Lynching in America,* 40, 43.

67. Frederickson, *The Black Image in the White Mind,* 272.

68. Wright, *Racial Violence in Kentucky;* Brundage, *Lynching in the New South;* Tolnay and Beck, *A Festival of Violence;* Carrigan, *The Making of a Lynching Culture;* Clegg, *Troubled Ground;* Wood, *Lynching and Spectacle.*

69. Gross, *Colored Amazons;* Harris, *Sex Workers, Numbers Runners, and Psychics;* Simmons, *Crescent City Girls,* 82–107; Flowe, *Uncontrollable Blackness;* Jett, *Race, Crime, and Policing in the Jim Crow South;* Shufelt, *The Uncommon Case of Daniel Brown.*

70. Skolnick and Fyfe, *Above the Law,* 23–88; Malka, *The Men of Mobtown;* Adler, *Murder in New Orleans;* Burnham, *By Hands Now Known.*

71. Prince, *The Ballad of Robert Charles,* 27.

72. Dray, *At the Hands of Persons Unknown,* 130; Prince, *The Ballad of Robert Charles,* 5; Hair, *Carnival of Fury,* 137.

73. Prince, *The Ballad of Robert Charles,* 5.

74. Philip Dray notes his actions constituted a "killing spree," but stops short of categorizing Charles as a spree murderer using the parameters set forth by law enforcement officials. See Dray, *At the Hands of Persons Unknown,* 136.

75. Behavioral Analysis Unit, *Serial Murder,* 9.

76. Prince, *The Ballad of Robert Charles,* 73.

77. Carrigan, *The Making of a Lynching Culture,* 134.

78. Carrigan, *The Making of a Lynching Culture,* 114; Brundage, ed., *Under Sentence of Death,* 49; Pfeifer, *Rough Justice,* 77.

1. The First Crimes

1. "Rayne Scene of Brutal Murder," *Daily Signal* (Crowley, La.), November 13, 1909.

2. "Rayne Scene of Brutal Murder," *Daily Signal* (Crowley, La.), November 13, 1909; "A Brute's Work," *Sedalia Democrat-Sentinel,* November 14, 1909; "Four Negroes Slaughtered," *Daily Picayune* (New Orleans, La.), November 14, 1909.

3. "Quadruple Murder," *Times-Democrat* (New Orleans, La.), November 14, 1909.

4. "Rayne Scene of Brutal Murder," *Daily Signal* (Crowley, La.), November 20, 1909; "Three Arrests," *Daily Signal* (Crowley, La.), November 20, 1909.

5. "A Brute's Work," *Sedalia Democrat-Sentinel,* November 14, 1909.

6. "A Brute's Work," *Sedalia Democrat-Sentinel,* November 14, 1909.

7. Carrigan, *The Making of a Lynching Culture,* 114.

8. "Four Negroes Slaughtered," *Daily Picayune* (New Orleans, La.), November 14, 1909.

9. "Quadruple Murder," *Times-Democrat* (New Orleans, La.), November 14, 1909.

10. Loftus, *Eyewitness Testimony.*

11. "Four Negroes Slaughtered," *Daily Picayune* (New Orleans, La.), November 14, 1909; "Quadruple Murder," *Times-Democrat* (New Orleans, La.), November 14, 1909.

12. "Four Negroes Slaughtered," *Daily Picayune* (New Orleans, La.), November 14, 1909.

13. "Rayne Scene of Brutal Murder," *Daily Signal* (Crowley, La.), November 13, 1909.

14. "Three Arrests," *Daily Signal* (Crowley, La.), November 20, 1909.

15. "New Officials Assume Office," *Daily Signal* (Crowley, La.), June 1, 1908; 1910 United States Census, Crowley City, Acadia Parish, Louisiana, digital image s.v. "Louis Fontent," Ancestry.com.

16. "Proceedings of District Court," *Daily Signal* (Crowley, La.), May 15, 1909.

17. "Quadruple Murder," *Times-Democrat* (New Orleans, La.), November 14, 1909.

18. 1900 United States Census, Rayne, Acadia Parish, Louisiana, digital image s.v. "Demosthene Opelousas," Ancestry.com.

19. "Quadruple Murder," *Times-Democrat* (New Orleans, La.), November 14, 1909.

20. "Quadruple Murder," *Times-Democrat* (New Orleans, La.), November 14, 1909.

21. "Rayne Scene of Brutal Murder," *Daily Signal* (Crowley, La.), November 13, 1909.

22. "Quadruple Murder," *Times-Democrat* (New Orleans, La.), November 14, 1909; "Four Negroes Slaughtered," *Daily Picayune* (New Orleans, La.), November 14, 1909.

23. "Three Arrests," *Daily Signal* (Crowley, La.), November 20, 1909; "The Latest News in All Louisiana," *Daily Picayune* (New Orleans, La.), November 16, 1909.

24. "Four Negroes Slaughtered," *Daily Picayune* (New Orleans, La.), November 14, 1909.

25. "Three Arrests," *Daily Signal* (Crowley, La.), November 20, 1909.

26. "Suspect Arrested," *Daily Signal* (Crowley, La.), November 19, 1909.

27. "Suspect Arrested," *Daily Signal* (Crowley, La.), November 19, 1909.

28. "Louisiana Affairs," *Times-Democrat* (New Orleans, La.), November 21, 1909.

29. "Big Blizzard on the Plains," *Daily Signal* (Crowley, La.), December 4, 1909; "Coldest Weather in Years," *Shreveport Times,* December 14, 1909.

30. "Railroad Time Tables," *Daily Signal* (Crowley, La.), January 3, 1910; Hofsommer, *The Southern Pacific*, 169.

31. "Life Sentence for Richard Lee Convicted of Double Murder," *Lake Charles Daily American-Press*, July 30, 1910.

32. "Life Sentence for Richard Lee Convicted of Double Murder," *Lake Charles Daily American-Press*, July 30, 1910; "Negro Arrested for Murder," *Tensas Gazette* (St. Joseph, La.), February 25, 1910; Jones, *Labor of Love, Labor of Sorrow.*

33. Sanborn Fire Insurance Map, Lake Charles, Calcasieu Parish, Louisiana, February 1909, Library of Congress.

34. "Negro Woman and Baby Found Murdered in Bed Today," *Lake Charles Daily American-Press*, February 11, 1910.

35. "Louisiana Affairs," *Times-Democrat* (New Orleans, La.), November 20, 1908.

36. "Negro Woman and Baby Found Murdered in Bed Today," *Lake Charles Daily American-Press*, February 11, 1910.

37. "Woman and Child Chopped to Death," *Shreveport Times*, February 13, 1910; "Negro Woman and Baby Found Murdered in Bed Today," *Lake Charles Daily American-Press*, February 11, 1910.

38. "Negro Woman and Baby Found Murdered in Bed Today," *Lake Charles Daily American-Press*, February 11, 1910.

39. "Woman and Child Chopped to Death," *Shreveport Times*, February 13, 1910.

40. "Woman and Child Chopped to Death," *Shreveport Times*, February 13, 1910.

41. "Negro Woman and Baby Found Murdered in Bed Today," *Lake Charles Daily American-Press*, February 11, 1910.

42. "Woman and Child Chopped to Death," *Shreveport Times*, February 13, 1910.

43. "Negro Woman and Baby Found Murdered in Bed Today," *Lake Charles Daily American-Press*, February 11, 1910.

44. U.S. Census Bureau, "Supplement for Louisiana," in *Thirteenth Census of the United States* (Government Printing Office, 1913), 574.

45. "Woman and Child Chopped to Death," *Shreveport Times*, February 13, 1910.

46. "Negro Woman and Baby Found Murdered in Bed Today," *Lake Charles Daily American-Press*, February 11, 1910.

47. "Woman and Child Chopped to Death," *Shreveport Times*, February 13, 1910.

48. "Negro Woman and Baby Found Murdered in Bed Today," *Lake Charles Daily American-Press*, February 11, 1910.

49. "Woman and Child Chopped to Death," *Shreveport Times*, February 13, 1910.

50. "Louisiana Affairs," *Times-Democrat* (New Orleans, La.), February 17, 1910; "Richard Lee Under Arrest," *Lake Charles Daily American-Press*, February 19, 1910.

51. "Richard Lee Under Arrest," *Lake Charles Daily American-Press*, February 19, 1910.

52. "Life Sentence for Richard Lee Convicted of Double Murder," *Lake Charles Daily American-Press*, July 30, 1910.

53. "Life Sentence for Richard Lee Convicted of Double Murder," *Lake Charles Daily American-Press*, July 30, 1910.

54. "Life Sentence for Richard Lee Convicted of Double Murder," *Lake Charles Daily American-Press*, July 30, 1910.

55. "Life Sentence for Richard Lee Convicted of Double Murder," *Lake Charles Daily American-Press,* July 30, 1910.

56. "Richard Lee Is on Trial Today," *Lake Charles Daily American-Press,* July 29, 1910.

57. "Life Sentence for Richard Lee Convicted of Double Murder," *Lake Charles Daily American-Press,* July 30, 1910.

58. "Life Sentence for Richard Lee Convicted of Double Murder," *Lake Charles Daily American-Press,* July 30, 1910.

59. "No. 18,455: State v. Lee."

60. "No. 18,455: State v. Lee," 267.

61. "No. 18,455: State v. Lee," 268.

62. "No. 18,455: State v. Lee," 267.

63. "Decisions in Higher Court," *Shreveport Times,* November 15, 1910; "Supreme Court Cases," *Times-Democrat* (New Orleans, La.), November 15, 1910.

64. Muhammad, *The Condemnation of Blackness;* Flowe, *Uncontrollable Blackness.*

65. Hickey, *Serial Murderers and Their Victims,* 4th ed.; Muhammad, *The Condemnation of Blackness;* Branson, "African American Serial Killers"; Flowe, *Uncontrollable Blackness.*

66. "Negro Woman Killed and Children Injured," *Charlotte Daily Observer,* November 14, 1909; "Family Butchered," *Tampa Morning Tribune,* November 14, 1909; "The Husband Is Accused," *Valdosta Daily Times,* February 12, 1910.

67. "The Town of Rayne," *Daily Picayune* (New Orleans, La.), February 9, 1887.

68. "Census Bulletin," *Daily Signal* (Crowley, La.), December 19, 1891.

69. U.S. Census Bureau, "Supplement for Louisiana," in *Thirteenth Census of the United States* (Government Printing Office, 1913), 574.

70. "Acadia as a Rice Parish," *Daily Picayune* (New Orleans, La.), January 28, 1890.

71. Mire, *Images of America.*

72. Mire, *Looking Back at Crowley's History,* 47–50.

73. "Cement Walks Ordinances Pass," *Daily Signal* (Crowley, La.), May 17, 1909; Corrales, "Prurience, Prostitution, and Progressive Improvements," 37–70.

74. "Woman's Petition Was Turned Down," *Daily Signal* (Crowley, La.), July 7, 1909.

75. "It Threatens Their Homes," *Daily Signal* (Crowley, La.), May 29, 1909.

76. "Woman's Petition Was Turned Down," *Daily Signal* (Crowley, La.), July 7, 1909.

77. "Cement Walks Ordinances Pass," *Daily Signal* (Crowley, La.), May 17, 1909.

78. Corrales, "Prurience, Prostitution, and Progressive Improvements," 46–47.

79. "Woman's Petition Was Turned Down," *Daily Signal* (Crowley, La.), July 7, 1909; Sanborn Fire Insurance Map, Crowley, Acadia Parish, Louisiana, March 1909, Library of Congress; Sanborn Fire Insurance Map, Crowley, Acadia Parish, Louisiana, January 1915, Library of Congress.

80. "Brutal Murder of Negro Family Is Discovered in West Crowley," *Daily Signal* (Crowley, La.), January 26, 1911.

81. Sanborn Fire Insurance Map, Crowley, Acadia Parish, Louisiana, March 1909, Library of Congress.

82. "Brutal Murder of Negro Family Is Discovered in West Crowley," *Daily Signal* (Crowley, La.), January 26, 1911; Sanborn Fire Insurance Map, Crowley, Acadia Parish, Louisiana, January 1915, Library of Congress.

83. "Crowley Negro, Wife and Child Brained with Ax as They Slept," *Daily Picayune* (New

Orleans, La.), January 27, 1911; Sanborn Fire Insurance Map, Crowley, Acadia Parish, Louisiana, January 1915, Library of Congress. Although four other Black Baptist churches had been established in Crowley by 1902, it is reasonable to conclude that the Byerses were members of the church where their funeral was held. Additionally, Morning Star Baptist was the first church for African Americans in the city, founded in 1889. Thus, mentions of "the Colored Baptist Church" likely refer to Morning Star Baptist.

84. "Brutal Murder of Negro Family Is Discovered in West Crowley," *Daily Signal* (Crowley, La.), January 26, 1911.

85. "Brutal Murder of Negro Family Is Discovered in West Crowley," *Daily Signal* (Crowley, La.), January 26, 1911.

86. "One Suspect Is Under Arrest," *Daily Signal* (Crowley, La.), January 27, 1911.

87. "Brutal Murder of Negro Family Is Discovered in West Crowley," *Daily Signal* (Crowley, La.), January 26, 1911.

88. "Brutal Murder of Negro Family Is Discovered in West Crowley," *Daily Signal* (Crowley, La.), January 26, 1911.

89. "One Suspect Is Under Arrest," *Daily Signal* (Crowley, La.), January 27, 1911.

90. "One Suspect Is Under Arrest," *Daily Signal* (Crowley, La.), January 27, 1911.

91. "One Suspect Is Under Arrest," *Daily Signal* (Crowley, La.), January 27, 1911.

92. "One Suspect Is Under Arrest," *Daily Signal* (Crowley, La.), January 27, 1911.

93. "Suspect Is Arrested," *Daily Signal* (Crowley, La.), January 31, 1911.

94. "Suspect Is Arrested," *Daily Signal* (Crowley, La.), January 31, 1911.

95. "One Suspect Is Under Arrest," *Daily Signal* (Crowley, La.), January 27, 1911.

96. "Funeral of Joe Barker," *Daily Signal* (Crowley, La.), October 26, 1910.

97. Mire, "Black History Month—Looking Back at Crowley History," *Crowley Post-Signal,* February 7, 2021; "Colored People in Strong Stand," *Daily Signal* (Crowley, La.), February 4, 1911.

98. "One Suspect Is Under Arrest," *Daily Signal* (Crowley, La.), January 27, 1911.

99. "Colored People in Strong Stand," *Daily Signal* (Crowley, La.), February 4, 1911.

100. "Byers Murder Case," *Daily Signal* (Crowley, La.), January 30, 1911. For additional context of such cooperation during the Jim Crow era, see Jett, *Race, Crime, and Policing in the Jim Crow South.*

101. "Colored People in Strong Stand," *Daily Signal* (Crowley, La.), February 4, 1911.

102. "Strictly Personal," *Daily Signal* (Crowley, La.), February 22, 1911.

103. "Four Negroes Murdered," *Alexandria Daily Town Talk,* February 27, 1911.

104. "Family of Four Negroes Murdered; Escaped Lunatic Is Suspected," *Daily Picayune* (New Orleans, La.), February 26, 1911.

105. "Family of Four Negroes Murdered; Escaped Lunatic Is Suspected," *Daily Picayune* (New Orleans, La.), February 26, 1911.

106. "Horrible Crime," *Lafayette Advertiser,* February 28, 1911.

107. "Family of Four Negroes Murdered; Escaped Lunatic Is Suspected," *Daily Picayune* (New Orleans, La.), February 26, 1911; Babin and Babin, Civil Engineering, Surveying, "1912 Map of Lafayette, La.," Drawer 7, Acadian Manuscript Collection, University of Louisiana at Lafayette; Mouton Engineering Co., "1905 Map of Lafayette, La.," Drawer 7, Acadian Manuscript Collection, University of Louisiana at Lafayette.

108. "Whole Family of Negroes Murdered in Lafayette Home," *New Orleans Item,* February 26, 1911.

109. "Horrible Crime," *Lafayette Advertiser,* February 28, 1911.

110. "Murder in Lafayette," *Daily Signal* (Crowley, La.), February 25, 1911; "Family of Four Negroes Murdered; Escaped Lunatic Is Suspected," *Daily Picayune* (New Orleans, La.), February 26, 1911; 1910 United States Census, Lafayette, Lafayette Parish, Louisiana, digital image s.v. "Alexander Andrus," Ancestry.com.

111. According to the 1910 United States Census, the Andruses had three additional children, all under the age of six. It is unclear where these children were on the night of the murder.

112. "Family of Four Negroes Murdered; Escaped Lunatic Is Suspected," *Daily Picayune* (New Orleans, La.), February 26, 1911.

113. "Family of Four Negroes Murdered; Escaped Lunatic Is Suspected," *Daily Picayune* (New Orleans, La.), February 26, 1911.

114. "Horrible Crime," *Lafayette Advertiser,* February 28, 1911.

115. "Family of Four Negroes Murdered; Escaped Lunatic Is Suspected," *Daily Picayune* (New Orleans, La.), February 26, 1911; "Whole Family of Negroes Murdered in Lafayette Home," *New Orleans Item,* February 26, 1911.

116. "Horrible Crime," *Lafayette Advertiser,* February 28, 1911.

117. "Horrible Crime," *Lafayette Advertiser,* February 28, 1911.

118. "Family of Four Negroes Murdered; Escaped Lunatic Is Suspected," *Daily Picayune* (New Orleans, La.), February 26, 1911.

119. "Family of Four Negroes Murdered; Escaped Lunatic Is Suspected," *Daily Picayune* (New Orleans, La.), February 26, 1911.

120. "Horrible Crime," *Lafayette Advertiser,* February 28, 1911.

121. "Whole Family of Negroes Murdered in Lafayette Home," *New Orleans Item,* February 26, 1911.

122. "Family of Four Negroes Murdered; Escaped Lunatic Is Suspected," *Daily Picayune* (New Orleans, La.), February 26, 1911.

123. "Family of Four Negroes Murdered; Escaped Lunatic Is Suspected," *Daily Picayune* (New Orleans, La.), February 26, 1911.

124. "Four Negroes Murdered," *Alexandria Daily Town Talk,* February 27, 1911.

125. "Four Negroes Murdered," *Alexandria Daily Town Talk,* February 27, 1911.

126. "No Clue Yet," *Lafayette Advertiser,* March 3, 1911.

127. "Horrible Crime," *Lafayette Advertiser,* February 28, 1911.

128. "Negro Arrested for Rayne Crime," *Daily Signal* (Crowley, La.), March 24, 1911.

129. Hollandsworth, *The Midnight Assassin.*

130. "Negro Arrested for Rayne Crime," *Daily Signal* (Crowley, La.), March 24, 1911; "Negro Arrested," *Lafayette Advertiser,* March 28, 1911.

131. "Negro Arrested," *Lafayette Advertiser,* March 28, 1911.

2. Unlikable Suspects

1. "Family of Five Murdered in Bed," *San Antonio Light,* March 22, 1911; "Murder Mystery Deepens," *San Antonio Express,* March 25, 1911.

2. Marriage Certificate, Lane and Castellow, February 18, 1885, Hays County Clerk of the

Court, accessed via FamilySearch; "Five in Family Killed While Asleep in Home," *San Antonio Express,* March 23, 1911.

3. "Five in Family Killed While Asleep in Home," *San Antonio Express,* March 23, 1911; "Murder Mystery Deepens," *San Antonio Express,* March 25, 1911.

4. "Five in Family Killed While Asleep in Home," *San Antonio Express,* March 23, 1911.

5. "Five in Family Killed While Asleep in Home," *San Antonio Express,* March 23, 1911.

6. "Five in Family Killed While Asleep in Home," *San Antonio Express,* March 23, 1911.

7. "Whole Family Is Buried Same Day," *Macon Daily Telegraph,* March 27, 1911.

8. Hobbs, *A Chosen Exile.*

9. "Family of Five Murdered in Bed," *San Antonio Light,* March 22, 1911; "Five in Family Killed While Asleep in Home," *San Antonio Express,* March 23, 1911.

10. "Family of Five Murdered in Bed," *San Antonio Light,* March 22, 1911.

11. "Five in Family Killed While Asleep in Home," *San Antonio Express,* March 23, 1911.

12. "Family of Five Murdered in Bed," *San Antonio Light,* March 22, 1911.

13. "Family of Five Murdered in Bed," *San Antonio Light,* March 22, 1911; "Five in Family Killed While Asleep in Home," *San Antonio Express,* March 23, 1911.

14. "Family of Five Murdered in Bed," *San Antonio Light,* March 22, 1911.

15. "Family of Five Murdered in Bed," *San Antonio Light,* March 22, 1911.

16. "Five in Family Killed While Asleep in Home," *San Antonio Express,* March 23, 1911.

17. "Family of Five Murdered in Bed," *San Antonio Light,* March 22, 1911.

18. "Five in Family Killed While Asleep in Home," *San Antonio Express,* March 23, 1911.

19. "House in Which Tragedy Occurs Appears Gloomy," *San Antonio Express,* March 25, 1911.

20. Zelime Vance Gillespie, "John Wallace Tobin: Bexar County Sheriff and San Antonio Mayor," *Handbook of Texas,* https://www.tshaonline.org/handbook/entries/tobin-john-wallace (last updated July 1, 1995).

21. Gillespie, "John Wallace Tobin: Bexar County Sheriff and San Antonio Mayor," *Handbook of Texas.*

22. "John W. Tobin, Mayor and Alumnus Dies," *The Rattler* (St. Mary's University, San Antonio), November 23, 1927.

23. "Five in Family Killed While Asleep in Home," *San Antonio Express,* March 23, 1911.

24. "Five in Family Killed While Asleep in Home," *San Antonio Express,* March 23, 1911; "Person Crazed," *Daily Advocate* (Victoria, Tex.), March 24, 1911.

25. "House in Which Tragedy Occurs Appears Gloomy," *San Antonio Express,* March 25, 1911.

26. "Family of Five Murdered in Bed," *San Antonio Light,* March 22, 1911; "House in Which Tragedy Occurs Appears Gloomy," *San Antonio Express,* March 25, 1911.

27. "Family of Five Murdered in Bed," *San Antonio Light,* March 22, 1911; "Five in Family Killed While Asleep in Home," *San Antonio Express,* March 23, 1911.

28. "Five in Family Killed While Asleep in Home," *San Antonio Express,* March 23, 1911.

29. "Person Crazed," *Daily Advocate* (Victoria, Tex.), March 24, 1911; "Murder Done by Someone Crazed by Problem of Miscegenation?," *San Antonio Light,* March 23, 1911.

30. "Five in Family Killed While Asleep in Home," *San Antonio Express,* March 23, 1911.

31. "Five in Family Killed While Asleep in Home," *San Antonio Express,* March 23, 1911.

32. "Person Crazed," *Daily Advocate* (Victoria, Tex.), March 24, 1911.

33. "House in Which Tragedy Occurs Appears Gloomy," *San Antonio Express,* March 25, 1911.

34. "Five in Family Killed While Asleep in Home," *San Antonio Express,* March 23, 1911.

35. "Murder Done by Someone Crazed by Problem of Miscegenation?," *San Antonio Light,* March 23, 1911.

36. "House in Which Tragedy Occurs Appears Gloomy," *San Antonio Express,* March 25, 1911.

37. "No Clue Found to Slayers of the Casaways," *San Antonio Express,* March 24, 1911.

38. "White Suspected," *Daily Advocate* (Victoria, Tex.), March 25, 1911.

39. "No Clue Found to Slayers of the Casaways," *San Antonio Express,* March 24, 1911.

40. "Among the Courts," *San Antonio Express,* March 25, 1911.

41. "House in Which Tragedy Occurs Appears Gloomy," *San Antonio Express,* March 25, 1911.

42. "House in Which Tragedy Occurs Appears Gloomy," *San Antonio Express,* March 25, 1911.

43. "Murder Mystery Deepens," *San Antonio Express,* March 25, 1911.

44. "Five in Family Killed While Asleep in Home," *San Antonio Express,* March 23, 1911.

45. "No Clue Found to Slayers of the Casaways," *San Antonio Express,* March 24, 1911; "Person Crazed," *Daily Advocate* (Victoria, Tex.), March 24, 1911; "Two Brothers Located," *San Antonio Express,* March 31, 1911.

46. "Murder Mystery Deepens," *San Antonio Express,* March 25, 1911.

47. "White Man is Suspected," *San Antonio Light,* March 24, 1911; "Murder Mystery May Be Solved," *San Antonio Light,* April 2, 1911; "White Suspected," *Daily Advocate* (Victoria, Tex.), March 25, 1911.

48. "City News," *San Antonio Light,* March 26, 1911; "Court Gives His Charge," *San Antonio Express,* March 28, 1911.

49. "Murder Mystery Deepens," *San Antonio Express,* March 25, 1911; "Two Brothers Located," *San Antonio Express,* March 31, 1911.

50. "Two Brothers Located," *San Antonio Express,* March 31, 1911.

51. "Think They Have a Clue," *San Antonio Express,* April 2, 1911.

52. "Does Not Report," *San Antonio Light,* April 9, 1911; "23 Indictments Against One Man," *San Antonio Light,* April 12, 1911; "Court Receives Report of Work by Grand Jury," *San Antonio Express,* April 30, 1911.

53. "Two Brothers Located," *San Antonio Express,* March 31, 1911; "$250 Reward Offered," *Fort Worth Star-Telegram,* March 30, 1911; "Governor Offers Reward," *Dallas Morning News,* March 31, 1911.

54. "Five in Family Killed While Asleep in Home," *San Antonio Express,* March 23, 1911.

55. "Gov. Colquitt Offers Reward," *San Antonio Light,* March 30, 1911.

56. "Negroes Will Raise Reward," *San Antonio Light,* March 28, 1911; "Subscribe to Reward," *San Antonio Light,* April 1, 1911.

57. "Negroes Will Raise Reward," *San Antonio Light,* March 28, 1911; "$250 Reward Offered," *Fort Worth Star-Telegram,* March 30, 1911.

58. "Allerlei," *Freie Presse Für Texas,* April 1, 1911.

59. "Subscribe to Reward," *San Antonio Light,* April 1, 1911.

60. "Casaway Murder Still a Mystery," *San Antonio Light,* March 25, 1911.

61. "Two Brothers Located," *San Antonio Express,* March 31, 1911.

62. "Unknown Defies Sheriff," *San Antonio Express,* May 28, 1911.

63. "'I Killed Casaway Family' Says Man in Letter to Sheriff," *San Antonio Light,* May 28, 1911; "Unknown Defies Sheriff," *San Antonio Express,* May 28, 1911.

64. "Held for Investigation," *San Antonio Express,* August 9, 1911.

65. *Directory of the City of San Antonio, 1910–1911,* 775; *Jules A. Appler's General Directory and Blue Book of Greater San Antonio,* 806.

66. Sanborn Fire Insurance Map, San Antonio, Bexar County, Texas, 1912, Perry-Castañeda Library Map Collection, University of Texas at Austin.

67. "Held for Investigation," *San Antonio Express,* August 9, 1911.

68. Headstone for William McWilliams, Oakwood Cemetery Annex, Austin, Travis County, Texas; "Held for Investigation," *San Antonio Express,* August 9, 1911.

69. "Arrested for Death of Family," *San Antonio Light,* August 8, 1911.

70. "Refuses to Discuss the Casaway Killing," *San Antonio Light,* August 9, 1911.

71. "With a Smiling Face Defendant Hears Evidence," *San Antonio Express,* August 15, 1911.

72. "M'Williams Asks Liberty," *San Antonio Express,* August 13, 1911; "McWilliams Asks His Release," *San Antonio Express,* August 14, 1911; "Seeks His Freedom," *San Antonio Light,* August 10, 1911.

73. "Man Charged with Murders Has Hearing," *San Antonio Light,* August 14, 1911.

74. "With a Smiling Face Defendant Hears Evidence," *San Antonio Express,* August 15, 1911.

75. "With a Smiling Face Defendant Hears Evidence," *San Antonio Express,* August 15, 1911.

76. "With a Smiling Face Defendant Hears Evidence," *San Antonio Express,* August 15, 1911.

77. "M'Williams Is Still Confined in County Jail," *San Antonio Express,* August 16, 1911; "Man Charged with Murders Has Hearing," *San Antonio Light,* August 14, 1911; "M'Williams Is Held for Five Murders," *San Antonio Light,* August 16, 1911.

78. "House in Which Tragedy Occurs Appears Gloomy," *San Antonio Express,* March 25, 1911.

79. "Think They Have a Clue," *San Antonio Express,* April 2, 1911.

80. "M'Williams Is Still Confined in County Jail," *San Antonio Express,* August 16, 1911.

81. "M'Williams Is Still Confined in County Jail," *San Antonio Express,* August 16, 1911; "Defense Will Endeavor to Purge Record," *San Antonio Light,* August 15, 1911.

82. "M'Williams Is Still Confined in County Jail," *San Antonio Express,* August 16, 1911.

83. "M'Williams Not Confined in Cell," *San Antonio Light,* August 18, 1911.

84. "Court Holds M'Williams," *San Antonio Express,* August 17, 1911.

85. "Opening of Fall Terms," *San Antonio Express,* October 1, 1911; "Man 70 Years Old Faces Murder Trial," *Fort Worth Star-Telegram,* October 2, 1911; "Grand Jury Convenes," *Austin Statesman,* October 3, 1911; "Prosecutors Have Tilt," *San Antonio Light,* November 14, 1911.

86. "Arrested for Death of Family," *San Antonio Light,* August 8, 1911.

87. "Thirty-Two Are Indicted," *San Antonio Express,* October 28, 1911; "Thirty-Two Indictments Handed Down," *San Antonio Light,* October 27, 1911.

88. "In Confession Negro Clears Up Murders," *San Antonio Light,* April 2, 1912.

89. Image 123, microfilm reel 1019350, Index to Probate Minutes, K-Z, 1836–1973, Probate minutes, Office of the County Clerk, Bexar County records, Archives and Information Services Division, Texas State Library and Archives Commission.

90. "Family Murdered," *Daily Telegram* (Long Beach, Calif.), March 22, 1911; "Entire Family Murdered," *News and Courier* (Charleston, S.C.), March 28, 1911.

91. “Killed Whole Family,” *Manitoba Free Press* (Winnipeg, Canada), April 3, 1911.

92. “Negro Arrested,” *Lafayette Advertiser,* March 28, 1911.

93. Federal Writers Project Collection, Folder 45, Cammie G. Henry Research Center, Northwestern State University, Natchitoches, Louisiana (hereafter cited as CGHRC).

94. Federal Writers Project Collection, Folder 45, CGHRC; 1910 United States Census, Police Jury Ward 7, Lafayette Parish, Louisiana, digital image s.v. “Antoine Bernabe,” Ancestry.com.

95. “Negro Held in Jail at Crowley for Butchery of Family of Four,” *Daily Picayune* (New Orleans, La.), September 3, 1911.

96. “Murder Suspect Is Jailed Here,” *Daily Signal* (Crowley, La.), September 2, 1911.

97. “Suspect Arrested,” *Lafayette Advertiser,* September 5, 1911.

98. “Negro Held in Jail at Crowley for Butchery of Family of Four,” *Daily Picayune* (New Orleans, La.), September 3, 1911.

99. “Suspect Arrested,” *Lafayette Advertiser,* September 5, 1911.

100. *State of Louisiana vs. Raymond Barnabette,* Deaccessioned Lafayette Clerk of Court Criminal Microfilm, Louisiana State Archives, Baton Rouge, Louisiana (hereafter cited as LSA).

101. “Kept Apart from Witnesses,” *Daily Picayune* (New Orleans, La.), September 3, 1911; “Suspect Arrested,” *Lafayette Advertiser,* September 5, 1911; “Murder Suspect Is Jailed Here,” *Daily Signal* (Crowley, La.), September 9, 1911.

102. *State of Louisiana vs. Raymond Barnabette,* LSA.

103. “Negro Arrested on Murder Charge,” *Beaumont Enterprise,* September 3, 1911; “Negro Held in Jail at Crowley for Butchery of Family of Four,” *Daily Picayune* (New Orleans, La.), September 3, 1911.

104. “The Latest News in All Louisiana,” *Daily Picayune* (New Orleans, La.), October 10, 1911.

105. *State of Louisiana vs. Raymond Barnabette,* LSA.

106. *State of Louisiana vs. Raymond Barnabette,* LSA.

107. *State of Louisiana vs. Raymond Barnabette,* LSA.

108. *State of Louisiana vs. Raymond Barnabette,* LSA.

109. *State of Louisiana vs. Raymond Barnabette,* LSA.

110. *State of Louisiana vs. Raymond Barnabette,* LSA.

111. *State of Louisiana vs. Raymond Barnabette,* LSA.

112. *State of Louisiana vs. Raymond Barnabette,* LSA.

113. *State of Louisiana vs. Raymond Barnabette,* LSA.

114. *State of Louisiana vs. Raymond Barnabette,* LSA.

115. *State of Louisiana vs. Raymond Barnabette,* LSA.

116. *State of Louisiana vs. Raymond Barnabette,* LSA.

117. *State of Louisiana vs. Raymond Barnabette,* LSA.

118. In this case, Louisiana Creole refers to a specific language of French origin, not a racial or cultural identity. Federal Writers Project Collection, Folder 45, CGHRC; Daniel Schnopp-Wyatt, “Ax Woman of the Sacrifice Sect: Clementine Barnabet and the Louisiana-Texas Ax Murders of 1909 to 1912,” unpublished manuscript, 2018.

119. *State of Louisiana vs. Raymond Barnabette,* LSA.

120. *State of Louisiana vs. Raymond Barnabette,* LSA.

121. “Bernabet Convicted,” *Lafayette Advertiser,* October 24, 1911; “Negro Murderer Was Convicted,” *Daily Signal* (Crowley, La.), October 28, 1911.

122. *The Code of Criminal Law of the State of Louisiana*, 12.

123. *State of Louisiana vs. Raymond Barnabette*, LSA.

124. "The Latest News in All Louisiana," *Daily Picayune* (New Orleans, La.), October 20, 1911.

125. "District Attorney Robira," *Daily Picayune* (New Orleans, La.), October 22, 1911.

126. "District Attorney Robira," *Daily Picayune* (New Orleans, La.), October 22, 1911.

127. "Jury Defends Its Verdict," *Daily Picayune* (New Orleans, La.), October 22, 1911; "Jurymen Launch Vigorous Protest," *New Orleans Item*, October 22, 1911.

128. "New Trial Denied," *Lafayette Advertiser*, October 27, 1911; "Judge Testified for a Negro," *Shreveport Times*, October 28, 1911; "Bernabet Gets New Trial," *Lafayette Advertiser*, October 31, 1911; *State of Louisiana vs. Raymond Barnabette*, LSA.

129. *State of Louisiana vs. Raymond Barnabette*, LSA.

130. *State of Louisiana vs. Raymond Barnabette*, LSA.

131. "Last Bernabet Note," *Daily Picayune* (New Orleans, La.), October 29, 1912.

3. Arresting Clementine

1. "Negro Murderer Was Convicted," *Daily Signal* (Crowley, La.), October 28, 1911.

2. Climatological Data for Lafayette Region AP, LA—December 1911, National Oceanic and Atmospheric Administration, www.weather.gov/wrh/Climate?wfo=lch (accessed August 28, 2025).

3. "Negro Family Murdered," *Lafayette Advertiser*, November 28, 1911; "Six Murdered in Lafayette," *Daily Signal* (Crowley, La.), November 27, 1911; 1910 United States Census, Lafayette City, Lafayette Parish, Louisiana, population schedule, Lafayette City, digital image s.v. "Norbert Randall," Ancestry.com.

4. "Six Murdered in Lafayette," *Daily Signal* (Crowley, La.), November 27, 1911.

5. "Negro Family Murdered," *Lafayette Advertiser*, November 28, 1911; "Butchery of Human Beings," *Monroe News-Star*, November 28, 1911; Federal Writers Project Collection, Folder 45, CGHRC.

6. "Six Murdered in Lafayette," *Daily Signal* (Crowley, La.), November 27, 1911.

7. "Negro Family Murdered," *Lafayette Advertiser*, November 28, 1911.

8. "Family of Six Butchered in Bed," *Daily Picayune* (New Orleans, La.), November 28, 1911; "Butchery of Human Beings," *Monroe News-Star*, November 28, 1911; "Whole Family Butchered," *Alexandria Daily Town Talk*, November 28, 1911.

9. "Family of Six Butchered in Bed," *Daily Picayune* (New Orleans, La.), November 28, 1911; "Louisiana Negress Admits She Murdered Family of Six," *Daily Herald* (Gulfport, Miss.), November 28, 1911.

10. "Family of Six Butchered in Bed," *Daily Picayune* (New Orleans, La.), November 28, 1911; "3 Crimes Charged to Barnabet Woman," *New Orleans Item*, November 28, 1911.

11. "Family of Six Butchered in Bed," *Daily Picayune* (New Orleans, La.), November 28 1911; "Five in Family Killed While Asleep in Home," *San Antonio Express*, March 23, 1911.

12. "Family of Six Butchered in Bed," *Daily Picayune* (New Orleans, La.), November 28, 1911.

13. "Family of Six Butchered in Bed," *Daily Picayune* (New Orleans, La.), November 28, 1911.

14. "3 Crimes Charged to Barnabet Woman," *New Orleans Item*, November 28, 1911.

15. "Family of Six Butchered in Bed," *Daily Picayune* (New Orleans, La.), November 28, 1911.

16. "Negro Family Murdered," *Lafayette Advertiser*, November 28, 1911.

17. "Ready for Visitors," *Lafayette Advertiser,* November 21, 1911; "Lambert Oran Clark, Pioneer Doctor, Dies," *Lafayette Advertiser,* May 8, 1959.

18. "Family of Six Butchered in Bed," *Daily Picayune* (New Orleans, La.), November 28, 1911.

19. "Family of Six Butchered in Bed," *Daily Picayune* (New Orleans, La.), November 28, 1911.

20. "3 Crimes Charged to Barnabet Woman," *New Orleans Item,* November 28, 1911; "Bernabe Woman May Be Insane," *Shreveport Times,* November 29, 1911; "No Confession from Negro Girl," *Times-Democrat* (New Orleans, La.), November 29, 1911.

21. "Family of Six Butchered in Bed," *Daily Picayune* (New Orleans, La.), November 28, 1911.

22. "Astounding Confession of Negress Solves 17 Murders; Her Own Story of Killings," *New Orleans Item,* April 2, 1912; "Six Murdered in Lafayette," *Daily Signal* (Crowley, La.), November 27, 1911.

23. "Six Murdered in Lafayette," *Daily Signal* (Crowley, La.), November 27, 1911; "Family of Six Butchered in Bed," *Daily Picayune* (New Orleans, La.), November 28, 1911.

24. "Negress Is Indicted for Murdering Family," *Daily Picayune* (New Orleans, La.), April 5, 1912; "Family of Six Butchered in Bed," *Daily Picayune* (New Orleans, La.), November 28, 1911.

25. "Family of Six Butchered in Bed," *Daily Picayune* (New Orleans, La.), November 28, 1911.

26. "Negro Woman May Be Murdress [*sic*] of a Dozen," *New Advocate* (Baton Rouge, La.), November 28, 1911.

27. "Family of Six Butchered in Bed," *Daily Picayune* (New Orleans, La.), November 28, 1911.

28. "No Confession from Negro Girl," *Times-Democrat* (New Orleans, La.), November 29, 1911.

29. "'Ordered by God,' Girl Slays Ten," *Cincinnati Post,* November 28, 1911.

30. *Convict Records, no. 6801–9900,* vol. 17, Louisiana State Penitentiary, LSA.

31. Gross, *Colored Amazons;* Haley, *No Mercy Here;* LeFlouria, *Chained in Silence.*

32. "Family of Six Butchered in Bed," *Daily Picayune* (New Orleans, La.), November 28, 1911. Zepherin established an alibi that he was in Broussard and was released. Edwin and Gregory were also released, though they were rearrested after the discovery of bloodstained underwear in Edwin's jail cell. "Young Negress Perpetrator," *Daily Picayune* (New Orleans, La.), November 29, 1911; "The Latest News in All Louisiana," *Daily Picayune* (New Orleans, La.), December 1, 1911.

33. "Family of Six Butchered in Bed," *Daily Picayune* (New Orleans, La.), November 28, 1911; "3 Crimes Charged to Barnabet Woman," *New Orleans Item,* November 28, 1911.

34. "Negro Woman May Be Murdress [*sic*] of a Dozen," *New Advocate* (Baton Rouge, La.), November 28, 1911; "Bernabe Woman May Be Insane," *Shreveport Times,* November 29, 1911; "The Latest News in All Louisiana," *Daily Picayune* (New Orleans, La.), November 30, 1911.

35. Ross, *The Great New Orleans Kidnapping Case.*

36. "Butchery of Human Beings," *Monroe News-Star,* November 28, 1911.

37. Skolnick and Fyfe, *Above the Law;* Niedermeier, *The Color of the Third Degree.*

38. Usage of the third degree was common throughout the early twentieth century. However, specific details as to what it entailed were not widely publicized until the National Commission on Law Observance and Enforcement, known as the Wickersham Commission, concluded its reports in 1931. Details about what Clementine could have experienced comes from these reports. Wickersham, "Report on Lawlessness in Law Enforcement," 19.

39. Wickersham, "Report on Lawlessness in Law Enforcement," 47.

40. Niedermeier, *The Color of the Third Degree,* 8.

41. Wickersham, "Report on Lawlessness in Law Enforcement," 47.

42. Wickersham, "Report on Lawlessness in Law Enforcement," 63–64.

43. Kassin et al., "Police-Induced Confessions," 6.

44. Roberts, *Killing the Black Body.*

45. Representative sample of articles published: "Wench Confesses to Ten Murders," *La Crosse Tribune,* November 28, 1911; "Girl Murders Ten," *Staunton Dispatch-News,* November 29, 1911; "Confesses She Killed Ten in Two Families," *Knoxville Sentinel,* November 30, 1911; "Girl Admits Killing Ten," *Star-Gazette* (Sallisaw, Okla.), December 8, 1911.

46. "Killed Ten for Church," *Olean Evening Times,* November 28, 1911.

47. "Negress Admits She Killed 10 with Axe," *Evening Record* (Windsor, Canada), November 28, 1911.

48. "'Ordered by God,' Girl Slays Ten," *Cincinnati Post,* November 28, 1911.

49. "Creole Tells of Murdering Ten," *Mahoning Dispatch,* December 1, 1911.

50. "Negress Confesses Murdering Family Over Church Row," *Wilkes-Barre Times Leader,* November 28, 1911; "'Order by God,' Girl Slays Ten," *Cincinnati Post,* November 28, 1911.

51. "Girl Says She Slew Ten in Two Families," *Philadelphia Inquirer,* November 29, 1911.

52. "Creole Tells of Murdering Ten," *Mahoning Dispatch,* December 1, 1911.

53. "Confesses Killing 10," *South Bend Tribune,* November 29, 1911.

54. "Creole Tells of Murdering Ten," *Mahoning Dispatch,* December 1, 1911.

55. "Creole Tells of Murdering Ten," *Mahoning Dispatch,* December 1, 1911.

56. "Louisiana Negress Admits She Murdered Family of Six," *Daily Herald* (Gulfport, Miss.), November 28, 1911; "Tells How Ten Negroes Were All Murdered," *Fort Wayne News,* November 28, 1911.

57. "Families Are Wiped Out; Jealousy and Fanaticism," *Washington Herald,* November 29, 1911; "Negress Used Ax on Family," *Daily Gate City* (Keokuk, Iowa), November 28, 1911.

58. "Negress Admits She Killed 10 with Axe," *Evening Record* (Windsor, Canada), November 28, 1911.

59. "Six Murdered in Lafayette," *Daily Signal* (Crowley, La.), November 27, 1911; "Negro Woman May Be Murdress [*sic*] of a Dozen," *New Advocate* (Baton Rouge, La.), November 28, 1911; "The Latest News in All Louisiana," *Daily Picayune* (New Orleans, La.), November 30, 1911.

60. "No Confession from Negro Girl," *Times-Democrat* (New Orleans, La.), November 29, 1911; "Girl Admits Killing Ten," *Belleville News Democrat,* November 29, 1911.

61. "Confesses to Murder of Family," *Lake Charles Daily Times,* November 28, 1911.

62. "Confesses She Murdered Ten!," *Buffalo Enquirer,* November 28, 1911; "Girl Confesses to Having Slain Ten," *Daily Journal-Gazette* (Mattoon, Ill.), November 28, 1911.

63. "Negress Laughs at Charge of Sextuple Murder," *Bellingham Herald,* November 28, 1911; "Negress Sent to Jail," *San Antonio Light,* December 1, 1911.

64. "Young Negress Perpetrator," *Daily Picayune* (New Orleans, La.), November 29, 1911; "The Latest News in All Louisiana," *Daily Picayune* (New Orleans, La.), November 30, 1911; "Doubt That One Person Could Have Butchered Six Victims," *Alexandria Daily Town Talk,* December 1, 1911.

65. Kassin et al., "Police-Induced Confessions," 14.

66. Kassin and Wrightsman, *The Psychology of Evidence and Trial Procedure,* 76–80; Walker, "False Confessions of Battered Women," 459–60.

67. Kassin et al., "Police-Induced Confessions," 14.

68. Kassin et al., "Police-Induced Confessions," 15.

69. *State of Louisiana vs. Raymond Barnabette*, LSA.

70. Kassin et al., "Police-Induced Confessions," 19; Cleary, "Applying the Lessons of Developmental Psychology to the Study of Juvenile Interrogations," 118–30; Cleary et al., "How Trauma May Magnify Risk of Involuntary and False Confessions Among Adolescents," 173–204.

71. *State of Louisiana vs. Raymond Barnabette*, LSA.

72. Arain et al., "Maturation of the Adolescent Brain," 449–61.

73. See the following studies that discuss similar versions of adulthood for young Black women in their late teenage years and those with fully developed brains. Gross, *Colored Amazons;* LeFlouria, *Chained in Silence.*

74. *State of Louisiana vs. Raymond Barnabette*, LSA; 1910 United States Census, Police Jury Ward 7, Lafayette Parish, Louisiana, digital image s.v. "Antoine Bernabe," Ancestry.com.

75. An April 1912 article claimed that Raymond left home once "after beating his wife." "Just Escaped Noose," *Daily Picayune* (New Orleans, La.), April 19, 1912.

76. *State of Louisiana vs. Raymond Barnabette*, LSA.

77. "Negro Charged with Murder of Family," *New Orleans Item*, September 3, 1911; "Negro Held in Jail at Crowley for Butchery of Family of Four," *Daily Picayune* (New Orleans, La.), September 3, 1911; "Sheriff Believes Negress' Story," *Times-Democrat* (New Orleans, La.), April 3, 1912.

78. Bethard, "Deadly Visitations," 6–12; Jack Crouchet, personal correspondence to James Wilson, October 6, 2006, private collection.

79. "Arrest 'Voodoo' Doctor in 17 Murders," *New Orleans Item*, April 3, 1912; "Real Names Demanded," *Times-Democrat* (New Orleans, La.), April 6, 1912.

80. Hunter, *To 'Joy My Freedom;* LaShawn Harris, "The *Commonwealth of Virginia vs. Virginia Christian*"; Simmons, *Crescent City Girls.*

81. "Louisiana Negress Admits She Murdered Family of Six," *Daily Herald* (Gulfport, Miss.), November 28, 1911.

82. "No Confession from Negro Girl," *Times-Democrat* (New Orleans, La.), November 29, 1911; "Young Negress Perpetrator," *Daily Picayune* (New Orleans, La.), November 29, 1911.

83. "Girl and Father Accused of Murder," *Fort Worth Star-Telegram*, December 1, 1911; "The Latest News in All Louisiana," *Daily Picayune* (New Orleans, La.), December 1, 1911.

84. "The Latest News in All Louisiana," *Daily Picayune* (New Orleans, La.), December 1, 1911.

85. "Blood and Brain from Living Person Spattered Girl's Clothes," *Times-Democrat* (New Orleans, La.), January 18, 1912; "Chemist Metz Says," *Lafayette Advertiser*, January 19, 1912; "Evidence Strong Against Negress," *Daily Signal* (Crowley, La.), January 20, 1912; "Louisiana State News," *Rice Belt Journal* (Welsh, La.), January 26, 1912; "Chemist Report on Blood Stains Fastens Crime for Murder of Six on Negress," *Daily Picayune* (New Orleans, La.), January 28, 1912.

86. "Chemist Metz Says," *Lafayette Advertiser*, January 19, 1912.

87. "Blood and Brain from Living Person Spattered Girl's Clothes," *Times-Democrat* (New Orleans, La.), January 18, 1912; "Chemist Metz Says," *Lafayette Advertiser*, January 19, 1912; "Evidence Strong Against Negress," *Daily Signal* (Crowley, La.), January 20, 1912.

88. Donaldson and Lamont, "Biochemistry Changes That Occur After Death," 1–10.

89. "Chemist Report on Blood Stains Fastens Crime for Murder of Six on Negress," *Daily Picayune* (New Orleans, La.), January 28, 1912.

90. "Chemist Report on Blood Stains Fastens Crime for Murder of Six on Negress," *Daily Picayune* (New Orleans, La.), January 28, 1912.

91. "Negro Woman and Four Children Murdered in Crowley Last Night," *Daily Signal* (Crowley, La.), January 19, 1912.

92. "Negro Woman and Four Children Murdered in Crowley Last Night," *Daily Signal* (Crowley, La.), January 19, 1912.

93. "Negro Family Killed in Crowley," *Lafayette Advertiser,* January 23, 1912.

94. "Negro Family Killed in Crowley," *Lafayette Advertiser,* January 23, 1912.

95. "Warner Murder Still a Mystery," *Daily Signal* (Crowley, La.), January 20, 1912.

96. 1910 United States Census, Crowley City, Acadia Parish, Louisiana, digital image s.v. "[ill] Warner," Ancestry.com.

97. "Negro Woman and Four Children Murdered in Crowley Last Night," *Daily Signal* (Crowley, La.), January 19, 1912.

98. Marie Warner, death certificate, 19 January 1912, file number 786, Louisiana State Board of Health, copy in possession of author.

99. "Warner Murder Still a Mystery," *Daily Signal* (Crowley, La.), January 20, 1912.

100. "No Arrests Made for Quadrangle Murder," *New Orleans Item,* January 21, 1912.

101. "Wholesale Murders Cause Panic Among the Colored Inhabitants," *Daily Signal* (Crowley, La.), January 22, 1912.

102. "Crowley Negress Is Held for Murder of Family," *New Orleans Item,* January 28, 1912; "Negro Woman Held in Connection with Ax Murders," *Lake Charles Daily Times,* January 27, 1912.

103. "Wholesale Murders Cause Panic Among the Colored Inhabitants," *Daily Signal* (Crowley, La.), January 22, 1912; "Sanders Offers $500 Reward," *Daily Picayune* (New Orleans, La.), January 23, 1912.

104. "Wholesale Murders Cause Panic Among the Colored Inhabitants," *Daily Signal* (Crowley, La.), January 22, 1912; "Crowley Negress Is Held for Murder of Family," *New Orleans Item,* January 28, 1912.

105. "The Latest News in All Louisiana," *Daily Picayune* (New Orleans, La.), January 21, 1912.

106. "Two More Held for Ax Murders," *Times-Democrat* (New Orleans, La.), January 30, 1912; "Negroes Charged with Murder," *Galveston Daily News,* January 31, 1912; "Guilty Negroes Are in Custody," *Alexandria Daily Town Talk,* February 1, 1912.

107. "The Latest News in All Louisiana," *Daily Picayune* (New Orleans, La.), February 3, 1912.

108. "Negroes, in Terror, on Guard Against 'Sacrifice Church,'" *New Orleans Item,* January 23, 1912.

109. "Confesses Killing 10," *South Bend Tribune,* November 29, 1911.

110. "Wholesale Murders Cause Panic Among the Colored Inhabitants," *Daily Signal* (Crowley, La.), January 22, 1912.

111. "Wholesale Murders Cause Panic Among the Colored Inhabitants," *Daily Signal* (Crowley, La.), January 22, 1912.

112. "Colored People to Aid Officers," *Daily Signal* (Crowley, La.), January 23, 1912.

113. "$250 Reward Offered," *Fort Worth Star-Telegram,* March 30, 1911; "Five in Family Killed While Asleep in Home," *San Antonio Express,* March 23, 1911.

114. "Louisiana Negress Admits She Murdered Family of Six," *Daily Herald* (Gulfport, Miss.), November 28, 1911.

115. "The Latest News in All Louisiana," *Daily Picayune* (New Orleans, La.), January 21, 1912.

116. "The Latest News in All Louisiana," *Daily Picayune* (New Orleans, La.), January 21, 1912.

117. "The Latest News in All Louisiana," *Daily Picayune* (New Orleans, La.), January 21, 1912.

118. "Family of Six Butchered in Bed," *Daily Picayune* (New Orleans, La.), November 28, 1911.

119. "The Latest News in All Louisiana," *Daily Picayune* (New Orleans, La.), January 21, 1912.

120. "3 Crimes Charged to Barnabet Woman," *New Orleans Item,* November 28, 1911; "No Confession from Negro Girl," *Times-Democrat* (New Orleans, La.), November 29, 1911.

4. Inevitable Crimes

1. Sanborn Fire Insurance Map, Lake Charles, Calcasieu Parish, Louisiana, February 1909, Library of Congress.

2. "Entire Family of Five Negroes Murdered Here Sunday Mor[n]ing," *Lake Charles Daily American-Press,* January 22, 1912.

3. "Entire Family of Five Negroes Murdered Here Sunday Mor[n]ing," *Lake Charles Daily American-Press,* January 22, 1912.

4. 1910 United States Census, Lake Charles City, Calcasieu Parish, Louisiana, digital image s.v. "Jacob C. Thibodeaux," Ancestry.com.

5. "Entire Family of Five Negroes Murdered Here Sunday Mor[n]ing," *Lake Charles Daily American-Press,* January 22, 1912.

6. "Five Are Killed in Beds with Ax," *Times-Democrat* (New Orleans, La.), January 22, 1912.

7. "Five Negroes Slain in Their Beds as They Lay Peacefully in Slumber; Skulls Crushed and Brained with Ax," *Lake Charles Daily Times,* January 22, 1912.

8. "Five Negroes Slain in Their Beds as They Lay Peacefully in Slumber; Skulls Crushed and Brained with Ax," *Lake Charles Daily Times,* January 22, 1912.

9. "Five Are Killed in Beds with Ax," *Times-Democrat* (New Orleans, La.), January 22, 1912; "Entire Family of Five Negroes Murdered Here Sunday Mor[n]ing," *Lake Charles Daily American-Press,* January 22, 1912.

10. "Five Are Killed in Beds with Ax," *Times-Democrat* (New Orleans, La.), January 22, 1912.

11. "Entire Family of Five Negroes Murdered Here Sunday Mor[n]ing," *Lake Charles Daily American-Press,* January 22, 1912.

12. Bill and Rachel James argue that the inscription is a verbatim line from Harriet Beecher Stowe's *Uncle Tom's Cabin.* This is an example of modern-day readers engaging in historical omnipotence. *Uncle Tom's Cabin,* although incredibly popular in the mid-nineteenth century, had waned in importance by the early 1900s. Moreover, Stowe's text had gained a reputation for being inaccurate and racist in the aftermath of Reconstruction, meaning that Black communities in the South would not necessarily have encountered this literary work, let alone committed a phrase from it to memory. Moreover, evidence suggests the inscription could have come from a different version of the Bible—perhaps one adopted by Protestant groups with millenarian leanings. Henry Allan Ironside's *The Midnight Cry,* for example, refers to the psalm without the phrase "he remembereth them." James and James, *The Man from the Train;* Ironside, *The Midnight Cry.*

13. Du Bois, *The Negro Church;* Frazier, *The Negro Church in America;* Blassingame, *The Slave Community;* Raboteau, *Slave Religion.*

14. "Entire Family of Five Negroes Murdered Here Sunday Mor[n]ing," *Lake Charles Daily American-Press*, January 22, 1912.

15. "Entire Family of Five Negroes Murdered Here Sunday Mor[n]ing," *Lake Charles Daily American-Press*, January 22, 1912.

16. "Sacrifice Sect Slaughters 26," *Daily Picayune* (New Orleans, La.), January 22, 1912.

17. "Entire Family of Five Negroes Murdered Here Sunday Mor[n]ing," *Lake Charles Daily American-Press*, January 22, 1912.

18. "Blood Atonement Claims Lives of 26," *Sun* (New York, N.Y.), January 25, 1912; "Voodooism Too Much for Law," *Alexandria Daily Town Talk*, January 25, 1912; "Human Life Sacrificed to Negro Superstition," *Daily Times News* (Ann Arbor, Mich.), January 27, 1912.

19. Greene-Hayes, "A Very Queer Case," 58–84.

20. "Negroes Revile Deity; Would Enslave Whites," *Times-Democrat* (New Orleans, La.), October 20, 1907.

21. Jenkins, *Mystics and Messiahs;* Morris, *American Messiahs;* Corrigan and Neal, eds., *Religious Intolerance in America*, 2nd ed.

22. Lifton, *Thought Reform and the Psychology of Totalism;* Lalich, *Bounded Choice;* Stein, *Terror, Love and Brainwashing.*

23. "Five Families Are Murdered[,] Police Without Single Clue," *Elmira Star Gazette*, January 25, 1912; "Voodooism Too Much for Law," *Daily Republican* (Rushville, Ind.), January 25, 1912.

24. "Five Families Are Murdered[,] Police Without Single Clue," *Elmira Star Gazette*, January 25, 1912; "Voodooism Too Much for Law," *Daily Republican* (Rushville, Ind.), January 25, 1912.

25. "Two Negro Preachers Are Accused of Crime," *Macon Daily Telegraph*, January 24, 1912.

26. Greene-Hayes, "A Very Queer Case," 65.

27. "Arrested as Suspect," *Lafayette Advertiser*, January 23, 1912.

28. "Arrested as Suspect," *Lafayette Advertiser*, January 23, 1912; "Murder May Be Work of Cranks," *Lake Charles Daily American-Press*, January 22, 1912.

29. "Entire Family of Five Negroes Murdered Here Sunday Mor[n]ing," *Lake Charles Daily American-Press*, January 22, 1912.

30. "Negro Family Murdered in Lake Charles," *Jennings Daily Times-Record*, January 23, 1912.

31. "Sacrifice Sect Slaughters 26," *Daily Picayune* (New Orleans, La.), January 22, 1912; "'Sacrifice Sect' Blamed for 26 Murders," *New Orleans Item*, January 22, 1912.

32. "Negroes, in Terror, on Guard Against 'Sacrifice Church,'" *New Orleans Item*, January 23, 1912; "Second Arrest Made of Negro Preacher in Connection with Human Slaughters," *Daily Picayune* (New Orleans, La.), January 23, 1912.

33. Sanders, *Saints in Exile;* Alexander, ed., *The Dictionary of Pan-African Pentecostalism*, 175.

34. "Negroes, in Terror, on Guard Against 'Sacrifice Church,'" *New Orleans Item*, January 23, 1912; "Second Arrest Made of Negro Preacher in Connection with Human Slaughters," *Daily Picayune* (New Orleans, La.), January 23, 1912.

35. Sanders, *Saints in Exile.*

36. "Negroes, in Terror, on Guard Against 'Sacrifice Church,'" *New Orleans Item*, January 23, 1912.

37. "Wholesale Murders Cause Panic Among the Colored Inhabitants," *Daily Signal* (Crowley, La.), January 22, 1912.

38. "Blood Atonement Claims Lives of 26," *Sun* (New York, N.Y.), January 25, 1912; "Human Life Sacrificed to Negro Superstition," *Daily Times News* (Ann Arbor, Mich.), January 27, 1912; "Blood Atonement Claims Lives of 26," *Daily Phoenix* (Saskatoon, Canada), February 10, 1912.

39. "Voodoo's Horrors Break Out Again," *Denver Post*, February 11, 1912.

40. "Blood Atonement Claims Lives of 26," *Sun* (New York, N.Y.), January 25, 1912.

41. "Blood Atonement Claims Lives of 26," *Sun* (New York, N.Y.), January 25, 1912; "Like the Jungles of Africa," *Saturday Globe* (Utica, N.Y.), February 17, 1912.

42. "Deaths Are Laid to Voodoo," *St. Albans Daily Messenger*, January 25, 1912.

43. Greene-Hayes, "A Very Queer Case," 69.

44. "Preacher Caught in Homes at Night Quotes Scriptures When Surprised," *Times-Democrat* (New Orleans, La.), February 2, 1912.

45. "Held for Investigation," *San Antonio Express*, August 9, 1911; "With a Smiling Face Defendant Hears Evidence," *San Antonio Express*, August 15, 1911.

46. 1900 United States Census, San Augustine City, San Augustine County, Texas, digital image s.v. "John Dove," Ancestry.com; 1910 United States Census, Beat No. 2, San Augustine County, digital image s.v. "John Dove," Ancestry.com.

47. "John Dove, Husband and Father of the Murdered Family, Arrives in City," *Beaumont Journal*, February 24, 1912; "Looking for His Son-in-Law," *Galveston Daily News*, February 25, 1912.

48. "Four Members of Negro Family Are Found Foully Murdered," *Beaumont Journal*, February 19, 1912; "John Dove, Husband and Father of the Murdered Family, Arrives in City," *Beaumont Journal*, February 24, 1912.

49. "John Dove, Husband and Father of the Murdered Family, Arrives in City," *Beaumont Journal*, February 24, 1912.

50. "John Dove, Husband and Father of the Murdered Family, Arrives in City," *Beaumont Journal*, February 24, 1912.

51. "Four Members of Negro Family Are Found Foully Murdered," *Beaumont Journal*, February 19, 1912.

52. "Four Members of Negro Family Are Found Foully Murdered," *Beaumont Journal*, February 19, 1912.

53. "Four Members of Negro Family Are Found Foully Murdered," *Beaumont Journal*, February 19, 1912.

54. "Negro Family of 4 Murdered," *Beaumont Enterprise*, February 20, 1912.

55. "Four Members of Negro Family Are Found Foully Murdered," *Beaumont Journal*, February 19, 1912; Robert Wooster, "History of Voth, Texas: From Sawmill Community to Annexation," *Handbook of Texas*, https://www.tshaonline.org/handbook/entries/voth-tx (last updated September 1, 2023).

56. "No Clue to Murderer Who Killed with an Axe Four Negroes Here Yesterday," *Beaumont Journal*, February 20, 1912.

57. "John Dove, Husband and Father of the Murdered Family, Arrives in City," *Beaumont Journal*, February 24, 1912.

58. "Four Members of Negro Family Are Found Foully Murdered," *Beaumont Journal*, February 19, 1912; "Looking for His Son-in-Law," *Galveston Daily News*, February 25, 1912.

59. "Looking for His Son-in-Law," *Galveston Daily News*, February 25, 1912.

60. "Crimes Charged to Own Son-in-Law," *Alexandria Daily Town Talk,* February 28, 1912.

61. "Four Members of Negro Family Are Found Foully Murdered," *Beaumont Journal,* February 19, 1912; "No Clue to Murderer Who Killed with an Axe Four Negroes Here Yesterday," *Beaumont Journal,* February 20, 1912.

62. "No Clue to Murderer Who Killed with an Axe Four Negroes Here Yesterday," *Beaumont Journal,* February 20, 1912.

63. "Negro Family of 4 Murdered," *Beaumont Enterprise,* February 20, 1912; "No Clue to Murderer Who Killed with an Axe Four Negroes Here Yesterday," *Beaumont Journal,* February 20, 1912.

64. Sanborn Fire Insurance Map, Beaumont, Jefferson County, Texas, 1911, Perry-Castañeda Library Map Collection, University of Texas at Austin.

65. "Negro Family of 4 Murdered," *Beaumont Enterprise,* February 20, 1912.

66. "Negro Family of 4 Murdered," *Beaumont Enterprise,* February 20, 1912; "No Clue to Murderer Who Killed with an Axe Four Negroes Here Yesterday," *Beaumont Journal,* February 20, 1912.

67. "Negro Family of 4 Murdered," *Beaumont Enterprise,* February 20, 1912.

68. "No Clue to Murderer Who Killed with an Axe Four Negroes Here Yesterday," *Beaumont Journal,* February 20, 1912.

69. "Negro Family of 4 Murdered," *Beaumont Enterprise,* February 20, 1912; "No Clue to Murderer Who Killed with an Axe Four Negroes Here Yesterday," *Beaumont Journal,* February 20, 1912.

70. "Louisiana Axman Invades Texas and Slaughters a Negro Family of Four," *Daily Picayune* (New Orleans, La.), February 20, 1912; "Beaumont Murders Cause Added Fear in Crowley," *Times-Democrat* (New Orleans, La.), February 21, 1912.

71. "Four Beaumont Negroes Victims of the Ax Fiend Monday Night," *Daily Signal* (Crowley, La.), February 20, 1912; "Chiefs to Confer," *Daily Picayune* (New Orleans, La.), February 22, 1912.

72. "Authorities United to Nab Axe-Slayer," *New Orleans Item,* February 22, 1912; "Chiefs to Confer," *Daily Picayune* (New Orleans, La.), February 22, 1912; "Discuss Murders," *New Orleans Item,* February 25, 1912.

73. "Sheriffs to Plan Systematic Course," *Times-Democrat* (New Orleans, La.), February 25, 1912.

74. "No Meeting of Sheriffs," *Daily Picayune* (New Orleans, La.), February 25, 1912. This about-face may have a reasonable explanation. Likely, as had been the case with Clementine Barnabet's November 1911 confession, someone close to the axman crimes was attempting to control what information was leaked to the media. After all, if the assailant followed any of the newspapers in the towns along the Southern Pacific Railroad, even the smallest details about the detectives' strategies ran the risk of tipping off the culprit(s).

75. "Four Members of Negro Family Are Found Foully Murdered," *Beaumont Journal,* February 19, 1912; "Negro Family of 4 Murdered," *Beaumont Enterprise,* February 20, 1912.

76. "No Clue to Murderer Who Killed with an Axe Four Negroes Here Yesterday," *Beaumont Journal,* February 20, 1912; "Negroes Offer Reward," *Houston Post,* February 22, 1912.

77. "No Clue to Murderer Who Killed with an Axe Four Negroes Here Yesterday," *Beaumont Journal,* February 20, 1912; "Beaumont Negroes Guard Against the 'Axman,'" *Galveston Daily News,* February 26, 1912; "Franklin Negroes Believe Chloroform Won't Pass Over Water," *Alex-*

andria Daily Town Talk, February 28, 1912; "Local Negroes Are Using New Method [to] Foil the Axe-Man," *Lake Charles Daily Times*, February 28, 1912; "Ready for the Ax Brute," *Assumption Pioneer* (Napoleonville, La.), March 9, 1912.

78. "House in Which Tragedy Occurs Appears Gloomy," *San Antonio Express*, March 31, 1911.

79. "Beaumont Negroes Guard Against the 'Axman,'" *Galveston Daily News*, February 26, 1912.

80. "Beaumont Negroes Guard Against the 'Axman,'" *Galveston Daily News*, February 26, 1912; "Franklin Negroes Believe Chloroform Won't Pass Over Water," *Alexandria Daily Town Talk*, February 28, 1912.

81. "Local Negroes Are Using New Method [to] Foil the Axe-Man," *Lake Charles Daily Times*, February 28, 1912; "Negroes Taking No Chances," *Alexandria Daily Town Talk*, February 29, 1912.

82. Payne, "The Criminal Use of Chloroform," 685.

83. "Says He Knows 'Ax Murderers,'" *Times-Democrat* (New Orleans, La.), February 27, 1912; "May Apprehend Ax Man," *Houston Post*, February 28, 1912; "Information about Murders," *Galveston Daily News*, February 29, 1912; "Acadia Sheriff Is Given a Tip," *Lake Charles Weekly American-Press*, March 1, 1912; "Says He Knows," *Lafayette Advertiser*, March 1, 1912.

84. "Says He Knows 'Ax Murderers,'" *Times-Democrat* (New Orleans, La.), February 27, 1912.

85. "Information About Murders," *Galveston Daily News*, February 29, 1912.

86. "Astounding Confession of Negress Solves 17 Murders; Her Own Story of Killings," *New Orleans Item*, April 2, 1912.

5. Self-Defense Strategies

1. "Colored People to Aid Officers," *Daily Signal* (Crowley, La.), January 23, 1912.

2. "Negroes Alarmed," *Lafayette Advertiser*, February 13, 1912; "In State of Terror," *Daily Picayune* (New Orleans, La.), February 13, 1912.

3. "Colored Citizens," *Lafayette Advertiser*, February 13, 1912.

4. "Negroes Offer Reward," *Houston Post*, February 22, 1912; "Negroes to Meet," *Times-Democrat* (New Orleans, La.), February 25, 1912; "No Meeting of Sheriffs," *Daily Picayune* (New Orleans, La.), February 25, 1912.

5. Hadden, *Slave Patrols*.

6. "Four Beaumont Negroes Victims of the Ax Fiend Monday Night," *Daily Signal* (Crowley, La.), February 20, 1912.

7. "Ax Fiend Scare Almost Proves Fatal to a Negro Intruder," *Lake Charles Daily American-Press*, February 5, 1912; "Sheriffs to Plan Systematic Course," *Times-Democrat* (New Orleans, La.), February 25, 1912; "Was Not the 'Axe Man,'" *Alexandria Daily Town Talk*, March 15, 1912.

8. "Beaumont Negroes Guard Against the 'Axman,'" *Galveston Daily News*, February 26, 1912; "Beaumont Negroes Are in Frenzy over the 'Axman,'" *Galveston Daily News*, February 27, 1912; "Many Negroes Fear the Axman," *Galveston Tribune*, March 2, 1912.

9. "Trace Crimes to Sacrificers," *Los Angeles Times*, January 30, 1912.

10. "Dove Murders Parallel Other Crimes," *Meriden Weekly Republican*, February 22, 1912.

11. "Beaumont Negroes Guard Against the 'Axman,'" *Galveston Daily News*, February 26, 1912.

12. *Directory of the City of Beaumont, 1912–1913*, 46.

13. "Mistaken for the Ax Fiend," *Daily Signal* (Crowley, La.), February 22, 1912.

14. "May Be the Axman," *Daily Picayune* (New Orleans, La.), March 2, 1912; "Police Officer Shoots a Negro," *Daily Signal* (Crowley, La.), March 2, 1912.

15. For discussion of self-defense claims by white policemen during the Jim Crow era, see Adler, "Cognitive Bias," 43–61.

16. "May Be the Axman," *Daily Picayune* (New Orleans, La.), March 2, 1912; "Letter Found in Dead Negro's Grip May Result in Important Arrest," *Lake Charles Weekly American-Press,* March 8, 1912.

17. "Letter Found in Dead Negro's Grip May Result in Important Arrest," *Lake Charles Weekly American-Press,* March 8, 1912.

18. While Voodoo was—and is—a distinct diasporic religion with specific rituals, practices, and beliefs, hoodoo was—and is—a way of interacting with the world through manipulation of natural and manmade objects. Hoodoo does not require belief in a larger cosmology, but simply a belief in a given practitioner and their remedies. Often overly simplified to "folk medicine," hoodoo—or conjure—is a complex spectrum that can embrace both formal religion and supernaturalism, depending on its regional distinctiveness. That A. E. Johnson was categorized as belonging to either of these diasporic communities simply due to the contents of his suitcase and the artifacts on his person suggests that axman hysteria had rendered the slightest anomaly suspicious—perhaps even fatally so. See the following literature for details: Davis, *American Voudou;* Long, *Spiritual Merchants;* Anderson, *Conjure in African American Society.*

19. "Deaths Are Laid to Voodoo," *St. Albans Daily Messenger,* January 25, 1912.

20. "4 New Murders Charged to Fanatic," *New Orleans Item,* February 20, 1912; "Louisiana Axman Invades Texas and Slaughters a Negro Family of Four," *Daily Picayune* (New Orleans, La.), February 20, 1912; "New Ax Murder Occurs in Texas," *Times-Democrat* (New Orleans, La.), February 20, 1912; "Slaughter of Negro Family Was Repeated at Beaumont," *Alexandria Daily Town Talk,* February 20, 1912.

21. "Negro Family of 4 Murdered," *Beaumont Enterprise,* February 20, 1912.

22. "24 Negroes Slain, 'Sacrifice' Sect Preacher Is Held," *St. Louis Post-Dispatch,* February 4, 1912.

23. "Deaths Are Laid to Voodoo," *St. Albans Daily Messenger,* January 25, 1912.

24. "Negroes Taking No Chances," *Alexandria Daily Town Talk,* February 29, 1912.

25. "Chemist Report on Blood Stains Fastens Crime for Murder of Six on Negress," *Daily Picayune* (New Orleans, La.), January 18, 1912.

26. "The Latest News in All Louisiana," *Daily Picayune* (New Orleans, La.), February 3, 1912.

27. "Negroes, in Terror, on Guard Against 'Sacrifice Church,'" *New Orleans Item,* January 23, 1912; "Local Negroes Are Using New Method [to] Foil the Axe-Man," *Lake Charles Daily Times,* February 28, 1912.

28. "No Clue to Murderer Who Killed with an Axe Four Negroes Here Yesterday," *Beaumont Journal,* February 20, 1912.

29. "'Ax Man' Visiting Capital the Report," *Shreveport Times,* March 23, 1912.

30. "Beaumont Negroes Guard Against the 'Axman,'" *Galveston Daily News,* February 26, 1912.

31. "Chemist Report on Blood Stains Fastens Crime for Murder of Six on Negress," *Daily Picayune* (New Orleans, La.), January 18, 1912.

32. "In State of Terror," *Daily Picayune* (New Orleans, La.), February 13, 1912.

33. "Wholesale Murders Cause Panic Among the Colored Inhabitants," *Daily Signal* (Crowley, La.), January 22, 1912.

34. "Beaumont Negroes Are in Frenzy over the 'Axman,'" *Galveston Daily News*, February 27, 1912.

35. "Negroes Terrorized," *Daily Signal* (Crowley, La.), February 17, 1912; "4 New Murders Charged to Fanatic," *New Orleans Item*, February 20, 1912.

36. "No Clue to Murderer Who Killed with an Axe Four Negroes Here Yesterday," *Beaumont Journal*, February 20, 1912; "Beaumont Negroes Are in Frenzy over the 'Axman,'" *Galveston Daily News*, February 27, 1912; "Ax Fiend Scare Almost Proves Fatal to a Negro Intruder," *Lake Charles Daily American-Press*, February 5, 1912; "Mistaken for the Ax Fiend," *Daily Signal* (Crowley, La.), February 22, 1912.

37. "Blood Atonement Claims Lives of 26," *Sun* (New York, N.Y.), January 25, 1912; "Trace Crimes to Sacrificers," *Los Angeles Times*, January 30, 1912; "Blood Atonement Claims Lives of 26," *Daily Phoenix* (Saskatoon, Canada), February 10, 1912.

38. "Negro Terror May Shorten Rice Crop," *New York Times*, March 3, 1912.

39. Painter, *Exodusters*, 184.

40. "Blood Atonement Claims Lives of 26," *Sun* (New York, N.Y.), January 25, 1912; "Traces Crimes to Sacrificers," *Los Angeles Times*, January 30, 1912; "Negro Terror May Shorten Rice Crop," *New York Times*, March 3, 1912; "A Wall Street Hoodoo," *Evening World-Herald* (Omaha, Nebr.), March 9, 1912; "Voodoo Doctors," *Tipton Daily Tribune*, March 18, 1912; "Negro Terror May Shorten Rice Crop," *Daily Journal-Gazette* (Mattoon, Ill.), April 8, 1912.

41. Painter, *Exodusters;* Lemann, *The Promised Land.*

42. "Negro Terror May Shorten Rice Crop," *New York Times*, March 3, 1912.

43. "A Wall Street Hoodoo," *Evening World-Herald* (Omaha, Nebr.), March 9, 1912.

44. "Voodoo Doctors," *Tipton Daily Tribune*, March 18, 1912.

45. "Negroes Are Frightened," *Daily Signal* (Crowley, La.), February 1, 1912; "Butchery Practised by 'The Sanctified Church,'" *Tampa Daily Times*, February 9, 1912; "Negro Receives Letter," *Houston Post*, February 24, 1912; "Orange Negroes Frightened," *Galveston Daily News*, February 24, 1912; "Franklin Negroes Believe Chloroform Won't Pass Over Water," *Alexandria Daily Town Talk*, February 28, 1912; "Ready for the Ax Brute," *Assumption Pioneer* (Napoleonville, La.), March 9, 1912; "O-ogh! the 'Axe Man' Is After Bad Darkies!," *Austin Statesman*, March 23, 1912; "Short Texas Specials," *Houston Post*, April 1, 1912.

46. "Texas Marriages, 1837–1973," FamilySearch, https://familysearch.org/ark:/61903/1:1:F6YC-MQX: 22 January 2020, Jim Fields, 1912.

47. 1910 United States Census, Precinct No. 1, Colorado County, Texas, digital image s.v. "Ida Booker," Ancestry.com.

48. 1880 United States Census, Precinct #4, Colorado County, Texas, digital image s.v. "Jim Fields," Ancestry.com.

49. 1880 United States Census, Precinct #4, Colorado County, Texas, digital image s.v. "Charlie Fields," Ancestry.com.

50. "Axman Deals Death to Six More Victims," *Galveston Daily News*, March 28, 1912; "Six Negroes Brained by Ax While Asleep at Glidden," *Houston Post*, March 28, 1912.

51. "Appalling Murder at Glidden," *Colorado Citizen*, March 29, 1912.

52. "Appalling Murder at Glidden," *Colorado Citizen,* March 29, 1912.

53. "Axman Deals Death to Six More Victims," *Galveston Daily News,* March 28, 1912; "Six Are Slain," *Galveston Tribune,* March 28, 1912.

54. "Axman Deals Death to Six More Victims," *Galveston Daily News,* March 28, 1912; "Appalling Murder at Glidden," *Colorado Citizen,* March 29, 1912.

55. "Six Negroes Brained by Ax While Asleep at Glidden," *Houston Post,* March 28, 1912.

56. "Appalling Murder at Glidden," *Colorado Citizen,* March 29, 1912.

57. "Six Negroes Brained by Ax While Asleep at Glidden," *Houston Post,* March 28, 1912.

58. "Appalling Murder at Glidden," *Colorado Citizen,* March 29, 1912.

59. "Appalling Murder at Glidden," *Colorado Citizen,* March 29, 1912; "Six Negroes Brained by Ax While Asleep at Glidden," *Houston Post,* March 28, 1912.

60. "Six More Killed by 'the Ax-Man,'" *Times-Democrat* (New Orleans, La.), March 28, 1912.

61. "Appalling Murder at Glidden," *Colorado Citizen,* March 29, 1912.

62. "Six Negroes Slain as They Slept," *Boston Daily Globe,* March 28, 1912; "Texas Negroes Fear Fanaticism," *Daily Herald* (Gulfport, Miss.), March 28, 1912; "Twelve Negroes Killed Recently in Texas," *Albuquerque Morning Journal,* March 28, 1912.

63. "Axman Deals Death to Six More Victims," *Galveston Daily News,* March 28, 1912; "Six More Killed by 'the Ax-Man,'" *Times-Democrat* (New Orleans, La.), March 28, 1912; "Six Negroes Brained by Ax While Asleep at Glidden," *Houston Post,* March 28, 1912; "Axman Deals Death to Six," *Daily Advocate* (Victoria, Tex.), March 29, 1912.

64. "Appalling Murder at Glidden," *Colorado Citizen,* March 29, 1912; "Victims of Ax Man Buried," *Houston Post,* March 29, 1912.

65. "Victims of Ax Man Buried," *Houston Post,* March 29, 1912.

66. "Ax Man Again," *Lafayette Advertiser,* April 2, 1912.

67. "Axman Deals Death to Six More Victims," *Galveston Daily News,* March 28, 1912.

68. "Six Negroes Brained by Ax While Asleep at Glidden," *Houston Post,* March 28, 1912.

69. "Axman Deals Death to Six More Victims," *Galveston Daily News,* March 28, 1912.

70. "Appalling Murder at Glidden," *Colorado Citizen,* March 29, 1912.

71. "Tells of Glidden Murders," *Galveston Daily News,* April 2, 1912.

72. "Tells of Glidden Murders," *Galveston Daily News,* April 2, 1912.

73. "Tells of Glidden Murders," *Galveston Daily News,* April 2, 1912.

74. Stein, "The Glidden Ax Murders," 308.

75. "Special Session of Court Ordered by Judge Kennon," *Colorado Citizen,* April 5, 1912.

76. "Special Session of Court Ordered by Judge Kennon," *Colorado Citizen,* April 5, 1912; *State of Texas vs. Jim Fields,* no. 3163, Colorado County District Court, Columbus, Texas.

77. *State of Texas vs. Jim Fields,* no. 3163, Colorado County District Court, Columbus, Texas.

78. "Alleged Axman Indicted," *Galveston Tribune,* May 20, 1912; "Negro Is Placed on Trial," *San Antonio Express,* May 28, 1912.

79. *State of Texas vs. Jim Fields,* no. 3163, Colorado County District Court, Columbus, Texas; "[Untitled]," *La Grange Journal,* June 6, 1912.

80. "Ax Murder Trial," *Fort Worth Record,* June 2, 1912.

81. "Not Guilty Verdict Given," *Dallas Morning News,* June 2, 1912.

82. Stein, "The Glidden Ax Murders," 311.

6. Clementine's Confession

1. "'Voodoolism [*sic*],'" *Mudgee Guardian* (Mudgee, Australia), April 4, 1912; "Hoodooism," *South Wales Echo,* April 3, 1912; "Confession of 17 Murders," *Derby Daily Telegraph,* April 4, 1912; "Seventeen Murders," *The Leader* (Allahabad, India), May 9, 1912; "Confession to 17 Murders," *Northern Advocate* (Whangarei, New Zealand), May 22, 1912.

2. "Negress Confesses," *Lafayette Advertiser,* April 5, 1912.

3. "Astounding Confession of Negress Solves 17 Murders; Her Own Story of Killings," *New Orleans Item,* April 2, 1912.

4. "Arrest 'Voodoo' Doctor in 17 Murders," *New Orleans Item,* April 3, 1912.

5. "The 'Axe Man' Is a Woman," *Alexandria Daily Town Talk,* April 2, 1912; "Probe Murders," *Daily Picayune* (New Orleans, La.), April 2, 1912; "Ogden Gets Notice," *Times-Democrat* (New Orleans, La.), July 14, 1912.

6. "Astounding Confession of Negress Solves 17 Murders; Her Own Story of Killings," *New Orleans Item,* April 2, 1912.

7. "Quadruple Murder," *Times-Democrat* (New Orleans, La.), November 14, 1909.

8. "Astounding Confession of Negress Solves 17 Murders; Her Own Story of Killings," *New Orleans Item,* April 2, 1912.

9. "Arrest 'Voodoo' Doctor in 17 Murders," *New Orleans Item,* April 3, 1912.

10. "Arrest 'Voodoo' Doctor in 17 Murders," *New Orleans Item,* April 3, 1912; "Indictments in Axe Murder Gases [*sic*]," *New Orleans Item,* April 4, 1912; "Sacrifice Secrets Found," *New Orleans Item,* April 6, 1912.

11. "Arrest 'Voodoo' Doctor in 17 Murders," *New Orleans Item,* April 3, 1912.

12. "Astounding Confession of Negress Solves 17 Murders; Her Own Story of Killings," *New Orleans Item,* April 2, 1912.

13. Long, *Spiritual Merchants;* Anderson, *Conjure in African American Society.*

14. "A Negro Charm Seller Held in the Ax Cases," *Daily Picayune* (New Orleans, La.), April 4, 1912.

15. "Amplifies Confession," *Times-Democrat* (New Orleans, La.), April 4, 1912; "Says She Slew Twenty Blacks," *Daily Picayune* (New Orleans, La.), April 2, 1912.

16. "Barnabet Woman to Be Tried Quickly," *New Orleans Item,* April 5, 1912.

17. "Amplifies Confession," *Times-Democrat* (New Orleans, La.), April 4, 1912; "Indictments in Axe Murder Gases [*sic*]," *New Orleans Item,* April 4, 1912; "A Negro Charm Seller Held in the Ax Cases," *Daily Picayune* (New Orleans, La.), April 4, 1912.

18. "Arrest Hoodoo Doctor," *Lafayette Advertiser,* April 5, 1912.

19. "Indictments in Axe Murder Gases [*sic*]," *New Orleans Item,* April 4, 1912.

20. "A Negro Charm Seller Held in the Ax Cases," *Daily Picayune* (New Orleans, La.), April 4, 1912; "Barnabet Woman to Be Tried Quickly," *New Orleans Item,* April 5, 1912.

21. "Voodoo Doctor Arrested," *Times-Democrat* (New Orleans, La.), April 4, 1912.

22. "Amplifies Confession," *Times-Democrat* (New Orleans, La.), April 4, 1912; "Voodoo Doctor Arrested," *Times-Democrat* (New Orleans, La.), April 4, 1912.

23. "Barnabet Woman to Be Tried Quickly," *New Orleans Item,* April 5, 1912.

24. "Indictments in Axe Murder Gases [*sic*]," *New Orleans Item,* April 4, 1912.

25. Anderson, *Conjure in African American Society,* 79.

26. "Indictments in Axe Murder Gases [*sic*]," *New Orleans Item,* April 4, 1912; "Barnabet Woman to Be Tried Quickly," *New Orleans Item,* April 5, 1912.

27. "Real Names Demanded," *Times-Democrat* (New Orleans, La.), April 6, 1912; "Sacrifice Secrets Found," *New Orleans Item,* April 6, 1912.

28. "New Arrest Made in 'Axe-Murders,'" *New Orleans Item,* April 9, 1912; "Wielder of Deadly Ax Not Arraigned," *Daily Picayune* (New Orleans, La.), April 9, 1912.

29. "New Arrest Made in 'Axe-Murders,'" *New Orleans Item,* April 9, 1912; "The Bernabet Case," *Lafayette Advertiser,* April 9, 1912.

30. "New Arrest Made in 'Axe-Murders,'" *New Orleans Item,* April 9, 1912.

31. "Wielder of Deadly Ax Not Arraigned," *Daily Picayune* (New Orleans, La.), April 9, 1912.

32. "Sacrifice Secrets Found," *New Orleans Item,* April 6, 1912; "Woman to Give New Axe-Murder Clues," *New Orleans Item,* April 10, 1912; "Sanctified Sect Teachings Now Revealed," *New Orleans Item,* April 7, 1912; "Not Certain Bernarbet Woman Will Be Tried at This Term of Court," *Daily Picayune* (New Orleans, La.), April 10, 1912; "Could Learn Nothing," *Lafayette Advertiser,* April 12, 1912.

33. "Says She Slew Twenty Blacks," *Daily Picayune* (New Orleans, La.), April 2, 1912; "Officials Think That Woman Had Accomplice," *Daily Picayune* (New Orleans, La.), April 3, 1912.

34. "Negress Is Indicted for Murdering Family," *Daily Picayune* (New Orleans, La.), April 5, 1912.

35. "Police on Trail of Negro Suspects," *Times-Democrat* (New Orleans, La.), April 7, 1912; "The Officials Stretch Dragnet and Get Woman," *Daily Picayune* (New Orleans, La.), April 7, 1912.

36. "Negress Is Indicted for Murdering Family," *Daily Picayune* (New Orleans, La.), April 5, 1912.

37. "Sheriff Has All Five," *Daily Picayune* (New Orleans, La.), April 24, 1912.

38. "Thomas Implicated," *Daily Picayune* (New Orleans, La.), April 27, 1912.

39. "Zepherin Barnabet Says He Took Part in Murders," *Times-Democrat* (New Orleans, La.), April 24, 1912.

40. "Girl Contradicts Self," *Daily Picayune* (New Orleans, La.), April 21, 1912; "Thomas Implicated," *Daily Picayune* (New Orleans, La.), April 27, 1912.

41. "Sheriff Has All Five," *Daily Picayune* (New Orleans, La.), April 24, 1912; "'Axe Gang' Are All Now in the Toils," *Shreveport Times,* April 24, 1912; "'Axe Gang' Are All Now in the Toils," *Alexandria Daily Town Talk,* April 24, 1912.

42. "Sheriff Has All Five," *Daily Picayune* (New Orleans, La.), April 24, 1912.

43. "Thomas Implicated," *Daily Picayune* (New Orleans, La.), April 27, 1912.

44. "Astounding Confession of Negress Solves 17 Murders; Her Own Story of Killings," *New Orleans Item,* April 2, 1912.

45. "Indictments in Axe Murder Gases [*sic*]," *New Orleans Item,* April 4, 1912.

46. "Says She Slew Twenty Blacks," *Daily Picayune* (New Orleans, La.), April 2, 1912.

47. "Amplifies Confession," *Times-Democrat* (New Orleans, La.), April 4, 1912.

48. "Says She Slew Twenty Blacks," *Daily Picayune* (New Orleans, La.), April 2, 1912.

49. Kopp, "Surgical Treatment as Sex Crime Prevention Measure," 692–706.

50. Hickey, *Serial Murderers and Their Victims,* 4th ed.; Ramsland, *Inside the Minds of Serial Killer;* Vronsky, *Female Serial Killers.*

51. "Astounding Confession of Negress Solves 17 Murders; Her Own Story of Killings," *New*

Orleans Item, April 2, 1912; "Real Names Demanded," *Times-Democrat* (New Orleans, La.), April 6, 1912.

52. "Sacrifice Secrets Found," *New Orleans Item*, April 6, 1912.

53. "Arrested as Suspect," *Lafayette Advertiser*, January 23, 1912.

54. "Sacrifice Secrets Found," *New Orleans Item*, April 6, 1912; "Sanctified Sect Teachings Now Revealed," *New Orleans Item*, April 7, 1912.

55. "Sacrifice Secrets Found," *New Orleans Item*, April 6, 1912.

56. "Not Certain Bernarbet Woman Will Be Tried at This Term of Court," *Daily Picayune* (New Orleans, La.), April 10, 1912.

57. "Woman to Give New Axe-Murder Clues," *New Orleans Item*, April 10, 1912.

58. "Arrest 'Voodoo' Doctor in 17 Murders," *New Orleans Item*, April 3, 1912.

59. "Amplifies Confession," *Times-Democrat* (New Orleans, La.), April 4, 1912.

60. "Officials Think That Woman Had Accomplice," *Daily Picayune* (New Orleans, La.), April 3, 1912.

61. "Real Names Demanded," *Times-Democrat* (New Orleans, La.), April 6, 1912.

62. "Discredits Woman's Story," *Daily Picayune* (New Orleans, La.), April 4, 1912.

63. "Sheriff Believes Negress' Story," *Times-Democrat* (New Orleans, La.), April 3, 1912; "Voodoo Doctor Is Put Under Arrest," *Evansville Courier*, April 4, 1912.

64. "Arrest 'Voodoo' Doctor in 17 Murders," *New Orleans Item*, April 3, 1912; "Negress Is Indicted for Murdering Family," *Daily Picayune* (New Orleans, La.), April 5, 1912.

65. "Negress Armed with Voodoo Kills 17," *Bellingham Herald*, April 2, 1912; "Cult Practiced Human Sacrifice," *Washington Herald*, April 3, 1912.

66. "Negress Murders to Save Her Soul," *Spokesman-Review* (Spokane, Wash.), April 3, 1912.

67. "Thirty-Four Lives 'Sacrificed' by Negro Fanatics," *Buffalo Courier*, April 3, 1912.

68. "Black 'Priestess' Tells of Killing 17 of Own Race," *Evening Gazette* (Cedar Rapids, Iowa), April 3, 1912.

69. "Negress Confesses to Killing Twenty Persons," *Arkansas Democrat*, April 2, 1912; "35 Are Slain by Negro Cult," *Asheville Gazette News*, April 2, 1912; "Forty Hideous Murders Charged to Negress, Who Says She Sought to Gain Immortality; Strange Woman Heads 'Church of Sacrifice,'" *Cincinnati Enquirer*, April 3, 1912.

70. "Negress Is Indicted for Murdering Family," *Daily Picayune* (New Orleans, La.), April 5, 1912.

71. "35 Killed by Negroes," *Santa Fe New Mexican*, April 2, 1912.

72. "Voodoo Priestess Admits 17 Murders," *Salt Lake Tribune*, April 3, 1912.

73. "Confesses to Foul Crime," *Fairmont West Virginian*, November 28, 1911; *State of Louisiana vs. Raymond Barnabette*, LSA.

74. "Amplifies Confession," *Times-Democrat* (New Orleans, La.), April 4, 1912.

75. "Negress Is Indicted for Murdering Family," *Daily Picayune* (New Orleans, La.), April 5, 1912.

76. "Real Names Demanded," *Times-Democrat* (New Orleans, La.), April 6, 1912.

77. Jones, *Labor of Love, Labor of Sorrow;* Hunter, *To 'Joy My Freedom;* Glymph, *Out of the House of Bondage;* Harris, "The *Commonwealth of Virginia vs. Virginia Christian*"; Simmons, *Crescent City Girls.*

78. "Real Names Demanded," *Times-Democrat* (New Orleans, La.), April 6, 1912.

79. "The Latest News in All Louisiana," *Daily Picayune* (New Orleans, La.), November 30, 1911.

80. "Bernarbet Girl Found to Be Sane," *Daily Picayune* (New Orleans, La.), October 22, 1912.

81. Jack Crouchet, personal correspondence to James Wilson, October 6, 2006, private collection.

82. "Creole Tells of Murdering Ten," *Mahoning Dispatch*, December 1, 1911.

83. "A Black Borgia," *Atchison Daily Globe* (Atchison, Kans.), April 2, 1912. This news story is representative of hundreds of similarly worded articles.

84. "Seventeen Killed by a Negress," *Durango Weekly Herald*, April 4, 1912. This news story is representative of hundreds of articles.

85. "Amplifies Confession," *Times-Democrat* (New Orleans, La.), April 4, 1912; "Real Names Demanded," *Times-Democrat* (New Orleans, La.), April 6, 1912.

86. Brattain, "Miscegenation and Competing Definitions of Race in Twentieth-Century Louisiana"; Hobbs, *A Chosen Exile*.

87. Hall, *Africans in Colonial Louisiana;* Brasseaux, Fontenot, and Oubre, *Creoles of Color in the Bayou Country;* Istre, *Creoles of South Louisiana.*

88. "Girl Head of Cult Led Many Murders," *New York Tribune*, April 3, 1912. This news story is representative of hundreds of articles.

89. "Amplifies Confession," *Times-Democrat* (New Orleans, La.), April 4, 1912.

90. Average ascertained based on women sentenced to the Louisiana State Penitentiary at the same time as Clementine Barnabet.

91. "Like the Jungles of Africa," *Saturday Globe* (Utica, N.Y.), February 17, 1912.

92. Gross, *Colored Amazons*, 101–126.

93. "Clementine Barnabet's Gruesome Story Confirmed in Many Details," *Lake Charles Weekly American-Press*, April 5, 1912.

94. "Frightful Story of Negro Girl," *Brownsville Herald*, April 3, 1912. This news story is representative of hundreds of articles.

95. "Real Names Demanded," *Times-Democrat* (New Orleans, La.), April 6, 1912.

96. "Believes Daughter's Story," *Times-Democrat* (New Orleans, La.), April 9, 1912.

97. "Terrible Story of Superstition," *Daily Telegraph* (London, United Kingdom), April 4, 1912.

98. "Human Butcher," *Owensboro Daily Inquirer*, April 3, 1912; "Negress Murderess Killed 35 People as a Sacrifice," *Evening Courier* (Bozeman, Mont.), April 3, 1912.

99. "Officials Think That Woman Had Accomplice," *Daily Picayune* (New Orleans, La.), April 3, 1912.

100. "Arrest 'Voodoo' Doctor in 17 Murders," *New Orleans Item*, April 3, 1912.

101. "Mulatto Murderess Smokes and Sings While in Jail," *Shreveport Times*, April 5, 1912.

102. John Henry Newman, "Lead, Kindly Light," in *Lyra Apostolica* (1836).

103. "To Try Barnabet Soon," *Times-Democrat* (New Orleans, La.), April 5, 1912.

104. Federal Writers Project Collection, Folder 45, CGHRC.

105. "To Try Barnabet Soon," *Times-Democrat* (New Orleans, La.), April 5, 1912.

106. "Negro Woman's Trial," *Waco Times-Herald*, April 5, 1912.

107. National Association for the Advancement of Colored People, *Thirty Years of Lynching in the United States*, 30.

108. Brundage, ed., *Under Sentence of Death,* 97, 138, 141.

109. According to one study of 188 confirmed Black female lynchings, only four of these killings were conducted by Black mobs. Baker and Garcia, "An Analytical History of Black Female Lynchings in the United States," 83–128.

110. Brundage, ed., *Under Sentence of Death;* Dray, *At the Hands of Persons Unknown;* Carrigan, *The Making of a Lynching Culture;* Armstrong, *Mary Turner and the Memory of Lynching;* Feimster, *Southern Horrors.*

111. "Real Names Demanded," *New Orleans Item,* April 6, 1912.

112. "Negress Is Indicted for Murdering Family," *Daily Picayune* (New Orleans, La.), April 5, 1912.

113. "Wielder of Deadly Ax Not Arraigned," *Daily Picayune* (New Orleans, La.), April 9, 1912.

114. "Mulatto Murderess Smokes and Sings While in Jail," *Alexandria Daily Town Talk,* April 13, 1912.

115. "Negress Expects to Be Hanged," *News Democrat* (Paducah, Ky.), April 7, 1912.

116. "Negress Admits Many Murders," *San Francisco Chronicle,* April 3, 1912. This news story is representative of hundreds of articles.

117. "Sheriff Believes Negress' Story," *Times-Democrat* (New Orleans, La.), April 3, 1912.

118. "Sheriff Has All Five," *Daily Picayune* (New Orleans, La.), April 24, 1912.

119. "Police on Trail of Negro Suspects," *Times-Democrat* (New Orleans, La.), April 7, 1912.

120. "Declared the Murders Will Continue," *Daily Sentinel* (Grand Junction, Colo.), April 3, 1912. This news story is representative of hundreds of articles.

7. Clementine's Prediction

1. "The 'Axe Man' Is a Woman," *Alexandria Daily Town Talk,* April 2, 1912.

2. "Killing of Five Negroes Puzzles the Authorities," *San Antonio Express,* April 13, 1912.

3. William Burton, Standard Certificate of Death, Texas State Board of Health, April 13, 1912.

4. "Negro Family of Five Slain with Axe as They Slept," *San Antonio Light,* April 12, 1912.

5. "Negro Family of Five Slain with Axe as They Slept," *San Antonio Light,* April 12, 1912.

6. "Five Negroes Slain by Ax," *Houston Post,* April 13, 1912.

7. "Negro Family of Five Slain with Axe as They Slept," *San Antonio Light,* April 12, 1912.

8. "Killing of Five Negroes Puzzles the Authorities," *San Antonio Express,* April 13, 1912.

9. "Negro Family of Five Slain with Axe as They Slept," *San Antonio Light,* April 12, 1912.

10. "Five Negroes Slain by Ax," *Houston Post,* April 13, 1912; "San Antonio Visited by Murderous Fiend," *Galveston Daily News,* April 13, 1912.

11. "Axeman Does Bloody Work in San Antonio," *Bryan Daily Eagle,* April 12, 1912. This news story is representative of hundreds of articles.

12. "Killing of Five Negroes Puzzles the Authorities," *San Antonio Express,* April 13, 1912; "5 Texas Negroes Added to 'Axeman' Victims," *New Orleans Item,* April 12, 1912.

13. "Whole Family Is Buried Same Day," *Macon Daily Telegraph,* March 27, 1911.

14. "Negro Family of Five Slain with Axe as They Slept," *San Antonio Light,* April 12, 1912; Hobbs, *A Chosen Exile.*

15. "Killing of the Five Negroes Is Still a Mystery," *San Antonio Express,* April 14, 1912; 1900

United States Census, La Grange City, Bexar County, Texas, digital image s.v. "Carrie Evers," Ancestry.com.

16. "Find Additional Evidence," *San Antonio Express,* April 15, 1912.

17. "Negro 'Voodoo' Doctors Held in Burton Case," *San Antonio Light,* April 13, 1912; "Find Additional Evidence," *San Antonio Express,* April 15, 1912.

18. "Negro Family of Five Slain with Axe as They Slept," *San Antonio Light,* April 12, 1912.

19. Carole E. Christian, "Hempstead, Texas: A Historical Overview," *Handbook of Texas,* https://www.tshaonline.org/handbook/entries/hempstead-tx (last updated September 16, 2020).

20. "'Ax Man' Works on Hempstead Negroes," *Austin Statesman,* April 15, 1912.

21. 1910 United States Census, Justice Precinct #1, Waller County, Texas, digital image s.v. "Ed Marshall," Ancestry.com.

22. "'Ax Man' Works on Hempstead Negroes," *Austin Statesman,* April 15, 1912.

23. Alice Marshall, Standard Certificate of Death, Texas State Board of Health, April 14, 1912.

24. "'Axe Man' Attacks Hempstead Family," *San Antonio Light,* April 15, 1912.

25. Ike Burney, Standard Certificate of Death, Texas State Board of Health, April 17, 1912.

26. Carrie Burney Turner, Standard Certificate of Death, Bureau of Vital Statistics, Texas Department of Health, May 21, 1938.

27. "This Axe Man Bungled Job," *Daily Signal* (Crowley, La.), April 20, 1912.

28. Hickey, *Serial Murderers and Their Victims,* 4th ed.; Vronsky, *Serial Killers;* Ramsland, *Inside the Minds of Serial Killers.* Even the most infamous serial killers had victims who survived. Whitney Bennett survived Richard Ramirez. Tracy Edwards survived Jeffrey Dahmer. Carol DaRonch survived Ted Bundy. The status of these individuals does not undermine the perpetrator's ability to kill repeatedly.

29. "Bundle of Rags Left by Ax Man; Negroes Aroused," *Austin Statesman,* April 16, 1912.

30. "This Axe Man Bungled Job," *Daily Signal* (Crowley, La.), April 20, 1912.

31. "Living in Dread of the Axeman," *Virginian Pilot* (Norfolk, Va.), May 5, 1912.

32. Lebsock, *A Murder in Virginia;* Hollandsworth, *The Midnight Assassin.*

33. "Two Arrests at Hempstead," *Daily Advocate* (Victoria, Tex.), April 17, 1912.

34. "Negroes Terrified by Deeds of Axman," *Brenham Daily Banner,* April 17, 1912.

35. "Negro Under Arrest," *Houston Post,* August 2, 1912.

36. Sanborn Fire Insurance Map, Hempstead, Waller County, Texas, 1912, Perry-Castañeda Library Map Collection, University of Texas at Austin.

37. George C. Werner, "History of the Houston and Texas Central Railway," *Handbook of Texas,* https://www.tshaonline.org/handbook/entries/houston-and-texas-central-railway (last updated March 14, 2017).

38. "Two Arrests at Hempstead," *Daily Advocate* (Victoria, Tex.), April 17, 1912.

39. "Blacks Terror Stricken," *Beaumont Journal,* April 15, 1912.

40. "Negro 'Voodoo' Doctors Held in Burton Case," *San Antonio Light,* April 13, 1912.

41. "Killing of the Five Negroes Is Still a Mystery," *San Antonio Express,* April 14, 1912.

42. "[Untitled]," *El Paso Herald,* April 20, 1912; "Offers Reward for Axman," *Galveston Tribune,* April 26, 1912.

43. "The Deadly Axman Did Dirty Work at Hempstead," *Brenham Daily Banner,* April 15, 1912.

44. "A Moral Pervert," *Guardian-Journal* (Homer, La.), April 10, 1912.

45. "Blood Atonement Claims Lives of 26," *Sun* (New York, N.Y.), January 25, 1912.

46. "Fear of the Axman Ruining Negro Labor," *Galveston Daily News*, April 18, 1912.

47. "Window Frame Cut by a Bold Intruder," *Beaumont Daily Journal*, April 16, 1912.

48. "Negro Becomes Insane," *Galveston Daily News*, April 28, 1912.

49. "Shooting Must Stop Says the Marshal," *Brenham Daily Banner*, April 17, 1912.

50. "Shooting Must Stop Says the Marshal," *Brenham Daily Banner*, April 17, 1912.

51. "Two Negroes Slain in Axe Man Panic," *Houston Post*, April 17, 1912.

52. "Two Negroes Are Killed, Mistaken for 'Axman,'" *Times-Democrat* (New Orleans, La.), April 18, 1912; "Hearing of 'Ax Man' Killers," *Austin Statesman*, April 24, 1912.

53. "Prowler Visits Negro's Home," *Palestine Daily Herald*, April 16, 1912.

54. "Axe Man Causes Restless Nights Among the Colored," *Examiner-Review* (Navasota, Tex.), April 18, 1912.

55. "Axe Man Causes Restless Nights Among the Colored," *Examiner-Review* (Navasota, Tex.), April 18, 1912.

56. "Axe Man Causes Restless Nights Among the Colored," *Examiner-Review* (Navasota, Tex.), April 18, 1912.

57. "Two Negroes Are Killed, Mistaken for 'Axman,'" *Times-Democrat* (New Orleans, La.), April 18, 1912.

58. "Lockhart Ax Man Scare," *Austin Statesman*, May 14, 1912.

59. "Strange Appearing Negress Arrested," *Temple Daily Telegram*, April 23, 1912.

60. "A 'Batty' Colored Woman," *Temple Daily Telegram*, May 29, 1912.

61. "Feared Axe Man Resisted Officers," *Marshall Messenger*, May 22, 1912.

62. "Texas Briefs," *Galveston Daily News*, April 21, 1912; "Lockhart Ax Man Scare," *Austin Statesman*, May 14, 1912.

63. "'Ax Man' Causes Terror," *Daily Picayune* (New Orleans, La.), April 19, 1912.

64. "The Ax Man in DeSoto," *Mansfield Enterprise* (Mansfield, La.), April 18, 1912.

65. "Negro Women Made Ill; Broken Glass Found in Soup," *Minneapolis Sunday Tribune*, May 5, 1912.

66. "The Negroes of Junction City," *Gazette* (Farmville, La.), May 15, 1912.

67. "Woman in Mortal Fear of 'Axman'; Police Find 'Dynamite' Old Battery," *Times-Democrat* (New Orleans, La.), April 18, 1912.

68. "Mississippi Matters," *Times-Democrat* (New Orleans, La.), May 4, 1912.

69. "Blood Atonement Claims Lives of 26," *Sun* (New York, N.Y.), January 25, 1912; "Traces Crimes to Sacrificers," *Los Angeles Times*, January 30, 1912; "Negro Terror May Shorten Rice Crop," *New York Times*, March 3, 1912; "A Wall Street Hoodoo," *Evening World-Herald* (Omaha, Nebr.), March 9, 1912; "Voodoo Doctors," *Tipton Daily Tribune*, March 18, 1912.

70. "This Axe Man Bungled Job," *Daily Signal* (Crowley, La.), April 16, 1912; "Fear of the Axman Ruining Negro Labor," *Galveston Daily News*, April 18, 1912; "'Ax Man' Causes Terror," *Daily Picayune* (New Orleans, La.), April 19, 1912.

71. "'Axe Man' Killings Have Texas Negroes in State of Terror," *Knoxville Sentinel*, April 18, 1912; "'Axe-Man' Terrifies Texas Negroes," *Charlotte News*, April 18, 1912; "Negro Night of Terror," *Tulsa Daily Democrat*, April 18, 1912. These stories are a representative sample of the breadth of publication locations.

72. "He May Know of Murder," *San Antonio Express*, April 17, 1912.

73. "Negro 'Voodoo' Doctors Held in Burton Case," *San Antonio Light,* April 13, 1912.

74. "Hempstead Axe Man May Be an Accomplice," *San Antonio Light,* April 15, 1912.

75. "Negroes Still on Qui Vive," *San Antonio Express,* April 18, 1912.

76. "He May Know of Murder," *San Antonio Express,* April 17, 1912.

77. "Axe Murderers Are White Men, Is Stated in Texas," *Lake Charles Daily Times,* April 20, 1912.

78. "Axe Murderers Are White Men, Is Stated in Texas," *Lake Charles Daily Times,* April 20, 1912.

79. "Negroes Still on Qui Vive," *San Antonio Express,* April 18, 1912.

80. "Negroes Again in Fear of Murder by 'Axman,'" *San Antonio Light,* May 20, 1912. For histories of Black police, see: Dulaney, *Black Police in America;* Forman, *Locking Up Our Own;* Jett, *Race, Crime, and Policing in the Jim Crow South.*

81. "Negro Deputy Sues Chief of Police Newnam," *San Antonio Light,* June 9, 1912.

82. "Sheriff and Police Jangle," *San Antonio Express,* May 20, 1912.

83. "Deputies Are Fined $100," *Austin Statesman,* May 21, 1912.

84. "Citizens' League Candidates Ask Voters' Suffrage," *San Antonio Express,* July 26, 1912.

85. "Sheriff and Police Jangle," *San Antonio Express,* May 20, 1912.

86. "Sheriff and Police Jangle," *San Antonio Express,* May 20, 1912.

87. "Tobin Resents Charge to the Grand Jury," *San Antonio Light,* June 3, 1912.

88. "Grand Jury to Hear Tobin," *San Antonio Express,* June 4, 1912.

89. "Sheriff Tobin to Explain," *San Antonio Express,* June 5, 1912.

90. Joseph Jr., Danielle, Margot, and Merryl (Joseph Dashiell's children), in Zoom discussion with the author, recording and transcript, February 22, 2022, personal collection.

91. "Negroes Wrought Up Over Attempt to Enter House," *San Antonio Express,* June 12, 1912.

92. "Axman Fails in Attempt to Murder Woman," *San Antonio Light,* August 16, 1912.

93. "Axman Fails in Attempt to Murder Woman," *San Antonio Light,* August 16, 1912.

94. See appendix B for more details.

95. "Axman Fails in Attempt to Murder Woman," *San Antonio Light,* August 16, 1912.

96. See appendix B for details about the oral history kept alive by the Dashiells' descendants regarding this case.

97. "Axman Fails in Attempt to Murder Woman," *San Antonio Light,* August 16, 1912.

98. "'Ax Man' Causes Terror," *Daily Picayune* (New Orleans, La.), April 19, 1912.

8. Clementine's Trial

1. "Court in Session," *Lafayette Advertiser,* October 8, 1912; "Heavy Criminal Docket in Lafayette Parish," *Daily Signal* (Crowley, La.), September 12, 1912; "Court in Session," *Lafayette Advertiser,* October 8, 1912.

2. "Resolutions of the Bar Association on the Death of Judge William Campbell," *Abbeville Meridional* (Abbeville, La.), May 5, 1928.

3. "Brained Negroes as Sacrifice to Church," *Daily Gate City* (Keokuk, Iowa), October 7, 1912; "Ax-Woman Tried for 17 Murders," *La Crosse Tribune,* October 7, 1912; "All Around the World," *Chicago Defender,* October 19, 1912.

4. Federal Writers Project Collection, Folder 45, CGHRC.

5. “Bernabet Woman Grilled by Jury,” *Daily Picayune* (New Orleans, La.), October 13, 1912.

6. Federal Writers Project Collection, Folder 45, CGHRC.

7. “Former Local City Official Dies at Age 84,” *Lafayette Daily Advertiser*, March 29, 1966.

8. “J. J. Fournet, St. Martinville Native Dies in Lafayette Sat.,” *Teche News* (St. Martinville, La.), December 22, 1966.

9. “John L. Kennedy’s Death Ends Career of Leading Lawyer,” *Crowley Daily Signal*, September 2, 1929.

10. “Jury to Take Up Bernarbet Case,” *Daily Picayune* (New Orleans, La.), October 8, 1912; “Says She Slew Twenty Blacks,” *Daily Picayune* (New Orleans, La.), April 2, 1912.

11. “Ask Commission to Examine ‘Ax Woman,’” *New Orleans Item*, October 17, 1912; “Lunacy Board May Examine Her Mind,” *Daily Picayune* (New Orleans, La.), October 17, 1912.

12. *State of Louisiana v. Clementine Barnabet*, Eighteenth Judicial District Court, Parish of Lafayette, Louisiana, no. 2900, Lafayette Parish Clerk of Court, hereafter cited as LPCC.

13. *The Code of Criminal Procedure of the State of Louisiana* (The New Advocate, 1910), 60; *Insane and Feeble-Minded in Institutions, 1910*, Department of Commerce, Bureau of the Census (Government Printing Office, 1914).

14. *State of Louisiana v. Clementine Barnabet*, LPCC.

15. *Insane and Feeble-Minded in Institutions.*

16. *Code of Criminal Procedure*, 60–61.

17. “Of Offenses Against the Person,” *The Code of Criminal Law of the State of Louisiana.*

18. “Ask Commission to Examine ‘Ax Woman,’” *New Orleans Item*, October 17, 1912.

19. “Lunacy Commission Named,” *Daily Picayune* (New Orleans, La.), October 18, 1912.

20. *New Orleans Medical and Surgical Journal* 62 (July 1909 to June 1910): 98.

21. Fortier, ed., *Louisiana*, 446–47.

22. *State of Louisiana v. Clementine Barnabet*, LPCC.

23. “Egamining [*sic*] Bernarbet Girl,” *Daily Picayune* (New Orleans, La.), October 21, 1912; “Lafayette Elks Give Annual Show,” *Weekly Times-Democrat* (New Orleans, La.), October 25, 1912.

24. Muhammad, *The Condemnation of Blackness.*

25. “Bernarbet Girl Found to Be Sane,” *Daily Picayune* (New Orleans, La.), October 22, 1912.

26. “Just Escaped Noose,” *Daily Picayune* (New Orleans, La.), April 19, 1912.

27. *State of Louisiana v. Noah Bernabet*, Eighteenth Judicial District Court, Parish of Lafayette, Louisiana, no. 2313, LPCC.

28. “Bernarbet Girl Found to Be Sane,” *Daily Picayune* (New Orleans, La.), October 22, 1912.

29. “Bernarbet Girl Found to Be Sane,” *Daily Picayune* (New Orleans, La.), October 22, 1912.

30. “Bernarbet Girl Found to Be Sane,” *Daily Picayune* (New Orleans, La.), October 22, 1912.

31. “Bernarbet Girl Found to Be Sane,” *Daily Picayune* (New Orleans, La.), October 22, 1912.

32. “Bernarbet Girl Found to Be Sane,” *Daily Picayune* (New Orleans, La.), October 22, 1912.

33. “Bernarbet Girl Found to Be Sane,” *Daily Picayune* (New Orleans, La.), October 22, 1912.

34. “Bernarbet Girl Found to Be Sane,” *Daily Picayune* (New Orleans, La.), October 22, 1912.

35. *State of Louisiana v. Clementine Barnabet*, LPCC.

36. “Clementine Barnabet Sane,” *Lafayette Advertiser*, October 22, 1912; “Bernarbet Girl Found to Be Sane,” *Daily Picayune* (New Orleans, La.), October 22, 1912.

37. Ellwood, “Lombroso’s Theory of Crime,” 716–23; Gross, *Colored Amazons;* Muhammad, *The Condemnation of Blackness.*

38. *State of Louisiana v. Clementine Barnabet,* LPCC.

39. Davenport, *Eugenics,* 14.

40. Peile, *Eugenics and the Church,* 6–7.

41. Castle, *Genetics and Eugenics,* 281.

42. Tuke et al., "Insanity," 597.

43. Tuke et al., "Insanity," 601.

44. Gross, *Colored Amazons;* Muhammad, *The Condemnation of Blackness.*

45. "Wrapping Chain Around Negress," *Daily Picayune* (New Orleans, La.), October 25, 1912.

46. "Brained Negroes as Sacrifice to Church," *Daily Gate City* (Keokuk, Iowa), October 7, 1912; "Ax-Woman Tried for 17 Murders," *La Crosse Tribune,* October 7, 1912; "All Around the World," *Chicago Defender,* October 19, 1912.

47. "Bernarbet Girl Found to Be Sane," *Daily Picayune* (New Orleans, La.), October 22, 1912.

48. "Wrapping Chain Around Negress," *Daily Picayune* (New Orleans, La.), October 25, 1912; "Barnabet Trial," *Lafayette Advertiser,* October 25, 1912; "Trial of 'Axe Woman,'" *Shreveport Times,* October 25, 1912; "Ax Woman on Trial," *Houston Post,* October 25, 1912; "Trial of 'Ax Woman' Possessed of Evil Eye," *Daily Clarion Ledger* (Jackson, Miss.), October 25, 1912.

49. "Went to Lafayette," *Daily Signal* (Crowley, La.), October 24, 1912; "Ax-Woman Gets Life Term," *Austin Statesman,* October 26, 1912; "To Open Up Stream," *Times-Democrat* (New Orleans, La.), October 26, 1912.

50. "Egamining [*sic*] Bernarbet Girl," *Daily Picayune* (New Orleans, La.), October 21, 1912; "Ax Woman Sane," *Daily Signal* (Crowley, La.), October 22, 1912.

51. "Bernarbet Girl Found to Be Sane," *Daily Picayune* (New Orleans, La.), October 22, 1912.

52. "Wrapping Chain Around Negress," *Daily Picayune* (New Orleans, La.), October 25, 1912.

53. "'Axwoman' Is Convicted," *San Antonio Express,* October 26, 1912; "Bernabet Girl Guilty," *Weekly Times-Democrat* (New Orleans, La.), November 1, 1912.

54. "Wrapping Chain Around Negress," *Daily Picayune* (New Orleans, La.), October 25, 1912; "Confessed Slayer of Twenty-Two Convicted," *New Orleans Item,* October 25, 1912.

55. Hine, "Rape and the Inner Lives of Black Women in the Middle West."

56. "Wrapping Chain Around Negress," *Daily Picayune* (New Orleans, La.), October 25, 1912.

57. At the same time, this victimization often further criminalized Black men. Freedman, "'Crimes Which Startle and Horrify'"; Henley, "'Devilish Deeds.'"

58. McGuire, *At the Dark End of the Street;* Williams, *They Left Great Marks on Me.*

59. Gross, *Colored Amazons;* Mustakeem, "'Armed with a Knife in Her Bosom.'"

60. "Wrapping Chain Around Negress," *Daily Picayune* (New Orleans, La.), October 25, 1912.

61. *State of Louisiana v. Clementine Barnabet,* LPCC.

62. "Wrapping Chain Around Negress," *Daily Picayune* (New Orleans, La.), October 25, 1912; "Official Promulgation," *Lafayette Advertiser,* February 2, 1908; "Family of Six Butchered in Bed," *Daily Picayune* (New Orleans, La.), November 28, 1911.

63. "Wrapping Chain Around Negress," *Daily Picayune* (New Orleans, La.), October 25, 1912.

64. "Wrapping Chain Around Negress," *Daily Picayune* (New Orleans, La.), October 25, 1912.

65. "Wrapping Chain Around Negress," *Daily Picayune* (New Orleans, La.), October 25, 1912.

66. "Bernabet Girl on Trial," *Times-Democrat* (New Orleans, La.), October 25, 1912.

67. "Bernabet Girl on Trial," *Times-Democrat* (New Orleans, La.), October 25, 1912.

68. "Wrapping Chain Around Negress," *Daily Picayune* (New Orleans, La.), October 25, 1912.

69. "Wrapping Chain Around Negress," *Daily Picayune* (New Orleans, La.), October 25, 1912.

70. "Bernabet Girl on Trial," *Times-Democrat* (New Orleans, La.), October 25, 1912.

71. "Wrapping Chain Around Negress," *Daily Picayune* (New Orleans, La.), October 25, 1912.

72. "Bernabet Girl on Trial," *Times-Democrat* (New Orleans, La.), October 25, 1912; "Life Term Given Bernarbet Woman," *Daily Picayune* (New Orleans, La.), October 26, 1912; Documents and Correspondences, Dec. 27 1890–June 23, 1899, Metz-Kahn Family Papers, Tulane University, New Orleans, Louisiana.

73. "Bernabet Girl on Trial," *Times-Democrat* (New Orleans, La.), October 25, 1912.

74. "Wrapping Chain Around Negress," *Daily Picayune* (New Orleans, La.), October 25, 1912.

75. "Family of Six Butchered in Bed," *Daily Picayune* (New Orleans, La.), November 28, 1911.

76. "Life Term Given Bernarbet Woman," *Daily Picayune* (New Orleans, La.), October 26, 1912.

77. "Wrapping Chain Around Negress," *Daily Picayune* (New Orleans, La.), October 25, 1912.

78. "The Latest News in All Louisiana," *Daily Picayune* (New Orleans, La.), January 21, 1912.

79. "Wrapping Chain Around Negress," *Daily Picayune* (New Orleans, La.), October 25, 1912.

80. "Jury to Take Up Bernarbet Case," *Daily Picayune* (New Orleans, La.), October 8, 1912.

81. "Seventeen Murders Were Confessed To," *Fort Wayne News*, October 25, 1912; "Murderess Is Guilty," *Bemidji Daily Pioneer* (Bemidji, Minn.), October 26, 1912; "Slayer of 22 Is Sentenced," *Mascoutah Herald* (Mascoutah, Ill.), October 30, 1912. These news stories are a representative sample of newspaper coverage.

82. *State of Louisiana v. Clementine Barnabet*, LPCC.

83. "Life Term Given Bernarbet Woman," *Daily Picayune* (New Orleans, La.), October 26, 1912.

84. "Life Term Given Bernarbet Woman," *Daily Picayune* (New Orleans, La.), October 26, 1912.

85. "Life Term Given Bernarbet Woman," *Daily Picayune* (New Orleans, La.), October 26, 1912.

86. "Life Term Given Bernarbet Woman," *Daily Picayune* (New Orleans, La.), October 26, 1912.

87. "Life Term Given Bernarbet Woman," *Daily Picayune* (New Orleans, La.), October 26, 1912.

88. "Life Term Given Bernarbet Woman," *Daily Picayune* (New Orleans, La.), October 26, 1912.

89. "Life Term Given Bernarbet Woman," *Daily Picayune* (New Orleans, La.), October 26, 1912.

90. "Life Term Given Bernarbet Woman," *Daily Picayune* (New Orleans, La.), October 26, 1912.

91. "Admits 17 Murders, Woman Is Sentenced to Prison for Life," *World* (New York, N.Y.), October 25, 1912; "Ax-Woman Held Dead Babes to Her Breast," *Omaha Daily News*, October 25, 1912; "Confesses but Says She Is Not Guilty of Murder," *Evening News* (Wilkes-Barre, Pa.), October 25, 1912. This is a representative sample of articles to show geographic diversity. More than fifty newspapers printed a version of Clementine's courtroom admission.

92. Title VI, Chapter 3, *The Code of Criminal Law of the State of Louisiana.*

93. "Life Term Given Bernarbet Woman," *Daily Picayune* (New Orleans, La.), October 26, 1912.

94. "Ax Woman Found Guilty of Murder," *Daily Signal* (Crowley, La.), October 26, 1912.

95. "Life Term Given Bernarbet Woman," *Daily Picayune* (New Orleans, La.), October 26, 1912; "Court News," *Lafayette Advertiser*, October 29, 1912. Hundreds of newspapers covered this verdict.

96. *State of Louisiana v. Clementine Barnabet*, LPCC.

97. "Life Term Given Bernarbet Woman," *Daily Picayune* (New Orleans, La.), October 26, 1912.

98. Gross, *Colored Amazons;* Harris, "The *Commonwealth of Virginia vs. Virginia Christian.*"

99. According to the Espy Project Execution Records, a digital project of the M. Watt Espy

Papers and the Espy File dataset (a flawed but oft-cited database of legal executions in the United States), eleven Black women and girls were executed nationwide after 1865 but before Clementine's trial. Although this number is likely incorrect, it confirms that Black females were not regularly executed. See Espy Project Execution Records, M. E. Grenander Special Collections and Archives, University at Albany, State University of New York, https://archives.albany.edu/espy/.

100. "The Perils of Murderous Mania," *Seattle Daily Times,* November 11, 1912.

101. "Bernabet Girl Guilty," *Times-Democrat* (New Orleans, La.), November 1, 1912.

102. "Looks for Angel in Fire Chariot," *New Castle News* (New Castle, Pa.), October 25, 1912; "Louisiana Murderess to Prison for Life," *Lincoln Daily News* (Lincoln, Nebr.), October 25, 1912; "Slayer of 17 Says She Is of Sacrifice Sect," *Cairo Bulletin* (Cairo, Ill.), October 26, 1912; "Negress Proposes to Rival Elijah," *Indiana County Gazette* (Indiana, Pa.), October 26, 1912.

103. 2 Kings 2:11 (King James Version).

104. 1 Kings 18:20–40 (KJV).

105. 1 Kings 17:17–24 (KJV).

106. 1 Kings 17:1–7 (KJV).

107. 1 Kings 18:41–46 (KJV).

108. 1 Kings 18:33–38 (KJV).

109. 2 Kings 1:9–15 (KJV).

110. Malachi 4:5–6 (KJV).

111. Taylor, *Brooding over Bloody Revenge;* Gross, *Vengeance Feminism.*

112. "Admits 17 Murders, Woman Is Sentenced to Prison for Life," *World* (New York, N.Y.), October 25, 1912; "Woman Ax Slayer of 17 Gets Life Sentence," *St. Louis Post-Dispatch,* October 25, 1912; "Confesses to Many Crimes," *Daily Telegram* (Long Beach, Calif.), October 26, 1912; "Woman Confesses to 17 Killings," *Spokane Press,* October 30, 1912. This is a representative sample of articles to show geographic diversity. More than one hundred newspapers printed a version of this story, indirectly linking Clementine to the murders of hundreds of people.

113. "Life Sentence for the 'Ax Woman,'" *Houston Post,* October 26, 1912.

114. "Axe Woman Confesses to Seventeen Murders," *Vancouver World* (Vancouver, Canada), October 26, 1912.

115. In the aftermath of Clementine's conviction, newspapers reported that the seemingly unthinkable had happened: the axman had murdered a family near Philadelphia, Mississippi. The white media quickly latched onto the Walmsley family's death as conclusive proof that the elusive assassin had "extended his operations to Mississippi." At the same time, the press readily linked this latest murder to those Clementine Barnabet had confessed to back in April. By November, however, she was sitting in prison hundreds of miles away from the crime scene. While Clementine might have been able to argue that her accomplices had visited her in jail to tell of their slaughters in Lake Charles and Beaumont, it was highly unlikely she was receiving covert intel in the remote hills of West Feliciana Parish. Still, that didn't stop the International News Service from running a story that Clementine had "knowledge of the killings" in Philadelphia. Even after her incarceration, it seemed news outlets could not resist making Clementine Barnabet into a master manipulator and puppeteering provocateur. They had spent months—arguably almost a full year—crafting her to be a cunning killer and a cult leader. Now, a murder that only had a threadbare connection to the others—namely the weapon of choice—was touted as part of her

purview. See: "'Axe Man' Strikes Again," *Sun* (New York, N.Y.), November 23, 1912; "Ax-Wielder Puts Family to Death," *Daily Picayune* (New Orleans, La.), November 23, 1912; "Entire Family Found Slain," *Allentown Democrat* (Allentown, Pa.), November 23, 1912.

116. "Court News," *Lafayette Advertiser,* October 29, 1912.

117. "Last Bernabet Note," *Daily Picayune* (New Orleans, La.), October 29, 1912.

118. "Bernarbet Woman Sentenced," *Daily Picayune* (New Orleans, La.), October 27, 1912.

119. "New Arrest Made in 'Axe-Murders,'" *New Orleans Item*, April 9, 1912; "Last Bernabet Note," *Daily Picayune* (New Orleans, La.), October 29, 1912.

120. "Negroes Fear the Ax-Men's Return," *Daily Signal* (Crowley, La.), November 6, 1912; "Another Bernarbet Affair," *Daily Picayune* (New Orleans, La.), November 5, 1912; "Negro Stabs Another," *Lafayette Advertiser*, November 5, 1912.

121. "Negro Stabs Another," *Lafayette Advertiser*, November 5, 1912; "Two Brothers of Ax-Woman Wanted," *Daily Signal* (Crowley, La.), November 5, 1912; "Negroes Fear the Ax-Men's Return," *Daily Signal* (Crowley, La.), November 6, 1912.

122. "Negroes Fear the Ax-Men's Return," *Daily Signal* (Crowley, La.), November 6, 1912.

123. "Two Brothers of Ax-Woman Wanted," *Daily Signal* (Crowley, La.), November 5, 1912; "Negroes Fear the Ax-Men's Return," *Daily Signal* (Crowley, La.), November 6, 1912.

124. "Last Bernabet Note," *Daily Picayune* (New Orleans, La.), October 29, 1912.

125. "Last Bernabet Note," *Daily Picayune* (New Orleans, La.), October 29, 1912.

126. Carleton, *Politics and Punishment;* "History of Angola," Angola Museum at the Louisiana State Penitentiary, Angola, Louisiana (hereafter cited as AMLSP), visited February 6, 2018.

9. Clementine's Incarceration

1. Lichtenstein, *Twice the Work of Free Labor;* Oshinsky, *"Worse than Slavery"*; Blackmon, *Slavery by Another Name;* LeFlouria, *Chained in Silence.*

2. Marianne Fisher-Giorlando, "The Walls."

3. Carleton, *Politics and Punishment;* Myers and Fisher-Giorlando, "Bad Girls, Convict Women, Part 1," 43–44.

4. Carleton, *Politics and Punishment,* 10; Derbes, "'Secret Horrors,'" 280–81; Hermann, "Specters of Freedom," 94.

5. Hermann, "Specters of Freedom," 65.

6. Myers and Fisher-Giorlando, "Bad Girls, Convict Women, Part 1," 50.

7. Myers and Fisher-Giorlando, "Bad Girls, Convict Women, Part 1," 52; Cardon, "'Less Than Mayhem.'"

8. Myers and Fisher-Giorlando, "Bad Girls, Convict Women, Part 1," 52; Hermann, "Specters of Freedom," 254; Reproduction of "Angola Plantation Bill of Sale, January 1, 1901," viewed at AMLSP, visited February 6, 2018. Original at Louisiana State Archives, Baton Rouge.

9. Carleton, *Politics and Punishment;* "History of Angola" and "The Other Side of the Story," AMLSP.

10. "The Other Side of the Story," AMLSP; Myers and Fisher-Giorlando, "Bad Girls, Convict Women, Part 2," 29.

11. Myers and Fisher-Giorlando, "Bad Girls, Convict Women, Part 2," 29; "A Female Ex-Convict," *Daily Picayune* (New Orleans, La.), June 25, 1887.

12. “The Other Side of the Story,” AMLSP.

13. Butler and Henderson, *Dying to Tell;* Carleton, *Politics and Punishment;* LeFlouria, *Chained in Silence;* Blackmon, *Slavery by Another Name;* Oshinsky, *“Worse than Slavery.”*

14. Carleton, *Politics and Punishment,* 20.

15. “Timeline: Louisiana State Penitentiary, 1835–1900,” AMLSP.

16. Myers and Fisher-Giorlando, “Bad Girls, Convict Women, Part 2,” 29.

17. “Convict Farmers of Louisiana,” Louisiana Works Progress Administration, Louisiana Digital Library, hereafter cited as LDL.

18. Myers and Fisher-Giorlando, “Bad Girls, Convict Women, Part 2,” 31.

19. Hermann, “Specters of Freedom,” 347.

20. Carleton, *Politics and Punishment,* 100.

21. Marianne Fisher-Giorlando, “The Walls.”

22. Myers and Fisher-Giorlando, “Bad Girls, Convict Women, Part 2,” 29.

23. “Convict Farmers of Louisiana,” LDL.

24. “Convict Farmers of Louisiana,” LDL.

25. Myers and Fisher-Giorlando, “Bad Girls, Convict Women, Part 2,” 29.

26. “Convict Farmers of Louisiana,” LDL.

27. Myers and Fisher-Giorlando, “Bad Girls, Convict Women, Part 2,” 33.

28. “Blood Lust Cut Out of Clementine Barnabet,” *New Iberia Enterprise,* August 9, 1913.

29. *Biennial Report, 1914–1915,* 19.

30. *Convict Records,* no. 1823–14594, vol. 24, 1902–1923, Louisiana State Penitentiary, LSA. Available via FamilySearch.

31. Carleton, *Politics and Punishment,* 93.

32. “Re-Planting Cane on Angola State Farm,” *True Democrat* (St. Francisville, La.), November 16, 1912.

33. *Convict Records,* vol. 24, Louisiana State Penitentiary, LSA. Available via FamilySearch.

34. *Convict Records,* vol. 24, Louisiana State Penitentiary, LSA. Available via FamilySearch.

35. *Convict Records,* no. 6801–9900, vol. 17, Louisiana State Penitentiary, LSA. Available via FamilySearch.

36. Women at the Louisiana State Penitentiary Dataset, October 1912 to April 1923, hereafter cited as Dataset, 1912–1923. Created by the author.

37. Dataset, 1912–1923.

38. *Biennial Report, 1914–1915,* 98.

39. According to Gwendolyn Midlo Hall, “grif” in colonial Louisiana referred to individuals of Black (African) and Native American ancestry. According to Walter Johnson, the term connoted someone who was lighter than the vague description of “black” but not fair enough to be considered “yellow.” Hall, *Africans in Colonial Louisiana,* 118; Johnson, “The Slave Trader, the White Slave, and the Politics of Racial Determination in the 1850s,” 13–38.

40. “Five Families Are Butchered by the ‘Human Five,’” *Calgary Daily Herald* (Calgary, Canada), February 13, 1912; “Capture Negress Murderess,” *Arkansas City Daily Traveler* (Arkansas City, Kans.), April 2, 1912; “35 Slain by Negro Cult,” *Asheville Gazette News,* April 2, 1912; “Negress Confesses Murder of Seventeen,” *Buffalo Evening News* (Buffalo, N.Y.), April 3, 1912.

41. *Convict Records,* no. 6801–9900, vol. 17, Louisiana State Penitentiary, LSA. Available via FamilySearch.

42. Dataset, 1912–1923.

43. Lombroso-Ferrero, ed., *The Criminal Man.*

44. Frances Kellor's 1901 seminal study, "The Criminal Negro," readily disproved Lombroso's theory. Frances A. Kellor, "The Criminal Negro: A Sociological Study," *The Arena* 25, nos. 1–5 (January–May 1901): 59–68, 190–97, 308–16, 419–28, 510–20.

45. Rafter, *Creating Born Criminals,* 110.

46. *Convict Records,* no. 6801–9900, vol. 17, Louisiana State Penitentiary, LSA. Available via FamilySearch.

47. Gross, *Colored Amazons.*

48. Lombroso-Ferrero, ed., "The Born Criminal," in *The Criminal Man,* 10–24.

49. *Oxford Dictionary of Dentistry,* "Cyanosis," published 2020, https://www.oxfordreference.com/view/10.1093/acref/9780191828621.001.0001/acref-9780191828621-e-1085.

50. Lombroso-Ferrero, ed., "Tattooing," in *The Criminal Man,* 45–48.

51. Hunter, *To 'Joy My Freedom.*

52. Gross, *Colored Amazons;* Hicks, *Talk with You Like a Woman;* Simmons, *Crescent City Girls.*

53. Gross, *Colored Amazons;* Blair, *I've Got to Make My Livin';* Harris, *Sex Workers, Psychics, and Numbers Runners.*

54. Richie, *Arrested Justice.*

55. Odem, *Delinquent Daughters;* McGerr, *A Fierce Discontent;* Stern, *Eugenic Nation;* Lombardo, *Three Generations, No Imbeciles;* Hicks, *Talk with You Like a Woman;* Muhammad, *The Condemnation of Blackness;* Leonard, *Illiberal Reformers;* Agyepong, *The Criminalization of Black Children.*

56. "Of Carnal Crimes," *The Code of Criminal Law of the State of Louisiana,* 15.

57. Dataset, 1912–1923.

58. "Of Offenses Against the Person," *The Code of Criminal Law of the State of Louisiana,* 11–12.

59. Dataset, 1912–1923.

60. Landau, *Spectacular Wickedness;* Simmons, *Crescent City Girls.*

61. "Of Offenses Against the Person," *The Code of Criminal Law of the State of Louisiana,* 12. The one woman not charged with murder or murder without capital punishment was instead charged with administering poison.

62. "Of the Trial and Its Incidents," *Code of Criminal Procedure,* 82.

63. "Negro Woman to Hang," *Monroe News-Star,* May 20, 1918; "Walter Lamana Avenged," *St. Landry Clarion* (Opelousas, La.), November 23, 1907.

64. Carleton, *Politics and Punishment,* 54; Hillyer, *A Wall Is Just a Wall,* 27–45.

65. Dataset, 1912–1923.

66. Act 112, *Acts Passed by the General Assembly of the State of Louisiana at the Regular Session* (New Orleans: Ernest Marchand, State Printer, 1890), 154.

67. Act 160, *Acts Passed by the General Assembly of the State of Louisiana at the Regular Session* (*The Advocate,* 1902), 305–6.

68. *Biennial Report, 1914–1915,* 73.

69. *Biennial Report, 1914–1915,* 25–26.

70. *Convict Records,* no. 6801–9900, vol. 17, Louisiana State Penitentiary, LSA. Available via FamilySearch.

71. *Register of Convicts Received,* vol. 10, no. 1–3800, 1901–1907, LSA; *Register of Convicts Received,* vol. 11, no. 3801–6800, 1907–1911, LSA.

72. *Register of Convicts Received,* vol. 11, LSA.

73. "A Short History of Prison Reform in Louisiana," LDL.

74. Derbes, "'Secret Horrors.'"

75. "Where Felons Pay Debts They Owe to Society," *Times-Picayune* (New Orleans, La.), September 4, 1920.

76. "Blood Lust Cut Out of Clementine Barnabet," *New Iberia Enterprise,* August 9, 1913; "Where Felons Pay Debts They Owe to Society," *Times-Picayune* (New Orleans, La.), September 4, 1920.

77. "Blood Lust Cut Out of Clementine Barnabet," *New Iberia Enterprise,* August 9, 1913; Fortier, ed., *Louisiana,* 418.

78. "Blood Lust Cut Out of Clementine Barnabet," *New Iberia Enterprise,* August 9, 1913; "Convict Farmers of Louisiana," LDL.

79. *Index to Prisoners Received,* no. 1–6799, vol. 3, LSA.

80. "Where Felons Pay Debts They Owe to Society," *Times-Picayune* (New Orleans, La.), September 4, 1920.

81. *Biennial Report, 1914–1915,* 18.

82. "Blood Lust Cut Out of Clementine Barnabet," *New Iberia Enterprise,* August 9, 1913.

83. "Blood Lust Cut Out of Clementine Barnabet," *New Iberia Enterprise,* August 9, 1913.

84. "Where Felons Pay Debts They Owe to Society," *Times-Picayune* (New Orleans, La.), September 4, 1920.

85. *State of Louisiana v. Clementine Barnabet,* LPCC.

86. Caruso and Sheehan, "Psychosurgery, Ethics, and Media," 1–8.

87. Whitaker, *Mad in America;* Horn, *Damnation Island.*

88. Ochsner, "Surgical Treatment of Habitual Criminals," 867–68; Mears, "Asexualization as a Remedial Measure in the Relief of Certain Forms of Mental, Moral and Physical Degeneration," 584–86.

89. "Blood Lust Cut Out of Clementine Barnabet," *New Iberia Enterprise,* August 9, 1913.

90. Beauchamp, "Informed Consent," 515–23.

91. Roberts, *Killing the Black Body;* Washington, *Medical Apartheid;* Skloot, *The Immortal Life of Henrietta Lacks;* Owens, *Medical Bondage.*

92. "Blood Lust Cut Out of Clementine Barnabet," *New Iberia Enterprise,* August 9, 1913.

93. "Blood Lust Cut Out of Clementine Barnabet," *New Iberia Enterprise,* August 9, 1913.

94. "Blood Lust Cut Out of Clementine Barnabet," *New Iberia Enterprise,* August 9, 1913.

95. Van Der Kolk, *The Body Keeps Score.*

96. *Convict Records,* no. 6801–9900, vol. 17, Louisiana State Penitentiary, LSA. Available via FamilySearch.

97. "The New Mill at Angola," *Louisiana Planter and Sugar Manufacturer* 47, no. 17 (1911): 269.

98. "Where Felons Pay Debts They Owe to Society," *Times-Picayune* (New Orleans, La.), September 4, 1920.

99. Hartman, "Venus in Two Acts."

100. Daniel Schnopp-Wyatt, "Ax Woman of the Sacrifice Sect: Clementine Barnabet and the Louisiana-Texas Ax Murders of 1909 to 1912," unpublished manuscript, 2018.

101. "Capture Negress Murderess," *Arkansas City Daily Traveler* (Arkansas City, Kans.), April 4, 1912.

102. Scheiner, *Negro Mecca;* Osofsky, *Harlem;* Spear, *Black Chicago.*

Epilogue

1. Chatelain, *South Side Girls;* Simmons, *Crescent City Girls.*

2. Gross, "Exploring Crime and Violence in Early-Twentieth-Century Black Women's History," 56–71.

3. Federal Writers Project Collection, Folder 45, CGHRC.

Bibliography

Primary Sources

ARCHIVES

Colorado County Clerk's Office, Columbus, Tex.

Fayette Heritage Museum and Archives, Fayette Public Library, La Grange, Tex.

Lafayette Parish Clerk of Court, Lafayette, La.

Louisiana Prison Museum and Cultural Center, Louisiana State Penitentiary, Angola, La.

Louisiana State Archives, Baton Rouge, La.

Louisiana State University, Louisiana and Lower Mississippi Valley Collections, Baton Rouge, La.

Nesbitt Memorial Library, Columbus, Tex.

Northwestern State University, Cammie G. Henry Research Center, Natchitoches, La.

Sanborn Maps Collection, Geography and Map Division, Library of Congress.

State Library of Louisiana, Baton Rouge, La.

Texas State Library and Archives Commission, Austin, Tex.

Tulane University, Metz-Kahn Family Papers, New Orleans, La.

University of Louisiana at Lafayette, Acadian Manuscripts Collection, Lafayette, La.

University of Texas at Austin, Perry-Castañeda Library Map Collection, Austin, Tex.

MAJOR NEWSPAPERS

Alexandria Daily Town Talk

Austin Statesman

Daily Advocate (Victoria, Tex.)

Daily Picayune (New Orleans, La.)

Daily Signal (Crowley, La.)

Houston Post

Lafayette Advertiser

Lake Charles American-Press

Lake Charles Times

New Orleans Item

San Antonio Express

San Antonio Light

Shreveport Times

Times-Democrat (New Orleans, La.)

PUBLISHED PRIMARY SOURCES

Act 112. *Acts Passed by the General Assembly of the State of Louisiana at the Regular Session.* Ernest Marchand, State Printer, 1890.

Act 160. *Acts Passed by the General Assembly of the State of Louisiana at the Regular Session.* The Advocate, 1902.

Ball, B. "La Folie Erotique." Translated by F. E. Chandler. *Medical Times and Register* 32, no. 5 (August 1896).

Biennial Report of the Board of Control. *Louisiana State Penitentiary, 1914–1915.* Baton Rouge, 1916.

Castle, W. E. *Genetics and Eugenics: A Text-Book for Students of Biology and a Reference Book for Animal and Plant Breeders.* Harvard Univ. Press, 1922.

Clay, William M., and E. Mead Wilcox. "Five Generations of an Inferior Family." *Journal of Heredity* 18, no. 3 (March 1927): 121–24.

The Code of Criminal Law of the State of Louisiana. The New Advocate, 1910. HathiTrust.

The Code of Criminal Procedure of the State of Louisiana. The New Advocate, 1910. HathiTrust.

Davenport, C. B. *Eugenics: The Science of Human Improvement by Better Breeding.* Holt, 1910.

Department of the Interior. "Minor Civil Divisions—Louisiana." In *Census Reports Volume 1, Twelfth Census of the United States Taken in the Year 1900, Population Part 1.* United States Census Office, 1901.

———. "Populations of Civil Divisions Less Than Counties—Louisiana." In *Statistics of the Population of the United States at the Tenth Census.* Government Printing Office, 1880.

———. "Table I: Population of the United States by States and Territories" and "Table V: Population by Race, Sex, and Nativity." In *Statistics of the Population of the United States at the Tenth Census.* Government Printing Office, 1880.

Directory of the City of Beaumont, 1912–1913. Morrison and Fourmy Directory Co., 1912.

Directory of the City of San Antonio, 1910–1911. Texas Publishing Company, 1910.

Ellwood, Charles A. "Lombroso's Theory of Crime." *Journal of Criminal Law and Criminology* 2, no. 5 (1912): 716–23.

Harris, William H. *Louisiana Products, Resources and Attractions, with a Sketch of the Parishes: A Hand Book of Reliable Information Concerning the State.* Times-Democrat Print, 1881.

Ironside, Henry Allan. *The Midnight Cry,* 4th ed. Loizeaux Brothers, 1928.

Jules A. Appler's General Directory and Blue Book of Greater San Antonio. Jules A. Appler, 1912.

Knox, Howard A. "Tests for Mental Defects." *Journal of Heredity* 5, no. 3 (March 1914): 122–30.

Kopp, Marie E. "Surgical Treatment as Sex Crime Prevention Measure." *Journal of Criminal Law and Criminology* 28, no. 5 (winter 1938): 692–706.

Lombroso-Ferrero, Gina. *The Criminal Man: According to the Classification of Cesare Lombroso.* Knickerbocker Press, 1911.

Mears, J. Ewing. "Asexualization as a Remedial Measure in the Relief of Certain Forms of Mental, Moral and Physical Degeneration." *Boston Medical and Surgical Journal* 161 (October 1909): 584–86.

National Association for the Advancement of Colored People. *Thirty Years of Lynching in the United States, 1889–1918.* NAACP National Office, 1919.

Newman, John Henry. "Lead, Kindly Light." In *Lyra Apostolica.* H. Mozley and Sons, 1836.

New Orleans Medical and Surgical Journal 62 (July 1909 to June 1910): iii–1048.

"No. 18,455: State v. Lee." In *Louisiana Reports: Cases Argued and Determined in the Supreme Court of Louisiana Sitting at New Orleans at Term Beginning First Monday of October, 1909, and at Term Beginning First Monday of October, 1910.* Edited by Charles G. Gill, 265–268. West Publishing Co., 1911.

Ochsner, A. J. "Surgical Treatment of Habitual Criminals." *Journal of the American Medical Association* 32, no. 16 (April 1899): 867–68.

Peile, J. H. F. *Eugenics and the Church.* Eugenics Education Society, 1909.

Shaler, Nathaniel S. "The Negro Problem." *Atlantic Monthly,* November 1884, 696–709.

Tuke, John B., John Macpherson, Lewis C. Bruce, Alexander W. Renton, and Frederick Peterson. "Insanity." In *Encyclopædia Britannica.* University of Cambridge, 1911.

U.S. Census Bureau. "Irrigation for Rice Growing: Louisiana, Texas, and Arkansas." In *Thirteenth Census of the United States.* Government Printing Office, 1913.

———. "Supplement for Louisiana." In *Thirteenth Census of the United States.* Government Printing Office, 1913.

———. "Supplement for Texas." In *Thirteenth Census of the United States.* Government Printing Office, 1913.

Wickersham, George W. "Report on Lawlessness in Law Enforcement." National Commission on Law Observance and Enforcement, 1931.

Secondary Sources

Adler, Jeffrey S. "Cognitive Bias: Interracial Homicide in New Orleans, 1921–1945." *Journal of Interdisciplinary History* 43, no. 1 (summer 2012): 43–61.

———. *First in Violence, Deepest in Dirt: Homicide in Chicago, 1875–1920.* Harvard Univ. Press, 2006.

———. "'A Low Caste White Man with Lust in His Heart': Race, Deviance, and Criminal Justice in Jim Crow New Orleans." *Journal of Southern History* 84, no. 2 (May 2018): 245–76.

———. *Murder in New Orleans: The Creation of Jim Crow Policing.* Univ. of Chicago Press, 2019.

———. "Murder, North and South: Violence in Early-Twentieth-Century Chicago and New Orleans." *Journal of Southern History* 74, no. 2 (May 2008): 297–324.

Aggrawal, A. "Mass Murder." In *Encyclopedia of Forensic and Legal Medicine*, edited by Jason Payne-James, Roger Byard, Tracey Corey, and Carol Henderson, 3:216–23. Elsevier Academic Press, 2005.

Agyepong, Tera Eva. *The Criminalization of Black Children: Race, Gender, and Delinquency in Chicago's Juvenile Justice System, 1899–1945*. Univ. of North Carolina Press, 2018.

Alexander, Estrelda Y., ed. *The Dictionary of Pan-African Pentecostalism*. Vol. 1, *North America*. Wipf and Stock Publishers, 2018.

Alison, Laurence, Craig Bennell, Andreas Mokros, and David Ormerod. "The Personality Paradox in Offender Profiling: A Theoretical Review of the Processes Involved in Deriving Background Characteristics from Crime Scene Actions." *Psychology, Public Policy, and Law* 8, no. 1 (March 2002): 115–35.

Anderson, Jeffrey E. *Conjure in African American Society*. Louisiana State Univ. Press, 2005.

Appleby, Sara C., Lisa E. Hasel, and Saul M. Kassin. "Police-Induced Confessions: An Empirical Analysis of Their Content and Impact." *Psychology, Crime & Law* 19, no. 2 (2013): 111–28.

Arain, Mariam, Maliha Haque, Lina Johal, Puja Mathur, Wynand Nel, Ranbir Sandhu, and Sushil Sharma. "Maturation of the Adolescent Brain." *Neuropsychiatric Disease and Treatment* 9 (April 2013): 449–61.

Armstrong, Julie Buckner. *Mary Turner and the Memory of Lynching*. Univ. of Georgia Press, 2011.

Babineaux, Lawson Paul, Jr. "A History of the Rice Industry of Southwestern Louisiana." Master's thesis, University of Southwestern Louisiana, 1967.

Baker, David V., and Gilbert Garcia. "An Analytical History of Black Female Lynchings in the United States, 1838–1969." *Journal of Qualitative Criminal Justice and Criminology* 8, no. 1 (2019): 83–128.

Bardes, John. *The Carceral City: Slavery and the Making of Mass Incarceration in New Orleans, 1803–1930*. Univ. of North Carolina Press, 2024.

Beauchamp, Tom L. "Informed Consent: Its History, Meaning, and Present Challenges." *Cambridge Quarterly of Healthcare Ethics* 20, no. 4 (2011): 515–23.

Behavioral Analysis Unit. *Serial Murder: Multi-Disciplinary Perspectives for Investigators*. Federal Bureau of Investigation, 2005.

Bennett, James B. *Religion and the Rise of Jim Crow in New Orleans*. Princeton Univ. Press, 2005.

Berlin, Ira. *Many Thousands Gone: The First Two Centuries of Slavery in North America*. Belknap Press, 1998.

Berstein, Robin. *Racial Innocence: Performing American Childhood from Slavery to Civil Rights*. New York Univ. Press, 2011.

Bethard, Alvin Y. "Deadly Visitations: The Southwest Louisiana Axe Murders." *À La Pointe: Quarterly Newsletter of the Pointe de l'Église: Acadia Genealogical and Historical Society, Inc.* 19, no. 1 (2008): 6–12.

Blackmon, Douglas A. *Slavery by Another Name: The Re-Enslavement of Black Americans from the Civil War to World War II.* Doubleday, 2008.

Blair, Cynthia M. *I've Got to Make My Livin': Black Women's Sex Work in Turn-of-the-Century Chicago.* Univ. of Chicago Press, 2010.

Blassingame, John W. *The Slave Community: Plantation Life in the Antebellum South.* Oxford Univ. Press, 1972.

Blevins, Brooks. *Ghost of the Ozarks: Murder and Memory in the Upland South.* Univ. of Illinois Press, 2017.

Bonn, Scott. *Why We Love Serial Killers: The Curious Appeal of the World's Most Savage Murderers.* Skyhorse Publishing, 2014.

Braithwaite, Oyinkan. *My Sister, the Serial Killer.* Doubleday, 2018.

Branson, Allan L. "African American Serial Killers: Over-Represented Yet Underacknowledged." *Howard Journal of Criminal Justice* 52, no. 1 (February 2013): 1–18.

———. *The Anonymity of African American Serial Killers: A Continuum of Negative Imagery from Slavery to Prisons.* Self-published, 2015.

Brasseaux, Carl A. *The Founding of New Acadia: The Beginnings of Acadian Life in Louisiana, 1765–1803.* Louisiana State Univ. Press, 1997.

Brasseaux, Carl A., Keith P. Fontenot, and Claude F. Oubre. *Creoles of Color in the Bayou Country.* Univ. of Mississippi Press, 1994.

Brattain, Michelle. "Miscegenation and Competing Definitions of Race in Twentieth-Century Louisiana." *Journal of Southern History* 71, no. 3 (August 2005): 621–58.

Brundage, W. Fitzhugh. *Lynching in the New South: Georgia and Virginia, 1880–1930.* Univ. of Illinois Press, 1993.

———, ed. *Under Sentence of Death: Lynching in the South.* Univ. of North Carolina Press, 1997.

Burnham, Margaret A. *By Hands Now Known: Jim Crow's Legal Executioners.* Norton, 2022.

Burton, H. Sophie, and F. Todd Smith. "Slavery in the Colonial Louisiana Backcountry: Natchitoches, 1714–1908." *Louisiana History* 52, no. 2 (2011): 133–88.

Butler, Anne M. "Still in Chains: Black Women in Western Prisons, 1865–1910." *Western Historical Quarterly* 20, no. 1 (February 1989): 18–35.

Butler, Anne, and C. Murray Henderson. *Dying to Tell: Angola, Crime, Consequence, Conclusion at Louisiana State Penitentiary.* Univ. of Louisiana at Lafayette Press, 1992.

Butler, Joseph T., Jr. "The Atakapa Indians: Cannibals of Louisiana." *Louisiana History* 11, no. 2 (spring 1970): 167–76.

Cahn, Susan K. *Sexual Reckonings: Southern Girls in a Troubling Age.* Harvard Univ. Press, 2012.

Camp, Stephanie M. H. "The Pleasures of Resistance: Enslaved Women and Body Politics in the Plantation South, 1830–1861." *Journal of Southern History* 68, no. 3 (August 2002): 533–72.

Canter, David V., Laurence J. Alison, Emily Alison, and Natalia Wentink. "The Organized/Disorganized Typology of Serial Murder: Myth or Model?" *Psychology, Public Policy, and Law* 10, no. 3 (September 2004): 293–320.

Cardon, Nathan. "'Less Than Mayhem': Louisiana's Convict Lease, 1865–1901." *Louisiana History* 58, no. 4 (fall 2017): 417–41.

Carleton, Mark T. *Politics and Punishment: The History of the Louisiana State Penal System.* Louisiana State Univ. Press, 1971.

Carrigan, William D. *The Making of a Lynching Culture: Violence and Vigilantism in Central Texas, 1836–1916.* Univ. of Illinois Press, 2004.

Cartwright, Keith. "Voodoo Hermeneutics/The Crossroads Sublime: Soul Musics, Mindful Body, and Creole Consciousness." *Mississippi Quarterly* 57, no. 1 (winter 2003): 157–70.

Caruso, James P., and Jason P. Sheehan. "Psychosurgery, Ethics, and Media: A History of Walter Freeman and the Lobotomy." *Neurosurgical Focus* 43, no. 3 (September 2017): 1–8.

Chatelain, Marcia. *South Side Girls: Growing Up in the Great Migration.* Duke Univ. Press, 2015.

Chireau, Yvonne P. *Black Magic: Conjure in the African-American Tradition.* Univ. of California Press, 2003.

Clark, Emily. *Masterless Mistresses: The New Orleans Ursulines and the Development of a New World Society, 1727–1834.* Univ. of North Carolina Press, 2007.

Cleary, Hayley M. D. "Applying the Lessons of Developmental Psychology to the Study of Juvenile Interrogations: New Directions for Research, Policy, and Practice." *Psychology, Public Policy, and Law* 23, no. 1 (2017): 118–30.

Cleary, Hayley, Lucy Guarnera, Jeffrey Aaron, and Megan Crane. "How Trauma May Magnify Risk of Involuntary and False Confessions Among Adolescents." *Wrongful Conviction Law Review* 2, no. 3 (December 2021): 173–204.

Clegg, Claude A., III. *Troubled Ground: A Tale of Murder, Lynching, and Reckoning in the New South.* Univ. of Illinois Press, 2010.

Cocuzza, Dominique. "Stella Blum Grant Report: The Dress of Free Women of Color in New Orleans, 1780–1840." *Dress: The Journal of the Costume Society of America* 27, no. 1 (2000): 78–87.

Corrales, Barbara Smith. "Deviant Women and the Politics of Privilege: Two Louisiana Murder Cases, 1911–1913." *Louisiana History* 48, no. 3 (summer 2007): 317–40.

———. "Prurience, Prostitution, and Progressive Improvements: The Crowley Connection, 1909–1918." *Louisiana History* 45, no. 1 (winter 2004): 37–70.

Corrigan, John, and Lynn S. Neal, eds. *Religious Intolerance in America,* 2nd ed. Univ. of North Carolina Press, 2020.

Cox, Karen L. *Goat Castle: A True Story of Murder, Race, and the Gothic South*. Univ. of North Carolina Press, 2017.

Curtis, L. Perry, Jr. *Jack the Ripper and the London Press*. Yale Univ. Press, 2001.

Davis, Natalie Zemon. *The Return of Martin Guerre*. Harvard Univ. Press, 1984.

Davis, Ron. *American Voudou: Journey into a Hidden World*. Univ. of North Texas Press, 1999.

Dawdy, Shannon Lee. *Building the Devil's Empire: French Colonial New Orleans*. Univ. of Chicago Press, 2009.

Derbes, Brett Josef. "'Secret Horrors': Enslaved Women and Children in the Louisiana State Penitentiary, 1833–1862." *Journal of African American History* 98, no. 2 (spring 2013): 277–90.

Deshane, Kenneth. "A Morphology for the Pentecostal Experience of Receiving the Baptism in the Holy Spirit." *Western Folklore* 62, no. 4 (autumn 2003): 271–91.

Desmangles, Leslie G. "Replacing the Term 'Voodoo' with 'Vodou': A Proposal." *Journal of Haitian Studies* 18, no. 2 (fall 2012): 26–33.

Dethloff, Henry C. "Rice Revolution in the Southwest, 1880–1910." *Arkansas Historical Quarterly* 29, no. 1 (spring 1970): 66–75.

Donaldson, Andrea E., and Iain L. Lamont. "Biochemistry Changes That Occur After Death: Potential Markers for Determining Post-Mortem Interval." *PLoS ONE* 8, no. 11 (November 2013): 1–10.

Downs, Jim. *Sick from Freedom: African-American Illness and Suffering During the Civil War and Reconstruction*. Oxford Univ. Press, 2012.

Dray, Philip. *At the Hands of Persons Unknown: The Lynching of Black America*. Modern Library, 2002.

Du Bois, W. E. B. *Black Reconstruction in America: An Essay Toward a History of the Part Which Black Folk Played in the Attempt to Reconstruct Democracy in America, 1860–1880*. Russell and Russell, 1935.

———. *The Negro Church*. Atlanta Univ. Press, 1903.

Dulaney, W. Marvin. *Black Police in America*. Indiana Univ. Press, 1996.

Egger, Steven A. *The Killers Among Us: An Examination of Serial Murder and Its Investigation*. Prentice Hall, 1998.

Elliott, Todd C. *Axes of Evil: The True Story of the Ax-Man Murders*. Trine Day LLC, 2015.

Equal Justice Initiative. *Lynching in America: Confronting the Legacy of Racial Terror*. 3rd ed. Equal Justice Initiative, 2017.

Fairclough, Adam. *Race and Democracy: The Civil Rights Struggle in Louisiana, 1915–1972*. Univ. of Georgia Press, 1995.

Farmer, Ashley D. "In Search of the Black Women's History Archive." *Modern American History* 1, no. 2 (2018): 289–93.

Feimster, Crystal N. *Southern Horrors: Women and the Politics of Rape and Lynching*. Harvard Univ. Press, 2011.

Fisher-Giorlando, Marianne. "The Walls." *64 Parishes*, December 2019, 64parishes.org/the-walls.

Fisher-Giorlando, Marianne, and Daniel Dotter. "Murder in Black and White: A Crime and Media Story in Antebellum Louisiana." *Women and Criminal Justice* 14, no. 2–3 (2003): 59–87.

Flowe, Douglas J. *Uncontrollable Blackness: African American Men and Criminality in Jim Crow New York*. Univ. of North Carolina Press, 2020.

Foley, Neil. *The White Scourge: Mexicans, Blacks, and Poor Whites in Texas Cotton Culture*. Univ. of California Press, 1997.

Foner, Eric. *Reconstruction: America's Unfinished Revolution, 1863–1877*. Harper and Row, 1988.

Forman, James, Jr. *Locking Up Our Own: Crime and Punishment in Black America*. Farrar, Straus and Giroux, 2017.

Forret, Jeff. "Before Angola: Enslaved Prisoners in the Louisiana State Penitentiary." *Louisiana History* 54, no. 2 (spring 2013): 133–71.

Fortier, Alcée, ed. *Louisiana: Comprising Sketches of Parishes, Towns, Events, Institutions, and Persons, Arranged in Cyclopedic Form*, vol. 3. Century Historical Association, 1914.

Frazier, E. Franklin. *The Negro Church in America*. Schocken Books, 1964.

Frederickson, George M. *The Black Image in the White Mind: The Debate on Afro-American Character and Destiny, 1817–1914*. Harper and Row, 1971.

Freedman, Estelle B. "'Crimes Which Startle and Horrify': Gender, Age, and the Racialization of Sexual Violence in White American Newspapers, 1870–1900." *Journal of the History of Sexuality* 20, no. 3 (September 2011): 465–97.

Friendly, Fred W. *Minnesota Rag: Corruption, Yellow Journalism, and the Case That Saved Freedom of the Press*. Univ. of Minnesota Press, 2003.

Fuentes, Marisa J. *Dispossessed Lives: Enslaved Women, Violence, and the Archive*. Univ. of Pennsylvania Press, 2016.

Gamber, Wendy. *The Notorious Mrs. Clem: Murder and Money in the Gilded Age*. Johns Hopkins Univ. Press, 2017.

Garrett, Brandon L. "Contaminated Confessions Revisited." *Virginia Law Review* 101 (2015): 395–453.

Gipson, Jennifer. "'A Strange, Ventriloquous Voice': Louisiana Creole, Whiteness, and the Racial Politics of Writing Orality." *Journal of American Folklore* 129, no. 514 (October 2016): 459–85.

Glymph, Thavolia. *Out of the House of Bondage: The Transformation of the Plantation Household*. Cambridge Univ. Press, 2003.

Goins, Charles Robert, and John Michael Caldwell. *Historical Atlas of Louisiana*. Univ. of Oklahoma Press, 1995.

Gomez, Michael A. *Exchanging Our Country Marks: The Transformation of African Identities in the Colonial and Antebellum South*. Univ. of North Carolina Press, 1998.

Gordon, Richard Lawrence. "The Development of Louisiana's Public Mental Institutions, 1735–1940." Ph.D. diss., Louisiana State University and Agricultural and Mechanical College, 1978.

Greene, Jack. *Pursuits of Happiness: The Social Development of Early Modern British Colonies and the Formation of American Culture.* Univ. of North Carolina Press, 1988.

Greene-Hayes, Ahmad. "'A Very Queer Case': Clementine Barnabet and the Erotics of a Sensationalized Voodoo Religion." *Nova Religio* 26, no. 4 (May 2023): 58–84.

Groneman, Carol. "Nymphomania: The Historical Construction of Female Sexuality." *Signs: Journal of Women in Culture and Society* 19, no. 2 (winter 1994): 337–67.

Gross, Kali Nicole. *Colored Amazons: Crime, Violence, and Black Women in the City of Brotherly Love, 1880–1910.* Duke Univ. Press, 2006.

———. "Exploring Crime and Violence in Early-Twentieth-Century Black Women's History." In *Contesting Archives: Historians Develop Methodologies for Finding Women in the Sources,* ed. Nupur Chaudhuri, Sherry J. Katz, and Mary Elizabeth Perry, 56–71. Univ. of Illinois Press, 2010.

———. *Hannah Mary Tabbs and the Disembodied Torso: A Tale of Race, Sex, and Violence in America.* Oxford Univ. Press, 2016.

———. *Vengeance Feminism: The Power of Black Women's Fury in Lawless Times.* Seal Press, 2024.

Hadden, Sally E. *Slave Patrols: Law and Violence in Virginia and the Carolinas.* Harvard Univ. Press, 2003.

Hair, William Ivy. *Carnival of Fury: Robert Charles and the New Orleans Race Riot of 1900.* Louisiana State Univ. Press, 1976.

———. "'Inquisition for Blood': An Outbreak of Ritual Murder in Louisiana, Georgia and Texas, 1911–1912." *Louisiana Studies* 11 (1972): 274–81.

Haley, Sarah. *No Mercy Here: Gender, Punishment, and the Making of Jim Crow Modernity.* Univ. of North Carolina Press, 2016.

Hall, Gwendolyn Midlo. *Africans in Colonial Louisiana: The Development of Afro-Creole Culture in the Eighteenth Century.* Louisiana State Univ. Press, 1992.

Hall, Julien A. "Negro Conjuring and Tricking." *Journal of American Folklore* 10, no. 38 (September 1897): 241–43.

Halttunen, Karen. *Murder Most Foul: The Killer and the American Gothic Imagination.* Harvard Univ. Press, 1998.

Harris, LaShawn. "The *Commonwealth of Virginia vs. Virginia Christian:* Southern Black Women, Crime and Punishment in Progressive Era Virginia." *Journal of Social History* 47, no. 4 (June 2014): 922–42.

———. *Sex Workers, Psychics, and Numbers Runners: Black Women in New York City's Underground Economy.* Univ. of Illinois Press, 2016.

Hartman, Saidiya. "Venus in Two Acts." *Small Axe* 12, no. 2 (2008): 1–14.

Haskins, Jim. *Voodoo and Hoodoo: The Craft as Revealed by Traditional Practitioners.* Original Publications, 1978.

Hayes, John. *Hard, Hard Religion: Interracial Faith in the Poor South.* Univ. of North Carolina Press, 2017.

Hazzard-Donald, Katrina. *Mojo Workin': The Old African American Hoodoo System.* Univ. of Illinois Press, 2013.

Headley, Bernard. *The Atlanta Youth Murders and the Politics of Race.* Southern Illinois Univ. Press, 1998.

Henley, Lauren Nicole. "Contested Commitment: Policing Black Female Juvenile Delinquency at Efland Home, 1919–1939." *Souls* 20, no. 1 (2018): 38–57.

———. "'Devilish Deeds': Serial Murder and Racial Violence in Austin, Texas, 1884–1885." *Journal of African American History* 105, no. 1 (winter 2020): 1–27.

Hermann, Christina Pruett. "Specters of Freedom: Forced Labor, Social Struggle, and the Louisiana State Penitentiary System, 1835–1935." Ph.D. diss., Michigan State University, 2015.

Herron, and A. M. Bacon. "Conjuring and Conjure-Doctors in the Southern United States." *Journal of American Folklore* 9 (1896): 143–47, 224–26.

Hickey, Eric W. *Serial Murderers and Their Victims,* 2nd ed. Thomson Wadsworth, 1997.

———. *Serial Murderers and Their Victims,* 4th ed. Thomson Wadsworth, 2006.

Hicks, Cheryl D. *Talk with You Like a Woman: African American Women, Justice, and Reform in New York, 1890–1935.* Univ. of North Carolina Press, 2010.

Higginbotham, Evelyn Brooks. "Beyond the Sound of Silence: Afro-American Women in History." *Gender and History* 1, no. 1 (spring 1989): 50–67.

———. *Righteous Discontent: The Women's Movement in the Black Baptist Church, 1880–1920.* Harvard Univ. Press, 1994.

Hill, Samuel S., ed. *Varieties of Southern Religious Experience.* Louisiana State Univ. Press, 1988.

Hillyer, Reiko. *A Wall Is Just a Wall: The Permeability of the Prison in the Twentieth-Century United States.* Duke Univ. Press, 2024.

Hine, Darlene Clark. "Rape and the Inner Lives of Black Women in the Middle West." *Signs: Journal of Women in Culture and Society* 14, no. 4 (summer 1989): 912–20.

Hobbs, Allyson. *A Chosen Exile: A History of Racial Passing in American Life.* Harvard Univ. Press, 2014.

Hofsommer, Don L. *The Southern Pacific, 1901–1985.* Texas A&M Univ. Press, 1986.

Hollandsworth, Skip. *The Midnight Assassin: Panic, Scandal, and the Hunt for America's First Serial Killer.* Holt, 2015.

Horn, Stacy. *Damnation Island: Poor, Sick, Mad and Criminal in 19th-Century New York.* Algonquin Books, 2018.

Huffard, R. Scott, Jr. *Engines of Redemption: Railroads and the Reconstruction of Capitalism in the New South.* Univ. of North Carolina Press, 2019.

Hunter, Tera W. *To 'Joy My Freedom: Southern Black Women's Lives and Labors After the Civil War.* Harvard Univ. Press, 1997.

Istre, Elista. *Creoles of South Louisiana: Three Centuries Strong.* Univ. of Louisiana at Lafayette Press, 2018.

James, Bill, and Rachel McCarthy James. *The Man from the Train: The Solving of a Century-Old Serial Killer Mystery.* Scribner, 2017.

Janssen, Diederik F. "From Libidines Nefandæ to Sexual Perversions." *History of Psychiatry* 31, no. 4 (2020): 421–39.

Jenkins, Philip. *Mystics and Messiahs: Cults and New Religions in American History.* Oxford Univ. Press, 2000.

———. "Serial Murder in the United States 1900–1940: A Historical Perspective." *Journal of Criminal Justice* 17, no. 5 (1989): 377–92.

———. *Using Murder: The Social Construction of Serial Homicide.* Aldine de Gruyter, 1994.

Jett, Brandon T. *Race, Crime, and Policing in the Jim Crow South: African Americans and Law Enforcement in Birmingham, Memphis, and New Orleans, 1920–1945.* Louisiana State Univ. Press, 2021.

Johnson, Walter. "The Slave Trader, the White Slave, and the Politics of Racial Determination in the 1850s." *Journal of American History* 87, no. 1 (June 2000): 13–38.

Jones, Jacqueline. *Labor of Love, Labor of Sorrow: Black Women, Work, and the Family from Slavery to the Present.* Basic Books, 1985.

Jones, Lindsey Elizabeth. "'The Most Unprotected of All Human Beings': Black Girls, State Violence, and the Limits of Protection in Jim Crow Virginia." *Souls* 20, no. 1 (2018): 14–37.

Kassin, Saul M., Steven A. Drizin, Thomas Grisso, Gisli H. Gudjonsson, Richard A. Leo, and Allison D. Redlich. "Police-Induced Confessions: Risk Factors and Recommendations." *Law and Human Behavior* 34 (2010): 3–38.

Kassin, Saul M., and Lawrence S. Wrightsman, eds. *The Psychology of Evidence and Trial Procedure.* Sage, 1985.

Kelleher, Michael D., and C. L. Kelleher. *Murder Most Rare: The Female Serial Killer.* Dell Publishing, 1998.

Kellor, Frances A. "The Criminal Negro: A Sociological Study." *The Arena* 25, nos. 1–5 (January–May 1901): 59–68, 190–97, 308–16, 419–28, 510–20.

King, Wilma. "'Mad' Enough to Kill: Enslaved Women, Murder, and Southern Courts." *Journal of African American History* 92, no. 1 (winter 2007): 37–56.

Krakauer, Jon. *Under the Banner of Heaven: A Story of Violent Faith.* Anchor Books, 2004.

Lalich, Janja. *Bounded Choice: True Believers and Charismatic Cults.* Univ. of California Press, 2004.

Landau, Emily Epstein. *Spectacular Wickedness: Sex, Race, and Memory in Storyville, New Orleans.* Louisiana State Univ. Press, 2013.

Larson, Erik. *The Devil in the White City: Murder, Magic, and Madness at the Fair That Changed America.* Crown, 2003.

Le Menestrel, Sara. "The Color of Music: Social Boundaries and Stereotypes in Southwest Louisiana French Music." *Southern Cultures* 13, no. 3 (fall 2007): 87–105.

Lebsock, Suzanne. *A Murder in Virginia: Southern Justice on Trial.* Norton, 2003.

LeFlouria, Talitha L. *Chained in Silence: Black Women and Convict Labor in the New South.* Univ. of North Carolina Press, 2015.

Lemann, Nicholas. *The Promised Land: The Great Black Migration and How It Changed America.* Knopf, 1991.

Leonard, Thomas C. *Illiberal Reformers: Race, Eugenics, and American Economics in the Progressive Era.* Princeton Univ. Press, 2016.

Leyton, Elliot. *Hunting Humans: The Rise of the Modern Multiple Murderer.* Penguin, 1986.

Lichtenstein, Alex. *Twice the Work of Free Labor: The Political Economy of Convict Labor in the New South.* Verso, 1996.

Lifton, Robert Jay. *Thought Reform and the Psychology of Totalism.* Norton, 1961.

Lockridge, Kenneth A. *A New England Town: The First Hundred Years.* Norton, 1985.

Loftus, Elizabeth F. *Eyewitness Testimony.* Harvard Univ. Press, 1979.

Logan, Trevon D. "Health, Human Capital, and African-American Migration Before 1910." *Explorations in Economic History* 46, no. 2 (April 2009): 169–85.

Lombardo, Paul. *Three Generations, No Imbeciles: Eugenics, the Supreme Court, and Buck v. Bell.* Johns Hopkins Univ. Press, 2008.

Long, Carolyn Morrow. *Spiritual Merchants: Religion, Magic and Commerce.* Univ. of Tennessee Press, 2001.

Malka, Adam. *The Men of Mobtown: Policing Baltimore in the Age of Slavery and Emancipation.* Univ. of North Carolina Press, 2018.

Martin, Denise. "African Mythic Science or Vodou Methodology." *Journal of Pan African Studies* 5, no. 4 (June 2012): 83–100.

McGerr, Michael. *A Fierce Discontent: The Rise and Fall of the Progressive Movement in America, 1870–1920.* The Free Press, 2003.

McGuire, Danielle L. *At the Dark End of the Street: Black Women, Rape, and Resistance—A New History of the Civil Rights Movement from Rosa Parks to the Rise of Black Power.* Vintage Books, 2010.

McLaren, Angus. *A Prescription for Murder: The Victorian Serial Killer of Dr. Thomas Neill Cream.* Univ. of Chicago Press, 1993.

Michel, Claudine. "Vodou in Haiti: Way of Life and Mode of Survival." *Journal of Haitian Studies* 8, no. 1 (spring 2002): 98–109.

Middleton, Billy. "Two-Headed Medicine: Hoodoo Workers, Conjure Doctors, and Zora Neale Hurston." *Southern Quarterly* 53, no. 3/4 (spring/summer 2016): 156–75.

Millner, Lyn. *The Allure of Immortality: An American Cult, a Florida Swamp, and a Renegade Prophet.* Univ. Press of Florida, 2015.

Mire, Ann. *Images of America: Crowley.* Arcadia Publishing, 2014.

———. *Looking Back at Crowley's History.* Self-published, 2015.

Mitchell, Michele. "Silences Broken, Silences Kept: Gender and Sexuality in African-American History." *Gender and History* 11, no. 3 (1999): 433–44.

Mjanes, Karin, Eric Beauregard, and Melissa Martineau. "Revisiting the Organized/Disorganized Model of Sexual Homicide." *Criminal Justice and Behavior* 44, no. 12 (December 2017): 1604–19.

Moehling, Carolyn, and Anne Morrison Piehl. "Immigration, Crime, and Incarceration in Early Twentieth-Century America." *Demography* 46, no. 4 (November 2009): 739–63.

Montgomery, William E. *Under Their Own Vine and Fig Tree: The African-American Church in the South, 1865–1900*. Louisiana State Univ. Press, 1993.

Morris, Adam. *American Messiahs: False Prophets of a Damned Nation*. Liveright, 2019.

Morrow, Diane Batts. *Persons of Color and Religious at the Same Time: The Oblate Sisters of Providence, 1828–1860*. Univ. of North Carolina Press, 2003.

Muhammad, Khalil Gibran. *The Condemnation of Blackness: Race, Crime, and the Making of Modern Urban America*. Harvard Univ. Press, 2010.

Murphy, Joseph M. *Working the Spirit: Ceremonies of the African Diaspora*. Beacon Press, 1994.

Murray, Thomas R. *Roots of Haiti's Vodou-Christian Faith: African and Catholic Origins*. ABC-CLIO, 2014.

Mustakeem, Sowande'. "'Armed with a Knife in Her Bosom': Gender, Violence, and the Carceral Consequences of Rage in the Late 19th Century." *Journal of African American History* 100, no. 3 (summer 2015): 385–405.

Myers, Kerry, and Marianne Fisher-Giorlando. "Bad Girls, Convict Women: The Historically Unseen of Louisiana's Prison System, Part 1: 1835–1901." *The Angolite* 36, no. 6 (December 2011): 42–55.

———. "Bad Girls, Convict Women: The Historically Unseen of Louisiana's Prison System, Part 2: 1901–1950." *The Angolite* 37, no. 1 (February 2012): 28–39.

Niedermeier, Silvan. *The Color of the Third Degree: Racism, Police Torture, and Civil Rights in the American South, 1930–1965*. Translated by Paul Cohen. Univ. of North Carolina Press, 2019.

Odem, Mary E. *Delinquent Daughters: Protecting and Policing Adolescent Female Sexuality in the United States, 1885–1920*. Univ. of North Carolina Press, 1995.

Ordover, Nancy. *American Eugenics: Race, Queer Anatomy, and the Science of Nationalism*. Univ. of Minnesota Press, 2003.

Orsi, Richard J. *Sunset Limited: The Southern Pacific Railroad and the Development of the American West, 1850–1930*. Univ. of California Press, 2007.

Osbey, Brenda Marie. "Why We Can't Talk to You about Voodoo." *Southern Literary Journal* 43, no. 2 (spring 2011): 1–11.

Oshinsky, David M. *"Worse than Slavery": Parchman Farm and the Ordeal of Jim Crow Justice*. Free Press Paperbacks, 1996.

Osofsky, Gilbert. *Harlem: The Making of a Ghetto-Negro New York, 1890–1930*. Harper and Row, 1966.

Owens, Deidre Cooper. *Medical Bondage: Race, Gender, and the Origins of American Gynecology*. Univ. of Georgia Press, 2017.

Painter, Nell Irvin. *Exodusters: Black Migration to Kansas After Reconstruction*. Knopf, 1977.

Pasquier, Michael. "Creole Catholicism Before Black Catholicism: Religion and Slavery in French Colonial Louisiana." *Journal of Africana Religions* 2, no. 2 (2014): 271–79.

Payne, J. P. "The Criminal Use of Chloroform." *Anaesthesia* 53, no. 7 (1998): 685–90.

Pelot-Hobbs, Lydia. *Prison Capital: Mass Incarceration and Struggles for Abolition Democracy in Louisiana*. Univ. of North Carolina Press, 2023.

Pfeifer, Michael J. *Rough Justice: Lynching and American Society, 1874–1947*. Univ. of Illinois Press, 2004.

Pfeifer, Michael J. "The Origins of Postbellum Lynching: Collective Violence in Reconstruction Louisiana." *Louisiana History* 50, no. 2 (spring 2009): 189–201.

Pinn, Anthony B. *Varieties of African American Religious Experience: Toward a Comparative Black Theology*. Fortress Press, 2017.

Pizza, Murphy. "Sacred Body in a Clear Mirror: A Comparison of Women's Theologies in Vodou and Neopaganism." *Journal of Haitian Studies* 13, no. 1 (spring 2007): 84–98.

Post, Lauren C. "The Rice Country of Southwestern Louisiana." *Geographical Review* 30, no. 4 (October 1940): 574–90.

Prince, K. Stephen. *The Ballad of Robert Charles: Searching for the New Orleans Riot of 1900*. Univ. of North Carolina Press, 2021.

Purkiss, Ava. "'Beauty Secrets: Fight Fat': Black Women's Aesthetics, Exercise, and Fat Stigma, 1900–1930s." *Journal of Women's History* 29, no. 2 (summer 2017): 14–37.

Raboteau, Albert J. *Slave Religion: The "Invisible Institution" in the Antebellum South*. Oxford Univ. Press, 1978.

Rafter, Nicole Hahn. *Creating Born Criminals*. Univ. of Illinois Press, 1977.

Ramsland, Katherine. *Inside the Minds of Serial Killers: Why They Kill*, 1st ed. Praeger, 2006.

Ressler, Robert K., Ann W. Burgess, and John E. Douglas. *Sexual Homicide: Patterns and Motives*. Lexington Books, 1988.

Reverby, Susan M. *Examining Tuskegee: The Infamous Syphilis Study and Its Legacy*. Univ. of North Carolina Press, 2009.

Richardson, Charlotte Mae. "Women in Prison: A Study of Social Relationships." Master's thesis, Louisiana State University and Agricultural and Mechanical College, 1959.

Richie, Beth E. *Arrested Justice: Black Women, Violence, and America's Prison Nation*. New York Univ. Press, 2012.

Ritterhouse, Jennifer. *Growing Up Jim Crow: How Black and White Southern Children Learned Race*. Univ. of North Carolina Press, 2006.

Roberts, Dorothy. *Killing the Black Body: Race, Reproduction, and the Meaning of Liberty.* Pantheon Books, 1997.

Ross, Michael A. *The Great New Orleans Kidnapping Case: Race, Law, and Justice in the Reconstruction Era.* Oxford Univ. Press, 2017.

Sanders, Cheryl J. *Saints in Exile: The Holiness-Pentecostal Experience in African American Religion and Culture.* Oxford Univ. Press, 1996.

Saxon, Lyle, Edward Dreyer, and Robert Tallant. *Gumbo Ya-Ya: Folk Tales of Louisiana.* Pelican Publishing Company, 1987.

Schechter, Harold. *Depraved: The Shocking Story of America's First Serial Killer.* Pocket Star Books, 1994.

Schechter, Harold, and David Everitt. *The A-Z Encyclopedia of Serial Killers.* Pocket Star Books, 1996.

Scheiner, Seth M. *Negro Mecca: A History of the Negro in New York City, 1865–1920.* New York Univ. Press, 1965.

Schmid, David. *Natural Born Celebrities: Serial Killers in American Culture.* Univ. of Chicago Press, 2005.

Seltzer, Mark. *Serial Killers: Death and Life in America's Wound Culture.* Routledge, 1998.

Sexton, Rocky L. "Rice Country Revisited: The Socioeconomic Transformation of a French Louisiana Subregion." *Louisiana History* 47, no. 3 (summer 2006): 309–32.

Shanabruch, Charles. "The Louisiana Immigration Movement, 1891–1907: An Analysis of Efforts, Attitudes, and Opportunities." *Louisiana History* 18, no. 2 (spring 1977): 203–25.

Sharpless, Rebecca. *Cooking in Other Women's Kitchens: Domestic Workers in the South, 1865–1960.* Univ. of North Carolina Press, 2010.

Shufelt, Gordon H. *The Uncommon Case of Daniel Brown: How a White Police Officer Was Convicted of Killing a Black Citizen, Baltimore, 1875.* Kent State Univ. Press, 2021.

Simmons, LaKisha Michelle. *Crescent City Girls: The Lives of Young Black Women in Segregated New Orleans.* Univ. of North Carolina Press, 2015.

Skloot, Rebecca. *The Immortal Life of Henrietta Lacks.* Broadway Paperbacks, 2010.

Skolnick, Jerome H., and James J. Fyfe. *Above the Law: Police and the Excessive Use of Force.* Simon and Schuster, 2010.

Slovenko, Ralph. "The Jury System in Louisiana Criminal Law." *Louisiana Law Review* 17, no. 4 (June 1957): 655–729.

Spear, Allan H. *Black Chicago: The Making of a Negro Ghetto, 1890–1920.* Univ. of Chicago Press, 1967.

Stein, Alexandra. *Terror, Love and Brainwashing: Attachment in Cults and Totalitarian Systems.* Routledge, 2016.

Stein, William Mark. "The Glidden Ax Murder." *Nesbitt Memorial Library Journal* 1, no. 10 (September 1991): 307–12.

Stern, Alexandra Mina. *Eugenic Nation: Faults and Frontiers of Better Breeding in Modern America.* Univ. of California Press, 2005.

Suddler, Carl. *Presumed Criminal: Black Youth and the Justice System in Postwar New York.* New York Univ. Press, 2019.

Tarver, John Reed. "The Clan of Toil: Piney Woods Labor Relations in the Trans-Mississippi South, 1880–1920." Ph.D. diss., Louisiana State University, 1991.

Taylor, Nikki M. *Brooding over Bloody Revenge: Enslaved Women's Lethal Resistance.* Cambridge Univ. Press, 2023.

Taylor, Nikki M. *Driven Toward Madness: The Fugitive Slave Margaret Garner and Tragedy on the Ohio.* Ohio Univ. Press, 2016.

Thompson, Robert Farris. *Flash of the Spirit: African and Afro-American Art and Philosophy.* Random House, 1983.

Thornton, John. *Africa and Africans in the Making of the Atlantic World, 1400–1800.* Cambridge Univ. Press, 1992.

Tolnay, Stewart E., and E. M. Beck. *A Festival of Violence: An Analysis of Southern Lynchings, 1882–1930.* Univ. of Illinois Press, 1995.

Touchstone, Blake. "Voodoo in New Orleans." *Louisiana History* 13, no. 4 (autumn 1972): 371–86.

Van Der Kolk, Bessel. *The Body Keeps Score: Brain, Mind, and Body in the Healing of Trauma.* Penguin, 2014.

Vicary, Amanada M., and R. Chris Fraley. "Captured by True Crime: Why Are Women Drawn to Tales of Rape, Murder, and Serial Killers?" *Social Psychological and Personality Science* 1, no. 1 (2010): 81–86.

Vronsky, Peter. *Female Serial Killers: How and Why Women Become Monsters.* Berkley Publishing Group, 2007.

———. *Serial Killers: The Method and Madness of Monsters.* Berkley Publishing Group, 2004.

———. *Sons of Cain: A History of Serial Killers from the Stone Age to the Present.* Berkley Publishing Group, 2018.

Walker, Lenore E. "False Confessions of Battered Women." In *The Battered Woman Syndrome,* 4th ed., 451–65. Springer Publishing Company, 2017.

Walkowitz, Judith R. *City of Dreadful Delight: Narratives of Sexual Danger in Late-Victorian London.* Univ. of Chicago Press, 1992.

Washington, Harriet A. *Medical Apartheid: The Dark History of Medical Experimentation on Black Americans from Colonial Times to the Present.* Harlem Moon, 2006.

Wawersik, J. "History of Chloroform Anesthesia." *Anaesthesiology und Reanimation* 22, no. 6 (1997): 144–52.

Wells-Barnett, Ida B. *A Red Record: Tabulated Statistics and Alleged Causes of Lynching in the United States.* Donohue and Henneberry, 1895.

Wells-Oghoghomeh, Alexis S. "'She Come Like a Nightmare': Hags, Witches and the

Gendered Trans-Sense Among the Enslaved in the Lower South." *Journal of Africana Religions* 5, no. 2 (2017): 239–74.

White, Deborah Gray. "Mining the Forgotten: Manuscript Sources for Black Women's History." *Journal of American History* 74, no. 1 (June 1987): 237–42.

White, Richard. *Railroaded: The Transcontinentals and the Making of Modern America.* Norton, 2012.

Whitaker, Robert. *Mad in America: Bad Science, Bad Medicine, and the Enduring Mistreatment of the Mentally Ill.* Perseus Publishing, 2002.

Wiley, B. I. "Salient Changes in Southern Agriculture Since the Civil War." *Agricultural History* 13, no. 2 (1939): 65–76.

Wilkins, Melinda Page. "A Comfortable Evil: Female Serial Murderers in American Culture." Ph.D. diss., Pennsylvania State University, 2004.

Williams, Heather Andrea. *Help Me to Find My People: The African American Search for Family Lost in Slavery.* Univ. of North Carolina Press, 2012.

Williams, Kidada E. *They Left Great Marks on Me: African American Testimonies of Racial Violence from Emancipation to World War I.* New York Univ. Press, 2012.

Wilson, Colin, and Donald Seaman. *The Serial Killers: A Study in the Psychology of Violence.* Carol, 1991.

Wood, Amy Louise. *Lynching and Spectacle: Witnessing Racial Violence in America, 1890–1940.* Univ. of North Carolina Press, 2011.

Woodward, C. Vann. *Origins of the New South.* Louisiana State Univ. Press, 1951.

———. *The Strange Career of Jim Crow.* Commemorative (2002). Oxford Univ. Press, 1955.

Wright, George C. *Racial Violence in Kentucky: Lynchings, Mob Rule, and "Legal Lynchings."* Louisiana State Univ. Press, 1990.

Zipf, Karin L. *Bad Girls at Samarcand: Sexuality and Sterilization in a Southern Juvenile Reformatory.* Louisiana State Univ. Press, 2016.

Index